Social Psychology
Experimental and Critical Approaches

Social Psychology
Experimental and Critical Approaches

Wendy Stainton Rogers

Open University Press

Maidenhead · Philadelphia

Open University Press
McGraw-Hill Education
McGraw-Hill House
Shoppenhangers Road
Maidenhead
Berkshire
SL6 2QL

email: enquiries@openup.co.uk
world wide web: www.openup.co.uk

and
325 Chestnut Street
Philadelphia, PA 19106 USA

First published 2003

A catalogue record of this book is available from the British Library

ISBN   0 335 21126 7 (pb)   0 335 21127 5 (hb)

Library of Congress Cataloging-in-Publication Data
The Library of Congress data for this book has been applied for from the Library of Congress

Printed in Great Britain by Bell and Bain Limited, Glasgow

This book is dedicated, with my love, my thanks and my admiration to TGM and, of course, with special thanks to the little fellow.

Contents

Preface

This book is an unusual one. As far as I know it is the only social psychology introductory textbook that seeks to bring together the mainstream approach – largely based upon experimental methods – and the emerging approach that I have called 'critical', but is also referred to as 'discursive' and 'social constructionist' social psychology. My purpose in bringing the two together was originally directed towards those introductory courses that are being taught by critical social psychologists. What they said they needed was a text that covered both, since students needed to learn about the mainstream before they could begin to get to grips with the critical. But, with encouragement from Justin Vaughan at Open University Press, it became gradually clearer that there was also a need being expressed by mainstream social psychologists to include coverage of critical work in their introductory courses.

What I have tried to do, therefore, is to construct a book that steers a rather difficult path – one that aims to do justice to each approach, that relates them to each other, but, crucially, does not pretend they can be integrated. The terminology I have used throughout the book is to say there is no 'fluffy bunny' solution to the conflict between them. By this I mean that it is not possible to achieve a comfortable compromise position that makes everybody feel all warm and cuddly – one where the 'best of both' can be brought together into some 'new, improved' social psychology. They are, fundamentally, incommensurable with and opposed to each other. As I set out in Chapter 2, they are based on two conflicting epistemologies (theories of the nature of knowledge and how it can be obtained) and two conflicting ontologies (theories of what things 'are' in the world, here, particularly, of the nature of the social world and people's relationship to it) that cannot be reconciled.

This has been, as they say, 'challenging' – or, to put it bluntly, incredibly difficult and at times frustrating. I have changed the structure of the book to accommodate this tension more times than I can bear to recall. The eventual design I have arrived at is as follows.

In the first part of the book, the first three chapters – I have called them 'Starting points' – set out the two approaches and clarify the main differences between them. Chapter 1 starts by reviewing the main 'bones of contention' between them – about whether or not social psychology should be a Science, about the ideological foundations of and issues raised by contemporary social psychology as it is taught and practised, and its aims to 'make the world a better place'. Next the chapter examines the two overarching paradigms within each approach is set – experimental social psychology in Modernism, and critical social psychology in Postmodernism. The rest of the chapter is devoted to tracing the historical development of each of them, in the process giving a brief history of social psychology from its origins in the late nineteenth century to the present.

Chapter 2 looks in more depth at the philosophical bases of each approach, specifically examining their epistemologies and ontologies. It does get in quite 'deep' – this is necessary to really get to grips with the radically different standpoints each one adopts on theory and research. I have used a framework taken from a number of sources but brilliantly put together (in my view) in a book by Blaikie (2000) that examines research through alternative 'logics of inquiry'. The chapter starts by examining this framework, and then goes systematically through three of its logics of inquiry – induction, deduction and abduction. By reference to a few illustrative social psychological studies, this chapter is intended to clarify precisely what is meant by each of these terms, and the way each of them delineates a different way of going about theory generation, development and refinement through different approaches to research.

Chapter 3 then gets back to the practical, examining the research methods and analytics used by social psychologists within the different approaches. This is not the usual 'how to do it' chapter on methodology (suggestions are made in the chapter about where to get this information). Rather it concentrates on giving information about the key elements of these methods and analytics in relation to how they are used within the different logics of inquiry.

The second part of the book moves on to 'Topics in social psychology' and this is where things get a bit more complicated. Chapter 4 is on 'Communication and language', and includes theory and research from both perspectives. I made it the beginning topic because language is an absolutely central issue and concern for critical social psychology, viewed through the broader theory of semiotics. This chapter, therefore, begins with the key theory and research on communication and language within experimental social psychology, and ends with a reasonably comprehensive introduction to semiotics and how this has been applied to critical social psychology.

However, the next two chapters – Chapter 5 on 'Understanding the social world', and Chapter 6 on 'Values and attitudes' – are written exclusively from the experimental perspective. Each chapter provides a basic introduction to mainstream, experimental social psychology's theory and research in these fields. This is then followed by Chapter 7 – 'Constructing the social world' – that is written from the critical perspective. This chapter begins by briefly introducing social constructionism, the theoretical framework within which critical social psychology is generally set. The chapter goes on to address the main criticisms made by critical social psychologists of mainstream approaches – especially the key areas of attribution and attitudes. It then sets out the critical camp's alternative approach. This is based on a fundamentally different conception – that the social world is not so much 'understood' as 'constructed'. My intention is that by the end of this chapter you should have a fair grasp of work in this field from both perspectives.

Chapter 8 on 'Selves and identities' goes back to covering both approaches together. It begins with – and later takes up again – an issue that is, by now, being developed in the book in a sustained manner: the issue of cultural variation (which first appeared in Chapter 6 in relation to values). This concerns the growing recognition by social psychologists that they have assumed that certain social processes and phenomena are universal when they are not. The 'self' is one of these areas where there are different conceptions, ranging from highly individualistic ones in western and northern cultures to much more relational ones in eastern and southern cultures. Next the chapter moves on to look at the early work in this field of James, Mead and Goffman. It then reviews, pretty briefly, alternative mainstream approaches, and ends by a couple of sections setting out the basic elements of the critical approach to the self. Chapter 9 goes back to a focus on experimental social psychology, reviewing its work on groups and group processes.

Chapter 10 provides an overview of the book, addressing the question of where social psychology should go next. In it I concentrate on two main issues. One takes up the theme of cultural diversity, and argues specifically that social psychology needs to take this seriously, in particular from the perspective of its ongoing racism. Social psychology has a highly racist history. In the late nineteenth and early twentieth centuries there were a number of social psychologists – most notably McDougall – who had an explicitly racist agenda; their research was directed towards demonstrating white supremacy. In this section I argue that while this overt racism has largely (but not entirely) been resigned to the history books, there still remains considerable institutional racism in the way social psychology is pursued. I make some suggestions about ways in which this aspect can be tackled.

The book ends by addressing the issue with which the book begun – the battle going on between the experimental and critical camps. Drawing on theory and research from Chapter 9 on group conflict, I suggest that it may be time for these two groups to stop behaving like two outgroups in a state of high conflict with each other, more concerned with distancing themselves from each other than seeking any engagement. Again, I make some suggestion about how this might be done, without (I hope!) resorting to a 'fluffy bunny' solution.

In certain places in the book I suggest that research in social psychology could benefit from being rather more creative than it is – taking risks, and creating situations where it is possible to genuinely make new discoveries and gain new insights. In other words, I argue for research being a 'launch-pad to an investigation' (Brown 1980: 39) where it is not known where touchdown will occur. To my real surprise, this book has turned out a lot like that. I have ended up in a rather different place from the one where I expected to land.

I was trained as a scientist (originally as a zoologist) and spent the first ten years of my career as a cognitive psychologist studying very short-term memory from a decidedly experimental perspective. I came to social psychology late and somewhat reluctantly, gaining entry into it as a critical social psychologist highly dubious about whether the social world *could* be studied experimentally. My writings and lectures in this field so far have been very much in the mode of a member of a low-status ingroup, hell bent to expose the inadequacies of experimental social psychology.

I began by accepting the need to include it in the book with a serious lack of enthusiasm. My arm was not exactly twisted, but it was certainly tweaked pretty firmly! But in its writing, I have learned a lot. I have ended it quite genuinely convinced that the future needs both approaches, and that we truly do have a lot to learn from each other, if only we could move beyond ritual name calling and into a more respectful scholarly debate. I sincerely hope that this book will make a contribution to that.

Wendy Stainton Rogers
Long Wittenham, April 2003

Acknowledgements

As I have written this book I have become increasingly aware of the immense intellectual debt I owe to Rex, my husband, co-author, co-researcher and co-conspirator for 27 years until he died in 1999. It was a bitter-sweet experience, as I was so often reminded as I wrote of his vivacious and incredibly diverse and erudite scholarship. These memories go back to some amazing, giggly, rather well-lubricated conversations with Gun Semin about 'risky shift' and 'cognitive dissonance' when both of them were young (and incredibly handsome!) lecturers finishing their doctorates. And end with memories of, in the week before he died, painstakingly working with Rex on the manuscript of our last book together when we thought he was recovering. It is far, far too little to say I could never have written a book like this without all he taught me about social psychology. Rex was a brilliant and charismatic teacher, and I was his most privileged student in so many ways. Nor could I have written this book without the support and love of all those who have helped me in the last three years to come to terms with Rex's death. My heart-felt thanks to all of you.

More specifically I would like to give particular thanks to Paul Stenner, Marcia Worrell, Kerry Chamberlain, and two anonymous reviewers who helped me prepare the design and content of the book. Special thanks go to Robin Long who took the manuscript all over the world and gave me such valuable (and tactful) feedback on it. I would like to thank the reviewers who helped me improve it once I had drafted it. It is a much shorter and a lot better book because of their advice. My thanks too to Carole Wheeler, Patricia Kelly and Ian Lowe for their support and help in finishing the manuscript.

Part I
Starting points

Chapter 1

What is social psychology?

Chapter contents

A route map of the chapter

The aim of this first chapter is to give you an overall picture of contemporary social psychology – where it is 'at' and where it is 'going'.

The first section – What the battle is about – describes three main bones of contention between the two camps – Science, ideology and the nature of the social world.

The next section then provides a context, briefly tracing the origins of social psychology. It is followed by two more focused sections, one reviewing the roots of experimental social psychology and the other the roots of critical social psychology.

The final section examines Modernism and Postmodernism. These provide the conceptual frameworks for the two approaches. Experimental social psychology is very much in the Modernist mould, whereas critical social psychology is sited in Postmodernism. This section considers two key questions from the two perspectives. Is social psychology a science? And should social psychology seek to make the world a better place?

Chapters 2 and 3 are then intended to help you develop your understanding of these two approaches to social psychology further. Chapter 2 examines their different theoretical and knowledge bases, and Chapter 3 their different research methods and analytics.

What the battle
is about

↓

The origins
of social
psychology

↓

The roots of
experimental
social
psychology

↓

The roots of
critical social
psychology

↓

Modernism and
Postmodernism

Learning objectives

When you have finished studying this chapter you should be able to:

1 Outline the three main elements of the battle between experimental and critical social psychology.
2 Trace the origins of social psychology through the work of McDougall and James, and the contributions made by *Völkerpsychologie* and crowd psychology.
3 Describe the main elements of Modernism and Postmodernism.
4 Identify the roots of and describe the historical development of both experimental and critical social psychology.
5 Explain how these two approaches are different, and why they cannot be integrated.

INTRODUCTION

What is social psychology? Actually, that's not an easy question to answer at the beginning of the twenty-first century. Contemporary social psychology is a fragmented and deeply divided discipline. There is not so much a lack of consensus – that is true for all academic disciplines – but a fierce fight going on between a sturdy Goliath (experimental social psychology) and a rather puny David (critical social psychology), with any number of skirmishes on the sidelines. So the answer to the question 'What is social psychology?' will depend on whom you ask.

Goliath is absolutely confident that social psychology is a **Science** (with a capital 'S'). David, a nimble and plucky (but, many would argue, misguided) little fellow, is equally confident that it is not – or, at least, that it shouldn't be, but something else entirely. There are some rather wet bystanders sitting on the fence who think that David and Goliath should sit down, talk peace, and work out a compromise (in academic terms, they should seek 'integration'). But the battle lines have been firmly drawn, and the majority of social psychologists identify themselves squarely in one camp or the other – with by far the largest group siding with Goliath.

Throughout the book, terms that are highlighted in bold are defined in the Glossary at the end.

WHAT THE BATTLE IS ABOUT

The argument between the two camps in social psychology is based on three main disputes, over:

- whether or not social psychology should be pursued as a Science
- ideology – that is, over whether or not social psychology is an objective, value-free endeavour, or one that promotes a particular ideological position
- what constitutes the social world and the relationship between the individual and the social phenomena, events and processes in which they are involved.

The battle over Science

What I mean by 'Science' here is what goes on in the **natural sciences** (such as physics, chemistry and biology). They seek to gain knowledge using Scientific method. Giving 'Science' a capital letter indicates a particular *version* of science, which conducts experiments using the **hypothetico-deductive method**. (We shall come on to look at other definitions of 'science' later in the chapter.)

Experimental social psychology is absolutely clear in its conviction that social psychology is a Science – indeed, I have adopted the term experimental social psychology because it takes this position:

> Social psychology employs the scientific method to study social
> behaviour . . . Science is a *method* for studying nature, and it is the
> method, not the people who use it, the things they study, the facts
> they discover or the explanations they propose, that distinguishes
> science from other approaches to knowledge. . . . The alternative to
> science is dogma or rationalism, where understanding is based upon
> authority: something is true ultimately because authorities (e.g. the
> ancient philosophers, the religious scriptures, charismatic leaders) say
> it is so.
>
> (Hogg and Vaughan 1998: 6–7, emphasis in the original)

Hogg and Vaughan's assertion makes it clear that experimental social
psychologists regard Science as the *only* valid way for social psychologists to go
about gaining knowledge. Everything else is 'dogma'.

For the other approach to social psychology I shall be using the term **critical
social psychology**. I toyed with several other possible labels – there are plenty
of them! But in the end I decided on this one for the simple reason that it is
both short and general.

Critical social psychology disputes the claim that Scientific method is the
only method that can be used to gain knowledge. This method, it says, is often
unsuited to studying the *social* aspects of people's behaviour and experience,
since these are so complex and fluid. There are, it claims, alternatives other
than 'dogma' that provide valid and useful ways of gaining knowledge. Critical
social psychology adopts an alternative logic of enquiry to Science, and uses
different ways of going about research

Logic of enquiry
is explained in
Chapter 2.

The battle over ideology

Following on from its conviction that Scientific method is the only valid means
to get knowledge, experimental social psychology regards this knowledge as
objective – unaffected by ideology and hence neutral in its values. Since
Science, in its view, makes it possible to get at 'the facts' (and facts are facts,
irrespective of politics, values, and so on), the Scientific basis of experimental
social psychology places it outside of and unaffected by ideology.

Critical social psychology disputes this. It argues for

> [a] social psychology which challenges social institutions and practices
> – including the discipline of psychology – that contribute to forms of
> inequality and oppression. . . . We are suggesting that psychologists
> should situate themselves and their work within society and develop
> a critical attitude towards psychological 'knowledge' and its
> applications.
>
> (Gough and McFadden 2001: 2–3)

It is this criticality that is the basis for my choosing critical social psychology as the label for this perspective. It views experimental social psychology as adopting an elitist ideological position that promotes the interests of the powerful (that is, the mainly white, Western, able-bodied, male Establishment) and hence contributes to the exploitation and oppression of less powerful groups.

The battle over the nature of the social world

This aspect of the battle is harder to get a handle on, so I shall, here, just describe it in terms of analogies. I hope these are helpful in at least beginning to get a sense of the differences between the two positions. They will become clearer, I promise, as you progress through the book.

Experimental social psychology has an image of the social world as something like an ocean, in which people swim like sea creatures. They may sometimes act together – like shoals of fish. They may even work cooperatively together and communicate (like dolphins do). But these are going on *within* the social world – the creatures are *immersed in* it, and it affects what they can do. It is an ocean with tides and currents that buffet and sweep the creatures along. Mostly these currents merely set them in motion in a particular direction and they still have volition about where they go (after their dinner, for example). Sometimes, though, the current will be so strong that it cannot be resisted. Crucial to this image of the social world is that the creatures and the ocean are *separate* from each other. The psychological processes going on in their minds interact with the social forces going on outside, and this interaction determines what they do.

Critical social psychology has a different image altogether. It views the social world as rather like music-making – that exists only when and because people are making it. All sorts of things may contribute to the music that is played and how it is performed. The musical instruments available, the skills and expertise of the players and singers, whether there is a conductor and, if so, their interpretation of the music – all of these will have an effect. Where and when, historically, the music is played will make a difference. Sometimes there will be a need to please a paying audience. Even, sometimes, there may be political constraints on what can be performed.

But it remains that without the players the musical instruments will be silent and there will be no music to hear. I shall not push this analogy too far, but it does give a sense the social world as something that is continually being created and recreated by people acting collectively together. It also carries the possibility of a diversity of social worlds if you think of different kinds of orchestras, musical bands and choirs throughout history and across the world, each making different kinds of music – from gamelan to rock, plainchant to jazz.

Crucial to this image of the social world is that it is not a separate milieu on the 'outside'. It is something people *do*.

There is no 'fluffy bunny' solution

You know how it is. Your friend is having a nightmare of a time, facing all sorts of dreadful problems and you don't know how to help. So you send them a card with a cute little fluffy bunny on the front, with words inside that tell them you care. (OK, so maybe it's not a fluffy bunny card, maybe you take them down the pub and buy them a pint, but you know what I mean.) It is a nice, kind, thoughtful thing to do, and they will appreciate it. But it glosses over the problems rather than doing anything to solve them.

This is what I mean by saying there is no 'fluffy bunny' solution to the conflict between experimental and critical social psychology. David and Goliath are doomed to battle on because there is no way to find a cosy resolution. In my view they are inherently antagonistic to each other and any attempt to integrate them is going to fail.

Why you need to get to know about both camps

You may wonder, then, why on earth I agreed to write a book that brings them together. I admit that there are times when I have asked myself precisely that! But here goes.

Many experimental social psychologists simply ignore critical social psychology altogether. They see it as a fringe activity conducted by an unruly rabble of misguided discontents, not really social psychology at all. You will find no mention of critical social psychology in the vast majority of standard textbooks in this field, let alone any attempt to cover its theory and research or address the criticisms it raises.

But, I would argue, critical social psychology cannot be ignored. Even though it is a fringe activity, it has become a force to be reckoned with. Since the mid-1990s it has gained a much stronger footing, in the UK in particular, but also in other parts of Europe, and in a few small outposts elsewhere in the world. The number of publications, courses and conferences devoted to it are steadily increasing. In the local situation of the UK it is now (somewhat) recognized in the research assessment exercise as a valid approach. And perhaps most notably, there is strong growth in the number of critical social psychological doctorates being pursued and awarded.

You have probably worked out by now that I belong to the 'unruly rabble' and can hardly be seen as dispassionate. But even though I have a stake in this, I do sincerely believe that anyone starting to get to grips with social psychology in the twenty-first century needs at least a basic grounding in *both* camps.

First, you need to know what the 'rabble' is up to if you are going to get a comprehensive grasp on the subject. My conviction here has grown as I have worked on the book. As I have been writing the different chapters, I was myself surprised at the effect of bringing them together. Once both approaches are applied to the various topics of social psychology, I found it striking just how much richer the picture gets. So, even if you decide to side with Goliath – if you do no more than look at what the critical approach has to offer and then say 'thanks, but no thanks' – your understanding of social psychology will be broader and deeper for getting to know about the opposition.

Alternatively, you may be persuaded by the critical arguments and become disillusioned about the experimental approach. Even so, learning about experimental social psychology is in no way a waste of time. For a start, you need to know what it is about to understand *what* is being criticized. It is also where the vast bulk of our current knowledge in social psychology comes from. So even if you accept the criticisms of how it was gained, this does not mean that you can dismiss this body of knowledge as useless. It most certainly is not. A critical approach should not persuade you to abandon experimental social psychology altogether.

So, no 'fluffy bunny' solution, then. If you go on to study social psychology further, you will have to make your mind up, sooner or later, which camp is for you. They cannot be cosily 'integrated', and so you cannot have a foot in each for long. Nor can you 'mix and match' them, any more than you could prepare a meal by cooking a single dish that combines, say, smoked fish and treacle pudding. Far from combining the delicious tastes of each, it would taste disgusting. Just as there are some foods that simply do not go together in the same dish, there are some ideas and approaches that only 'work' when they are kept separate.

However, what I do believe is possible at this stage – indeed, essential – are two things. First, I think it is essential for any student of social psychology to gain a good grasp of and grounding in *both* experimental *and* critical social psychology. I believe this book is the first to attempt such broad coverage, and is why I wrote it. Second, while integration between the two is not possible, I believe social psychology would gain considerable benefit from a more constructive dialogue between them. Currently they seem to either ignore each other, or they simply defend their opposing positions without listening to each other's arguments. If social psychology is going to continue as a vibrant and influential discipline, we need to do better than that. I make some suggestions about how we might pursue a more constructive agenda in Chapter 10.

The battle over science

There are two competing approaches to social psychology.

Experimental social psychology
- Asserts that the only valid way to gain valid knowledge about social phenomena, processes and events is by using Scientific method
- claims this knowledge is ideologically neutral
- views the social world as separate from the individual people acting within it.

Critical social psychology
- Asserts that Scientific method is not the only way to get knowledge and often not the best way to do it in social psychology
- regards all knowledge – including that of experimental social psychology – as inherently positioned ideologically
- views the social world as produced by people interacting with each other.

These alternative approaches to social psychology are antagonistic and cannot be integrated. But to gain a good grasp of social psychology, you need to have a grounding in both.

THE ORIGINS OF SOCIAL PSYCHOLOGY

The human sciences as we now know them began to be established during the late nineteenth and early twentieth centuries. The discipline boundaries were very fluid at this time, both between them and with philosophy (from which many of them had derived). Looking back there seems to have been a fair amount of jockeying for position and arguments over 'territorial' boundaries. Psychology was something of a 'late developer', having to fight hard to carve a place out for itself. This situation was rather quaintly described by one of its earliest historians like this: 'psychology was little more than a waif knocking now at the door of physiology, now at the door of ethics, now at the door of epistemology' (Murphy 1929: 172).

McDougall's social psychology

Social psychology's territory resulted from a harder – and later – fight still. According to William McDougall (1908), a vigorous proponent for social psychology in its early days, its disciplinary field had to be reclaimed from sociology and anthropology. McDougall argued that social psychology should be recognized as the rightful domain in which to study 'the springs of human action, the impulses and motives that sustain mental and bodily activity and regulate conduct' (McDougall 1919: 3). He argued specifically that 'intellectual processes' (what we would now call cognitive processes) are 'but the servants, instruments or means' by which they are processed and stored. In this he was making a specific criticism of the psychology of the time, which, he said, was almost entirely pre-occupied with cognition at the level of the individual. He attributed this to a misappropriation by other social sciences of much of the subject matter he considered to rightly be psychology's, forcing psychology to accept 'too narrow a view of its scope and methods and applications' (McDougall 1919: 6).

McDougall argued for a scientific approach to psychology and, crucially, for studying the impact of social processes, such as the process by which societies move from 'primitive' to 'civilized'. Central to McDougall's theorizing was the primacy of instinct. He viewed 'human nature' as the product of a set of instinctive tendencies – 'primitive urges' that, while they may be modified by the civilizing force of social and ethical mores, are nonetheless the primary basis of behaviour.

In this he was influenced by Darwinian evolutionary theory, which, at the time, was a dominant theme in sociology and anthropology. He specifically argued for an evolutionary psychology (McDougall 1919: 5). It is important to place this in historical context. At that time **Western** scholarship took a crude supremacist stance. When applying evolutionary theory to the social sciences, this was based on the belief that 'modern, civilized' (that is Western) societies had evolved from 'primitive, savage' ones through a process of civilization. All 'other' societies (that is the ones studied in 'outlandish' places by anthropologists) were regarded as being at a lower, less-developed stage of evolution. It is in this sense that McDougall was arguing for an 'evolutionary psychology', and it formed the basis of his theorizing.

He took as his fundamental axiom that human action arises out of biologically pre-programmed instincts, but that this conduct is modulated through the influence of social regulations operating in the society to which a person belongs and, in civilized societies, by an individual's socially acquired self-control. It is basically, then, a three-stage process:

| Instinct ———————→ | alone is what determines ———————→ | people's conduct in primitive, pre-social societies |

| Instinct + social ———→ regulation | together determine ———————————→ | people's conduct in traditional societies |

| Instinct + social regulation | + the capacity for self-regulation through the acquisition of higher moral judgement | → together determine | → people's conduct in advanced, modern societies |

What McDougall meant by an 'evolutionary psychology' then is not what we mean by this term today. Rather he was prescribing a social psychology that sought to understand *social* evolution – that is, the progressive stages that had led (in his view) to the pinnacle of human civilization, a Western world in which a person's actions are determined by each individual's higher moral judgement. The racist supremacy of this worldview is clear. As you move through this book you will see how this worldview still continues to influence mainstream social psychology, albeit in a way that is implicit rather than explicit, a point I take up in Chapter 10.

William James' social psychology

William James' books – *The Principles of Psychology* (published in 1890) and *Psychology* (published in 1907) – were general rather than specifically social psychology texts. However, they included extensive theorization about social psychology and were highly influential in its establishment. In many ways his ideas prefigured many aspects of critical social psychology.

James was critical (as was McDougall) of the **introspectionism** of early general psychology. However, this was not because he was concerned that it was 'unscientific' in its focus on subjective experience (as McDougall was), but because it failed to capture the connectedness of human thought. To describe this concept James invented a term for which he has become famous: the **stream of consciousness**. In a person's stream of consciousness, James proposed, all manner of thoughts, emotions, states, feelings, images, and ideas continually coexist at some level. At any one moment the vast majority of these are only immanent – outside of our awareness and at the 'back of our minds'. James called this state **transitivity**. In human consciousness, James said that moment by moment we become aware of just some of these – we notice, we realize, we recognize, we become aware of *something*. James called this **substantivity**.

To explain what he meant, he used an analogy of a flock of birds whirling and weaving around in the air, never still, always moving, so that it is impossible to tell where they are. But every now and then each bird will come to rest – to sit on a post or somewhere. At that moment we can locate it – it moves from a transitive to a substantive state. James emphasizes that it is only in its substantive state that we can pin down what a thought or whatever 'is'. He wrote that to try to examine thoughts or feelings or impressions in their transitive states is like holding a snowflake in our hand in order to look at it. It immediately turns it into something else – a droplet of water. James applied these ideas, in particular, to the ways in which people know themselves as 'me' (that is the self-as-known) and how they know themselves as 'I' (that is the self-as-knower).

These ideas are described more fully in Chapter 8, when we come on to look at the social psychology of the self.

Two contrasting images of the person

In the late nineteenth and early twentieth century writings of McDougall and James we can see the origins of two competing images of the person that persistently run through social psychological theorizing and research.

McDougall's image of people was that they are the largely products of their innate, biological instincts and drives, moulded by social and cultural forces into civilized members of society. This image portrays people as passive and lacking self-awareness. Even though they have, in civilized society, gained the ability to make moral judgements and thus behave ethically, this is through the internalization of civilized codes of conduct. Consequently, they lack free will.

James, in contrast, held an image of the person as a self-aware, self-conscious and self-determined being, who actively and purposively *makes* sense of the world in a connected manner, and, crucially, has the capacity for free will.

> Of course we measure ourselves by many standards. Our strength and our intelligence, our wealth and even our good luck, are things that warm our heart and make us feel ourselves a match for life. But deeper than all such things, and able to suffice unto itself without them, is the sense of the amount of effort which we can put forth. Those are, after all, but effects, products and reflections of the outer world within. But the effort seems to belong to an altogether different realm, as if it were the substantive thing that we *are*, and those are but externals that we *carry*.
>
> (James 1907: 458)

At its heart, McDougall's social psychology sees people as pieces in a chess game between external forces (in his case biological and social forces). Whether pawns or kings and queens, their destiny is in the hands of these external forces. But in James' social psychology, people are the players. While other influences (whether biological, psychological, social or whatever) may set the rules within which *people* play the game of life, people may play well or badly, they may play to win or give up when the going gets tough, but it is *they* who play the game.

The difference between these two is that in McDougall's social psychology it is an easy and straightforward matter to determine universal, causal laws of human nature since causes can be identified within external forces (external to the essential person, that is – often they are seen as internal, psychological forces). In James' social psychology it is not anywhere as easy – if possible at all – to determine causal laws of human nature, since to do so involves getting to grips with the human will. This is ultimately a matter of metaphysics and ontology – about the nature of being-in-the-world – and hence, James argues:

> When, then, we talk of 'psychology as a natural science' we must not assume that that means a sort of psychology that stands at last on solid ground. It means just the reverse: it means a psychology particularly fragile, and into which the waters of metaphysical criticism leak at every joint, a psychology all of whose elementary assumptions and data must be reconsidered in wider connections and translated into other terms.
> . . . What we have is a string of raw facts; a little gossip and wrangle about opinions; a little classification and generalization on the mere descriptive level; a strong prejudice that we *have* states of mind, and that our brain conditions them: but not a single law in the sense that physics shows us laws, not a single proposition from which any consequence can causally be deduced. . . . This is no science, it is only the hope of a science.
>
> (James 1907: 467–8)

This statement reads as highly prescient. It could almost have been written today, by a critical psychologist. In other words, the questions and issues raised by James' claim that 'This is no science, it is only the hope of a science' are as hotly debated today as they were when he wrote it – indeed, more so. In this chapter and those that follow you will be tracing this argument through social psychology's history and development over the nearly 100 years since James first raised it.

Early movements in social psychology

Social psychology was born out of aspirations to recapture certain aspects of 'the social' from sociology and 'the cultural' from anthropology. While there were earlier attempts to develop a 'psychology of society' (Lindner 1871), social psychology had its main roots in two movements in European psychology that predated the work of McDougall and James: German *Völkerpsychologie* and French and Italian work on 'crowd psychology'.

Völkerpsychologie

Völkerpsychologie is not that easy a term to translate; 'folk psychology', with its associated images in English of folklore and folk singing, is rather misleading. Its literal translation is 'a psychology of the people', which is somewhat better – though 'a psychology of ordinary people' is possibly closer. It was developed as a specifically psychological discipline by proposing that people who belong to particular *social* groups tend to think in a collective rather than individual manner; to hold the same opinions and beliefs, and to share the same values. To put this into today's terms, consider, say, members of a religious sect or an issue-based political group (such as the Taliban or Animal Rights activists). They can sometimes come across as though they have lost their capacity for independent judgement and to 'think as one'.

Like most psychological movements, *Völkerpsychologie* was a product of the prevailing concerns of its time and place. When it was first developed in Germany in the late nineteenth century, it was to try to understand what was going on as the nation state of Germany was being created from many small provinces and principalities. This was well before both world wars, remember. In this context *Völkerpsychologie*'s originators were mainly interested in discovering what it was that marked off a specifically *German* national character.

Murphy (1929) identifies Steinthal and Lazarus as its founders; they established its journal *Zeitschrift für Völkerpsychologie und Sprachwissenschaft* in 1900. But Wilhelm Wundt, the founder of modern experimental psychology, was its best-known proponent. Although he is generally most remembered as the 'father' of experimental psychology, according to Murphy, Wundt 'devoted some of his best energies' (Murphy 1929: 172) to the topic and completed five volumes of *Völkerpsychologie* between 1900 and 1920.

In some ways *Völkerpsychologie* was ahead of its time, in that its theories proposed a link between culture and language (see Chapter 4). Wundt, for instance, suggested that the vocabulary and grammar of a particular language profoundly affect the way people think and perceive the social world, and hence argued that language can provide a unifying medium for group identity and membership.

Crowd psychology

Crowd psychology also arose from social and political concerns of the time in which it was originated – here the broader social upheavals that had occurred in Europe in the previous century, such as the French Revolution. In particular it was devised to seek to understand how and why, when large masses of people act together, they seem to function as an entity – a 'crowd' or a 'mob'– rather than as individuals. Its foremost proponent was the French theorist Gustave Le Bon, who brought these ideas together in a book, *Crowd Psychology* (published in 1895).

Its central idea was in many ways parallel to that of *Völkerpsychologie*; that of a 'group mind'. Le Bon suggested that in certain situations, a 'mob' can best be seen as acting as a single, primitive entity, operating on a lower intellectual and moral plane than even its average member would usually adopt. Le Bon's writing was vivid, portraying 'the mob' as subject to collective madness and savagery. He drew upon the work of Charcot on hypnosis and suggestability, arguing that mob leaders (or even the mob itself) exert psychic pressure that strips the mob's members of their individual wills and coerces them to act as one – for good or ill.

Another influential theorist in this field was Tarde. In his book *The Laws of Imitation* (published in 1890) he also drew heavily on the concept of suggestibility, though his work was more comprehensive than Le Bon's. For example, Tarde speculated about the impact of cities upon outlying regions, with progress in popular opinion originating in cities and then diffusing out to the population as a whole. He also explored what happens when one nation is conquered by another, and how the values, opinions and practices of the conquerors tend to become adopted by the conquered. He suggested similar processes may occur between elite groups and the general population. As we shall see later, these ideas have been taken up more recently in theorization about social representations (also see Chapter 7).

The parting of the ways

In Western antiquity there were two main strands of philosophical thought about the relationship between the individual and society: Platonic – emphasizing the primacy of the state over the individual; and Aristotelian – emphasizing individual autonomy and freedom. Graumann (2001) calls these the individuo-centred and the socio-centred approaches.

- The **individuo-centred approach** focuses on the ways in which social grouping, social institutions and social forces are determined by the behaviour of individuals and the processes going on within individual minds. It is from this approach that psychology emerged as a discipline, focusing on what goes on within individual minds. Politically this approach is **liberal individualism**, that, as you have seen, stresses individual autonomy and freedom.

- The **socio-centred approach** focuses on the ways in which the behaviour and experiences of individual people are strongly determined by their membership of social groups and social institutions. The underlying philosophy of this approach is found, for example, in the writings of Hegel (1770–1831), who viewed the state as the ultimate form of society and the basis of the social mind to which individuals belong. It is from this approach that sociology emerged, and social psychological work on the 'group mind' also followed from this tradition. Politically this approach is **liberal humanism**, stressing the responsibility of individuals to contribute to the good of society through collective effort.

These two philosophies and traditions underpin two different approaches to social psychology – usually called **psychological social psychology** and **sociological social psychology** (Stephan and Stephan 1990). These labels convey the different emphases of each and their different disciplinary origins. Each has its own history and its own pioneers and heroes, and, to a certain extent, their power bases are located in different places. Speaking very broadly, the 'movers and shakers' of sociological social psychology have been and are European whereas psychological social psychology almost entirely dominates the subject in the USA.

As you have probably worked out by now, these two approaches are, to a degree, the progenitors of experimental and critical social psychology. However (sorry!) it is rather more complicated than that. What I am going to do next is trace the historical development of each of them and show how psychological social psychology gave rise to experimental social psychology and sociological social psychology gave rise to critical social psychology. Notice, though, that they are offshoots. Not all psychological social psychologists are experimental social psychologists, and not all sociological social psychology are critical social psychologists.

As you move through the book you will come up against some 'minor players' – other approaches to social psychology that do not fall neatly into either the experimental or critical camps. Space does not allow me to include them in this chapter. I shall give some basic details about them as they arise throughout the book.

The origins of social psychology

- *Völkerpsychologie* and crowd psychology were early progenitors of social psychology.
- From its beginnings, social psychology was a divided discipline: psychological social psychology (arising from early psychology,

and taking an individuo-centred approach) and sociological social psychology (emerging from early sociology and taking a socio-centred approach).

- The roots of experimental social psychology are in psychological social psychology. They can be traced back to the work of William McDougall, whose image of the person was of a passive subject of external forces, lacking free-will.
- The roots of critical social psychology are in sociological social psychology and can be traced back to the work of William James, whose image of the person was of an active, purposeful agent with free will.

THE ROOTS OF EXPERIMENTAL SOCIAL PSYCHOLOGY

Even before McDougall published his *Introduction to Social Psychology* (McDougall 1908) a turn to experimentation had begun. Interestingly there seems to have grown up something of a myth about what was the first social psychological experiment, but it is usually attributed to Norman Triplett (1898).

Triplett's study of dynamogenic influence – the making of a myth

When he was studying the cycling records of the Racing Board of the League of American Wheelmen (a cycling organization) of 1897, Triplett noticed that the times recorded for cyclists racing against each other were faster than when they raced alone against the clock. This intrigued him, and he tried to work out why. He surmised that there must have been some kind of 'energizing force' – a sort of psychological dynamo – that arises from competition. From this he formed the general hypothesis that the presence of others has a 'dynamogenic' influence on an individual's behaviour; that is, it leads to a speeding up of performance. To test this hypothesis he carried out an experiment.

In the experiment Triplett gave fishing rods to forty 8 to 17-year-old boys and girls and asked them to wind them up as fast as they could. As in all good experiments (see Chapter 3) he had a control group (children winding on their own) and an experimental group (children winding with others). As the dependent variable he used the speed at which the children wound the reel, since it was something he could objectively measure. His results were not all that clear-cut. When in the presence of another, some children wound faster, some slower than when they were reeling on their own. He attributed the faster reeling of the children who speeded up to 'the arousal of their competitive instincts and the idea of faster movement' and the slower reeling of the children who went less fast as them being over-stimulated by the task and 'going to pieces' (Triplett 1898: 526). There were not the statistical techniques we have today to sort out what was going on, so it is interesting that this study is generally reported as clearly supporting the hypothesis that the presence of others improves performance.

Hogg and Vaughan (1998) argue that Triplett's study is not a very good candidate for social psychology's first experiment, since it was not recognized as such at the time. They suggest that what is going on here is an 'origin myth'. As the story of Triplett's study has been told and retold, it has got **reified** as 'the first psychological' experiment (for example, Allport 1954; Sears *et al.* 1991) and simplified to tell a good story. Smith and Mackie, for example, clearly state categorically, '[s]ure enough, children's performance improved in the presence of others' (Smith and Mackie 2000: 7).

It was certainly not the first study of social influence. For instance, in an earlier study by Ringleman, a French agriculturalist, the results he obtained showed that when people work together to pull on a rope they tend to expend less effort than when pulling alone. Later work on **social influence** (as this area of social psychology is called) has shown that the situation is actually a highly complex one. But nonetheless Triplett seems to have found his place in history.

What is most important here, though, is that Triplett did adopt experimental method to provide evidence for developing his theory. Writing in 1929 Murphy commented: 'Probably the most striking event in contemporary social psychology is the introduction of experimental method' (Murphy 1929: 298). To us today it may not seem at all a radical thing to do – but it was pretty daring at the time. In so doing Triplett was seeking to identify social psychology as a Science, acquiring for it the legitimacy of being based upon objective evidence. This was a very significant turning point, one that has led to a situation today where experimental social psychology has come to be the dominant approach in the field.

Behaviourism

While its origins were European, once experimental social psychology took root in the USA it very much made its home there. From about 1890 to 1910, the USA became the centre for experimental research in psychology generally. In those 20 years, 31 universities in the USA set up experimental psychology faculties and departments (Ruckmick 1912). As an indication of just how dominant the position of the USA later became, it has been estimated that by the 1950s there were more social psychologists in the University of Michigan than in the whole of western Europe at that time (Smith and Harris Bond, 1993)!

Where social psychology was studied at the turn of the twentieth century, this was very much within the approach to general experimental psychology that was dominant in the USA at the time – **behaviourism**. The shift in approach was dramatic. When read these days, McDougall's (1908) *Introduction to Social Psychology* is nothing like we would recognize as a social psychology textbook. It comes across as rambling, opinionated and highly speculative, constantly making unsubstantiated claims about 'human nature'. By contrast Floyd Allport's *Social Psychology* (1924) looks much more familiar, even though it was published back at the beginning of the twentieth century.

Allport proposed that social psychology needed to become an experimental science if it was to be taken seriously. The book set out this agenda, based on Behaviourist principles. For example, in it Allport claimed that children develop language through conditioning. At its core, Behaviourism assumes that *all* behaviours are stimulated by instinctive drives and learned though the contingencies with which those drives were either rewarded or punished. Allport argued that this applies just as much to social behaviour. He emphatically rejected the foreign notion of a 'group mind'. Groups cannot think or behave, he argued, only individuals can.

Social influence, he said, is just one of the factors that shapes the motivations and perceptions of individuals. Allport conducted a number of experiments on this topic (see, for example, Allport 1920) and in his 1924 book he was the first to adopt the term 'social facilitation' (Hollander 1971: 59). This interest in the influence of others led Allport to study **attitudes**, which he did very much from within the Behaviourist tradition.

Social Learning theory

A good illustration of the how the Behaviourist approach became modified into Social Learning theory in the 1950s is a description written by Hilgard:

> Social motives may be acquired in the course of social behaviour. . . .
> [S]ocial behaviour is learned, in the first instance, in the course of
> satisfying physiological drives in a cultural setting. Once social motives
> are acquired, they become the basis of further learning.
>
> (Hilgard 1953: 127)

Hilgard then went on to argue that this leads to the establishment of 'social drives' (such as a autonomy, achievement and aggression), which stimulate people to behave in certain ways and create the conditions for learning (that is by the reinforcement of the behaviours that reduce the drive). He recognized that, unlike instinctive drives, social drives vary from one social group to another, seeing social learning as the means by which children become socialized according to the social drives of their social group.

Gestalt psychology

In the 1930s a significant number of social psychology's most distinguished thinkers fled from Europe to the USA. Many were Jews escaping from Nazisim. Indeed, so marked was this diaspora that one psychologist, Cartwright (1979), has claimed that the person who had the most impact upon the development of social psychology in the USA was Adolf Hitler!

The European refugees had been trained in **Gestalt psychology,** an approach that views context as a crucial driver for the way people perceive objects. Founded by Wertheimer in 1912 (Ellis 1938), Gestalt psychology used phenomenological methods (where people are asked to report their experiences) to gain insight into what and how people perceive.

Gestalt is another German word that does not translate very well into English, but means something like 'configuration' where the whole is more than the sum of its parts. An example is the famous image that can be seen either as two faces or a candlestick (Figure 1.1). Whichever you 'see', it is only visible through the relationship between the figure and ground – in this case they are reversible.

Figure 1.1
The candlestick/faces image is a well-known example of a Gestalt configuration, in which the figure constructs the ground and vice versa

When these refugees got to the USA and found social psychology dominated by Behaviourism, there was something of a rebellion; émigré social psychologists like Kurt Lewin and Mustafa Sherif refused to go along with Behaviourism's demand that mental states must be excluded from study since they cannot be objectively observed.

The emergence of experimental social psychology

These émigrés developed the experimental social psychology that we know today. They did so by moving away from behaviourist concepts (such as 'drives') to ones based on social influence.

Lewin is generally considered the 'founding father' of experimental social psychology. His particular interest was in the effects of social groups and group dynamics (Lewin 1947a, 1947b). Lewin developed **Field theory** based on Gestalt principles (Lewin 1951). In it he proposed that behaviour is influenced by the 'psychological field' or 'social climate' in the same way that the perceptual field influences what a person sees (Lewin *et al.* 1939). Sherif also developed a range of elegant experimental studies on social norms (Sherif 1936) and social judgement (Sherif and Hovland 1961).

You will look in more detail at Sherif's work on groups in Chapter 9.

The first book called *Experimental Social Psychology* was published by Murphy and Murphy (1931). By no means were all of the studies included in it experimental, but all were based upon hypothetico-deductive method. It is this that holds experimental social psychology together. Its status as a science is warranted by its use of scientific method.

> Social psychology is a science because it uses the scientific method to construct and test theories. Just as physics has concepts such as electrons, quarks and spin to explain physical phenomena, social psychology has concepts such as dissonance, attitude, categorisation, and identity to explain social psychological phenomena. The scientific method dictates that no theory is 'true' simply because it is logical and makes internal sense. On the contrary, a theory is valid on the basis of its correspondence with fact. Social psychologists construct theories from data and/or previous theories and then conduct empirical research in which data are collected to test the theory.
>
> (Hogg and Vaughan 1998: 3)

The roots of experimental social psychology

- A number of social psychological experiments were carried out in the late nineteenth century. Triplett's may not have been the first, but it is the best known. His experiment investigated what he

→

called a 'dynamogenic' influence on the speed at which children wound fishing rods – what we would now call 'social influence'.

- Experimental social psychology soon became established in the USA, located, at the beginning, in behaviourism and later in **Social Learning Theory**.

- However, experimental social psychology as we now know it was originated by Gestalt psychologists such as Lewin and Sherif, who emigrated to the USA in the 1940s. They expanded its scope to take in concepts like group dynamics and **group norms**, and introduced its main topics: **social perception**, social influence and **social interaction**.

THE ROOTS OF CRITICAL SOCIAL PSYCHOLOGY

Sociological social psychology grew out of sociology, based upon the traditions set by Emil Durkheim (1858–1917). Durkheim believed that 'social facts' are largely independent and outside of individual consciousness, and that it is the **collective representations** shared *between* people that determine how people understand and make sense of the world rather than individual representations, what we now call **intersubjectivity**.

Both *Völkerpsychologie* and crowd psychology stimulated the development of sociological social psychology. Tarde's work, for example, was highly influential upon the sociologist Ross, who published his text, *Social Psychology*, in 1908. Ross saw the discipline as the study of the 'planes and currents that come into existence among men in consequence of their association' (Ross, 1908: 1).

The theories
of Mead and
Goffman are
described in
Chapter 8.

Yet while Durkheim had called for a 'collective psychology' separate from individual psychology, there was actually very little activity in this field within psychology itself until the 1960s. It was sociologists like George Herbert Mead and Erving Goffman who pursued subjects like identity (Mead 1934a, 1977a, 1934b, 1977b; Goffman 1959) and behaviour in public (Goffman 1963).

Social representations theory

Social
representations
theory and
research is
described in
Chapter 7.

The turning point came at the beginning of the 1960s, although its impact was limited until the 1970s when work done in France was translated into English. A major stimulus was provided by Serge Moscovici when he published his pioneering study *La Psychoanalyse: son image et son public* (Moscovici 1961, 1976). Moscovici presented this as a study of **social representations**, which he saw as intermediate between collective and individual representations. He wanted to know how psychoanalytic terms (like 'complex') had come to be used by ordinary people. His interest lay in looking at how the knowledge of experts – their ideas about, concepts of and explanations for madness – had seeped out of the domain of expert knowledge and into what 'everybody knows'. Social representations research is now flourishing and influential in its own right (see, for example, Flick 1998). It is, in many ways, the contemporary site where sociological social psychology continues to operate – Flick calls it 'the psychology of the social'.

The branching off of critical social psychology

By the 1970s there was a distinct shift, with a number of social psychologists calling on their colleagues to 'put the social back into social psychology', including Rom Harré (see Harré 1979; Harré and Secord 1972), Henri Tajfel (1972) in the UK and Ken Gergen in the USA (Gergen 1973; Gergen and Gergen 1984). This shift became something of a landslide by the 1980s (albeit a relatively small and local one). Again there were several influential people, including Henriques and his colleagues (Henriques *et al*. 1984) and Jonathan Potter and Margaret Wetherell (Potter and Wetherell 1987). By the end of the decade Ian Parker – another leading light of the new movement – was calling the shift 'the crisis in modern social psychology' (Parker 1989) and arguing that it needed to be resolved.

At this point I need to change my metaphor from geology to biology, as what was going on by now was not so much a shift as a branching off. What had started out as a social psychology with a socio-centred focus was becoming something else – or actually, more like a number of different something elses! For Reason and Rowan (1981) among others, it was turning into a 'new paradigm'. For Gergen it was turning into social constructionist social psychology. For Potter and Wetherell it was becoming a **discursive psychology**. And for Henriques *et al*. and Parker it was a revolutionary movement turning into critical psychology. New alignments were being made, allying this new species of social psychology variously with symbolic interactionism, sociology of knowledge, semiotics, poststructuralism, and postmodern theory.

These aspects are described in Chapter 2, and taken up again in Chapter 7.

The roots of critical social psychology

Sociological social psychology has its roots in sociology, and focuses on the ways in which people's thinking and actions are socially mediated and operate at a social level.

- Sociological social psychology has been heavily influenced by sociological theory, including those of Emile Durkheim, George Herbert Mead and Erving Goffman.

- Up until the 1970s, psychologists generally did not pursue sociological social psychology. It first gained momentum as a serious alternative to experimental social psychology through the work of Serge Moscovici on social representations.
- In the 1970s and 1980s a number of psychologists such as Ken Gergen, Rom Harré, Jonathan Potter, Margaret Wetherell, and Ian Parker began to draw new theories into social psychology – mainly Social constructionism, Postmodernism and discourse analysis. These provided the basis for what I have called in this book critical social psychology.

MODERNISM AND POSTMODERNISM

In the previous section you have seen that experimental and critical social psychology developed from two different traditions. However, the division goes further than this. They draw on two fundamentally different philosophies – Modernism and Postmodernism. So, to understand where each of them are 'coming from', you need to start by understanding a bit about these two.

Modernism

Modernism is the name given to a set of theoretical and ethical beliefs and values, practices and endeavours, that were developed in Europe and the USA during the historical period of the Enlightenment in the eighteenth century. Modernism is based on four main principles:

- *Democracy*: the rights of citizens to determine their own destiny.
- *Liberal individualism*: the rights of citizens to autonomy and freedom from state power.
- *Liberal humanism*: a commitment to human betterment.
- *Science*: an empirical approach to gain rational knowledge

Democracy

Modernism gave birth to democracy. Key events in the founding of Modernism were the French and American Revolutions, where people took up arms in order to challenge the authority of rulers (in France the king and aristocracy, in the USA the colonial power of England). They fought for the democratic rights of ordinary people to be treated as citizens rather than subjects.

Liberal individualism

They also fought to challenge the power of any state – whether democratic or not – to interfere in people's private lives, and for the rights of individuals to, among other things, freedom of religion and freedom of speech. This aspect of Modernism champions the rights of the individual and seeks to limit the power of the state.

Liberal humanism

However, Modernism was not just pursued through armed conflict. These revolutions were inspired by the great thinkers of the day. Modernism is sometimes called the post-Enlightenment project, since it was (and is) motivated by the conviction that people can – and, crucially, *should* – create a better world through their *own* efforts (rather than, say, relying upon the benevolence of God). This aspect of Modernism is prepared to restrict some elements of individual freedom to maintain a well-ordered, well-functioning society (for example, to prevent crime). It therefore accepts that the state can have some power, so long as it uses it to serve human interests and protect human rights.

Science

At the very core of Modernism is the conviction that only science has the capacity to discover true knowledge. Modernism challenged the capacity of mysticism, superstition and religion to define what constitutes knowledge. It sought to replace irrationality and disorder with reason and rationality. It adopted **empiricism** in order to progress from knowledge based on subjective beliefs (those of religion, magic or the arcane) to knowledge gained by rational means, through scientific methods of empirical inquiry.

Epistemological evolution

Modernism is usually presented as the pinnacle of an evolution of **epistemology** (the theory of knowledge, covered in more detail in Chapter 2) (Douglas 1966):

First of all there was	a primitive world where knowledge was based on magic and superstition.
This was superseded by	a pre-modern world where knowledge was based upon religious belief – where an all-knowing God was viewed as the sole authority of what constitutes true knowledge.

| Which was itself then superseded by | a modern world where knowledge is based on rationality, where empiricism is held to be the means to obtain objective, factual, accurate knowledge. |

This 'up the mountain' tale of epistemological progress (Rorty 1980) views science as the supreme source of knowledge. It regards all other sources (such as magic, religion and traditional folklore) as not really knowledge at all, but merely 'beliefs' and 'myths'.

Postmodernism

Postmodernism is a major influence on critical social psychology. The word reads as though it follows on from Modernism, a fourth stage in the progression set out above, but this is misleading. It is neither a historical period nor a stage following on from Modernism. It is a reaction against and challenge to it. Here we need to concentrate on its challenge to Science – the radically different position Postmodernism takes on what knowledge is and how it can be gained. Postmodernism views knowledge as constructed rather than discovered, as multiple rather than singular, and as a means by which power is exercised.

Knowledge is constructed, not simply discovered

Modernism assumes that Science is capable of discovering the real things and real happenings that are 'out there' in the real world. Postmodernists do not deny the existence of a real, material world – a world of 'death and furniture' (Edwards *et al.* 1993). But they *do* deny that this real world can ever be simply '*dis*-covered' – as if all that needs to be done is to gradually strip off the veils of human ignorance to reveal the facts about the-world-as-it-really-is. Postmodernism stresses that the knowledge obtained by Science is – like all other knowledge – a *representation* of the 'real-world', influenced by what scientists chose to observe, how they interpret what they find, and, crucially, the stories they tell about what they have observed and found.

Donna Haraway describes Science as a story-telling craft. Scientists make their mark, she says, by telling clever and convincing stories about their data. And, she stresses, the 'story quality of the sciences . . . is not some pollutant that can be leached out by better methods, say by finer measures and more careful standards of field experiment. . . . The struggle to construct good stories is a major part of the craft' (Haraway 1984: 79–80). Postmodern theory views scientific knowledge – just like any other knowledge – as a product of human inventiveness, intuition, insight, and creativity.

There is not just one true knowledge

Since, according to Postmodern theory, there is no way to get *direct* knowledge about the real world, then there will never be one single reality (that is one true knowledge). Rather people construct a variety of different knowledges. Each of these knowledges is made – and made real – by human meaning-making.

Postmodernists accept that some forms of knowledge may be more useful than others, according to the situation. Since Scientific method constructs knowledge in a rigorous and systematic way, Postmodernists acknowledge that it can be particularly functional in situations where it 'works' – where, for example, it tests different materials for their strength and durability and what they can do. All of the technology that makes modern life possible – from vacuum cleaners to jet planes, mobile phones to skyscrapers – have been developed using scientific knowledge.

But Postmodernists point out that there are circumstances where scientific knowledge is not so useful. For instance, many of the diseases of modern life – stress, pre-menstrual tension, chronic fatigue syndrome – cannot be diagnosed through scientific tests, because they are socially and culturally constructed, defined and experienced.

An example here is a disorder that is, in Scientific terms, called 5α-reductase deficiency. This definition describes a genetic 'bug' that gives rise to a child being born who *looks* female, but is genetically male. The deficiency prevents the male foetus developing a penis and testicles. But, once the hormones of puberty 'kick in' they override the deficiency sufficiently for the boy's penis and testicles to develop – although they are small and the individual is infertile.

What the disorder means and signifies – both to the person concerned and the others around them – differs according to where it occurs. The condition is called *kwolu-aatowol* in Papua New Guinea, which means 'neither male nor female'. As it is a genetic condition that occurs more frequently (though still quite rarely) in New Guinea, it is usually recognized at birth. The baby is accorded a 'third' gender – neither male nor female – and is brought up as neither a boy nor a girl. As such the individual is excluded from the usual rites of passage that mark transition into adulthood, and *kwolu-aatowol* tend to live on the margins of their community.

The condition is also found in the Dominican Republic, where it is called *uevedoces* ('penis-at-twelve'), *machihembra* ('male-female') or *guevotes* ('penis-and-eggs'). The difference in this society is that such individuals can, however, gain male status at puberty. Even though they are infertile they can become heads of households and participate in male life. An alternative today is that some individuals go to the USA to have surgery, to 'reconstruct' them as women (see Lorber 1994 for a more detailed discussion).

In this example we can see that scientific knowledge can tell us about the biological mechanisms at work. But it cannot tell us about the meaning of the disorder, how it will be experienced, and how the affected person will be treated. For this other forms of knowledge about human meaning-making are required.

Knowledge and power

Postmodernism offers an extensive and elaborate body of theorization about the relationship between knowledge and power. It regards scientific knowledge as a particularly powerful form of knowledge, since Science claims it has the authority of truth. Postmodernists argue that we need to be very wary of this claim and the power this gives to Science to tell us what is and what is not true. This is especially so when dealing with social actions and phenomena, since scientists are human and hence will always have a stake in the stories they tell about human interests and concerns.

SOCIAL PSYCHOLOGY, MODERNISM AND POSTMODERNISM

Historically, social psychology (and, indeed, psychology in general) is very much a product of Modernism. In particular it has adopted two of the central principles of Modernism:

- its principle that Science is the route to knowledge, and hence the view that social psychology should be a Science
- its liberal humanistic principle of human betterment, and hence the view that social psychology should seek to make the world a better place.

This section looks briefly at each of these claims, in relation to the positions taken by experimental social psychology and critical social psychology.

Is social psychology a science?

The answer to this question is – it all depends what you mean by science! Social psychology is usually seen as a **human science** – one of a number of disciplines that study people. Human sciences are usually taken to include anthropology (people in culture), economics (people and money), geography (people and places), history (people over time) and sociology (people in society). However, in all these human sciences, there are different interpretations of the word 'science'.

In this book, I have used two different terms, to highlight the different interpretations. I use the uncapitalized term 'science' to refer to its general meaning: 'an effort to make accurate observations and valid causal inferences, and to assemble these observations and inferences in a compact and coherent way' (Brickman 1980: 10). By contrast I use the capitalized term 'Science' to refer to the use of Scientific (that is, hypothetico-deductive) method.

Social psychologists differ in the position they take on whether social psychology is a 'science' (that is, is based on rigorous and empirical methods) or a 'Science' (is based on Scientific method). Some social psychologists see it as a 'science' – as a rigorous, empirical form of inquiry, but not necessarily needing to use any particular method: 'contrary to what is sometimes asserted, science is a question of aim, not method' (Brickman 1980: 10). Others, however stress the centrality of Scientific method: 'Social psychology is a science because it uses the scientific method to construct and test theories' (Hogg and Vaughan 1998: 3).

Generally experimental social psychologists adopt the second position – they regard social psychology as a Science, based on Scientific method. Critical social psychologists take the first position, viewing social psychology as a 'science' – a rigorous and systematic means of conducting research and developing theory. They deny that social psychology is a 'Science', because, they argue, Scientific method is not the only or even the best way to be rigorous and systematic.

Just to give one example, semiotics was defined by Saussure, its originator, as a 'science that studies the life of signs within a society' (Saussure 1959: 16). Semiotics is one of the main theoretical frameworks adopted by critical social psychologists to study human communication. It does not use Scientific method, but rather a close scrutiny of the signs and symbols through which meanings are made and managed. Semiotics is a good approach to use to understand the social and cultural aspects of 5α-reductase deficiency because it deals with symbols, meanings and significance.

Semiotics is addressed in Chapter 4.

Should social psychology try to make the world a better place?

From its Modernist beginnings, social psychology has had what Tiffin *et al.* (1940) termed a 'humaneering' mission:

> The value of learning more about ourselves and human nature is obvious. Our social, political and economic theories rest ultimately upon our understanding of human nature. Upon sound knowledge of human nature depends the possibility of directing social changes, so as to make social institutions and practices better suited to human needs. As citizens, then, we need to make our beliefs about human nature as sound and rational as possible. The nineteenth century was marked by great achievements in engineering. Advances in psychology, sociology, and

physiology should lead to as striking advances in 'humaneering' during the twentieth century.

(Tiffin *et al.* 1940: 23–4)

Critical social psychologists would agree that social psychologists have a duty to 'change the world'. However, they are often highly critical of institutionalized social psychology. Many of them go further, by using their study of the discipline as a form of political activism to challenge oppression.

> Social psychology should be about changes in the real world. It should also, though, be concerned with how people can collectively *change* the order of things for themselves. Unfortunately, social psychology as an academic institution is structured in such a way as to blot out that which is most interesting about social interaction (language, power and history) and to divert attention from efforts to de-construct its oppressive functions in a practical way.

(Parker 1989: 1, emphasis in the original)

These studies are described in Chapter 7.

You will generally find that the topics studied by critical social psychologists are ones concerned in some way with the abuse of power. Sometimes they specifically address issues of domination, exploitation and abuse. Examples include Wetherell and Potter's (1992) study of racism, and Kitzinger and Frith's (1999) study of how men exploit women's difficulties in rejecting unwanted sexual advances.

Stenner's study of jealousy is described in Chapter 3.

In others the topics may appear less overtly 'political' (an example here is Stenner's 1993 study of jealousy). However, the analysis applied always has a 'political' undercurrent. A term introduced by Michel Foucault – the **micropolitics of power** – is useful here. It neatly describes the main aim of much critical research: to tease out how the micropolitics of power are being exercised and resisted in people's relations with one another, whether as individuals or as groups.

So, as you can see, again there is general agreement that social psychology should seek to 'make the world a better place'. However, there are significant differences in how this should be pursued, and what should be the targets for change.

Social psychology, Modernism and Postmodernism

- *Modernism* is based on the assumption that science is the only way to gain rational knowledge.
- *Postmodernism* is based on the assumption that knowledge is constructed rather than discovered, multiple rather than singular, and a means by which power is exercised.

- *Is social psychology 'scientific'?* It depends on your definition. Both approaches agree that it should be rigorous, empirical and systematic. But experimental social psychology views it as a Science, based on Scientific method. Critical social psychology regards Scientific method as just one possible means to gain knowledge, and often not the best one.
- Both experimental and critical social psychology have a commitment to *'making the world a better place'*, but they have radically different ideas what this entails. Experimental social psychologists seek to promote liberal values, such as freedom, love and the pursuit of happiness. Critical social psychologists have a much more 'political' agenda – such as fighting oppression and exposing exploitation.

FURTHER READING

Experimental social psychology

Hogg, M.A. and Vaughan, G.M. (1998) *Social Psychology,* 2nd edn. Hemel Hempstead: Prentice Hall.

> You will find the introductory chapter (Chapter 1) to this book particularly helpful if the basis of Scientific method as adopted by psychology is unfamiliar to you. It contains a comprehensive section on Scientific method on pages 7–16, which clearly explains its basis, its goals and its various forms. Overall this first chapter is an excellent exposition of experimental social psychology, including a short critique of critical social psychological approaches.

Smith, E.R. and Mackie, D.M. (2000) *Social Psychology.* Philadelphia, PA: Taylor and Francis.

> If you are after a straight US text, this one is probably the clearest and the best. Its first chapter is not as detailed or erudite as Hogg and Vaughan, but it gives a much broader introduction to the topics and approaches than I have been able to do. It is particularly good at introducing social psychology's applied topics.

Critical social psychology

Gough, B. and McFadden, M. (2001) *Critical Social Psychology: An Introduction.* Basingstoke: Palgrave.

> As far as I know, this is the only textbook (as opposed to edited collection) specifically dealing with critical social psychology. At this

stage you may find it a bit too detailed, but it is well written and clear. If this approach has 'grabbed' you already, this book should keep you contentedly busy for some time.

Gergen, K. (1973) Social psychology as history, *Journal of Personality and Social Psychology*, 26: 309–20.
>This was a highly influential article at the beginnings of critical social psychology and still worth reading today.

Sociological social psychology

Flick, U. (ed.) (1998) *The Psychology of the Social*. Cambridge: Cambridge University Press.
>This is the best source if you want to find out where sociological social psychology is 'at' these days. Flick's introductory chapter sets this out cogently.

QUESTIONS

1 'Social psychology has always had a mission to "make the world a better place".' Compare and contrast the stance taken by experimental and critical social psychology in relation to this claim.
2 Is social psychology scientific? Should it be?
3 'Postmodernism is not a development from modernism, it is a reaction against it.' Do you agree?
4 What are the origins of the concept of 'group mind'? Say why you think this concept was rejected by experimental social psychology.
5 'Social psychological theories are the products of the times and places in which they are developed.' Discuss this statement, with illustrations from the early movements in social psychology, from experimental social psychology in the 1940s and from the emergence of critical social psychology in the 1970s and 1980s.

Chapter 2

Social psychology's two paradigms

Chapter contents

A route map of the chapter

The first section systematically works through experimental social psychology's ontological and epistemological assumptions. It distinguished between inductive and deductive logics of inquiry. In particular it focuses on Scientific method – **hypothetico-deductivism**. The second section describes critical social psychology's ontological and epistemological assumptions. In critical social psychology the pursuit of knowledge is usually framed within social constructionism, and its basic principles and approaches are outlined here. The section goes on to compare the critical realist and critical relativist approaches, and then focuses on abduction as a logic of inquiry. Sometimes abduction is deployed in Science – it is the basis of discovery in Science (Kuhn 1970). In social constructionist research, however, it is used more strategically, and this section describes and illustrates abductory research. Both uses are described in this section. The chapter ends with a review, briefly summarizing the main differences between the two paradigms.

Epistemology and ontology in experimental social psychology

⬇

Epistemology and ontology in critical social psychology

⬇

Comparing and contrasting the two paradigms

Learning objectives

When you have finished studying the chapter you should be able to:

1 Outline the ontological and epistemological assumptions upon which experimental social psychology is based.
2 Describe the key elements of the inductive and deductive logics of inquiry, and define the difference between them.
3 List the main stages of hypothetico-deductive method, illustrating this with reference to a study of the effects on problem solving of expressing the problem in abstract or meaningful terms.
4 Outline the ontological and epistemological assumptions of critical social psychology.
5 Describe the basic principles of social constructionism, and compare critical realist and critical relativist approaches to gaining knowledge.
6 Define abduction as a logic of inquiry, describe how it can be the basis of discovery in Science and give an account of its strategic use in social constructionist research.
7 Summarize the main differences between the two paradigms of experimental and critical social psychology, in particular in relation to their approaches to gaining knowledge, how they deal with complexity, and their position on objectivity.

INTRODUCTION

In order to understand the differences between the experimental and critical approaches to social psychology it is necessary to get your head round two philosophical concepts – ontology and epistemology.

- **Ontology** is the branch of philosophy that addresses what things are and their being-in-the-world. Applied to social psychology, it is about the assumptions made about the nature of the social world – what it consists of, what units make it up and how they interrelate to each other.
- **Epistemology** is the branch of philosophy that considers the nature of knowledge – what counts as valid knowledge, and how it can be gained. Applied to social psychology, it is about the assumptions made about what constitutes valid knowledge about the social world (as opposed to beliefs or opinions) and how social psychologists should go about gaining it.

Blaikie identifies four main strategies for human science research, based on four different 'logics of inquiry' (Blaikie 2000: 9). They take different positions on ontology and epistemology and have different aims. The four strategies are summarized in Figure 2.1.

As you can see, there is a lot going on here. Don't panic – it all gets explained as we move through the chapter. Simply look through for now and get an over-all sense of the different strategies.

These two analogies of the social world and an ocean and as making music are described in full on pages 8–9.

As you have seen in Chapter 1, experimental social psychology regards the social world – the world in which people live together and interact with each other – as external to and separate from human action. It is rather like an ocean, in which social events (like social interaction and group processes) and social phenomena (such as prejudice and intergroup conflict) happen and arise through social processes. That is, it is a system of lawfully related elements. Two different epistemologies are pursued within this paradigm. Both have the aim to discover the universal laws by which the social world 'works'.

Critical social psychology is based on a different ontology altogether. It regards the social world as constructed through human action – as a product of people producing and reproducing it, like an orchestra making music. Once more two different epistemologies are pursued, but again there is a common aim. It is to gain understanding and insight into how and why particular social realities are constructed in the way they are.

EPISTEMOLOGY AND ONTOLOGY IN EXPERIMENTAL SOCIAL PSYCHOLOGY

Experimental social psychology is broadly based upon an epistemological position called **positivism**. At its purest and most simple, positivism holds that

Figure 2.1
Social psychology's research strategies

	Ontology	Epistemology	Research aim	Dominant paradigm
Inductive	The social world exists 'out there' in nature, separate from human action. It consists of discrete and observable social events and phenomena that are lawfully related.	Positivism	To observe the social world and identify systematic regularities in causes and effects, in order to develop universal laws.	Modernism
Deductive		Rationalism	To develop theories to discover universal laws, by testing hypotheses in ways that allow them to be falsified.	
Retroductive	There is no social world 'out there' in nature. It is socially constructed, through human meaning-making – through people's efforts to make sense of it and navigate their selves and lives within it.	Critical Realism	To gain insight and understanding of social reality through observing regularities and generating models to explain them.	Postmodernism
Abductive		Critical Relativism	To discover how and why different social realities are constructed and deployed in order to gain understanding and insight into the purposes to which they are put.	

Source: After Blaikie 2000

there is a straightforward one-to-one relationship between things and events in the outside world and people's knowledge of them. The goal of experimental social psychology is to get as close as possible to this ideal – to discover reliable, factual knowledge about the social-world-as-it-really-is.

Today few scientists claim that this is ever entirely possible. They accept that since human perception and understanding are fallible, people will always be somewhat selective and biased by their preconceptions (Chalmers 1999). However, most scientists – including experimental social psychologists – take the position that by using Scientific method they can progressively pin down 'the facts' and get close enough to reality to develop working models of how processes and phenomena 'work' in systematic, lawful ways.

The goal of experimental social psychology is to unravel the lawful relationships between the different elements of the social world, and so to explain how they 'work'. To pursue this goal, experimental social psychologists seek to discover knowledge through Scientific method; that is, through the systematic collection and analysis of things that can be directly observed.

So let's now look at how Science goes about discovering knowledge and, in particular, how experimental social psychologists have worked within the Scientific paradigm to gain knowledge. In this section I shall refer to a range of studies to illustrate how Scientific method has been applied to experimental social psychological theorizing and research.

Hypothetico-deductivism

Contemporary Scientific method is based upon Popper's (1959) hypothetico-deductivism – put more simply, the process of making deductions from the testing of hypotheses. Underpinning this obscure language are some simple but powerful ideas. As an illustration I am going to begin by looking at a study of what happens when people try to solve logical problems.

Wason's selection task problem

If you want to know more about this research, see the Further Reading section at the end of this chapter.

The study I have chosen was carried out by Cosmides (1989). In it she examined whether people find it easier to solve logical problems if the problem is expressed in a meaningful way that relates to their social knowledge about the world, compared with when the problem is expressed in abstract terms. To do this she used a problem-solving task called the **selection task problem**, originally devised by Peter Wason (1966, 1968). She was by no means the first person to explore the impact of meaningfulness on people's ability to solve the problem, but hers is one of the easiest to follow.

Wason, a cognitive psychologist, was particularly interested in the errors people make in their reasoning. To investigate this he devised a number of highly creative problems of logic – problems that appear to be simple but are actually fiendishly difficult. Of these, the selection task problem is probably his most famous (it is one of the exhibits in the Psychology section of London's Natural History Museum).

Figure 2.2
Wason's selection task problem in abstract form
Source: Wason 1966

The selection task problem in its abstract form

Rule: If a vowel is on one side,
an even number is on the other side.

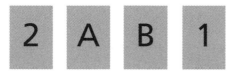

In his 1966 chapter Wason describes how he got some of his students to try the problem. He placed before them four cards, as shown in Figure 2.2. Each card had a letter on one side and a number on the other. Comparing these allows a rule to be tested. The problem the person has to solve is to identify which cards *must* be turned over to see if the rule is true or not.

Try it for yourself

Wason commented that the problem 'proved to be particularly difficult' to solve (Wason 1966: 146). Try it for yourself and see how you get on. It really is worth experiencing the surprising difficulty of the task for yourself, so don't cheat by looking at the answers in the text. Spend a few minutes thinking about the rule and what is on the cards, and then write down your answers.

I wonder if, like almost all of Wason's students, you picked the A and the 2? The A is a right answer, but the 2 is wrong. You should have picked the A and the 1. Not convinced? Then take it slowly. You need to turn over the A because an odd number on the other side of the card would *disprove* the rule. But you don't need to turn over the 2 because it does not matter what is on the other side. The rule says: 'If there is a vowel on one side, there is an even number on the other.' It says nothing about what kind of number may be on the other side of a consonant. So even if on the other side of the 2 there is a B, the rule is not disproved.

Equally you don't need to turn over the B, since it does not matter what's on the other side. But you do need to turn over the 1, because if there is a vowel on the other side it *disproves* the rule.

Try it for yourself

Still not convinced? Then try Cosmides' meaningful version. This (in somewhat modified form) is shown in Figure 2.3 below.

This version is very much easier to solve, as the alternatives are expressed meaningfully. This tells you that you don't need to look at the cards about John being sober and John taking a taxi – they are obviously irrelevant. All you need to know to test the rule is whether or not John, when he drove his car, was drunk or sober (the second card); and whether, when he was drunk, he took a taxi or drove his car (the last card). If you are still unconvinced about the abstract version, go back now and look at it again. It usually helps to have done the social knowledge question – it makes it easier to see what is at stake in the abstract one.

Constructing a hypothesis

A hypothesis is a specific, operational prediction about an outcome from a Scientific study, that you can test empirically. Devising a hypothesis consists of a series of stages.

Figure 2.3
Wason's selection task problem in its meaningful form
Source: Modified from Cosmides 1989

The selection task problem in its meaningful form

Rule: If John is drunk,
John must leave his car and take a taxi.

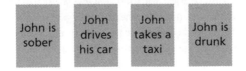

Stage 1: Making a general prediction

In Scientific method, in order to gain empirical knowledge, it must be possible to make logical and unequivocal predictions about cause and effect. To do this you need to have in mind one or more potential answers to your research question. What you have in mind will be guided by the theory you are working from.

The general prediction in this case is pretty obvious. Our theory claims that thinking works most efficiently when using meaning. So our general prediction in this study will be that when people solve the selection task problem, they will perform better if it is expressed in meaningful terms than if it is expressed in abstract terms. Notice what has gone on here. We started with a theory about the influence of meaning. From this we predicted what would happen, in a way that enables us to make an observation about whether the prediction 'works'. We moved from the *abstract* idea of problem solving being 'helped' by meaning to the *practical* prediction that people would 'perform better'.

Stage 2: Specifying an experimental hypothesis

Performance is something we can test empirically by observing and, crucially, *measuring* how people perform. We could, for example, measure the number of errors people make, or the speed at which they respond or even the degree of certainty they have about their answers. It is usual to go for the easiest and most unequivocal thing to measure. In this case it would be the number of errors they would make – how many of the wrong cards they turned over and how many of the right cards they did not. So now we can specify an experimental hypothesis into a formal statement, in which the prediction has been operationalized – described in terms of an outcome that can be measured. The hypothesis is:

> People will make fewer errors when solving a problem if it is expressed in meaningful terms than if it is expressed in abstract form.

Stage 3: Establishing significant difference and the null hypothesis

However, this is not yet exact enough – how much fewer is few enough to test the hypothesis? At this point we need to make recourse to statistics. You may already be familiar with the concept of **significant difference**. Basically, it is a matter of comparing the experimental hypothesis with the alternative – the **null hypothesis**. This states that there will be no difference that can be attributed to the problem being expressed meaningfully.

The basic idea behind 'significant difference' is that a difference will be found that is sufficiently large that it is extremely unlikely that the null hypothesis is true. The question is, how 'extremely unlikely' does it have to be? A small difference could be a matter of coincidence. Consider the situation where 10 people tried to solve the problem in each condition. Now, let's assume that only 2 of the 10 who tried the problem in its abstract form got the right answer and made no errors, but in the meaningful form 4 people got it right. Is this just coincidence? Well, maybe. But let's say 100 people tried each condition, and with the abstract form 2 got it right but with the meaningful form 80 got it right. The difference here is much more convincing – the chance that this is just a fluke is much, much smaller.

Statistical procedures enable you to estimate the probability of this. For example, a 0.001 level of significance means that the difference has only one chance in 1000 of being a coincidence. The calculation takes account of the number of observations that are made of the hypothesis being tested – in this case this would be about how many people were asked to solve the problem. So here is the hypothesis in full:

> People will make significantly fewer errors when solving a problem expressed in meaningful terms than if it is expressed in abstract form.

Induction and deduction

This deals with the 'hypothetico-' bit of hypothetico-deductivism, but we are not there yet. We need to deal with the 'deductivism' part. It's here that Popper's work is most important. A philosopher of science, Popper (1959) argued that just because a prediction made in the hypothesis is supported by the observations made, this does not mean that the theory is proved. However many observations you make, and however convincing the significance level, there is always, logically, a small but nonetheless real possibility that the pattern of results is a matter of chance.

Induction

Induction is drawing inferences from observations, in order to make generalizations. Drawing on Blaikie (2000), induction can be seen as consisting of four main stages:

1 Facts are observed and recorded, without any attempt to be selective.
2 These facts are analysed, compared and classified, without reference to any hypothesis.
3 From this analysis, generalizations are inferred about the relationships between the facts.
4 These generalizations are tested, by further observation of the facts.

Wason's original experiment was like this. He devised the problem, made up the cards, gave them to his students, told them the rule, and then watched what they did. He had a hunch that they would find the original abstract form difficult, and so they did. He observed them making lots of errors, and speculated from this about why they kept turning over the even number card, even after they were told it was irrelevant.

As you will see in Chapter 3, some experimental social psychology research uses an inductive approach like this. Such studies are usually referred to as **descriptive research**. In them a situation is created or a naturally occurring event is observed, and the researcher seeks merely to record what happens in a dispassionate manner. When used by experimental social psychologists, this approach is usually intended to stimulate hypothetico-deductive research. By observing regularities in what happens – that, for example, people tend to make errors in the selection task problem – such studies offer a stimulus for generating hypotheses that can be tested. This is what Cosmides did. She speculated that the problem with the problem was that it was expressed in abstract form. So she set out to test it by an experiment in which she compared the abstract form with a meaningful form, following the hypothetico-deductive method we have followed in this section.

Induction is a common practice in everyday life. We make inferences such as 'the kids are always cranky around teatime' or 'I'm definitely not a morning person' all the time, and use them to organize the way we run our lives. As such, induction can be pretty much automatic.

Actually, I used Wason's selection task problem as my illustration deliberately. It gave you a chance to experience at first hand just how powerful a grip induction has on the way we think. When Wason's students made further attempts to solve the problem again they soon learned to look at the odd number card. But even when he gave them a careful explanation that they did not need to turn over the even number card, they still went on doing it. Wason commented that 'In spite of explicit instructions to the contrary, [it seems] they cannot inhibit a tendency to see whether the statement is "true"', and concluded that 'this implies that the need to establish the "truth" of the statement predominates over the instruction' (Wason 1966: 146–7).

Deduction

Popper argued specifically that induction can generate hypotheses but it cannot test them. To test a hypothesis it is necessary to use a deductive approach. Deduction, as shown in Wason's selection task problem, is based on **falsification** – putting a rule or a theory's predictions to the test, in ways that allow for them to be disproved. This may still seem to you an odd thing to do. Was Popper really arguing that researchers should set out to deliberately prove that their theories are wrong? Not at all. Rather he was saying that studies must be designed in such a way that the hypothesis *can* be falsified.

Again drawing on Blaikie (2000) Popper's argument (as applied to social psychology) can be summarized as follows:

1   The social world operates in a lawful manner, and the aim is to discover these laws.
2   This is done by generating theories and testing hypotheses about cause and effect, in order to be able to explain why people think, feel and act as they do.
3   However, it is not possible to unequivocally establish these laws. All that can be done is to eliminate false theories, thereby moving gradually closer to the truth.
4   But we have no way of knowing for certain when we have arrived at a true theory, so even those theories that have survived testing must be regarded as provisional.

I have summarized the differences between induction and deduction in Figure 2.4 to make the distinction between them clear.

Figure 2.4
Comparison of inductive and deductive approaches to research

	How does it assume that knowledge can be gained?	What is the purpose of gaining evidence?	What is the evidence gathered intended to do?	How is progress to be made?
Inductive approach	Making inferences from observations	To look for regularities and patterns in the events observed	Establish generalizations	To use these generalizations to develop hypotheses that can be tested deductively
Deductive approach	Testing hypotheses	To put hypotheses to the test in ways that allow them to be falsified	To provisionally support the theory that the hypothesis was designed to test	To exclude theories that have been falsified, and develop and refine those that have not

The epistemology and ontology of experimental
social psychology

- Experimental social psychology adopts either an inductive or
  deductive research strategy.
- It is based on an ontology in which the social world is external
  to and separate from human action. It consists of discrete and
  observable social events and phenomena that are lawfully
  related.
- Its epistemology is that knowledge can be gained about the
  universal laws of human behaviour and experience using
  hypothetico-deductive method. Theory is used to generate an
  experimental hypothesis that can be tested by falsification (that is
  deduction not induction).
- Where the predictions of a theory are falsified, the theory is
  abandoned. However, what generally happens is that research
  is used to gradually accumulate valid and reliable
  empirical evidence for theories that offer the best explanation
  for the causes of the processes or phenomena in
  question.

EPISTEMOLOGY AND ONTOLOGY IN CRITICAL SOCIAL PSYCHOLOGY

If you look back at Figure 2.1 you will see that critical social psychology is based on an ontology in which there is seen to be no social world 'out there' in nature. Rather the social world is constructed through people's actions – through their efforts to make sense of it and navigate and negotiate their selves and lives within it. This approach is called **social constructionism**. It is a theoretical framework informed by Postmodernism, but applied specifically to human sciences, most notably sociology and critical psychology.

Social constructionism

Though, as usual, its roots go back much further, social constructionism arose from a theory called the sociology of knowledge. The key text was Berger and Luckmann's (1967) *The Social Construction of Reality*. In it they theorized that social reality is constructed through three 'moments': externalization, objectification and internalization.

- **Externalization** is about the way that cultures, societies and social groups of different kinds make sense of – and therefore 'make' – their social worlds, including a whole range of social institutions and constructs.
- **Objectification** is how those constructs and social institutions then get to be perceived as real. This is also referred to as **reification**. An uglier but in some ways more transparent term is '**thingification**' – the process whereby ideas get turned into *socially* real things.
- **Internalization** is where the objectified social world becomes known, understood and adopted by individuals through processes of socialization and enculturation.

Berger and Luckmann saw these three moments as in constant interplay, as shown in Figure 2.5.

Chapter 7 explores social constructionism in more depth. For now what you need to take on board is that it is a theoretical position based on an ontology

Figure 2.5
Berger and Luckmann's three moments through which social reality is constructed

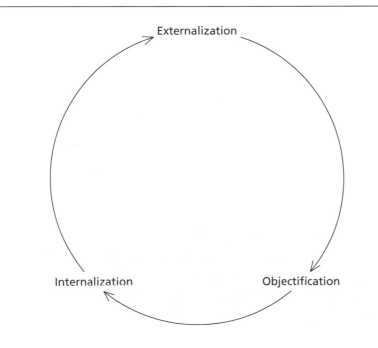

that regards social reality as constructed by way of human meaning-making, and operating by way of human meaning-interpretation and application.

The Critical Realist approach

It is in this sense that one branch of Postmodern theory is called 'Critical Realism' – it refers not to a natural reality, but to *social* reality. Blaikie (2000) describes the Critical Realist 'take' on this ontology thus:

> Social reality is viewed either as a socially constructed world in which social episodes are the products of the cognitive resources social actors bring to them (Harré, 1977), or as social arrangements that are the products of material but unobservable structures of social relations (Bhaskar, 1979).
>
> (Blaikie 2000: 108)

Critical Realist epistemology works from observations of people acting within the social world and making sense of it. Analysis of these observations is used to build hypothetical models that can account for what is going on. Critical Realist research views social actions and phenomena as produced by social structures (such as structural inequality) and mechanisms (such as patriarchy). It uses **retroduction** to identify systematic regularities in social action or social phenomena, in order to gain insight and understanding of the structures and mechanisms that produce them.

Harré and Secord (1972) divide the retroductive strategy – they call it ethogenic – into two phases. First is the step of identifying an observed regularity that is intriguing and offers the promise for insight. They call this *empirical studies*, an exploratory stage. Then follows a second stage of *theoretical studies*, the aim of which is to generate explications of the semiotic mechanisms and structures that produce the regularity (Harré and Secord 1972: 69–71).

The Critical Relativist approach

Critical Relativism (see Stainton Rogers 1995) is often called interpretativism, especially in sociology.

> Interpretative social science seeks to discover why people do what they do by uncovering the largely tacit, mutual knowledge, the symbolic meanings, motives and rules, which provide the orientations for their actions. Mutual knowledge is knowledge that is largely unarticulated; it is constantly being used and modified by social actors as they interact with each other; and it is produced and reproduced by them in the course of their lives together. It is the everyday beliefs and practices,

> mundane and taken for granted, which have to be grasped and
> articulated by the social researcher in order to provide an understanding
> of these actions.
>
> (Blaikie 2000: 115)

In many ways it appears, at first sight, to be very similar to Critical Realism. However, there is an important difference. Whereas Critical Realism views social reality as arising from underlying structures and mechanisms, Critical Relativism considers there to be a multiplicity of dynamic and changing social realities.

> Social reality [from this approach] is regarded as the product of
> processes by which social actors together negotiate the meanings for
> actions and situations; it is a complex of socially constructed mutual
> knowledge – meanings, cultural symbols and social institutions. These
> meanings and interpretations both facilitate and structure social
> relationships. Social reality is the symbolic world of meanings and
> interpretations. It is not some 'thing' that may be interpreted in
> different ways; it is those interpretations.
>
> (Blaikie 2000: 116)

Crucially, from this epistemological standpoint, there is no independent 'benchmark' that can be used to establish which social reality is 'true'. Critical Relativist research does not seek to discover the 'facts' of social life, social processes or social phenomena, since it regards this as a wild goose chase leading nowhere. It simply is not possible to do so. Hence the term relativism'.

Abduction

Abduction is a term most associated with the writings of the philosopher Charles Sanders Peirce (see, for example, Peirce [1940] 1955). He defines it as 'the process of forming an explanatory hypothesis' (Peirce 1955: 42). The aim of abductive research is to work on hunches to *construct* new theory rather than test it. To understand what is at stake here, we need to start from Peirce's (1955) formal statement of the logic behind abduction (such a statement is called a syllogism):

Result   The surprising fact, C, is observed.
Rule   But if A were true, C would be a matter of course.
Case   Hence, there is reason to suspect that A is true.

Now let's convert this into something easier to understand. Skilful hunters get their prey through having extensive knowledge about how to track and find them. They need to be able to identify different hoof marks and droppings and to recognize different smells and different patterns of broken twigs. What happens when they notice something surprising, such as a smell they have not come across before? They have to try to work out what kind of animal this smell comes from. They do this by drawing on the knowledge they already have.

Let us assume that they have hunted in this terrain for many years, and they have not encountered any new animals in all that time. So it is unlikely that some new beast has suddenly moved in (this is possible but unlikely). What do they make of the new smell? Their best hunch might be that the smell must come from a familiar animal that they already know about. Something therefore must have happened to bring about this smell.

Now the hunters have to consider what that could be. To do this they need to draw upon their existing knowledge again, and this may include the observation that the only circumstances where they have noticed animals giving off different smells before has been during their mating season. Although this is something that they have not come across with all the animals they are familiar with, they have observed it before in some cases. So, they will conclude, the most likely explanation is that this is the mating-season smell of an animal they know, but have not observed during the mating season before. This cuts their work considerably. All they now need to do is work out which are the animals for which they do not already know about their mating-season smell. Then they know that the smell must come from one of these. Shank (1998) re-expresses the syllogism like this:

Result   This is an unusual smell.
Rule   It is reasonable to suppose that animals give off unusual smells
           during their mating season.
Case   This quite possibly is the smell of a familiar animal during the mating
           season.

Critical social psychology uses an abductory approach in order to gain insight and understanding. It does this by deliberately looking for ways to make the surprising and the unexpected happen. The political scientist, Steven Brown, has described this kind of research as

> a launch pad for an investigation, an entrée into a phenomenon, the scientist's best initial guess as to how a particular administrative situation, social consciousness, or whatever operates. The data gathered . . . may lead in quite different directions. . . . There is never any guarantee, in other words, that splash-down will occur in the same area as the point of departure.
>
> (Brown 1980: 39)

Blaikie argues that this approach is therefore limited to descriptive research – simply gaining insight and understanding into the social realities that are 'real' to those who inhabit them. However, critical social psychologists who adopt a Critical Relativist position would take issue with him.

First, as social psychologists, they are interested not just in gaining descriptions of alternative social realities, but, crucially, in gaining insight into and understanding of the means by which they are constructed and deployed.

> It is through the daily interactions between people in the course of social life that our versions of knowledge become fabricated. Therefore social interaction of all kinds, and particularly language, is of great interest to social constructionists. The goings-on between people in the course of their everyday lives are seen as the practices during which our shared versions of knowledge are constructed. Therefore what we regard as 'truth' (which of course varies historically and cross-culturally), i.e. our current accepted ways of understanding the world, is a product not of objective observation of the world, but of social processes and interactions in which people are constantly engaged with each other.
>
> (Burr 1995: 4)

Second, critical social psychologists are profoundly concerned to gain insight into the social consequences of social reality being constructed in particular ways, and, most importantly, the impact this has upon how people can act and how they are treated. They therefore ask different questions. They believe the question 'Is this version of reality true?' to be unanswerable. Rather they ask questions like: what actions does this version of social reality make possible? In what ways does it constrain what people can do? Who gets their own way? Who gets exploited?

Blaikie's interpretation of abduction is also problematic, since he limits it to social science, and regards its aim as 'to generate social scientific accounts of social actors' accounts; . . . deriving technical concepts and theories from lay concepts and interpretations of social accounts' (Blaikie 2000: 114).

In my view abduction is less about generating theories from lay accounts and more a means to achieve insight and to make discoveries. Critical social psychology purposively pursues abductory research as its main strategy. But it is also adopted more serendipitously by natural as well as human scientists, and by experimental as well as critical psychologists.

Abduction as a means to discovery

The scientific discoveries that really capture our attention are where a real breakthrough is made. Alexander Fleming's discovery of penicillin was just such a discovery. The story goes that he was preparing culture dishes of bacteria in order to be able to study the effects of various chemicals. One day he came into the lab and noticed that one of them had gone mouldy. He was about to throw it away when he noticed something odd. Around the mould was a clear area. Strange, he thought, what is going on? He looked a little more carefully, and, sure enough, the mould seemed to be killing off the bacteria. The rest, as they say, is history – a history, for what its worth, in which countless lives have been saved by antibiotics.

Kuhn (1970) argued specifically that important scientific discoveries are not made through the incremental fine-tuning of knowledge through ever more meticulous hypothetico-deductive method, but through anomalies and surprises:

> Normal science . . . is a highly cumulative enterprise, eminently
> successful in its aim, the steady extension of the scope and precision of
> scientific knowledge. . . . Yet one standard product of the scientific
> enterprise is missing. Normal science does not aim for novelties of fact
> or theory and, when successful, finds none. New and unsuspected
> phenomena are, however, repeatedly uncovered by scientific research,
> and radical new theories have again and again been invented by
> scientists. History even suggests that the scientific enterprise has
> developed a uniquely powerful technique for producing surprises of this
> sort.
>
> (Kuhn 1970: 52–3)

What Kuhn is going on about here is a logic that is different from induction and deduction – abduction. Scientists use abduction in order to develop new theories. They look for the surprising and unusual, the data that don't fit, and they try to explain these anomalies. They develop hunches about why the anomalies have arisen, develop theories from those hunches, and *then* they use hypothetico-deductive method to test out their theories. In Kuhn's terms, they 'learn to see nature in a different way' (Kuhn 1970: 53) and, thereby, they make progress in a way not possible by incremental 'normal' scientific method. In other words, hypothetico-deductive method is only one part of the story. While necessary and useful, it is not necessarily the most interesting or even the most useful means to make major theoretical advances.

Theory development using abduction

Abductive research involves either homing in on disjunctions and discrepancies – that which is surprising or intriguing because it does not fit into pre-existing frameworks – or creating conditions where researchers can be surprised. Just as

Sherlock Holmes would always reach a point of identifying the crucial clue – such as 'the dog that did not bark' – abductory research looks for anomalies, inconsistencies and incongruities in what has been examined. And just like Sherlock Holmes, the researcher now has to puzzle out what can possibly account for the anomaly.

One of the most persistent and powerful advocates of abductive research in psychology is Gary Shank (for example Shank 1994, 1998). Shank argues that psychologists should give up on proliferating ever more detailed models and theories and, instead, concentrate on developing the craft tools to pursue research into meaning. And abduction, he says, is the way to go. To do this, he says, researchers do not need to wait to be surprised – though they should treasure serendipitous surprises when they come across them. Surprises can be made to happen, for instance, by juxtaposing things (such as of areas of study) that, at first sight, appear to be entirely unconnected in any way. New paths to insight and discovery, he claims, can be gained by attempts to reconcile – to come up with a working hunch to explain – the dislocation that is highlighted by this kind of juxtaposition.

One of Shank's own uses of juxtaposition was to compare scientific research reports with medieval bestiaries. These are books where a whole mishmash of things – plants, animals, minerals – were described and classified, and moral and/or religious lessons drawn. For example, the nature of the hippopotamus was used to show the moral inferiority of sloth and laziness, while the nature of a lion was used to demonstrate the moral superiority of courage. In looking at the strengths and weaknesses as 'ways of knowing' of these two very different kinds of text Shank was able to envision new and better ways of writing empirical reports.

As Shank himself acknowledges, such juxtapositioning of arbitrary and unusual ideas to gain insight is neither new nor uncommon. It is, for instance, frequently used in art – from movies to science fiction novels – and by market researchers to stimulate creative thinking. Rather, Shank makes the point that juxtaposition is an unusual research technique that has much to offer.

Interestingly, Blaikie (2000) uses the term abductive research to describe the kind of interpretative approach Shank is promoting:

> Interpretativists argue that statistical patterns or correlations are not understandable on their own. It is necessary to find out what meanings (motives) people give to the actions that lead to such patterns. . . . For Interpretativism, the social world *is* the world interpreted and experienced by its members, from the 'inside'. Hence, the task of the Interpretative social scientist is to discover and describe this 'insider' view, not to impose an 'outsider' view on it. Interpretative social science seeks to discover why people do what they do by uncovering the largely

tacit, mutual knowledge, the symbolic meanings, motives and rules, which provide the organization for their actions.

(Blaikie 2000: 115)

Shank claims that 'we tend to see the world not in terms of truth, but in terms of significance. This means that we experience not a world of facts, but of signs' (Shank 1998: 856). And so, he argues, social psychologists should devise methods based upon **semiotics** – the study of signs, symbols and meaning. Shank recommends 'a semiotic strategy that uses an abductive focus' since this is 'general enough to address basic issues, while being sensitive enough to the complex and manifold issues of meaning' (Shank 1998: 853).

The way critical social psychologists go about this is described and discussed in detail in Chapters 3 and 4.

Originally a branch of linguistics, as you saw in Chapter 1, semiotics was defined in that context as 'the science of the life of signs in society' (Saussure 1974). As it is now utilized in fields like media studies (see Hodge and Kress 1988, for example) it has been adapted as an analytic – 'social semiotics'. It is used to gain insight into the ways in which meaning is produced, communicated and understood and, in particular, to scrutinize how meaning-making is deployed strategically.

The epistemology and ontology of critical social psychology

Critical social psychology is based on an ontology in which there is seen to be no social world 'out there' in nature. It is socially constructed, through human meaning-making – through people's efforts to make sense of it and navigate and negotiate their selves and lives within it.

Berger and Luckmann (1967) suggest that reality is constructed through three main 'moments': externalization, objectification and internalization.

Critical realist research
- Views social actions and phenomena as produced by social structures (such as structural inequality) and mechanisms (such as patriarchy)
- Uses retroduction to identify systematic regularities in social action or social phenomena, in order to gain insight and understanding of the structures and mechanisms that produce them.

Critical relativist research
- Considers there to be a multiplicity of dynamic and changing social realities

→

- Specifically seeks to use abduction to pursue its research and theory development.

Abduction
- Is an essential part of the scientific endeavour alongside hypothetico-deductive method
- Works by noticing or looking for surprises – inconsistencies, contradictions or anomalies – and then generating hypotheses to explain them
- Provides a 'launch pad' for the generation of new theories.

COMPARING AND CONTRASTING THE TWO PARADIGMS

As you have seen in this chapter, experimental and critical social psychology differ in their 'take' on epistemology and ontology. Broadly, these differences boil down to three main disputes over

- the nature and status of knowledge
- how to deal with complexity
- the ability to be and desirability of being objective.

The nature and status of knowledge

Experimental social psychology is based on the assumption that it is possible to gain factual knowledge about human behaviour and experience in social settings. It assumes it is possible to identify and to study processes and phenomena that are universal. These processes and phenomena are seen as operating at a psychological level – that is, at the level of the individual who may be influenced by the social context but who, ultimately, operates as a self-contained entity. The psychological processes are held to be working *inside* the individual's mind. These days they are generally seen as cognitive processes – such as strategically directing attention.

Critical social psychology is based on the assumption that all knowledge is a product of human meaning-making, and hence it differs according to the historical time and the social or cultural location in which it is being used. It therefore rejects the claim that it is possible to arrive at an objective knowledge that transcends history and culture. It regards that all that it is possible for social psychology to achieve are contingent accounts of the particular social conventions operating in specific times and places. Thus it does not regard psychological processes or phenomena as ultimately operating within individual minds, but as operating intersubjectively – *between* people, *within* those shared conventions and mediated by and through the meanings that are shared by people who, for example, have a common culture or social relationship with each other.

How to deal with complexity

Based on the assumption that it is possible to gain objective knowledge, experimental social psychology seeks to produce **nomothetic** (that is universally lawful) **explanations** about the general laws that govern psychological processes and phenomena, and to develop these through the gradual refinement of theory using hypothetico-deductive method. Explanation provides a cause-and-effect account of how and why something happens – to explain means, literally, to 'smooth out'. Complexity is dealt with by smoothing it out. Using experimental method, a limited, specified set of variables are selected for study and extraneous influences are excluded.

Based on the assumption that knowledge is inevitably contingent, critical social psychology seeks to produce **idiographic** (that is specific to particular instances) **explications**. An explication does not seek to account for cause and effect. Rather it provides a 'teasing out' – explicate means, literally, to 'unfold'. Explication teases out the *particular* social and cultural conventions that govern social interaction in *particular* circumstances, and that mediate the ways that people make and interpret meaning and significance in *particular* situation.

Complexity is dealt with both through this specificity and through abduction, which is used to identify anomalies. This allows researchers to home in on those aspects of, say, an interaction between people (such as a conversation) that are most likely to be productive of insight and, ultimately, theory.

The ability to be and desirability of being objective

Experimental social psychology has one very important thing going for it - its agreement about what constitutes valid and reliable knowledge, and what kinds of research are appropriate for gaining it. Critical social psychologists have found sophisticated and clever ways to study meaning. But in denying the possibility of objectivity, they do open themselves up to the accusation that their work is 'politics by other means' – highly subjective and biased, more hot polemic than cool, considered scholarship. The tendency of critical social psychologists to work from ideological positions (such as feminism and Marxism) tends to feed this perception: that however clever and convincing their analyses and interpretations of their data, they are still (and self-admittedly) highly *subjective* accounts.

The main differences between the two paradigms are summarized in Table 2.1.

Thus deciding which approach is 'best' is in part about deciding what you think matters most – objectivity or the ability to deal with meaning.

Table 2.1
The main differences between experimental and critical social psychology

Experimental social psychology	Critical social psychology
Operates within Modernism	Operates within Postmodernism
Views the social world as 'out there' external to and separate from people	Views the social world as made by people, and not separate from them
Views knowledge as based on facts that are 'out-there-in-the-world' waiting to be discovered	Views knowledges as constructed through people's meaning-making
Asserts there is only one true, objective knowledge that transcends time and cultural location	Accepts that there are multiple knowledges, and that knowledge is highly contingent on time and cultural location
Asks of knowledge 'is it true?'	Asks of knowledge 'what does it do?', 'how can it be used – by whom, and to what ends?', 'whose interest does it serve?', 'what does it make possible?'
Seeks to gain knowledge primarily through hypothetico-deductive testing of theory	Seeks to gain knowledge primarily through abduction – looking for anomalies and trying to puzzle them out
Seeks to provide nomothetic cause-and-effect explanations	Seeks to provide idiographic explications that offer insight into specific social events and phenomena
Seeks to be dispassionate and apolitical	Is often motivated by ideology and makes no claim to be objective or dispassionate
Has a long tradition and established standards of what constitutes valid research	Is relatively new and as yet is only beginning to establish standards of what constitutes valid research

Crucially, it involves deciding whether you believe that objectivity is ever possible.

Here I want to remind you of my assertion in Chapter 1 that there is no 'fluffy bunny' resolution between the two paradigms – fundamentally they are, in Kuhn's terms, incommensurable with each other. There is, in that sense, a real feeling in each camp that 'if you are not with us, you are against us'.

However, I hope that this chapter has shown that at a more pragmatic level there are actually some important commonalties between them. In particular the growing interest in abduction has the potential for more informed dialogue and debate between experimental and critical social psychologists. This is not going to lead to any resolution of the conflict over epistemology and ontology – the two positions are mutually exclusive. But maybe it will lead to an acknowledgement that we are engaged in the same enterprise, and debate can move away from mutual derision and name-calling to a more informed discussion.

This argument is taken up and developed in Chapter 10.

FURTHER READING

Classic texts

There are two classic texts that you should consult if you want to get to grips with the basis of Scientific method. These are:

Popper, K. (1959) *The Logic of Scientific Discovery*. New York: Basic Books.

Kuhn, T.S. (1970) *The Structure of Scientific Revolutions*. Chicago: University of Chicago Press.

Research strategies

Blaikie, N. (2000) *Designing Social Research: The Logic of Anticipation*. Cambridge: Polity.

> This book is not (simply) a 'how to do it manual' – though it does offer detailed and relatively comprehensive (if a bit quirky) advice and information on all stages of the research processes used in social psychology. It is unusual in two ways. First, it covers both Scientific and social constructionist approaches to research. Second, it really tries to get to grips with the underlying philosophical issues. In relation to this chapter, his Chapter 4 'Strategies for answering research questions' is worth reading – though note that he takes a contentious line on abduction. In my view Shank's (1998) article (see below) is both more accurate and easier to follow.

Experimental social psychology

You have two choices here. First, try any US general textbook on social psychology, and you will find its methodology chapter sets out the basic tenets and approaches of the experimental paradigm. They are usually written in highly user-friendly prose, and pretty easy to digest. A somewhat more onerous choice is the Methodology chapter by Manstead and Semin.

Manstead, A.S.R. and Semin, G. (2001) Methods in social psychology: tools to test theories, in M. Hewstone, and W. Stroebe (eds) *Introduction to Social Psychology*, 3rd edn. Oxford: Blackwell.
> The book is written almost exclusively by European experimental social psychologists. It is more scholarly and detailed, and harder work generally. But in my view it gives a more balanced account, that addresses the drawbacks and problems rather than offering the kind of 'mission statement' for experimental social psychology you find in US textbooks.

Critical social psychology

Gough, B. and McFadden, M. (2001) *Critical Social Psychology: An Introduction*. Basingstoke: Palgrave.
> Chapter 2 of this text presents a mixture of some of the history we covered in Chapter 1 and a critique of experimental social psychology that is more polemical and goes into a lot more detail than I can here.

Abduction

Shank, G. (1998) The extraordinary ordinary powers of abductive reasoning, *Theory and Psychology*, 8(6): 841–60.
> This is the best entrée I have found into the use of abduction in social psychology. It is clearly written and while the ideas expressed *are* complicated, you should be able to get a reasonably good understanding of what it is and its potential from this paper.

The selection task problem

Poletiek, F. (2001) *Hypothesis-testing Behaviour*. Hove: Psychology Press.
> Chapter 4 of this book provides an excellent review of the very substantial body of theorization and research associated with Wason's selection task.

QUESTIONS

1 What are the main ontological and epistemological assumptions on which Scientific method is based?
2 Compare and contrast the approaches taken by experimental and critical social psychology to research.
3 What are the common assumptions about ontology shared by Critical Realism and Critical Relativism? How do they differ in their epistemological approaches?
4 Define induction, deduction and abduction, and explain the differences between them.
5 If Sherlock Holmes had been a social psychologist, what kind of social psychologist do you think he would have been? Explain the reasons for your answer.

Chapter 3

Methods and analytics

Chapter contents

A route map of the chapter

This chapter briefly sets out the methods and analytics used in social psychology research. The first section looks at descriptive research, as conducted by both experimental and critical social psychologists. The remainder of the chapter is devoted to the specific approaches of each paradigm, starting with research as pursued in experimental social psychology and followed by research carried out by critical social psychologists.

Descriptive research

↓

Methods and analytics in experimental social psychology

↓

Methods and analytics in critical social psychology

Learning objectives

When you have completed your study of this chapter, you should be able to:

1 Describe what is meant by 'descriptive research', giving one example of it from the experimental approach and another from the critical approach.
2 Describe the main elements of a social psychological experiment and the different settings in which experiments are pursued.
3 Explain what is meant by the terms 'construct' and 'operalization', and distinguish between independent and dependent variables.
4 Outline the main techniques for collecting data in experimental social psychological studies and the different kinds of measures that can be used.
5 Explain what is meant by 'qualitative research' and the different ways it is used by experimental and critical social psychologists.
6 Compare the usefulness of laboratory experiments, field experiments and surveys in relation to issues of control, realism and representativeness.
7 Explain why analytics are more important than methods in social constructionist research.
8 Define the two main forms of discourse analysis and illustrate their different approaches with examples.
9 Outline the main elements of the grounded theory approach to research.
10 List two different ways of collecting data for social constructionist research.

INTRODUCTION

Social psychology gains its knowledge and refines and tests its theories through research – by gathering and analysing data. It is an empirical endeavour that:

• seeks to answer research questions	These may be framed in a variety of ways, from a hypothesis to be tested through to wanting to gain insight into and understanding of a particular topic. But research always seeks specific outcomes.
• is empirical	To find out about these questions it collects data based on observations of what people do and/or say in particular circumstances.
• is analytic	The data gathered are analysed and interpreted in order to answer these questions.
• is directed	The methods by which the data are collected and the forms analysis used are chosen as appropriate to the research question(s).

Methods are how data are gathered and **analytics** are the analytical means by which these data are processed and interpreted. This chapter takes you through the research methods and analytics associated with each paradigm. Its aim is to give you basic information about how each is done and why it is done in the way it is.

DESCRIPTIVE RESEARCH

Descriptive research is carried out within both paradigms, and is done to 'provide the researchers with an accurate description of the phenomenon in question' (Manstead and Semin 2001: 76).

Descriptive research in experimental social psychology

The first of Stanley Milgram's studies of obedience to authority (Milgram 1963) is a good example of descriptive research. In it he demonstrated that ordinary people can be persuaded to act extremely callously in a situation where there is strong pressure to obey. Milgram was motivated to do this study, in part, by reports of the trials of Nazis who had been involved in the mistreatment and torture of people during the Second World War. When they appeared in these trials they gave every impression of being mild-mannered and courteous people. They said they had simply been 'following orders'. Milgram wanted to investigate how such apparently ordinary people came to act in such barbaric ways.

Milgram's original study of obedience

Milgram put advertisements in newspapers to recruit people to take part in a study that was ostensibly about the effects of punishment on learning. In fact it was an elaborate deception. The subjects of the study (40 men, aged between 20–50) were led to believe they were giving electric shocks to another person. In fact they were giving no shocks at all. The other person was a **stooge** – a member of the experimental team, briefed to act as if he were being hurt in predetermined ways throughout the study.

The recruited subjects came to the laboratory and met the second man whom, they were told, was another subject. They were informed that one of them would be the learner and the other the teacher in a study of memorizing paired words. The teacher would give electric shocks to the learner when he made mistakes, as a means to learning. Both then drew lots to decide who would be the 'learner' and who the 'teacher'. The lots were rigged so that the stooge always got the role of learner; the actual subject of the study always got the role of teacher.

The subjects then saw the 'learner' being strapped to a chair and having electrodes attached to his arm with paste (Figure 3.1). They

Figure 3.1
The learner is strapped into the chair and the electrodes are attached to his wrist
Source: From the film *Obedience* © 1965 Stanley Milgram and distributed by Penn State University Media Sales. Permission granted by Alexandra Milgram

Figure 3.2
Scale on Milgram's shock generator
Source: Hogg and Vaughan 1998: 206

| 1 | 2 | 3 | 4 | 5 | 6 | 7 | 8 | 9 | 10 | 11 | 12 | 13 | 14 | 15 | 16 | 17 | 18 | 19 | 20 | 21 | 22 | 23 | 24 | 25 | 26 | 27 | 28 | 29 | 30 |

```
15 ----------- 75 -------------- 135 ------------- 195 -------------- 255 -------------- 315 ------------- 375 ------------- 435  450

|Volts|30|45|60|Volts|90|105|120|Volts|150|165|180|Volts|210|225|240|Volts|270|285|300|Volts|330|345|360|Volts|390|405|420|Volts|Volts|

Slight ------ Moderate -------- Strong ----------- Very ----------- Intense --------- Extreme --------- Danger: ------------  X X X
shock          shock            shock            strong            shock           intensity          severe
                                                 shock                               shock             shock
```

heard the experimenter explain that this paste was to prevent
blistering and burning, and that while the shocks that would be
administered might be painful they would not cause any permanent
damage. They also heard the learner telling the researcher he had a
slight heart condition. The subjects were then taken into another
room containing a dummy shock generator, which had a scale on it
from 'slight shock' to 'XXX' – a point beyond 'Danger: severe shock'
(Figure 3.2).

In this original study the subjects were not able to see the learner
(who was in another room) but could hear his responses to the
learning tasks and his (fake) reactions to the shock. They were told to
administer progressively larger shocks to the learner each time he
made a mistake. The study began and the learner gave some correct
answers but also made mistakes. Soon the subject was apparently
giving 'mild shocks' and could hear the learner grunting. At 120V the
learner cried out that the shocks were becoming painful. At 150V he
demanded to be released from the study and at 180V that he could
not stand the pain any longer. The learner went on crying out in
apparent pain, raising to an agonized scream at 250V. At 300V the
learner fell silent, and the subject was told to take this as a mistake
and continue giving ever-increasing shocks.

From the start of the study, subjects were agitated and soon began
to tell the experimenter they wanted to stop. The researcher gave a
predetermined response: 'Please continue'. As the subjects became
more and more distressed at giving greater and greater shocks, the
instructions to continue became increasingly stern – moving to 'It is

absolutely essential that you continue' and then 'You have no other choice, you must go on'. Many subjects expressed concern about causing real harm to the learner, but were told: 'The responsibility is mine. Please continue'.

In this study Milgram found that more than 60 per cent of the subjects were prepared to go on giving what they believed were extremely severe shocks – 450V – to a plump middle-aged man. They did this even though they heard the man begging for the experiment to stop and screaming in pain, even though he had finally gone silent, and even though they had earlier heard him tell the experimenter he had a heart complaint.

Another similar study by Philip Zimbardo and colleagues (Haney *et al.* 1973; Zimbardo *et al.* 1973) gave a similar demonstration that, given certain circumstances, ordinary men are capable of acting callously. Zimbardo and his colleagues set up a 'mock prison' and randomly assigned the subjects they had recruited to be either 'guards' or 'prisoners'. So aggressive and punitive did the 'guards' become that the study was ended less than half-way through its planned duration.

Neither study had a hypothesis as such. The data gathered in each case were *descriptive*. Therefore these descriptive studies did not – and could not – give any evidence to explain *why* the men in their studies behaved in the way they did. Writing from within the scientific paradigm, Manstead and Semin argue that for this reason 'social psychological research rarely stops at this point' (Manstead and Semin 2001: 77).

Descriptive research in critical social psychology

However, some social constructionist research does seek to do no more – methodologically at least – than generate descriptions as valuable ends in their own right. The primary goal is to gain insight into the specific ways in which a topic or issue is understood *by the account-giver*. This is the version of 'abductive' research that Blaikie (2000) describes (see Chapter 2).

Underpinning this approach is usually a strong commitment to enabling those who belong to marginalized groups (such as those with learning difficulties, who are diagnosed as schizophrenic or are survivors of sexual abuse) to be heard and their views taken into account. Researchers using this form of discourse analysis actively strive to avoid imposing their own ('expert') interpretation. Rather they seek to 'give voice' to the views being expressed.

A good example is a study of gender differences carried out by Wendy Hollway (1989). She described her approach as **descriptive interviewing**, its purpose being to be able to 'present extracts which "speak for themselves"':

> The researcher's role has been to organize this material so that it conforms to an essentially descriptive theory. The value of the approach is typically that the researcher should not presume to question the truthfulness of the account and this position is usually coupled with the view that a person's own account is most relevant for research because it is meaningful to the teller. Once an account is given, it assumes the status of *the* expression of the person's experience in relation to a particular topic.
>
> (Hollway 1989: 40)

Descriptive research

Social psychologists working in both the scientific and social constructionist paradigms do descriptive research.

- Milgram's first study of obedience is an example of descriptive research in the Scientific paradigm. It showed that ordinary people can be induced to act callously when put under pressure to obey by an authority figure. The study provides a demonstration of obedience, but no explanation as to how or why the obedience is induced.
- Hollway's use of descriptive interviewing is an example of descriptive research in the social constructionist paradigm. Its purpose is to 'give voice' to people's own understanding of their experiences and opinions.

METHODS AND ANALYTICS IN EXPERIMENTAL SOCIAL PSYCHOLOGY

I start this section with a fairly detailed examination of experimental method, since this is the benchmark standard against which all other Scientific methods are judged. I then briefly review other approaches used within this paradigm.

The purpose of an experiment is to find an explanation for a social influence, social process or social phenomenon by identifying the cause(s) of particular effects. As you saw in Chapter 2, using Scientific method this is done by starting with a theory and devising a hypothesis from it. The hypothesis is then tested by systematically varying one or more specific elements and measuring their effects. From analysis of the effects, a causal explanation is generated.

Experimental settings

In the natural sciences experiments are usually conducted in laboratories, although in some (such as earth sciences) they are carried out 'in the field' – **field experiments**. Social psychologists also sometimes do field experiments if this is the best way to create the experimental conditions.

Field experiments

A good example – the **scary bridge study** – is a study of the attribution of emotion. In it Dutton and Aron (1974) tested the theory that arousal can be interpreted in different ways in different settings. They hypothesized that it can, in the right circumstances, be experienced as sexual attraction.

In order to test their hypothesis they had an 'attractive' woman interview young men when they were on a footbridge. When the interview was complete the woman gave the man a card with her phone number on it so that, ostensibly, he could call up to find out the results of the study. What was actually counted was how many of the men called to ask the woman for a date. That, by inference, was seen as a measure of sexual arousal associated with the interview. This experiment manipulated arousal by the nature of the footbridge. In the 'low-arousal condition' the bridge was just an ordinary one. In the 'high-arousal condition' it was an incredibly scary wooden suspension bridge over a deep crevasse – scary because it sways alarmingly as you walk on it (I know, I tried it!) and the ground is a very, very long way down.

Another way of thinking about field experiments is that they are where researchers capitalize upon situations in which relevant factors are being varied naturally. Instead of seeking to vary anxiety in the laboratory (for example, by giving subjects drugs that raise anxiety) Dutton and Aron capitalized on the different effects of walking on the two bridges. Such studies are therefore sometimes called **quasi-experiments**, since in them there is less ability to control the experimental conditions than in the laboratory. A key principle of experimental design is that you must *randomly* allocate subjects to the different conditions to avoid the possibility that differences in the characteristics of the people in each group are what caused the effect, not your experimental manipulation. In the scary bridge study the researchers had no control over which men walked on which bridge. Maybe they were different – only men who liked taking risks went on the scary bridge, and risk-liking men are also more likely to ask women for dates.

Laboratory experiments

Laboratory experiments are conducted in controlled settings. In social psychology the 'laboratory' is often no more than an ordinary room, albeit one where people can be isolated from the outside world. This is because an experiment seeks to remove – or at least reduce as far as possible – as many extraneous influences as they can, so that it is only (or at least mainly) those that are manipulated by the experiment that exert an influence. However, as you will have already seen in Milgram's study, sometimes doing this requires a fair amount of staging. Milgram went on to conduct a number of proper experiments to try to explain why the people in his first descriptive study were obedient to authority. Like that one, these experiments required an elaborate **experimental scenario** in order to create the experimental conditions. Since he was seeking to convince the subjects that they were participating in an experiment (albeit not the one they were actually taking part in) it needed to look like one. And the manipulation of creating a strong authority figure meant that for the experimenter to look like one he wore a white laboratory coat and acted with great authority.

Other research settings

Not all experimental social psychology uses experiments. Hypothetico-deductive method can be used in other research settings. The main one is **survey research**, where data are gathered by asking people to fill in questionnaires or they are interviewed – face to face, by telephone or even by e-mail.

Testing the hypothesis

Following his descriptive study, Milgram went on to conduct a series of experiments to explore what was causing the obedience (Milgram 1965). In them he varied things like the gender of the subjects, the dress and demeanour of the experimenter, and whether the laboratory was sited in a university or in a scruffy downtown office. But for our purpose – to understand the basic format of an experiment – we will look at just one of these experiments: where Milgram deliberately set out to test the hypothesis that the closer the proximity between the subject and the learner, the less obedient the subject would be. In it Milgram tested four levels of proximity (see Figure 3.3).

Figure 3.3
Milgram's four levels of proximity

Level of proximity	Low	Moderate	High	Very high
Experimental condition	Subject cannot see or hear the learner	Subject can hear the learner but cannot see him	Subject can see and hear learner	Subject sits beside learner and holds his hand down onto a metal plate for the shock to be delivered

(*Below*) Still from 1965 film *Obedience*, showing the touch-proximity condition
Source: © 1965 Stanley Milgram and distributed by Penn State University Media Sales. Permission granted by Alexandra Milgram

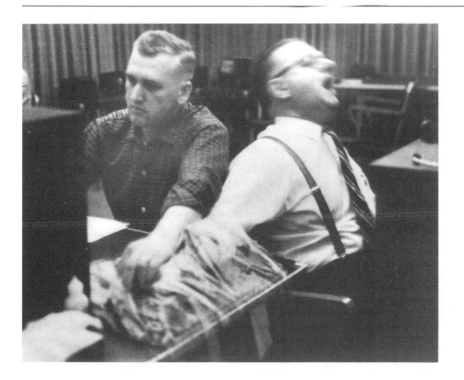

As far as it was possible, all other conditions were kept the same, so that any differences between the behaviour of the subjects could be attributed to the differences in the level of proximity. The results from the study were as shown below.

Level of proximity	Low	Moderate	High	Very high
Percentage of subjects who went up to the 450V limit	65	62.5	40	30

These data provide pretty convincing evidence that proximity does affect participants' obedience. Milgram's later studies were able to show that other factors exert an influence too: the behaviour and dress of the experimenter and the location of the experimental setting both had significant effects. However, what he found to be the most important influence was the presence of other 'teachers' (that is, additional stooges) and, in particular, their behaviour. If they refused to comply with instructions to go on giving shocks, then subjects almost always refused too. But if the others went on doing as they were told, then subjects generally did so as well.

Terminology

Milgram's (1965) experiment gives us the chance to get to grips with some important terminology used in relation to experiments. **Construct** is the term used to describe the abstract, theoretical concepts being studied – in the study we just looked at, these were obedience to authority and social proximity. **Operationalization** describes the way a construct is 'made operational' (that is, usable) in the form of variables that can be measured in a particular study. Hence the term **variable** describes the aspect of the construct that can be defined and/or measured. In this case, obedience to authority was measured by the point on the scale at which the subject refused to go on administering shocks, and proximity was measured by the level of proximity (low, moderate, high and very high) between the subject and the learner.

Variables come in one of two forms. The **independent variable** is the one the researcher varies to test the hypothesis. In Milgram's experiment the independent variable was the level of proximity which he varied in four steps. The experiment therefore had four **conditions**. The **dependent variable** is the one that is used to assess the impact of the independent variable (that is its magnitude depends upon the effect of the independent variable). In Milgram's experiment the dependent variable was the point on the scale at which the subject refused to go on administering shocks. The relationship between the constructs, variables and measurements in this experiment are thus:

Construct	Variable	Definition/measurement
Proximity	Independent	Low, moderate, high, very high
Obedience	Dependent	75V–450V

Data collection techniques

In experimental research there are three main ways in which measurable data can be collected (Table 3.1).

Observational measures

Observational measures are those taken from direct observation of the behaviour of subjects that is relevant to the research question. The behaviour can be in a form that is directly measured: for instance, the duration of eye gaze in seconds is frequently used as a measure of intimacy in relationships (Kleinke 1986). Or behaviours can be classified through a predetermined coding frame. Bales and Slater (1955), for instance, coded what people said in group discussions (for example requests for information, suggestions for action) and used these data to determine group members' roles in the group (for example 'facilitator', 'leader').

Table 3.1
Three data collection techniques

Measures	Definition	Examples
Observational	Recording actions directly relevant to the research question	Length of direct eye gaze; distance between people when they are interacting; categories of response such as wearing college sweat shirts
Self-report	Subjects' responses to questions	Questionnaire responses, responses in interviews
Implicit	Recording actions that imply an underlying effect	Response times to classifying items (for example as belonging or not belonging to a category like 'attractive')

Self-report measures

Many areas of social psychological research depend on **self-report measures**. Most research into people's attitudes, opinions and social cognition is done in this way. Reports may be in the form of answers to a scale or questionnaire, or in response to interview questions. In both cases the questions can be closed-ended (that is, where the question pre-specifies the responses that can be made) or open-ended (that is, where the question asks for an answer in the subject's own words). Closed-ended responses are coded through the instrument used. For example many use a **Lickert scale** with boxes to tick ranging, say, from 'strongly agree' to 'strongly disagree'. In experimental research, open-ended responses are pre-coded in relation to the hypothesis being tested. In the Bales and Slater study, for example, the coding frame was based on the hypothesis that facilitators and leaders would tend to make different contributions to the group discussion.

Implicit measures

Self-report measures rely on subjects giving accurate and honest answers to the questions they are posed. But they may not do so – for example, a subject may be unwilling to be seen as self-interested. In the 1992 general election in Britain the opinion polls indicated that Labour would win. But when people actually voted (as opposed to saying how they intended to vote) the Conservative Party won the election. Commentators speculated that many people did not want to be seen as selfish when asked about their voting intentions on the doorstep. So they lied and said they would vote for the party (Labour) with policies based on social welfare. But when they came to vote, they voted for the party they believed would best serve their own interests by keeping taxation low.

Social psychologists have therefore developed a range of **implicit measures**, from which a person's thinking (including their unconscious thinking) can be inferred indirectly. An example is a study of racial prejudice by Gaertner and McLaughlin (1983). They sat subjects in front of a computer screen, flashed up pairs of words (for example White–smart, Black–smart) and asked the subjects to press a button if they thought there was an association between the two words. The implicit measure that Gaertner and McLaughlin used was the speed at which subjects responded. On average White subjects in the experiment responded significantly faster to the White–smart pairing than the Black–smart one. From this the researchers inferred that these people were exhibiting racial prejudice.

Qualitative research

Kidder and Fine (1987) distinguish two meanings of the term **qualitative research**. They use the term '**little q**' to refer to the incorporation of non-numerical data in hypothetico-deductive research. An example is an open-ended question within a survey, another is what is said in a discussion group. However, this data is 'qualitative' only in the sense there is no direct measurement. The data are always coded in some way, since experimental studies always need to use dependent variables that can be measured or counted, as described above.

I have used the term 'experimental social psychology' to refer just to social psychology that adopts that position. But if you recall from Chapter 2, not all social psychologists do so. In particular those working within a sociological social psychological paradigm use other methods that are, in Kidder and Fine's (1987) terms, '**Big Q**'. These are qualitative methods that are to some degree abductive and explore meaning and, as such, will be discussed in the next section.

However, we should briefly note that it is not quite that simple. As I mentioned, scientists use abduction too, and there are some social psychologists who are *experimental* in their epistemological position but include 'Big Q' qualitative methods in their repertoires. For example, they may begin a study with open-ended interviews or group discussions in order to gather a general sense of what people think and say about a topic, for instance, as part of the process of designing a questionnaire.

Research strategies

When experimental researchers plan social psychological studies they need to take three considerations into account:

- the representativeness of the data collected
- realism – how far the study can reflect real life
- the amount of control that can be exerted over the experimental conditions.

Representativeness

Representativeness involves trying to make sure that the people taking part in the study are representative of the people you want to find out about or your theory is about. So, for instance, if your theory is about 'people in general', you need to make sure that the people taking part (in experiments they are called the **experimental subjects**, in surveys they are called **respondents**) are able to represent the population as a whole. Many (perhaps most) social psychological studies use students as experimental subjects, since they are, in effect, a 'captive market' (in many Psychology departments being a subject for the research of the people who work there is a course requirement). This is usually justified by the claim that students are sufficiently representative in the qualities relevant to the study for it not to matter that they are a specific group and not representative of the population as a whole.

In other settings, such as survey research, respondents are selectively sampled to be representative of the qualities held to matter in the study in question – for instance, in terms of social class, age and gender. Survey research is the best strategy when the research question is primarily a descriptive one and relates to public attitudes. **Opinion polls** (especially in the lead-up to elections) and **market research** are common examples, where what is wanted is to get an accurate description of trends and/or the differences between, say, different socio-economic groups.

Studies of market segmentation, for instance, are used to identify different kinds of customers, particularly when a new product is launched and companies want to know where to direct advertising. Where researchers want to find out about a specific sub-group, then they will seek to target just these people. Examples here are studies conducted by political parties, where they want to target just 'floating voters'. They use a questionnaire to identify such people and then invite just these to take part in **focus groups** about which policy initiatives 'go down well' with floating voters. Market researchers use both qualitative and quantitative methods, according to the research questions they are paid to answer.

Realism

Realism has to do with the extent to which it matters that the setting in which your study is conducted and the design of the study are close to 'real life'. In the Zimbardo study the 'real life' being constructed was designed to be as close as possible to a real prison (Zimbardo *et al.* 1973). In this study the researchers saw realism as a crucial element in the variables they wanted to study. But in Wason's (1966, 1968) selection task study that you looked at in Chapter 2, the 'realism' of the setting was not seen as relevant.

Control

Control is crucial to hypothetico-deductive method, in that it can work only if the researcher can isolate extraneous variables, closely control the manipulation of the independent variable(s) and accurately measure the dependent variable(s). The more important it is for a study to follow hypothetico-

Table 3.2
Suitability of different research strategies

	Research settings		
	Laboratory experiments	Field experiments	Surveys
Control	High	Medium	Lows
Realism	Lows	High	Irrelevant
Representativeness	Varies	Low	High

deductive method, the more crucial it is to have high levels of control. Thus control is relatively unimportant in descriptive research, but central to explanatory research.

Research design

When designing studies, researchers have to balance out these three factors. By and large greater realism means less control. The scary bridge study is a good example (Dutton and Aron 1974). It was fairly realistic – in that anxiety varied naturally between the two experimental settings. But the researchers had no control over which men walked across which bridge. This meant they could not be sure that the two samples were comparable. Researchers also have to be pragmatic, since greater representativeness usually means that subjects must be selected more carefully, and this can be time-consuming, difficult and often costly.

Different research strategies are used according to the relative salience and importance of representativeness, realism and control. Broadly these are as shown in Table 3.2.

From this it can be seen that where control is the most salient, laboratory experiments are best. Where realism is important then field experiments are best. And where representativeness is crucial, then surveys are best. Of course these are over-generalizations, but this is a broad rule of thumb that works most of the time.

Methods and analytics in experimental social psychology

Experimental social psychologists use Scientific methods. Just as in the natural sciences, these are based on a hypothetico-deductive

→

logic of inquiry. They adopt different strategies according to the relative salience of realism, representativeness and control.

- Experiments are the most rigorous form of experimental method, and **laboratory experiments** the most rigorous of all, since they allow considerable **control** to be exerted over the manipulation and measurement of variables and conditions.
- **Field** or **quasi-experiments** are not so rigorous – there is less control – but they allow for a greater degree of **realism**.
- **Surveys** are also less rigorous in the control they can exert over variables and conditions, but they offer greater potential for **representativeness**.

METHODS AND ANALYTICS IN CRITICAL SOCIAL PSYCHOLOGY

As you saw in Chapter 2, critical social psychology has adopted social constructionism as its theoretical framework for research. Willig (2001) defines it like this:

> Research from a social constructionist perspective is concerned
> with identifying the various ways of constructing social reality that
> are available in culture, to explore the conditions of their use and
> to trace their implications for human experience and social
> practice.

(Willig 2001: 7)

There are a variety of ways by which social constructionist research gets hold of the 'something' to which to apply its analytics – in other words, data collection. We shall not look at those first though, as they are not that important (we come on to look at them later the section). With a social constructionist approach, analysis is where the serious work is done. As the task is to seek understanding rather than to explain in cause-and-effect terms, there is no need to turn constructs into variables, or work out how to measure some things, control others and exclude the rest. As there is no claim to objectivity, researchers are not particularly concerned about representativeness, realism or control. Experimentalists sometimes see this as methodological sloppiness, but they are missing the crucial point: that different research questions are being asked and different kinds of answers sought, for which these methodological features are largely irrelevant.

Don't get this wrong: social constructionist research is not (or certainly should not be) sloppy. It always needs to be done with insight and in most cases needs to be done very meticulously. Conversation analysis (see Chapter 7), for example, requires high-quality, high-tech equipment to record every 'um', 'ah' pause and inflection in the conversations being scrutinized. It involves painstaking transcription, and both transcribers and those who do the analysis (often the same person) need to develop high-grade skills in recording and interpreting what has gone on.

Just as in the previous section I concentrated on experimental method as the foundation of Scientific method, here I begin with a detailed examination of **discourse analysis**. This is by far the most popular social constructionist research approach. There are several others (such as social representations, grounded theory and Q method) which we shall look at later. But discourse analysis is by far the best known and the most frequently used analytic within social constructionist research in social psychology.

Discourse analysis

Discourse is a term that was drawn originally from linguistics, where it is used to refer to a section of speech or writing. Within social constructionist social psychology it is used to describe something more specific. Here a discourse is defined as the product of constructing and the means to construct meaning in a particular way.

Social constructionist social psychologists have developed a number of different versions of discourse analysis. There are two main strands: **discursive practices** and **discursive resources**. Some discourse analysts (Billig 1997; Wetherell 1998) see these strands as differing only in emphasis or focus, while others (Parker 1997; Potter 1996) regard them as distinct, having different theoretical frameworks, different historical roots and research traditions, and each designed to address different kinds of research questions.

The analysis of discursive practices

This is probably the best known form of discourse analysis, initiated by Jonathan Potter and Margaret Wetherell in their classic book *Discourse and Social Psychology: Beyond Attitudes and Behaviour* (Potter and Wetherell 1987). As an analytical method, Willig defines it as a form of discourse analysis that is 'primarily concerned with how people use discursive resources in order to achieve interpersonal objectives in social interaction' (Willig 2001: 91). It is an analysis based on the following assumptions:

- language is the main symbolic system through which people construct their social realities.
- people deploy language purposefully and strategically, to achieve particular outcomes or goals.

- language use is therefore always a discursive practice – 'discursive' in the sense of meaning-making, and a 'practice' in the sense that it is behaviour.

Discursive practices are deployed at many different levels: at the individual level (for example when people have arguments); at the level of social groups and collectives (for example when they develop their own slang); and at the level of culture and society (for example where a particular worldview is so embedded into the language that it becomes taken for granted).

A discursive practices discourse analytic study of racism

Read the three extracts below, taken from an interview conducted as part of a study on racism. This was carried out in Aoteoroa with participants who were from the pakeha ethnic group living there. The interviews were about these participants' views of 'Polynesian immigrants'.

Extract 1
I'm not anti them at all you know, I, if they're willing to get on and be like us; but if they're just going to come here, just to be able to use our social welfares and stuff like that, then why don't they stay home.

Extract 2
What I would li . . . rather see is that, sure, bring them into New Zealand, right, try and train them in a skill, and encourage them to go back again.

Extract 3
I think that if we encouraged more Polynesians and Maoris to be skilled people they would want to stay here, they're not, um, as, uh, nomadic as New Zealanders are [*interviewer laughs*] so I think that would be better.

What do you think is going on here? Do you think the person who said these things is being racist? Discourse analysis of these extracts identifies two main discursive practices in use:

- **Disclaiming**, where, at the beginning of the first extract, the participant says 'I'm not anti them at all you know', using this disclaimer as a strategic practice to deny they are racist.
- **Extreme case formulation**, where the participant uses the most extreme situation – '*just* going to come here, *just* to be able to use our social welfares'. The speaker is using another discursive practice here for another reason – exaggerating in order to justify a particular prescription for action (that they should 'stay home'). Expressing the worst case scenario – that the immigrants have no motivation for

'coming here' other than to sponge off social welfare – enables the speaker to justify the claim that they should stay home.

These are two examples of the strategic use of discourse – discursive practices deployed to achieve particular outcomes. Much of this form of discourse analysis consists of identifying such strategies and practices and then seeking to 'best guess' the tactical purpose of each one. Abduction is being used here, as you can see, in two ways: by homing in on those sections of text that stand out as needing to be explained; and by asking the question 'what is the speaker *doing* with it?' In this way researchers can begin to build up an understanding of the practices involved in people's use of discourse. Notice too that what is going on is what you observed Shank suggesting in Chapter 2 – researchers using their own 'effort after meaning' skills as a 'rich and complex tool of inquiry' (Shank 1998: 856).

However, you may also have noticed that the second two extracts contradict each other. Extract 2 says that immigrants should be encouraged to go back, Extract 3 is about it being better for them to stay once they have arrived. When contradictions can be spotted (that is, there are obvious *surprises* in the text – anomalies and dislocations), this offers a particularly valuable opportunity to use abductive reasoning. Just as with Shank's juxtaposition (described in Chapter 2), the contradictory sections of text can be compared to see how discourse is being deployed differently. To gain insight into what may be going on, researchers carefully scrutinize the different contexts in which each statement is made.Here are extended versions of Extracts 2 and 3 within the text as a whole. I have italicised the bits you have seen already.

Extract 1

Interviewer: [do] you think that, say, immigration from the Pacific Islands should be encouraged [ ] to a much larger extent than it is? It's fairly restricted at the moment.

Respondent: Yes. Um, I think that there's some problems in, in encouraging that too much, is that they come in uneducated about our ways, and I think it's important they understand what they're coming to. I, *what I would li . . . rather see is that, sure, bring them into New Zealand, right, try and train them in a skill, and encourage them to go back again* because their dependence upon us will be lesser: I mean [ ] while the people back there are dependent on the people being here earning money to send it back, I mean that's a very very negative way of looking at something. [ ] people really should be trying, they should be trying to help their own nation first.

Extract 2

Respondent: Polynesians, they are doing jobs now that white people wouldn't do. So in many sectors of the community or or life, um, we would be very much at a loss without them, I think. Um, what I would like to see is more effort being made to train them into skills, skilled jobs, because we are without skilled people and a lot of our skilled people, white people, have left the country to go other places. *I think that if we encouraged more Polynesians and Maoris to be skilled people they would want to stay here, they're not, um, as, uh, nomadic as New Zealanders are* [interviewer laughs] *so I think that would be better.*

Now the reason for the contradiction becomes clearer. In Extract 2 the participant is expressing concern about the outflow of money from the New Zealand economy. In Extract 3 they are expressing concern about the skills shortage in New Zealand, given so many skilled New Zealanders move away and the potential for immigrants to make up the shortfall. This kind of analysis shows, among other things, that when people speak, they shift from one concern to another, and therefore in order to understand how they are using discourse we need to look at how it is organized to achieve different functions. Mick Billig expresses this well:

> Instead of mining the discourse for the respondents' underlying 'true' attitude or 'real' view, discursive psychologists view respondents' comments as discursive acts that can only be understood in context.
>
> (Billig 1997: 44)

Textbook writing as a discursive practice

Before we move on to considering the features of discursive resources discourse analysis, stop for a moment and think about *my* authorial discourse (that is, my discursive practice in the way I am writing this text for you). My plan was to give you an 'abductory moment', so I deliberately seeded a surprise for you – can you work out what it was? When I first began to describe the study, unless you knew the terms already you may have assumed that *Aoteoroa* was some obscure country and *pakeha* some exotic group of people. But I suspect you soon worked out that Aoteoroa is the original name of New Zealand, and pakeha the original name for the ethnic group that is non-Maori. Both words are taken from the Maori language.

By prioritizing the Maori terms, I was strategically deploying *my* language. Maybe you speculated about why I did so. You may have seen it as a form of 'politically correct' showing off. Maybe I wanted to impress my friends and colleagues in Aoteoroa/New Zealand by demonstrating that I am aware of the argument that it is more respectful to the Maori (given they are the indigenous people) to use their terminology rather than the imperialist use of English. Or maybe you saw it as a genuine attempt on my part to avoid being racist.

Now you can see that it was also a deliberate writerly, teacherly strategy. I hope you agree it is a good example of a 'surprise' that made you think. In making you wonder why I imported this terminology, I hope you began to ask questions about what I was 'getting at'. My purpose was to make you think about the preconceptions people often have about culture – that 'we' (whoever 'we' are) are 'ordinary people' outside of culture, whereas 'they' (whoever 'they' are) are 'exotic others' who have culture.

The term pakeha is used by Maori in Aoteoroa to define people by what they are *not* (*not* Maori). What white people often mean by the term 'black' is not so much to do with skin colour as with being not-white (that is, 'not like us'). If you are 'black' (including Maori) you do not need me to tell you what it feels like to be called a 'member of an ethnic group'. But if you are 'white' I hope being called a 'member of an ethnic group' (known as pakeha) was at least a little bit surprising, and maybe even disconcerting. That 'white' people are unused to this is a consequence, in part, of their lack of language skills. There are similar words in a number of languages (Rom and Japanese for example) but most 'white' people do not understand them.

The main elements of the discursive practices approach

The analysis of discursive practices concentrates on specific instances of language in use. The research questions posed are 'what is *this* person, in *this* part of the conversation, seeking to achieve? And what discursive practices are they using to do so?' Its primary goal is to explicate the functions to which discourse is put in different situations. Burman and Parker (1993) see it as discourse analysis focused on 'repertoires and dilemmas', highlighting Potter and Wetherell's preferred unit of analysis – **linguistic repertoires.**

The discourse studied is usually extracts from naturally occurring **talk** such as transcriptions of meetings or counselling sessions. The things that people say in such conversations are viewed as constructed from a pre-existing, shared manifold of linguistic repertoires, predicated upon collectively shared and understood ideas (that is discourses). These are seen to act as resources from which people weave arguments, explanations, descriptions and so on, to meet different rhetorical purposes and functions, which shift as the conversation progresses. The analysis usually consists of detailed scrutiny of the discursive practices going on in short extracts of talk.

Conversation analysis

A particularly fine-tuned form of discursive practice analysis is now conventionally called **conversation analysis** (see, for example, Psathas 1995). Its

Conversation
analysis is
described in more
detail and
examples
examined in
Chapter 7.

origins can be traced to the work of Harvey Sacks in the 1960s (see Sacks 1995) within the broader field of **ethnomethodology**. Conversation analysis uses very fine-grained classification and notation of interactive talk in order to examine what people are doing and seeking to achieve in the *way* they use language. It focuses on the units and forms of talk – such as conversational openings and closings and turn-taking. For example, it often examines in very fine detail the timing of talk – when people interrupt and speak over each other, or, alternatively, pause before they respond. Through this analysis researchers seek to determine how talk is being used and interpreted strategically.

The analysis of discursive resources

This form of discourse analysis works at a different level. Instead of looking in fine-grained detail at the strategic use of discourse *within* a particular piece of text, it takes a broader-brush perspective. It examines how discourses work *across* situations and settings. Analysis is concerned both with the **textuality** of discourse – its functions, uses and ability to wield power; and its socio-cultural **tectonics** – the ways in which discourse is produced, maintained and promoted, how discourses vie against and impinge upon one another (Curt 1994).

This approach is less concerned with what particular individuals say in particular settings than with the way discourse operates more generally and more globally as a social and cultural resource to be used in human activities and endeavours. Thus data collection techniques are more varied and analysis is more taxonomic. This form of analysis seeks to identify and describe, for a particular topic or issue, what are the main discourses in play, how they jockey with and exert power over each other, and how they vary and shift over time and from one discursive location to another. In discursive resources discourse analysis, the research questions are: what discourses operate in relation to this topic? Where do they come from? How and why were they constructed? How are they deployed and what can they be used to achieve?'

Here the discourse analytic work draws extensively from French theory, especially the work of Foucault and his concern with the relationships between power and knowledge. Indeed, this is why Willig (2001) calls it 'Foucauldian':

> From a Foucaultian point of view, discourses facilitate and limit, enable and constrain what can be said, by whom, where and when. . . .
> Foucaultian discourse analysts focus on the availability of discursive resources within a culture – something like a discursive economy – and its implications for those who live within it.
>
> (Willig 2001: 107)

A discursive resources analysis of jealousy

Using a variety of methods of data collection, Paul Stenner has conducted a discursive resourrces analytic study into discourses of jealousy (Stenner 1993, Curt 1994). Read the four short extracts from his study (taken from Curt 1994: Chapter 7) given below, and think about what is similar between Extracts 1a and 1b, and Extracts 2a and 2b, and what is different between them.

Paul Stenner is a member of the collective author, Beryl Curt.

Extract 1a
There was this young married couple called Scott . . . and Charlene . . . who went on holiday. While on holiday they became friends with a man called Steve . . . who was from the same town as them. Unfortunately after a couple of days Scott became ill so he couldn't go out or enjoy the holiday, but not wishing for his wife's holiday to be spoilt insisted that she go around with Steve to keep her company. So seeing what it meant to him that she was happy, she spent a lot of time with Steve sight-seeing. But as the week went on and Scott saw so little of his wife, he became very bad tempered and resentful of Steve because he was seeing more of her than he was, and she was his wife!

Extract 1b
The man who has not been jealous, beaten his mistress, torn her clothes; he has yet to be in love

Extract 2a
Jealous woman: 'I don't know why Fred [her boyfriend] wants me when he's had Wilma [his ex]. She's got a beautiful face, lovely skin, straight teeth and a perfect figure, I think he is just with me because he can't have her any more.
Friend: If Fred didn't want you he wouldn't be with you now, I don't know why you worry. You've got a lot to give.
Jealous woman: But if I was more pretty and had a better figure he might want me more than he wanted her.
Friend: I think you should just get on with living in the present and forget what's happened in the past.
Jealous woman: I'm not living in the past, it's just, I've always wanted good skin and I've put on weight and I'm not as tall as Wilma and I've always wanted longer legs. It's just so unfair that some people have got what I've always wanted.

Extract 2b
Jealousy is always the same no matter where you find it: (a) a neurotic need for approval, and (b) an intense feeling of inferiority. If you conquer those two conditions, nothing, not even having someone sleep

with your partner, can make you jealous. In fact, you could have several
people sleep with your partner on a regular basis and still not feel
jealous if you did not have problems with inferiority feelings and a
neurotic need for approval.

Stenner got the accounts of jealousy given in extracts 1a and 2a by asking
groups of students to work together to write a short scenario in which jealousy
is played out. Using Q methodology (described later in this section) he
identified them as describing two distinctly different discourses of jealousy.

Extract 1a he identifies as an account of 'jealousy as natural'. This discourse,
he says, usually relates to sexual (or, if you prefer, romantic) jealousy. In this
discourse jealousy is seen as a sign of true love, and is thought of as a kind of
'emotional glue' which holds a loving relationship together. Extract 1b is
another account of 'natural jealousy', taken from the historical writings of
Lucian in *Scenes of Courtesans* (quoted in Gonzalez-Crussi 1988). So Extracts 1a
and 1b are similar in that they depict jealousy in the same way. But they are
different in that Extract 1a is contemporary data gathered through getting
people to write a scene, whereas Extract 1b is a historical account.

Stenner identifies Extract 2a as an account of 'jealousy as psychological
immaturity'. This discourse, Stenner suggests, is much more recent in origin,
arising from psychodynamic ideas. This discourse explains that a jealous type
of person is insecure because of a lack of mother-love in childhood, and who
was not trained properly as a young child to cope with jealousy – to deal, for
example, with 'sibling rivalry'. Extract 2b is taken from a psychology text
(Hauck 1981: 35). So Extracts 2a and 2b are once more similar because they
articulate the same discourse of 'jealousy as psychological immaturity', and
different because they are drawn from different kinds of sources.

In his detailed analysis of these two alternative discourses (Stenner 1992,
1993; Curt 1994), Stenner draws on a diversity of sources to 'build up a picture'
of what each sees jealousy as being like and why it occurs. He explicates what
each one can be used to achieve – that they justify taking different moral
positions on whether jealousy is a good or bad thing, and they warrant
different kinds of action – violence in one case and sexual infidelity in the
other.

Grounded theory

As its name implies, **grounded theory** is not so much a method as an approach
to the way in which theory and method relate to each other. It argues that
instead of using methods to test theories, it is more functional to use methods
to generate them. You are already familiar with this argument, as it is the
basis of abductory research. However, I have included brief mention of the

methodological approach in this chapter, since you may well hear about it and wonder how it 'fits in' to social constructionist research.

Grounded theory as a method was devised by two sociologists Barney Glaser and Anslem Strauss (Glaser and Strauss 1967). Like discourse analysis, grounded theory starts with 'something to scrutinize' (most often interviews) and seeks to develop a theory about what is going on through detailed analysis. It is closest to discursive resources discourse in that it is less concerned with specific use of discourse analysis in specific pieces of text, and more interested in identifying common themes. Basically it comprises four key analytic strategies:

- coding
- constant comparative analysis
- theoretical sampling
- theoretical saturation.

Coding

Text is scrutinized to look for categories of meaning and code them. Some categorization is descriptive. For example, statements about 'anger', 'anxiety' and 'guilt' can be categorized as 'emotions'. Some categorization is more abstract. For instance, 'getting drunk', 'going shopping' and 'having a massage' might be categorized as 'indulgences'. Such categorization is quite different from content analysis (used in 'little q' research) that uses a predetermined coding scheme designed to test a hypothesis. In grounded theory categorization is derived *from* the scrutiny of the text.

Coding is the process of identifying categories. It is done by researchers 'immersing' themselves in the data – transcribed talk, mostly – by listening to it and reading and rereading it, over and over again. By this process they gradually identify categories, refine them and reassign them, slowly building up a network of categories, with some superordinate over others. The aim is to develop new, context-specific, superordinate categories that do not fit in with existing theory. Hence they will allow new theoretical insights to be made.

Constant comparative analysis

This is a process of refining categories. Having identified a new superordinate category, the researcher goes back to the transcripts and looks for instances they missed last time around. Comparing these with the ones already identified, it may be possible to identify meaningful sub-categories. For example, having identified 'getting drunk', 'going shopping' and 'having a massage' as 'indulgences', a researcher might, on more careful scrutiny, begin to detect a pattern where such instances are linked to escaping from problems in their lives. They find some more instances – 'burying myself in housework', 'playing computer games' and 'sorting out my tax' that are not so much forms of indulgence as ways of occupying oneself so you do not have to think. But both seem to serve the purpose of escaping from stress. Thus the coding frame is changed, with a new superordinate category – 'escape' and two sub-categories – 'indulgent escapes' and 'mind-numbing escapes'. Researchers must also look for negative cases – instances that do not fit, which mean the categorization needs to be amended and fine-tuned. Together these processes allow researchers to add depth and density to their analysis, incrementally building up a categorization that reflects the full complexity and diversity of the data they are scrutinizing.

At this stage it is not unusual to go out and collect more data. Often researchers begin with just, say, three or four interviews. They then code and do comparison analysis on them, to give them inspiration about new questions they might ask, or different kinds of people they might include in their study.

Theoretical sampling

This is the point at which the analysis moves from being descriptive to analytic. In grounded theory the researcher constantly asks questions of their data, using abduction to speculate about potential reasons why people say what they say and describe the issues around the topic in the ways in which they do.

Theoretical sampling is a strategic and purposive scrutiny of the categorization achieved so far, and comparing it with the data overall, sampling incidents and extracts that may either challenge or elaborate it. The coding stage is pursued in an open-ended, open-minded manner, dipping here and dipping there to see what can be got. Theoretical sampling is concerned with refinement and rigour – of checking out in a systematic way that the categorization is as good as it can be. And it is not unusual at this stage to again collect more data, if the theoretical sampling throws up questions that the data collected so far do not allow to be fully explored.

Theoretical saturation

Theoretical saturation is where, after numerous iterations of the three analytic strategies, the researcher reaches the point where no new categories are being identified. This is often more of an aspiration than something that is fully achieved. Most researchers stop at the point where they have a 'good enough' categorization to have been able to articulate a meaningful and useful theory.

Data collection techniques

In this section I cover two main ways of collecting data for social constructionist research – gathering text and Q method.

Gathering text

Discourse analysis is an analytic applied to a **text**. Usually text is defined as a human product or action that signifies something (signification is dealt with in detail in Chapter 4). It is usually a segment of language, but can also be an object (such as a building or a sculpture), a depiction (such as a painting or photograph) or even a performance (such as a piece of music, a dance routine or sporting performance). Usually, social constructionists apply discourse analysis to language – talk such as conversations, interviews or discussions, and written language that can be anything from the text on a toothpaste carton, through a bureaucratic document to a section of a novel or a textbook.

As you might imagine, there are lots of ways of collecting these texts. Stenner got some of his by asking groups of students to construct a jealousy scenario. I obtained data once by keeping a notebook and listening to conversations in places like queues in the post office and while having my hair cut. Clearly the kind of discourse analysis you want to do determines where you can get your talk. Conversation analysis, for instance, needs very accurately recorded talk, and so requires the use of high-grade recording equipment and agreement from participants to have their talk recorded. This is not always possible. Worrell (2000) for example got some of her data from observing therapy sessions with sexual offenders in prison, and other data from being a participant-observer in a self-help group. In neither case was it possible to make recordings, either technically or ethically.

Q method

Q method is something of an oddball to include as a means for obtaining text to which to apply discourse analysis, but bear with me. Most people think it is more suited to the experimental paradigm (on the basis that it uses numbers and statistics). However, Q method does not set out to measure anything objectively. Rather, it offers people taking part in a study opportunities to express their viewpoints or beliefs or whatever by the way they sort a number of items. Their sorting patterns (for example along a dimension from 'strongly agree' to 'strongly disagree') are numerically *coded*, to enable the statistical analysis. But this is not an attitude scale and no measurement is implied.

Usually the items sorted are statements but cartoons, photographs and musical extracts have also been used. The task of the researcher is to supply participants in the study with a set of items to sort (sometimes called a Q-sample) which, as far as possible, reflects the broad range of ideas, statements and arguments about the topic in question. It is generally done rather differently in the USA, but elsewhere the preparation of a Q-set is based on other social constructionist methods – such as interviews, focus groups and media analysis (such as looking at newspapers and movies, poems and academic texts).

Q methodology was invented by William Stephenson. He was working with Charles Spearman during the time when Spearman was formulating and refining the statistical technique of factor analysis. Stephenson had been trained as a physicist and active at a time when quantum physics was being developed. With this background, he was fascinated by the alternative possibilities of the statistical technique. He made what was at the time a very radical suggestion – that factor analysis could be 'inverted' to look at something different from what Spearman was interested in (looking for underlying, universal traits in areas like intelligence).

Stephenson's idea was twofold. First, he suggested that instead of applying the technique to data gained from objectively measured tests of ability, they could be applied to a person's own, subjective ideas and judgements (he called these 'self-referent' measures). Second, he suggested that instead of looking for lawful *patterns across a population* of people, the technique could be used to compare each individual's whole pattern of response with the whole pattern of each other person's responses. Spearman developed factor analysis to see if intelligence is a single capacity, or breaks down into a number of elements operating independently (such as verbal intelligence and mathematical intelligence, where people could be good at one and bad at the other). Stephenson's suggestion was that by 'inverting' the way data are fed into factor analysis, it is possible to look for systematically different ways of responding *as a whole*.

An example helps to show what he was getting at. Stephenson collected together some pictures of vases. He gave the set to different people and asked them to order them along a dimension from 'most aesthetically pleasing' to 'most unaesthetic' (we might use different terms, like 'most stylish' to 'most lacking in style'). With data from a number of people Stephenson performed the inverted factor analysis, and got factors that identified different patterns of response. One pattern focused on shape, where slim and elegant vases were seen as aesthetic and fat, round ones rather ugly. Another pattern concentrated on the amount of decoration. This was a bi-modal factor. Some people thought that the elaborately embellished vases were the most aesthetic and the plain ones were, well, just awfully plain! Others thought the simple, plain ones were the most aesthetic and saw the highly patterned ones as horribly overblown and ugly. Beauty, in this approach, was very much in the eye of the beholder.

Figure 3.4
Carrying out a Q sort

Q method has gradually (and a bit grudgingly) been accepted as useful for social constructionist research (see, for example, Stainton Rogers 1991; Senn 1996). It does have an explicitly abductory quality in that the classification comes out of gathering the data, rather than being put into it, it usually tells you something you did not know already, and it can generate real surprises. There is not the space to go into great detail about the history and methodological niceties of Q methodology here. If you want to know more I have offered suggestions in the Further Reading section at the end of the chapter.

The outcome of a Q analysis is a set of factors, each identifying an alternative sorting-pattern for the statement. These factors are then interpreted by looking at the pattern, often backed up by written and/or spoken comments from the people who did the sorting and sometimes by biographical information about them (see Figure 3.4).

Methods and analytics in critical social psychology

In critical social psychological research, analytics are more important than methods. This is because research is abductory, and seeks to build theory and generate hypotheses from scrutinizing data.

The most usual analytic is discourse analysis, which is pursued in two forms: discursive practices and discursive resources.   →

Discursive practices research focuses on specific segments of text in specific incidents of language use.

- It seeks to discover what *this* person, in *this* part of the conversation, is seeking to achieve, and thereby to develop theories about what people *do* with language.
- Conversation analysis is a variant of discursive practices research that focuses on speech style – things like paused and butting in – to explore how language is used strategically.

Discursive resources research takes a broader-brush approach, looking at how discourse operates *across* situations and settings, and through cultural forms (like the media).

- It applies **Foucauldian analytics** to look, in particular, at the semiotic relationship between discourse and power. It traces the textuality and tectonics of discourse, for example how they are moulded by historical forces.

Grounded theory is an analytic approach derived from sociology that specifically seeks to derive theory from close scrutiny of data.

Methods of data collection
- Discourse analysis and grounded theory use texts of various kinds, derived from interviews, naturally occurring talk (such as counselling sessions) and written material of all kinds.
- Q methodology collects data by presenting people with items – usually statements – and asking them to sort them evaluatively. Using a form of factor analysis it identifies different sorting patterns, and from this identifies alternative discourses. As such, it is generally used as a means to conduct discursive resources discourse analysis.

FURTHER READING

The Scientific paradigm

You are likely to find plenty of textbooks on experimental approaches to social psychology in your library and in academic bookshops.

Manstead, A.S.R. and Semin, G. (2001) Methods in social psychology: tools to test theories, in M. Hewstone and W. Stroebe (eds) *Introduction to Social Psychology*, 3rd edn. Oxford: Blackwell.

This chapter gives an excellently readable, detailed and comprehensive coverage of the research methods used in social psychology. It is mainly written from within the scientific paradigm, but it also offers a critique of some of the problems with experiments. It sets out a clear rationale for research design and is a good source for planning your own research project.

Oppenheim, N. (1992) *Questionnaire Design, Interviewing and Attitude Measurement*. London: Pinter.

This remains the standard 'how-to-do' text for these data collection techniques. It offers detailed and clear advice about designing and administering questionnaires and analysing and interpreting the data collected.

Social constructionist paradigm

Willig, C. (2001) *Introducing Qualitative Research in Psychology: Adventures in Theory and Method*. Buckingham: Open University Press.

Not only does this book give a thorough and clear exposition of social constructionist methods, it also includes a brilliant introduction to this paradigm and the rationale for it. It includes thought provoking 'boxes' that discuss various methodological issues, and good examples of undergraduate projects.

QUESTIONS

1 Using the knowledge you have gained from this chapter, go back to Triplett's study of 'dynamogenic influence' (described in Chapter 2) and illustrate how it follows the basic design and principles of an experiment.

2 Giving illustrations in each case, describe how laboratory experiments, field experiments and surveys differ in relation to their capacity to manage control, realism and representativeness in their design.

3 Following the events of 11 September 2001, many commentators have argued that these events fundamentally 'changed the way people see the world'. Briefly outline a design for a social psychological study that examines some aspect of this contention, *either* using scientific *or* social constructionist methods.

4 What are the main similarities and differences between the *discursive practices* and *discursive resources* approaches to discourse analysis?

5 Outline the main elements of the grounded theory approach to research.

Part II
Topics in social psychology

Chapter 4

Communication and language

Chapter contents

A route map of the chapter

The chapter begins with a section on basic communication theory. The next two sections set out – in highly condensed form – the key ideas and studies of experimental social psychology in this field, looking first at its studies of non-verbal communication and then at its theorization about and research into language.

Language, as I have already mentioned, is central both to critical psychology's theorizing and to its research. The final section introduces semiotic theory, that is the main conceptual paradigm within which language is addressed by critical social psychology.

Communication theory

↓

Non-verbal communication

↓

The study of language by experimental social psychology

↓

Semiotics

Learning objectives

When you have completed studying this chapter, you should be able to:

1 Outline the main features of communication theory, and list the ways in which human communication differs from the ways in which machines (such as telecommunication systems) communicate.
2 Describe the different forms that non-verbal communication can take, their role in human communication, and how non-verbal behaviour can give cues that a person is lying.
3 Define and explain linguistics, psycholinguistics and sociolinguistics.
4 Explain what is meant by 'paralanguage' and 'speech style', giving examples of each.
5 Outline the key assumptions and elements of semiotic theory, and define 'sign', 'symbol' and 'sign system'.
6 Describe the role of the mass media as a means of intersubjective communication.
7 Outline the approach taken by semiotic theory to language.

INTRODUCTION

This chapter explores the different ways that social psychology has theorized and conducted research into how people communicate with each other and the role this plays in social interaction. It focuses in particular upon the most important means by which people communicate – through language. Language is not just important as a topic in itself. As you will recognize from Chapter 3, the study of how language is used is at the very heart of critical social psychology's approach and mission. Hence this chapter is crucial to all those that follow. You need to get a good grasp of the theorization about language so you can understand how critical psychology approaches topics like attitudes and understanding the social world.

Before we start, it is important to recognize that communication is profoundly affected by its cultural setting. Indeed, as you will see, from a semiotic perspective culture is *the* medium through which people are seen to communicate. A conversation between a teacher and a pupil, for example, will be different in an elite private school in Scotland compared with in a progressive school in Sweden, a missionary-run school in Thailand or a public school in Singapore. In each location there are different rules and norms about the appropriate verbal and non-verbal communication between pupils and their teachers. These will dictate what can and cannot be said, the demeanour in which something is said, how people look at each other, and so on.

Cultural diversity at the core of communication poses problems for experimental social psychology because of its aim to discover nomothetic universal laws. Since most of its studies have been conducted in only a limited range of cultural settings – the vast majority in the USA – mostly they tell us about the communication customs and conventions *of the particular culture in which the studies were carried out*. They do not necessarily tell us about communication in other cultures.

And there is another problem. Customs and convention change over time. Many of the studies described in this chapter were carried out in the twentieth century, many in the 1960s and 1970s. Since then relationships between men and women have changed and many communities are becoming much more ethnically diverse. These mean that *your* world is almost certainly a different one from that in which most of the classic studies of communication were carried out. Bear these points in mind as you read the chapter.

COMMUNICATION THEORY

Communication theory was originally developed to help understand the workings of mechanical communication systems like telecommunications. Basing his ideas on the operation of computers, the mathematician Shannon

Figure 4.1
Shannon and Weaver's model
Source: Based on Deaux and Wrightsman 1988: 109

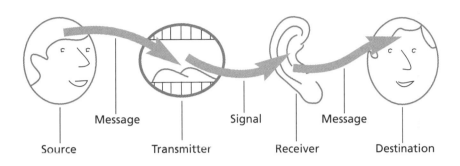

(1948) measured the transmission capacity of systems by calculating the rate at which information could be conveyed. Shannon and Weaver (1949) constructed a basic model of communication, shown in Figure 4.1.

Through the 1950s and 1960s psychologists applied this theorization to human information processing and communication (see, for example, Miller 1953; Posner 1966). However, by the end of the 1960s the 'cognitive revolution' in psychology (see Chapter 5) led to the recognition that people process and communicate information in a way that is very different from how machines do so. Shannon and Weaver's model was highly mechanistic and hence of limited value to understanding human communication. Cognitive models stressed that:

- human communication is not based (as machines are) upon the transmission of 'pure' information, but upon the transmission of meaning
- human communication is a *social activity*, actively involving two or more people and influenced by the nature of the relationship between them
- human communication is *ongoing and dynamic*, working sequentially and building upon what went before
- human communication usually works by *multiple encoding*, where, for example, a message is transmitted by both verbally and non-verbally encoded information together.

However, communication theory has given us much the basic terminology we use to understand human communication. It defines communication as involving six main elements: an information source, a transmitter or sender, a message, a communication channel, a receiver and a destination. Information transmission involves encoding and decoding, and is always subject to interference from noise.

Communication theory

- Communication involves six main elements: an information source, a transmitter or sender, a message, a communication channel, a receiver and a destination.
- Human communication is different from the mechanical forms of communication, such as telecommunication. It is active, meaningful, social and dynamic. It is also generally multiply encoded.

NON-VERBAL COMMUNICATION

Speaking is almost always accompanied by non-verbal communication. Even on the phone we tend to smile and frown, even though the other person cannot see us. Usually non-verbal cues complement and reinforce the message being conveyed verbally, and are an important aid to effective communication. In negotiations, for example, we can get cues about whether the other person is being honest by looking at their **body language**. Even when people control what they say and the way they speak so they sound as if they are being genuine, their gestures and stance can let them down (Argyle 1988).

Non-verbal communication includes a range of behaviours and serves a number of functions:

- supplementing verbal communication – for example, by giving information about feelings and emotions, and hence motives and intentions
- replacing verbal communication – for example, using hand gestures to someone who cannot hear you
- expressing things more effectively – such as the intimacy conveyed by a kiss or the touch of a hand
- helping to manage verbal communication – for instance by signalling when someone wants to speak.

Facial expression

Facial expression is important for expressing emotion. Experimental social psychologists claim that the signalling of emotion is universal from one culture to another, at least in conveying the basic emotions of happiness, surprise, sadness, fear, disgust and anger. This conclusion comes from studies carried out in 12 different countries, where people were asked to look at photographs and say what emotion was being expressed. These basic emotional expressions are associated with distinctive facial muscle activity (see Figure 4.2). Surprise, for

Figure 4.2
Some faces used in studies of emotional expression
Source: Smith and Harris Bond 1993: 59

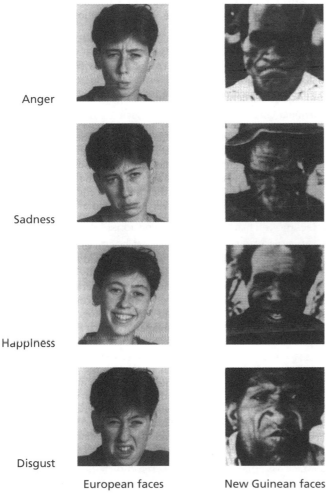

Anger

Sadness

Happiness

Disgust

European faces   New Guinean faces

example, involves raised eyebrows, dropped jaw, a wrinkled forehead, and a widening of the eyes.

This cultural universality (Ekman *et al.* 1987) has been interpreted as evidence for an innate basis to the use of facial expression for signalling emotion. This is supported by evidence of some continuity between humans and primates (Van Hooff 1972) and by the observation that people born deaf, blind and without hands still express basic emotions in much the same way as others. The most likely explanation is that certain emotions trigger a reflex in the facial muscles.

However, it needs to be noted that in virtually all cross-cultural studies of facial expression of emotion, participants were given words to label the pictures, and these words were translated from English. When people are merely asked to describe the emotions being displayed in their own words, the agreement was very much lower, and varied sharply between emotions. Joy and surprise, for example, were usually recognized, but shame and interest were not (Izard 1971).

However, there are, nonetheless, cultural conventions – called display rules – governing the way people display emotion. For example, in northern Europe and Asia men, in particular, are expected to 'damp down' emotional expression in general. Women are expected not to 'be emotional' in professional settings. In Japan both men and women learn to cover up the expression of certain negative emotions – for example, to use smiles to conceal anger or distress (Ekman 1973). Smiling, in particular, is an emotional expression that people learn to use for display purposes. In certain jobs – mainly those serving customers – staff are required to appear charming and cheerful, irrespective of what they may be feeling. Such work is called **emotional labour**, pointing to the effort involved in presenting a cheery face for hours on end, however obnoxiously the customers are behaving.

Gaze and eye contact

Gaze, in this context, refers to the time spent looking directly at another person (it has a totally different meaning in Postmodern theory). Eye contact refers to mutual gaze, when people 'catch each other's eyes'. Gaze and eye contact are used in five main ways: as a means of communication in their own right, to signal status, to signal interest and sincerity, to manage conversations and to exert control.

We sometimes say things like 'his thunderous look spoke volumes' or talk about when 'our eyes met across a crowded room'. A 'knowing look' can be used to comment to a friend about something somebody else has said. Lovers use glancing eye contact to signal mutual but secret knowledge. Gaze and eye contact are powerful ways of communicating in their own right.

The use of gaze in conversation varies by cultural convention. For example, in some cultures people in subordinate positions are expected to keep their eyes lowered when speaking to a superior. But in other cultures a lot of eye contact goes on between both speakers. Argyle and Ingham (1972) estimated that when two white British people are conversing together they spend about 60 per cent of the time gazing, each gaze lasting about three seconds. Of this, eye contact occupies about 30 per cent of the time, and each one lasts less than a second.

Social rules and cultural conventions about eye contact not only differ between cultures, but also are very powerful. Transgressing them can lead to miscommunication and can therefore be highly disturbing. In white British culture, eye contact is more used to signal interest and sincerity than status. Consequently someone who makes little eye contact will be regarded as 'shifty eyed', and the inference made that they are lying or 'up to no good'. In a culture where direct eye contact is used more to signal status, high levels of eye contact by a subordinate will be viewed as that person being 'uppity' and deliberately rude.

Most studies of gaze and eye contact have been conducted in cultures where they are regarded as signalling interest, openness and honesty. Not surprisingly, then, these studies have found that people tend to look more at those they like than at those they dislike, and for gaze and eye contact to be more frequent the more intimate the relationship (see Kleinke 1986 for a review). But even in such cultures, they are sensitive to status, though the pattern is different. Given that in such cultures gaze indicates interest, the person of lower status tends to gaze more, especially when listening to the person of higher status. Women, for example, tend, overall, to engage in more gazing than men do (Henley 1977).

Gaze and eye contact are also used to manage conversations. The main way people initiate a conversation is to make eye contact, and evading eye contact is the main way to avoid getting into conversation when you don't want to. Gaze is also used to manage turn taking. African Americans usually spend more time gazing when talking (LaFrance and Mayo 1976) whereas white people spend more time gazing while listening (Argyle and Ingham 1972). Changing the pattern (whichever one it is) acts as a cue that you want to speak, or to stop speaking. The differences can make for difficulties when black and white people speak together, though in increasingly ethnically mixed communities people are learning to accommodate to them. Rather as people adjust their speech style to suit the person they are talking with, people can learn to adjust their gazing behaviour to improve communication.

Finally, gaze can be used to exercise control, using what is called **visual dominance behaviour**. Being 'stared out' can be highly intimidating, making it hard to resist acting subserviently. But even a higher intensity of gazing can give the impression of authority. People who do so are evaluated as having greater leadership qualities than people who do not (Exline *et al.* 1975).

Postures and gesture

Postures are ways of positioning the body or certain parts of it, such as slouching in a chair or kneeling in prayer. Gestures are body movements such as bowing or pointing. Both postures and gestures are under more conscious control than facial expressions and more regulated by cultural norms and conventions. Most cultures have developed elaborate rules of etiquette about both the meaning and appropriate use of repertoires of behaviour – such as greeting people of different status. In Japan there are formal rules about the degree to which one should bow, and Chinese business people present their professional cards in a specific manner according to status. Less formally most cultures have more subtle rules about posture, often to do with status or intimacy (Mehrabian 1972)

In order to try to classify postures and gestures, they have been divided into illustrators and emblems. An **illustrator** is a posture or gesture that accompanies speech, generally reinforcing its message, such as using your hand to point directions. An **emblem** is a gesture that stands in for speech, such as a soldier's salute or a police officer's upheld hand signalling 'stop'. Some emblems are widely recognized across cultures. Others are culture specific. I remember well the difficulty I had talking with an Albanian once, for whom a nod meant 'no' and a sideways shake of the head meant 'yes', the exact opposite of the gestures I am used to. Just how much meaning can be packed into a gesture is shown by the observation that to represent suicide in the USA the gesture is usually a finger pointed to the temple with the hand clenched to represent a gun. In New Guinea it is more likely to be a hand clenched to the throat, pushing up to represent hanging. And in Japan it most likely to be plunging the fist to the stomach to represent hara-kiri or a finger across the neck to represent throat slitting.

Interpersonal distance

Interpersonal distance is about the distance people adopt when communicating with each other, the study of which is sometimes called **proxemics**. Since the closer people are to each other the more they can perceive non-verbal cues, and so non-verbal communication may be made easier. Consequently interpersonal distance can be used to signal and regulate privacy and intimacy.

Hall (1966) looked for systematic rules about the closeness/nature of the relationship between two people and how far they stand or sit from each other when interacting. From extensive observations, mainly in the USA, he identified four interpersonal zones.

- an *intimate zone* (about 0.5m), limited to intimate relationships
- a *personal zone* (up to about 1.5m) for friends and acquaintances
- a *social zone* (from about 1.25 to 3.5m) for formal interactions, such as doing business
- a *public zone* (about 3.5–7.5m) for public events.

Interpersonal distance is culturally mediated and virtually all studies have been done in the English-speaking world. Where different cultures have been compared, systematic differences are evident. A later study, also conducted in the USA, found that black and working-class children tend to stand closer when talking to each other than white and middle-class children (Aiello and Jones 1971). Interestingly, it seems that language acts as the cue to determine which norms are followed. In a study of bilingual French Canadians, Grujic and Libby (1978) found that when they were speaking French, subjects in the study sat closer at the beginning of the conversation and moved closer as it progressed than they did when speaking English.

What does appear to be universal is that people are disconcerted when the local rules are broken. This is illustrated by one of what has to be social psychology's most professionally risky field experiments (Middlemist *et al.* 1976). In it a confederate of the researchers loitered outside an empty male urinal until a man went into it. When he did, the confederate took up a predetermined position alongside the man, varying in distance from him. The results of the study showed that the closer the proximity, the longer the man took to start urinating and the faster he completed. One wonders what might have happened if the local police had been tipped off about what was going on! These results are taken to show the effects of over-close proximity. To me the study says more about the way that proximity is interpreted as meaning and cultural conventions, given that many nightclubs now provide female 'toilets for two'.

Touch

Like gestures and postures, touch can be illustrative (reinforce language) or emblematic (act in its stead). It is a powerful means of communication:

- to show affection, reassurance, appreciation and nurturance
- to communicate humour and playfulness
- to express anger and aggression
- to draw attention or gain compliance
- to follow etiquette or perform rituals
- to show or demonstrate action.

Most social psychology textbooks are rather coy about sexual touch. This is not really surprising given the potential for embarrassment and the diversity of meanings that can be attached to it, from expressing love, compassion and comfort, through signalling dominance or submission, to expressing anger and aggression. Sexual touch is rather a minefield of a topic, and it would take a whole chapter in itself to do it justice. So I have decided it is safest to leave it at that, merely noting that it is an extremely potent means of communication!

The use of touch is highly culture and context sensitive. For a start there are wide variations in how much it is acceptable for people to touch each other at all. A classic study was conducted in the 1960s by Jourard (1966) who simply watched couples in cafés in different countries and counted how many times they touched each other. In a one-hour period Jourard observed not a single touch in London, 2 in Florida, 110 in Paris and 180 in Puerto Rico. Times have changed and English-speaking cultures have become more 'touchy-feely' since then. But I suspect differences would still be found, don't you?

Most cultures, however, have prohibitions limiting touch between strangers, except in certain discount situations. For example, in Western biomedicine it is acceptable for medical professionals to touch patients, even parts of the body that would usually be regarded as off limits. Otherwise, touch is usually restricted to interactions between people who know each other (such as family members and close friends) and in social rather than professional situations, other than in exceptional circumstances. As with other non-verbal communication, culture specific rules operate about who touches whom, varying in terms of intimacy, status, gender, sexuality and age.

Touch can have surprisingly strong effects, although *what* effects seem highly context specific. For example, Crusco and Wetzel (1984) found that waitresses who glancingly touched the hands of customers received higher tips than those who did not. This was true for both men and women customers. It looks like both men and women interpreted the touch positively in this situation. But in another study the results were different. Whitcher and Fisher (1979) varied whether nurses gave a brief and 'professional' touch to patients during an interview prior to their operation. When women patients were interviewed after the operation, those who had been previously touched reported less fear and anxiety and had lower blood pressure readings than those who had not been touched. However, men patients who had been previously touched reported more anxiety and had higher blood pressure. Here it looks as though the touches were interpreted differently by men and women – as having quite different meanings.

As I said earlier, sexual touch is rather a minefield of a topic, beyond the scope of a chapter like this. Also we are hampered by the fact that almost all work in this field – as in psychology generally – has been conducted in the English-speaking world, mainly the USA. While culturally diverse, it has its

Figure 4.3
Males' and females' reported pleasantness of being touched on
various parts of the body
Source: Hogg and Vaughan 1998: 548

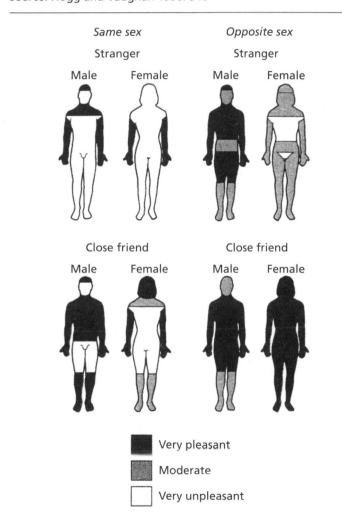

own distinct mores shared, especially, among younger people. Hence the data
to which we have access about gender differences are more a reflection of a
specific set of cultural rules than universal laws about, for example, where it is
acceptable and desirable for men to touch women and vice versa (Burgoon
et al. 1989). The results are not at all surprising – see Figure 4.3.

For me these data come across as too homogenous and obvious. Since the diagrams represent averages, they obscure what I think must have been considerable variation. For a start a proportion of the people taking part in the study must have been gay and, presumably, would have expressed quite different preferences.

Finally, as mentioned earlier, even within cultures, touch is highly context specific, both in the conventions governing what is acceptable and in terms of the meaning attached to a particular touch. A kiss – even a fleeting, tiny one – can mean everything or nothing. It can mean no more than a familiar greeting of no real significance, or signal a changing-point in a person's life, where nothing will ever be the same again.

Smell

I am not sure if this another example of coyness, but while most textbooks include touch as a means of non-verbal communication, none as far as I can tell include smell. And yet evolutionary psychologists, in particular, regard smell as a critical means by which people communicate with each other – albeit usually unconsciously and instinctively. For example, smell is held to be a very powerful element in sexual attraction.

It is well known that many animals communicate in this way. Chemicals called **pheromones** are used to send olfactory signals – for example, to male dogs that a female is 'in season' and hence instinctively primed to be sexually available. The speculation about humans using pheromones as signals is based upon the identification of genetic material called the **major histocompatibility complex (MHC)** that contains information that allows for the recognition of genetic similarity. It is the basis of the immune response, that allows an organism to detect bacteria, for example, as being alien and therefore needs to be destroyed. Humans are able to detect MHC from smelling the urine of mice, showing that they have the capacity to discriminate very subtle genetic differences through their sense of smell (Stoddart 1990).

Evolutionary psychologists have carried out studies to discover whether this ability could be used in the ways people select their sexual partners. The argument goes like this. One element of evolutionary theory proposes that people are instinctively primed to seek to have children that are as genetically dissimilar as possible, since genetic diversity is a positive evolutionary strategy. Hence, it is argued, women gain an evolutionary advantage if they can detect a potential father for their child who is genetically dissimilar from themselves.

Wedekind *et al.* (1995) tested this by getting men to wear T shirts for 48 hours – long enough to become impregnated with the man's sweat and hence his pheromones. Young women were given the T shirts to smell, and asked to choose which one they found most attractive. Generally they chose the

T shirts from men with the most different MHC from their own – except, that is, when the women were taking the contraceptive pill, when they chose the T shirts of men whose MHC was most like their own. Since taking the pill mimics the physiological state of pregnancy, Wedekind *et al*. (1995) concluded that women choose men in ways that have an evolutionary advantage for them. If they are able to get pregnant, they choose men who are genetically dissimilar, since this is most likely to produce genetically diverse offspring. But if they are pregnant or unable to get pregnant, they choose men who are genetically similar to them, since this way they are more likely to get support and help from male kin.

Non-verbal cues to deception

As you have seen, while facial expression appears to be at least somewhat instinctive, most non-verbal communication is learned. As such it may *seem* automatic and beyond conscious control, but this is more a matter of well-learned habit. Therefore people have an ability to modify it, to a greater or lesser extent. Mostly, though, it is so well consolidated as a habit that they are unaware of it. As a consequence, a skilled observer can use non-verbal cues to work out whether, say, a person is being honest in what they say or seeking to deceive. Freud put this elegantly: 'He that has eyes to see and ears to hear may convince himself that no mortal can keep a secret. If his lips are silent he chatters with his fingertips; betrayal oozes out of him at every pore' (Freud 1905: 76). This phenomenon of non-verbal clues giving the lie to what a person says is called **leakage**.

Research studies (mainly US) suggest that when people are lying, their deception does tend to 'leak out' in their non-verbal behaviour. For example, they tend to touch their face more often (Ekman and Friesen 1974), and to fiddle more with their hands and things like glasses and necklaces (Knapp *et al*. 1974). The trouble is that people are not very effective at detecting deception. Even those people whose job it is to spot dishonesty – such as police and customs officers – are not that good at it (Kraut and Poe 1980). However, overall people seem slightly better able to recognize deception than to perpetrate it (Zuckerman *et al*. 1981).

Non-verbal communication

Non-verbal communication is a means of communication in its own right; but it also supplements, augments and helps to manage verbal communication. There are a number of modes of non-verbal communication: facial expression, gaze and eye contact, postures and gestures, interpersonal distance and touch.

→

- *Facial expression*: given that there is considerable cultural commonality in the facial expressions used to display basic emotions, it is likely these have an innate basis. The most likely explanation is that certain emotions trigger a reflex in the facial muscles. However, there are also culture-specific display rules governing, for example, whether people seek to cover up or display their feelings.
- *Gaze and eye contact* are used in five main ways: as a means of communication in their own right, to signal status, to signal interest and sincerity, to manage conversations and to exert control. They vary by cultural convention. In some cultures, for instance, people in subordinate positions are expected to keep their eyes lowered when speaking to a superior.
- *Postures and gestures* can either be illustrators to reinforce speech, or emblems that stand in for speech. Some emblems are widely recognized across cultures, others are culture specific. In some, for example, a nod of the head means 'yes' but in others it means 'no'.
- *Interpersonal distance* tends to reflect the closeness of the relationship and its context. Intimates get up close, friends less so, and strangers prefer to keep their distance. The rules are culturally mediated, but people are disconcerted when they are broken.
- *Touch* is a powerful means of communication. It can be used to show affection, reassurance or appreciation; to communicate humour and playfulness; to express anger and aggression; to draw attention or gain compliance; to follow etiquette or perform rituals; or to show or demonstrate action.
- *Smell* in the form of pheromones may influence certain instinctive elements of communication, such as sexual attraction.
- Non-verbal behaviour can act as a cue to *deception* – sometimes called leakage. Learning these cues can help spot when somebody is dissembling or lying.

THE STUDY OF LANGUAGE BY EXPERIMENTAL SOCIAL PSYCHOLOGY

Language 'lies at the very heart of social life' (Mead 1934b). The study of language in experimental social psychology is called **sociolinguistics**. It is based upon linguistics and **psycholinguistics**, and we look briefly at these first.

Linguistics

Linguistics is the study of language itself. It begins by specifying the components of language. The basic, meaningless sounds are called **phonemes** – sounds like the 'th' at the beginning of 'think, or the 'oo' at the end of 'kangaroo'. The 'phonetic' qualities of language are to do with its sounds. Phonemes are connected together into **morphemes**. Generally these are words – basic units of meaning. Morphemes are then connected together through **syntactic rules** into sentences. So the syntactic qualities of language are to do with how words are fitted together.

Phonemes ➜ Morphemes ➜ Sentences

The meanings of words, sentences and utterances are determined by **semantic** rules. The semantic qualities of language are to do with its meanings. Semantic rules are highly complex and operate at different levels. For example, if you were sitting on a bench in a park with a friend and said 'It's getting cold', then the surface content of what you have said is purely descriptive – a comment on temperature. But it is quite likely that you intend this statement to convey depth content – that you are getting cold, and want to make a move (Chomsky 1957).

Psycholinguistics

Psycholinguistics is the study of the interrelationship between language and thought. One of its earliest and best known theorists was Vygotsky (1962), who claimed that language is the main medium in which people think.

> Thought is not merely expressed in words; it comes into existence through them. Every thought tends to connect to something else, to establish a relationship between things. Every thought moves, develops, fulfils a function, solves a problem.
>
> (Vygotsky 1962: 125)

Vygotsky argued that while we may have some thoughts that are vague and not verbalized, and we may sometimes say things automatically without conscious thought, most of our thinking consists of a kind of 'inner speech' that is interdependent with external speech. He depicted this diagrammatically, as shown in Figure 4.4.

Consequently, Vygotsky claimed, a person's capacity to think depends upon the linguistic resources they have available to them. This is a version of a theory proposed by Sapir and Whorf – the Sapir–Whorf theory of linguistic relativity (Whorf 1956). If you recall from Chapter 1, this was not

Figure 4.4
Vygotsky's model of the relationship between language and thought
Source: Lindesmith *et al.* 1999: 90

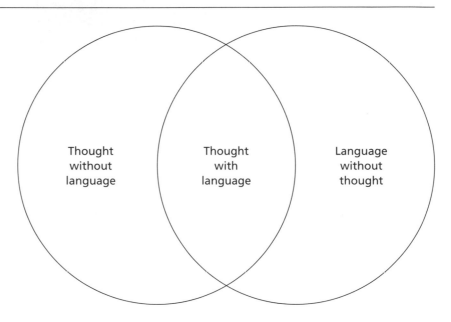

a new idea. It had already been proposed by Wundt some 60 or more years earlier.

Linguistic relativity

The theory of linguistic relativity claims that language determines thought – people cannot think about something for which they have no linguistic term. It is, literally, 'unthinkable'. The theory was built upon observations that different languages reflect different thought-worlds. For example, the language of Hopi Indians is very precise about, for example, how people travel, having different verbs for different kinds of travelling (going to and coming from, for example). But it does not differentiate between living and non-living flying things – all are called by the same name. English differentiates between birds, bats, aeroplanes and so on, because they are salient and meaningful in its thought-world.

The Sapir–Whorf theory is now regarded as too extreme. People are constantly developing language by constructing new words and phrases as the need arises to express new concepts. We can see this in the way that one language appropriates words from another. The French speak of '*le week-end*' and the English speak of a '*raison d'être*', since such phrases depict concepts more succinctly than they could be expressed in the original language. This shows that people can think about things they do not have a simple word for.

Nonetheless, as you will see as this chapter unfolds, it is equally clear that language powerfully moulds thought. Being given words to describe concepts is an important way of learning about a new topic, This is the main reason why this book (like most textbooks) gives you a lot of new words (or familiar ones used for new meanings) and defines them for you. It is one of the main ways you will get to know and understand the thinking behind social psychology's ideas and theories.

Sociolinguistics

Sociolinguistics focuses on how language is used in social situations: 'how speech (and other language in use) simultaneously influences social interaction and has its "meaning" constrained by its interactive context' (Grimshaw 1981: 241). Experimental social psychologists studying language have been less concerned with what is said than *how* it is said – with paralanguage and speech style rather than speech content (Hogg and Vaughan 1998).

Paralanguage and speech styles

Language does not just communicate by what is said, but also by *how* it is said. **Paralanguage** refers to the non-linguistic elements of speech – things like ums and ahs, grunts and sighs, speed, tone and pitch of voice, and so on. These are important aspects of how a message is imparted. Paralinguistic elements are also important in conveying emotion. In English low pitch typically communicates sadness or boredom, whereas high pitch communicates anger, fear or surprise (Frick 1985).

Equally, people use a range of **speech styles** in different contexts. For instance a woman will use different speech styles when talking to her children, with her mother-in-law and with her husband – and different styles with him when they are with friends, with his boss and when they are in bed together. Speech style has been extensively studied by experimental social psychologists (see Giles and Coupland 1991 for a review) since it is a sensitive marker of how people respond to social context. For example, Brown and Fraser (1979) have mapped out a diverse range of influences on speech style, including both contextual (such as the setting, the activity the person is involved in and who else is present) and personal (the person's mood, their personality and interests).

In particular, cues are given by a person's speech style – their accent and/or the slang or jargon they use – about such things as social class, status and, of course, nationality. A person's accent usually says a lot about where they grew up, their peer group in childhood and adolescence and the social group to which they belong. Speech contains social markers that are usually highly recognizable. Consequently it is an important influence on the way individuals are perceived and hence how others respond to them. Many languages have a high status version. In respect to English spoken in Britain this is referred to as **received pronunciation**. This is the speech style used by, for example, younger members of the royal family and that predominates in high-status professions like the law. Non-standard accents include regional accents (for example Yorkshire) and urban accents (for example Birmingham) and minority ethnic accents (for example Caribbean in Britain).

The impact of speech style has been studied using the **matched-guise technique** (Lambert *et al.* 1960). In it a series of tape-recorded speech extracts are recorded, all spoken by the same highly skilled actor but each one in a different accent or dialect. Subjects in the study give their impression of the speaker by responding to different evaluative dimensions. Lambert *et al.* (1960) for example, varied what they called status variables (for example intelligence and competence) and solidarity variables (for example warmth and friendliness). In their studies they found that subjects did indeed respond to the speech style cues. Received pronunciation was usually evaluated more favourably on status variables, whereas non-standard accents was usually evaluated more favourably on solidarity variables.

Radio and television programme makers respond to this tendency in their choice of presenters. When they want the person speaking to be perceived as serious and authoritative – commentating on a funeral, for example, or in 'serious' documentaries – they choose presenters who speak received pronunciation. But for 'youth' programmes, or programmes on subjects where they want to promote an image of friendliness and warmth, they are more likely to choose a presenter with a non-standard accent. And sometimes they make a deliberate play on the distinction. The BBC's television programme *Homefront*, for instance, uses the contrast between the faux aristocratic (and slightly 'camp') speech style of the interior designer Laurence Llewelyn-Bowen and the warm and friendly Irish brogue of garden designer Diarmuid Gavin to give the programme its unique dynamic 'buzz'.

Speech style, social groups and social identity

Experimental social psychology has developed extensive theorization about relationships between social groups, group membership and social identity. Experimental social psychologists working in this field talk of **ethnolinguistic**

groups – groups defined by their ethnic commonality and their use of a common **patois**. A patois is a developed and inclusive way of talking that has not only a particular accent, but also its own grammar and terminology. Rastafarian is a good example where, for example, the term 'I' is used differently from received pronunciation, as well as a strong accent and many specific words and phrases.

Chapter 9 examines this work in more detail. For now we just need to note that speech style is a highly effective marker of group membership and hence social identity, especially in terms of ethnicity.

The study of language by experimental social psychology

- The experimental social psychological study of language is called sociolinguistics, which is based upon linguistics and psycholinguistics.
- *Linguistics* is the study of language itself. It examines how language works as a means of communication, through the rules of syntax (how the different elements of language are structured) and the rules of semantics (how meaning is encoded into and decoded from language).
- *Psycholinguistics* views language as the main medium for thought, and examines the ways in language affects thinking. Its theory of linguistic relativity argues that each language makes some discriminations easier to make than others, and, therefore, make some ideas easier to think about than others.
- *Sociolinguistics* focuses on how language is used in social situations. Experimental social psychologists studying language have been less concerned with what is said than *how* it is said – with paralanguage and speech style rather than speech content.
- *Paralanguage* concerns the non-linguistic elements of speech – things like ums and ahs, interruptions and pauses, grunts and sighs, speed, tone and pitch of voice, and so on.
- *Speech style* is the manner in which people speak in different contexts (for example talking to children or adults). Aspects like accent and vocabulary act as social markers, often indicative of a person's status, social identity (for example as a member of an ethnic group) and role.
- Language is not only a social marker, but also a key factor in *social identity*. It provides a socio-cultural 'glue' which plays a significant role in sustaining social and cultural groups.

SEMIOTICS

Originated by Ferdinand de Saussure (1959) semiotics is about 'the organis-ation of shared meanings' (Parker 1989: 49) and how those shared meanings act as a kind of 'glue' that holds the social and cultural world together. Its theory is used by critical social psychologists to understand the systems by which meanings are organized, shared and communicated.

What makes it different from the approach taken by experimental social psychology is that in semiotics the systems for organizing meaning are not seen to be working solely within individual minds but within culture as well. In this perspective, instead of culture merely being viewed as an *influence* on communication, culture is seen as the medium and the means, itself, by which and within which communication works. Semiotic theory views culture as 'socially organised productions and flows of meaning and meaningful forms, related to likewise socially organised forms of power, material resources, time and space' (Fornäs 1995: 136). Meaning, by this definition, is not a subjective interpretation made by individuals, but is intersubjective; it operates *between* people.

Intersubjectivity

You may find it hard to grasp what is being claimed here. For people brought up in an individuo-centred culture, semiotic theory is not so much hard to understand because its ideas are difficult, but because it is counter-intuitive – it's not how they are used to thinking. But an example should help. The one Parker uses is a study by Marsh *et al.* (1974) on the regalia worn on the terraces by Oxford City (OCFC) football supporters:

> A scarf has a particular meaning as a sign, and would call into being for an observer the idea of the category of fan who was wearing it. It also brings into play a whole range of meanings and relationships through connotation. The scarf carries meaning as a sign by virtue of its relations with other items of clothing, not because the signified is in some magical way woven into the wool.
>
> (Parker 1989: 51)

What Parker (1989) is pointing to here is that the OCFC scarf is instantly recognizable, but only to football fans. If you are a football fan, you *know* what it means. If you are not a football fan, then you are much less likely to recognize it. But this 'knowing what it means' is not some simple, isolated act of individual recognition. It works because it is part of a whole system of knowing, that is, itself, part of being a football fan. And being a football fan is belonging to a community of football fans who share a common interest in and understanding of, not just of the game of football, but also of being a fan of football. This is what is meant by saying that culture is the means and the medium of communication. Meanings (like the meaning of an OCFC scarf) are not individually made and sustained, but collectively made and sustained. If we think of being a football fan as belonging to a particular subculture, then knowing what the OCFC scarf means is part of being a member of the subculture of football fans – at least to the extent of following football and being interested in it (as opposed to those of us who don't even watch the World Cup and couldn't recognize an OCFC scarf if it came up and hit us).

Signs and sign systems

A sign has two elements: the **signifier** – the physical characteristics of the sign (in this case the material entity of the scarf) – and the **signified** – what it is intended to *mean* (in this case, that the wearer supports Oxford City Football Club). Thus clothes are signifiers in that they communicate particular meanings, whether worn, spoken or about or depicted (Barthes [1957] 1967).

Words, gestures and body language operate as signs too. They transmit meaning among those who can interpret them, operating as **sign systems** – systems of signifiers and signifieds whereby messages about meaning are communicated. The process of using signs is called **signification**. Perinbanayagam (1985) uses the term **signifying act** to describe when a person expresses a symbol by the articulation of a message. People, he argues, communicate and interact with one another through signifying acts, that work through the expression of signs and, thereby, their meanings.

Saussure stressed that signs are arbitrary and specific. They are different in different cultures and subcultures, and each one is fully meaningful only to the people who belong to that particular culture or subculture. Being a football fan is one example. Another is what the gay community calls **gaydar** – a kind of cultural radar that allows gay people to recognize whether another person is gay or straight. Within gay communities, subtle signs are encoded into speech style, dress, demeanour and body language, that allow members of those gay communities to transmit and receive meanings that are not generally understood by straights.

Signs express value

Crucially, Saussure pointed out, signs not only signify (tell us what something is), but also express value (tell us in what way it should be appreciated). Consider the word 'madam'. In French *madame* is used in the way English would use Mrs and conveys little explicit value, either positive or negative. But In English 'madam' takes a number of differently valued meanings. It can be used as a polite term – used, for example, for a customer in a snooty boutique ('Would madam like to try on the dress?) or at a meeting ('Madam chairman'). But it can also refer to the woman who runs a brothel, or one who tells fortunes, and it can be applied to a girl child who is behaving precociously ('She was a right little madam'). The value attached to each use is quite different.

Signs, symbols and structuralism

Both signs and a symbols represent meaning, but a sign is a particular instance whereas a **symbol** is a sign where its meaning is based upon a shared ideology or institution. It is not hard to think of some powerful symbols – national flags, religious symbols like the holy cross, clothes such as football insignia and uniforms. People can be symbols – a queen, a pope, a pop idol. What symbols signify transcends time and place. But symbols can be used as specific signs too, when used to signify something different according to context. A man who wears a uniform can be signalling that he is 'on duty'. But the band Queen sometimes wore sailor's uniforms to signal messages about being gay. In the first case the uniform was a symbol, in the second a sign.

Semiotics is the study of how sign systems are structured, and hence is a form of **structuralism**. Another way of putting this is that it is the study of the *architecture* of meaning – of what meanings can be constructed, by whom and how and why and from what. It explores how particular meaning structures create particular meaning environments and how these shape the ways in which people experience their worlds in which they live and determine what they can and cannot do. This is what I meant earlier by saying that semiotics is the study of how meanings are organized. Geertz suggests that culture is made up of 'webs of significance' (Geertz 1975: 5). The purpose of structuralism is to understand how the organization of meaning – the way its 'webs of significance' are structured – enables it to work as the medium of communication.

This is why semiotics is useful for critical social psychologists. It allows them to 'step beyond the consciousness of the individual 'subject' and back from the personal meanings held by the members of a community' (Parker 1989: 52) and to look at the broader picture: to explore how sign systems 'work' inter-subjectively. Henriques *et al.* (1984) put it like this. Instead of reducing meaning to 'a problem of the "influence" of the social environment on the unitary individual', semiotic analysis 'interiorizes differences within the social process of signification, accounting for them by reference to differences of power and gender and different canalizations of desire' (Henriques *et al.* 1984: 149). In other words, it opens up the analysis of meaning to move it beyond meaning as it is apperceived by the individual subject, and links it into broader theories, such as political theories about power, feminist theories about gender and psychosocial theories about desire.

Mass media communication

An illustration of this kind of analysis is to look at the way that the **mass media** (that is television, newspapers, and so on) construct meaning for us. Take television news broadcasts, that, typically, consist of a series of short 'news items'. These purport to be factual, a straightforward telling-it-like-it-is. But semiotic theorists claim they are anything but factual. Rather, they are *made* meaningful *for* viewers by being constructed as illustrated narratives – news *stories*. 'The message comes already interpreted; they overflow with meaning' (Lindesmith *et al.* 1999: 15).

To understand what is going on in the telling of 'news stories', you need to think what the mass media are trying to achieve. Are they simply seeking to inform us about what is going on in the world? Or do they have other motives? A Marxist analysis (that is, one that is, among other things, critical of capitalism) would argue that it is these 'other motives' that are most important. Smythe (1994), for example, claims that the mass media have four main goals; they seek to create audiences that:

- are motivated by 'possessive individualism' – the desire to acquire the goods and services that are provided by capitalism
- become and remain consumers of advertised products
- support the strategies and policies of the state that sustains capitalism
- are unaware they are being manipulated.

A Marxist analysis views the mass media as an institutionalized sign system promoting a particular ideology (state capitalism) for a particular set of motives (creating politically passive consumers). You do not need to endorse this particular analysis to see that it at least provides a different understanding of human communication from that of experimental social psychology.

If we accept the claim of semiotics that meaning 'works' *through* culture, and is not merely an individual, personal interpretation *of* culture, then it follows that those who have any control over the way that culture is constructed also have some control over the way meaning is interpreted and understood by individuals. They are powerful in that they have the capability to construct a person's social reality for them.

Go back to the example of football fans for a moment and think about this. Their subculture is not simply the product of what football fans say and do. It is powerfully constructed through the broadcasting of football games and news reports and programmes about football; through newspaper and magazine reports of not only football matches but also footballers' personalities, wives and lives. It is also constructed through the aggressive marketing of consumer goods like football regalia; through the travel industry organizing trips to football competitions, and so on. There would be no football fans, as we currently understand this term, without the vast commercial and mass media infrastructures that create, support and sustain football fandom.

In this analysis, the 'trick' of the mass media – where it is really clever – is that it makes all this seem so very natural and real. In so doing it creates in people the sense that they are free and autonomous when, in truth, they are not. They are living in a world created for them in order that their behaviour serves the interests of those with the power and resources to create it. They think they are interpreting meaning when, in truth, they are consuming meaning that has already been pre-digested for them.

But ideas like this come not just from Marxist analysis. From the opposite side of the fence – management studies – Fenton-O'Creevy (2001) makes the claim that the key quality of leadership is the ability to manage meaning:

> Studies of leadership have sought to understand leadership as a social process rather than as an attribute of the individual or even an interaction between individual and situation. Within this perspective the characteristic function of leadership is seen as 'the management of meaning'.
> (Fenton-O'Creevy 2001: 7)

By this he means that leaders 'transform the needs, values, preferences and aspirations of followers' (Fenton-O'Creevy 2001: 9) and hence inspire them to abandon self-interest and serve the interests of the wider group. They provide vision and a sense of mission, instil pride and gain respect and trust. Leaders, he argues, give new meaning to people's lives and actions. His description fits both religious and political leaders, and this makes the point that meaning-making can be for both good and for ill. Contrast, for example, the leadership of Nelson Mandela and Osama Bin Laden. Both provided their followers with vision and a sense of mission, instilled pride in them and gained their respect and trust. The outcome for one was a (relatively) bloodless revolution, for the other a sea change in the practice of terrorism and its massive impact, not only on international politics but also on ordinary lives. The ability to make meaning is, in human society, an incredibly effective way to wield power. While making things (like buildings, steam engines and computers) clearly plays a part in history, it is by making meaning that history's seismic shifts have been brought about.

A semiotic account of language

Language is the most complex and sophisticated – and hence the most powerful – sign system, a system of signification. Actually as English speakers we are hampered here, since we have only one word for language. In French (the language in which Saussure wrote) there are two words: *langue* (language as a system that operates in a speech community, such as English or French), and **parole** (language as it is used in communicating messages). We have to take the somewhat confusing option of arbitrarily imposing technical definitions. The convention in English is to use the term language to mean *langue*: the abstract system of syntax and semantics that is 'virtual and outside of time' (Ricoeur 1955: 530); and to use **speech** to mean *parole*: that which is particular to the use of language in a specific situation.

Semin illustrates the difference by reference to the sentence 'the sun is rising'. At the level of language, it is a comment about the sunrise. But as speech it can be used to say different things. For two lovers having an affair it could say 'we better get up, my spouse will be home soon', whereas to a farmer it could say 'we better get up and feed the animals' (Semin 1997: 296). Language and speech operate in **dialectical** relation to one another, by which is meant, they only achieve full meaning only through their reciprocal relationship to each other (Barthes [1957] 1967).

Language constructs reality

In signifying both meaning and value, social constructionist theory argues that language is the most powerful means by which reality is socially constructed. Each language (*langue*) constructs and conveys particular assumptions about the relative worth of the social groups that make up the speech community that uses it – about class, gender, sexuality, race, disability and so on. We can see this, for instance, in the debate about 'political correctness'. It is a 'war of words' (Dunant 1994) where attempts are being made to change the way that language is used. Those who seek change do so in order to challenge the way that the conventions of language attach negative value to certain groups.

Within semiotics, language is a system of signs (words, phrases) connected together through a set of rules (syntax) that convey meaning and value. Language is such a powerful sign system because of these relational elements. It allows the signification of complexity, and not just knowing what something signifies but also being able to relate that signification to other more abstract significations. A cat or a dog can respond to the red glow of embers, avoiding it because they associate it with being burnt. But only a human can know it *means* heat, and that heat has to do with temperature, that heat and cold have a relationship to each other, and that this relationship can also be applied to a person's manner or character, because only humans have the sign system of language that allows them to do this.

Semiotics

- Semiotics is the study of signs and sign systems. Its main concern is with the organization of shared meanings, and is used by social constructionist social psychologists to find out how meaning 'works' and how it is structured.
- Semiotics sees meaning not individually but collectively made and sustained. Thus meaning is intersubjective – it 'works' within culture, not within individual minds. Instead of culture merely being viewed as an *influence* on communication, culture is seen as the medium and the means by which and within which communication works.
- A sign has two elements: the signifier (the physical characteristics of the sign) and the signified (its meaning and significance). Signs transmit meaning within sign systems – systems of signifiers and signifieds that communicate meaning through a process of signification.
- Signs not only signify (tell us what something is), but also express value.
- A symbol is a sign where its meaning is based upon a shared ideology, institutional system or worldview. Symbols are very powerful signs that encapsulate meaning and convey it strikingly.
- Language is the most complex, sophisticated and powerful sign system. As a social institution and a system of values that gives meaning to words, it is the main medium through which human social realities are constructed.
- The mass media and charismatic leaders use their power to construct meaning to influence how people see the world and hence how they behave.

FURTHER READING

Experimental social psychology

Again most mainstream textbooks will give you lots of extra detail about the enormous amount of social psychological research and theorization that has been applied to communication, language and social interaction.

Giles, H. and Coupland, N. (1991) *Language: Contexts and Consequences.* Buckingham: Open University Press.

This book provides a very readable and comprehensive account of mainstream social psychological research into and theorization about language and its relationship with social processes and phenomena.

Critical social psychology

Lindesmith, A.R. Strauss, A.L. and Denzin, N.K. (1999) *Social Psychology*, 8th edn. London: Sage.

> This is a remarkable textbook, in that its general title gives no hint that it is, in fact, a very unusual one, based primarily on symbolic interactionism. It is the best source I have found for an introduction of semiotics as applied to social psychology.

QUESTIONS

1 What are the main elements of communication theory? Why was it abandoned by social psychologists as a theory to explain *human* communication?
2 What are the main elements of non-verbal communication?
3 What evidence is there for cultural differences in the way people communicate with each other?
4 Compare and contrast psycholinguistic and semiotic theories of language.
5 What does it mean to say communication is intersubjective? Illustrate your answer by reference to the role of the mass media.

Chapter 5

Understanding the social world

Chapter contents

A route map of the chapter

The chapter has five sections. The first looks at early information processing models of how people understand the social world. I have illustrated this by a classic set of studies by one of experimental social psychology's founders, Solomon Asch, in which he explored the processes going on when people form 'first impressions' of another person.

The next section moves on to models of social cognition. To see where these came from, there is a brief review of the origins of general cognitive theory in psychology. Then we see how the social cognition approach theorizes about the way that people's understanding is a product of cognitive processes and structures.

In the third section we look at attribution theory from the perspective of experimental social psychology. Attribution has been one of the most fertile and enduring subjects studied by experimental social psychologists.

The fourth section then looks at recent theoretical developments in this field – processing-depth models of social cognition. These have mainly been developed by European social psychologists, driven by its greater focus on the role of language as a medium through which social cognition operates and also a desire to examine it in more real-life settings. The basic claim here is that most everyday processing is pretty mindless. Only when situations are unusual or decisions are important (or both) do people bother to process information in depth.

The final section moves into a different paradigm – personal construct theory. This is outside of experimental social psychology, and is better seen as located in the more general psychological social psychology framework. This is because it regards psychological processes and phenomena as primarily personal – operating within individual minds.

Critical social psychologists adopt a radically different approach, in which understanding the social world is seen in semiotic terms – as within the inter-subjective social construction of reality. This approach is set out in Chapter 7, taken together with the critical approach to attitudes and attitude change.

Information processing models

↓

Social cognition

↓

Attribution theory

↓

Processing-depth models of social cognition

↓

Personal construct theory

Learning objectives

When you have completed your study of this chapter, you should be able to:

1 Outline the key features of the information processing approach and illustrate it by reference to a study of impression formation.
2 Describe how the social cognition approach is different from that of information processing.
3 Define and describe the main processes of social cognition, outline some of the ways in which social cognition is constrained by information processing limits, and describe how social cognition processes information strategically.
4 Define what is meant by the terms 'schema' and 'script' and describe their roles in social cognition.
5 Provide a brief historical account of the origins of attribution theory, outline its main elements, and define the main 'attribution errors' to which social cognition is prone.
6 Define what is meant by 'processing-depth models of social cognition', and explain the main reasons for their development.
7 Outline the key features of personal construct theory, and some of the criticisms levelled against it.

INTRODUCTION

As you saw in Chapter 1, from the very earliest studies of social influence, social psychologists have been fascinated to discover how people acquire their knowledge of the social world, how they make sense of this knowledge, and how they use it to guide their actions and interactions with others. They want to understand how different social contexts are perceived and recognized, and how they influence the way that people behave. This chapter examines the main theories that experimental social psychologists and those working in personal construct theory have devised to explain how people gain knowledge and understanding of the social world, and use how they use them to navigate their own behaviour within it.

INFORMATION PROCESSING MODELS

One of the main things we need to be able to make sense of the social world is to understand other people (indeed, we also need to understand ourselves, but we come on to that in Chapter 8). It is important to know who another person is in order to know how to treat them – think of the problems you would have if you talked to your boss or your tutor as if they were your younger sister. We need to have some idea about what kind of person somebody is – can we trust them, or do we need to be wary? We have to be able to predict how other people will react – will they take a smile as being friendly or a 'come on'?

Impression formation

A good example of an information processing approach to how people gain understanding of other people is Asch's classic work on **impression formation** – how people form first impressions of others (Asch 1946). Information processing models view people's thinking as limited in the amount of information that can be processed. Asch developed a configural model – a general theory that when people form their impressions of another person, they do so by 'homing in' to just the most significant qualities (he called these 'central traits') that overshadow all the rest. One example he used was warm/cold. If a person is described as 'warm', he argued, then this will have a disproportionate impact on how they are perceived, making them more likely to be seen in a favourable light. The opposite would happen if the person is described as 'cold'.

Asch's hypothesis was therefore that central traits (like warm/cold) will have more effect on impression formation than other less important traits (like polite or blunt – we would probably use the word 'rude' here). To test his hypothesis Asch gave some of his students lists of seven trait descriptions (for example, intelligent, skilful, industrious, warm, determined, practical, cautious).

Figure 5.1
Lists used in Asch's experiment

List 1	List 2	List 3	List 4
• Intelligent	• Intelligent	• Intelligent	• Intelligent
• Skilful	• Skilful	• Skilful	• Skilful
• Industrious	• Industrious	• Industrious	• Industrious
• **Warm**	• **Cold**	• **Polite**	• **Blunt**
• Determined	• Determined	• Determined	• Determined
• Practical	• Practical	• Practical	• Practical
• Cautious	• Cautious	• Cautious	• Cautious

Figure 5.2
The results Asch obtained in his study expressed in the percentage of
students endorsing additional traits as a function of the trait included
in the list

Additional traits	Traits inserted into the list			
	Warm	Cold	Polite	Blunt
Generous	91	8	56	58
Wise	65	25	30	50
Happy	90	34	75	65
Good-natured	94	17	87	56
Reliable	94	99	95	100

He varied the trait descriptions included in the lists and asked the students to describe their impression of the individual described. Look at the four lists in Figure 5.1 and you can see the kind of thing he did. As you can see, he used four experimental conditions – inserting into the list either warm, cold, polite or blunt. These are illustrated in Figure 5.1

The students read the lists through. Then, in order to assess the impression they gained of the person being described they were given five more traits – generous, wise, happy, good-natured and reliable – and asked to say whether or not they thought the person had each of these qualities. The results Asch obtained are given in Figure 5.2.

As you can see, just by looking at the data, when the word 'warm' was in the list, the great majority of students endorsed the positive additional traits. When the word was 'cold' (except for 'reliable'), the great majority did not. The difference was most marked in relation to generous, happy and good-natured. By contrast, the differences between responses to polite/blunt were much less marked. Asch concluded that these results supported his hypothesis – central traits have a disproportionately large influence upon impression formation.

Later research by Rosenberg *et al.* (1968) led to viewing impression formation as more complex than this: that the centrality of a trait differs according to context. Rosenberg *et al.* (1968) therefore contested Asch's one-dimensional formulation and proposed, instead, that in different settings people use one of two alternative dimensions for evaluating character – either good/bad in *social* terms or good/bad in *intellectual* terms. Warm/cold, they argued, is clearly a social evaluation. Since Asch mainly used other social traits (like generous, wise, happy and good-natured) to assess the favourability of the impression, it is not surprising that varying warm/cold had more effect than varying polite/blunt.

Primacy and recency effects

Asch also found a **primacy effect**; that is, the earlier traits appear on a list, the greater the influence they have on the impression formed. If all the positive traits are at the beginning, the impression is more favourable compared with when all the negative traits are at the beginning. Later studies (for example Jones and Goethals 1972) also found some evidence of a **recency effect**, where traits later in the list had more impact. This happened when subjects were distracted or tired. However, primacy effects are more common, suggesting that first impressions are most important.

Negative and positive bias

Experimental research also produced empirical evidence to suggest that people tend to form positive impressions of others unless there is specific information to the contrary (Sears 1983). However, if people are told anything negative about the person at all, this tends to have a disproportionate effect. It immediately turns a good impression into a bad one (Fiske 1980). Moreover, once a negative impression is formed about someone, it tends to persist. Impression formation thus has a **negative bias** (see, for example, Hamilton and Zanna 1972).

The information processing approach

Information processing models of how people understand the social world envisaged people as operating rather like a sophisticated computer. They stressed the limitations imposed by both 'hardware' and 'software' on the amount of information that can be processed.

- Asch's experiments on impression formation provided evidence that people cope with these limits by focusing on just some information – central traits.
- Later work showed that information processing limits have some effect. For example, people tend to take more notice of information they receive first.
- However, it gradually became recognized that context is important – processing is determined by the kinds of evaluation people are making, and for what purpose.

SOCIAL COGNITION

In Chapter 4 I described how a shift was made in the 1960s and 1970s from theories of communication based on information processing models to psycholinguistic theory. This was a general shift undergone by experimental social psychology at that time. Its greatest influence was in the subject area of this chapter, heralding a radically new paradigm for studying how people make sense of the social world – social cognition. The study of social cognition within social psychology arose from ideas and theories developed from general cognitive psychology. We shall look at this briefly first.

General cognitive theory

Cognitive psychology's 'founding father' is generally agreed to be Ultric Neisser (1966), although he acknowledged its historical roots in the work of Bartlett (1932b) 30 years earlier. Neisser argued that information processing models took a far too mechanistic view of human thinking. They assumed that people play very little role in the *making* of the realities they experience, but simply take in the information they receive from their senses, process it in certain ways and then respond to it. It was this mechanistic image of human thinking that Neisser's new cognitive psychology was designed to challenge. The shift was towards a theory of people's thinking that stressed their capacity to *construct* complex images and models of the world through effortful thought, and their capacity to process information strategically rather than automatically.

Neisser saw sensory data from the outside as both processed bottom-up and top-down. The world that people perceive, understand, and with which they interact is a product of them *both* taking in information from the world *and* their own interpretation of this information through reference to the knowledge they have stored in memory about it. Through **top-down processing**, sensory input always gets to be imbued with meaning, and it is this *meaning* that gets processed, not the sensory input itself. Vision, for example, should not be seen as working like a camera, where the eye simply records patterns of light that it sends as mental pictures to the brain. Rather, vision is a two-way process, with top-down and **bottom-up processing** in combination enabling people to make sense of what they see around them.

Social cognition

These principles were incorporated into the social cognition paradigm. It was a reaction against the machine-like models of the person in social learning theory and information processing approaches. Its intention was to reconstruct psychology's image of people. Instead of seeing them as the passive puppets of, say, social conditioning, social cognition views them as active, purposive thinkers who strive to make sense of their social world and bring to this endeavour complex, sophisticated models-of-the-world in order to interpret it. This was a very significant shift – from the image we can trace back to William McDougall to the one proposed by William James (see Chapter 1).

Let's look at a specific example (Jenny) to see what this means.

Jenny

Jenny works in telesales, selling women's lingerie for a company that specializes in up-market but somewhat racy lines – silk G-strings, basques and suspenders are their best-selling products. Last night Jenny had a row with her partner, and it's preying on her mind. They've got a date tonight, and she's worried that it could be the end of the relationship. And to make things worse, it's turning out to be a nightmare day. Just two weeks before Valentine's day, and the phone lines are going mad.

Receiving information is a process of recognition

Jenny's job is to take calls from customers, answer their queries and take their orders. In terms of sensory inputs, she only has the words they say and the sound of the customers' voices to go on. But, as you saw in Chapter 4, these are enough for her to make a lot of inferences. By drawing on her prior knowledge she can recognize important cues about the caller. For example, she'll pick up subtle voice cues and conversational content to distinguish between a man who is confident about ordering a gift for his girlfriend and one who is cautious and shy.

As she's on commission Jenny wants to make as many sales as possible, and to do this she'll need to 'read' the different kinds of customers and treat them differently. In cognitive terms, this is much more complex than just reading the cues about paralanguage and speech style that you met in Chapter 4. She will need to judge their motives in the context of what she is selling. Lingerie is a somewhat unusual product, in that it carries with it an especially complex web of meanings and associations. For Jenny to be an effective salesperson she'll need to have access to a lot of highly specific social knowledge to do so, so she can interpret what they are saying and not just how they are saying it. Once she has recognized what kind of customer she is dealing with and the context of their purchase, Jenny can shift into the right repertoire. For example, with a confident customer she will engage in extended repartee to try to sell extra products, but with a shy one she will act 'cool and efficient' and stress the confidentiality of the service her company provides.

Constraints on processing

However, human cognition is fallible. If you have done a job like Jenny's (maybe not in telesales, but in any job that involves dealing with large numbers of other people such as working in a pub or a fast-food chain) you'll know just how easy it is to make mistakes, especially when the pressure builds up. Jobs like these involve coping with all sorts of information coming at you from lots of different directions at once, and responding to each one correctly. And you'll know that when the pace hots up beyond a certain point, your performance suffers.

It gets worse when there is a 'lot going on' in your head at the same time. Jenny's worries about the row with her partner are almost certain to undermine her performance. She will be prone to making mistakes – not always hearing accurately what her customers say and making a lot of keyboard errors, for instance. Numerous experimental social psychological studies have shown that when people are dealing with 'information overload', they make mistakes. Manstead and Semin (1980) attributed errors in task performance when in the presence of others to having to divide attention. Overload happens, in particular, when people have to deal with highly emotive inputs (see, for example, Lazarus 1991).

Social cognition continues to recognize that the human cognitive system has some fundamental limits on its capacities. Just like any other mechanism, limits are imposed by the material constraints of its 'hardware'. In the case of humans, these constraints arise from the biological make-up of the sensory organs, the nervous system and the brain. At its most basic this includes things like only being able to perceive certain bands of light and certain pitches of sound.

But 'software' sets limits too. In terms of social cognition some of the constraints are imposed by the particular ways in which knowledge is stored and processed in the human brain (as compared to a computer, for example). Nisbett and Ross (1980) introduced the term **cognitive miser** to describe how a person processes information. This rather negative view of the human cognitive system sees it as having a very limited capacity to deal with information, and of therefore of having to resort to all kinds of bodges, dodges and short-cuts to cope.

Telesales companies develop strict repertoires for their staff to follow, both in order to improve performance (in terms of accuracy and customer service) and to meet legal requirements. Workers are trained to use these, and, as they become experienced, the repertoires become effectively automatic. Manstead and Semin (1980) found that automatic tasks are much easier to perform accurately in a situation where a person is distracted. What we can see here is a tactic being adopted specifically to cope with the limitations of human cognition. Learning her script 'by heart' – mainly by constant repetition until she is word perfect – allows Jenny to perform accurately, even when under stress. Despite her preoccupations, she's unlikely to make any serious errors in reproducing the repertoire she has learned.

However, Jenny's performance will probably become a lot more 'wooden' when she relies on her ability to process automatically. In doing so she will miss out on the more subtle cues in the caller's voice, and be less able to generate the subtlety of response that makes her come across as responding naturally. Her judgement will also be impaired, as she will fall back more heavily on stereotypical images and assumptions and so be less able to respond to unusual or distinctive information. Much of the skill in doing a job like Jenny's involves being able to use higher cognitive functions – like being intuitive and insightful, so she can make her well rehearsed repertoire *seem* like a natural and lively conversation rather than a script. It is these capabilities that get compromised when she gets overloaded and shifts, strategically, into 'automatic' mode.

Processing strategically

This more flattering view of human cognition stresses that it is not so much limited as strategic (Showers and Cantor 1985). It's an image of the person as a **motivated tactician**: 'a fully engaged thinker who has multiple cognitive strategies available and chooses among them based on goals, motives and needs' (Fiske and Taylor 1991: 13). In many ways these two images of 'cognitive miser' and 'motivated tactician' are two sides of the same coin.

Compared to machines, people certainly do badly on long-running, repetitive tasks. They get bored, tired and all too easily distracted. They constantly take in a lot of information, but most of it decays before it ever gets recorded. Unlike a computer that can take in and store information at an incredible rate, humans rapidly get overloaded if expected to deal with too much information too fast.

But people are much more effective than computers at dealing with the complexities of human life, mainly because the information that does get retained is encoded much more efficiently – more efficiently, that is, in terms of being able to recall it and use it. This is because the information is encoded differently – human cognition operates with information that is encoded *meaningfully*. This allows the cognitive system to take short-cuts and work on hunches. The meaningfulness of the information means that gaps can be filled and errors rectified. This allows human cognition to be strategic – to home in on what really matters and cut out a lot of irrelevant and redundant work. In her work Jenny uses this capacity constantly. Within the cacophony of the call centre she concentrates on her own calls, filtering out all the spurious noise and action going on around her.

Try it for yourself

You can experience this for yourself by setting up a tape or minidisk recorder next time you go to a crowded place (for example, when you are with a group of friends – though do remember to check they are OK about you doing this). Let it run for, say, ten minutes while you are chatting to your friends. Then listen to the recording once you get somewhere quiet. You are likely to find the recording pretty unintelligible – just a rumbling hubbub of noise with just the occasional catches of conversation coming through at random. Then think back to what you experienced when you were sitting beside the recorder listening for yourself. You should be able to recall hearing the conversation with your immediate neighbours with clarity. This was because you were selectively attending to that particular conversation and filtering out most of the background noise.

You may not be too impressed by this demonstration as you have probably tried something like it before. (Most students find that they can get a good enough recording of a lecture for it to be useful, but soon give up on trying to record seminars when lots of people are talking.) What may intrigue you more is to know that you were actually processing the background noise to a surprising degree.

Have you ever had the experience of chatting in a crowded place like that, and suddenly, out of the hubbub of noise around you, you hear your own name being mentioned? This is called (rather quaintly these days) the **cocktail party phenomenon**. In order to be able to pick up on your name, you must have been unconsciously processing the conversations going on in the background. The human cognitive system has the capability to detect words that are personally salient (such as one's own name) or other inputs that are distinctive or unexpected, even when they are not consciously attending to them (Broadbent 1958). People can strategically switch their attention, and this makes them much more efficient than any recording machine so far invented – though work continues to be done to design one that can match human capacities. When, say, a documentary maker wants to record a group conversation, they need a lot of equipment and, crucially, a sound technician to do the switching between inputs.

Selective attention is just one way in which human cognition operates strategically. As we go through the chapter you will see that the study of social cognition is very much the study of what these strategies are and how they function.

Basic processes in social cognition

Looking in depth at what Jenny's job entails brings home the amazing amount of knowledge and ability to encode and process it that are required to do even quite simple tasks. It brings home that cognition always involves making inferences from one's own knowledge of people and situations – that people, unlike machines, process meaning, not just 'bits' of information. Whereas machines like computers mainly gain processing efficiency because of the sheer magnitude of information that they can handle and the speed at which they operate, human cognition 'works' because

- it draws upon an immense stock of social knowledge, stored in long-term memory, that has been built up through the life-span
- of the complexity and subtlety of the way that this stored knowledge has been categorized and organized so that it is meaningful
- of the way that its component processes are fine-tuned to work with this meaning.

Categorization

The basic process by which input information is made meaningful is through **categorization**. A category is where similar things are classified together and treated as an entity. 'Lingerie', for example, is a category that covers items of women's underwear, its defining characteristics being underwear that is particularly feminine in style – frilly and lacy – and that has associations with being 'sexy'. If I gave you a list of items – boxer shorts, basques, handbags and vests – you shouldn't find it too hard to recognize which of these is lingerie and which is not. But some items are easier to reject than others. The handbag isn't even underwear, so that one is obvious. But what about the boxer shorts and the vest? Both are underwear, but are they lingerie? Given its characteristic of being 'feminine', the boxer shorts are out then – men don't (usually) wear female clothing. So, what about the vest? Actually in some department stores their 'Lingerie Section' brings together all women's underwear. So it depends upon your definition and the situation. Categories are like that – they are influenced by context and can be quite fuzzy.

Stereotyping

However, categorization has its down side. In allowing us to treat particular instances as a single class, it can lead to wrong inferences. Think about the assumptions you've made about Jenny. Conjure up an impression of her in your mind's eye. Maybe your image of her is a pretty feminine one; a bit 'sassy' possibly, given the job she's got, but rather 'girlie' nonetheless. Probably you picture her as young (most people who work in telesales are) and almost certainly you think it's her boyfriend she's worried about.

But what if I told you that Jenny was a lesbian, and in her 50s – that she got the job because she has a husky and rather sexy voice? Suddenly the image shifts dramatically. What was going on before is called **stereotyping**. Categorization is a process of 'going beyond the information given' (Bruner 1957), and quite often that information is wrong. Plenty of young, heterosexual women are anything but 'girlie', and there are certainly older, lesbian women who are!

Have you heard the joke about the Irish labourer who goes for a job on a building site and is given an interview by the foreman. 'Paddy,' the foreman asks 'what's the difference between a girder and a joist?' Paddy thinks for a minute and then says 'Well, Mick, that's an easy question to answer. It's Goethe who wrote *Faust*, and it's Joyce who wrote *Ulysses*.' The joke is funny simply because it challenges the stereotype of the ignorant Irish labourer. A psychological study by Haire and Grune (1950) found empirical evidence that demonstrated this kind of stereotyping in practice. When subjects in the study were asked to write sentences about a 'working man' in which they were told to incorporate stereotype-consistent descriptions (such as 'ignorant') they found this easy. It was much harder, they found, to incorporate stereotype-inconsistent ones (such as 'intelligent').

The encoding of categories

Some cognitive psychologists have theorized that categories are encoded and processed as **prototypes** (see, for example, Barsalou 1985). Prototypes are abstract representations of idealized categories – rather like mental blueprints. Others (such as Smith and Zaraté 1992) contest this idea, arguing that encoding is **exemplar-based**, where memory storage and processing are based on specific exemplars.

Associative networks

Categorization is a rather simple, essentially semantic operation. In cognitive social psychology it is recognized that the representation of meaning requires something considerably more sophisticated, whereby not only is information categorized but also, crucially, categories are *associated with each other*. Whatever the basis for category encoding, cognitive social psychologists agree that social knowledge is organized hierarchically. Taking our illustration of 'lingerie', its hierarchical organization is shown in Figure 5.3.

Formulations like these allow us to see how cognitive processes and structures influence behaviour. Their influence is not only to do with *what* is encoded, but also with how the *interconnections* between them are structured. General cognitive psychology has developed sophisticated models of these. Fiedler and Bless (2001) describe **associative networks**, where the connections between categories are organized semantically. An illustration is given in Figure 5.4.

Figure 5.3
The hierarchical organization of 'lingerie' as a category

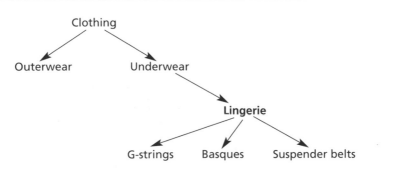

Figure 5.4
Illustration of an associative network

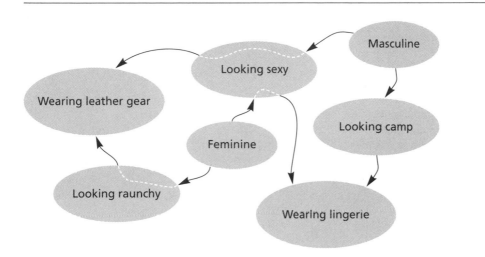

Schema

However, a more radical model moves beyond semantic interconnections, and portrays social knowledge as represented by way of **schema**: 'a cognitive structure that represents knowledge about a concept . . . including its attributes and the relations among these attributes' (Fiske and Taylor 1991: 98).

The term schema was first developed in the 1930s by Bartlett (1932b) to describe the conceptual frameworks through which people perceive and make sense of the world around them. Bartlett was interested, particularly, in how memory works. He conducted a number of studies on how people remember stories. He found that when asked to recount a story they had heard some time ago (anything from a day or so to years ago), people tended to tell a distorted version. Their account not only got shorter (a lot of detail got left out). At the same time, aspects of the original story that were at all strange or unfamiliar got 'ironed out' – made more plausible according to the individual's own worldview and experience.

Bartlett saw this as providing evidence that when people take in information they interpret it through their existing knowledge, and store this *interpreted* version in their memory. He suggested that the way in which this is done is that remembered knowledge is organized into schemas, and that it is these schemas that enable us to *make* sense of what happens around and to us.

Strictly *schema* is the singular form and *schemata* the plural; in practice the terms 'schema' and 'schemas' have become the most widely used.

Schemas are thus more powerful than mere categories. They not only represent semantic information about what things 'are' but also *schematic* information about how concepts and ideas relate to each other and analytical information that acts as a basis for interpretation and reasoning. Thus schemas can 'guide information processing by structuring experiences, regulating behaviour, and providing bases for making inferences and interpretations' (Martin and Halverson 1981: 1120).

Jenny's line of work draws heavily on her gender schemas, for example. As Janoff-Bulman and Frieze (1987) have argued 'our gender schemas represent deeply embedded assumptions that we hold about maleness and femaleness in our society, and that we use to evaluate ourselves as well as others' (Janoff-Bulman and Frieze 1987: 169). To be any good at selling lingerie, Jenny needs to have a good understanding of the range of masculinities and femininities that may bring people to call up her company. She needs to be able to use this to infer what products she is likely to sell to what customers and in what circumstances.

In social contexts, schemas not only encode information about different sorts of people and groups of people, but also do so for different forms of social interaction. A specific term used here is **scripts** (see, for example, Abelson 1981). (You met this earlier in Chapter 4.) Hogg and Vaughan (1998) define scripts as 'schemas about events'. Examples here might include making a sale and sending a Valentine gift. Like other kinds of schemas, scripts provide conceptual linking frameworks that class a number of items into an entity. A script like 'going on a date', for instance, sets up a variety of expectations about the sequence of events, what each person should and shouldn't do, and so on. Further differentiation ('a first date', 'a Valentine date') specifies still further.

Schemas are thus very potent encoding devices because they carry so much information. Consequently they are seen to play an important role in making cognition efficient. They make communication faster and more effective, since a lot can be conveyed in a single word or phrase. They aid problem solving by turning complexity into meaningful, manageable chunks that can then be processed more easily. They act as major organizing frameworks for perception and memory.

A highly oversimplified analogy is to see schemas as working a bit like the text-prediction function on a mobile phone. It can make text messaging a lot less onerous, and works well if the words you want to use are familiar ones. But it's not much use when the words you want to key in are at all out of the ordinary. Schemas work a bit like this. Once invoked they 'lock in' rapidly and save you the effort of having to think too hard about the immediate situation by filling in any gaps from your prior knowledge and preconceptions. Or, to put it more formally 'schemas facilitate top-down, conceptually driven or theory-driven processing, as opposed to bottom-up or data-driven processing'

(Hogg and Vaughan 1998: 50). Schemas are therefore very useful, especially when you need to assess a situation and respond to it rapidly. But they do lead to stereotypical thinking, which can be a problem when dealing with situations that *seem* familiar but aren't.

Social cognition

Cognitive psychology is a radically different paradigm from information processing for conceptualizing how people understand the world. Its basic principles are as follows:

- When taking in information from the outside, people don't just soak it up like a sponge, or passively record it like a computer. They actively seek to understand it through a process of recognition (that is, *re*-cognition), that encodes the information in terms of its meaning and salience.
- The design characteristics of the human cognitive system are such that it works best with meaningfully encoded information. This places limits on the speed, accuracy and efficiency with which information can be processed.
- However, encoding meaningfully brings enormous benefits. It enables people to be insightful and intuitive. In particular it allows people to be selective and therefore strategic – to direct cognitive effort to achieve particular goals.

Social cognition draws on this theorization and applies it to cognition in relation to social situations, processes and phenomena.

- It acknowledges that there are processing limits on people's ability to deal with information, but sees them as adopting a range of active and purposeful **cognitive strategies** to do so in ways that help them achieve social goals.
- There are different views of the effects of this strategic processing. Some theorists see people as needing to be cognitive misers, others as motivated tacticians.
- It stresses that information is encoded in ways that make it meaningful – categorization; and in ways that link concepts and ideas together semantically – by way of **associative networks**, scripts and schema.
- However, while such encoding makes cognition more efficient, it can have its problems. For instance stereotyping can lead to prejudice.

ATTRIBUTION THEORY

Attribution theory became the favourite area for experimental research in social cognition in the 1960s and 1970s. Charles Antaki called it the 'jewel in the crown' of the social cognition approach (Antaki 1988). While it has its critics it is still regarded by experimental social psychologists as an extremely important theoretical field, and of considerable value in applied settings. '[R]esearch on motivation, clinical psychology and close relationships demonstrates the continued vitality of attribution research, and the tremendous impact of attribution theory in advancing our understanding of applied problems' (Fincham and Hewstone 2001: 237).

Heider's theories of phenomenological causality

Attribution theorists acknowledge Fritz Heider (1953) as their 'founding father'. Apparently Heider devised his theory as a result of spending a very cold and hungry period just after the First World War writing up his doctoral thesis. This experience got him wondering why people become 'touchy and petulant' with one another (perhaps not the grandest basis for theory making, but certainly a reaction that many of us who have written doctorates can sympathize with very sincerely, as can the people around us when we were doing it).

Although the overall term Heider used for his theory was **phenomenological causality**, he carefully distinguished between attributions of causes and agency more generally, setting the scene for a continuing debate about the nature of how ordinary people understand cause and effect, and the errors they may make in doing so. Heider distinguished between specific and general explanations, explanations of what happened in the past and predictive explanations. Although he was primarily concerned with social perception (that is the ways people explain their own actions and those of others) he also reviewed theories of the way people account for events and influences from the physical environment too.

A man 'ahead of his time'?

Even though Heider's work has been the basis for attribution theory, Heider himself was much broader in his theorizing, and much more philosophical in his approach. He regarded the process of explanation as something which both differs *between* people according to particular personal characteristics (such as personality) and something that is dynamic *within the individual*, changing according to circumstances (on mood, for example). Heider was another psychologist 'ahead of his time' in that his formulations anticipated social constructionism. He argued that the explanations that people use to explain the world are both products of the way they 'structure the world' and at the same time contribute to that structuring. Heider's theorization also anticipated discursive psychology. He suggested that a person's explanations of the world may be deployed for different purposes, for example that they may be used for self-justification.

Heider argued that explanation needed to be studied at a common-sense level. He stressed that people do not respond directly to how the world *actually* works but according to their *perceptions* of the workings of the world. The explanations that individuals use to structure their world are crucial to making sense of the strategies they adopt in responding to it. He argued that we can begin to develop psychological theories about the way people act only after we have gained access to the explanatory framework within which they operate.

Social psychology, Heider asserted, needed to study people as 'naive physicists' who have developed theories to predict and to understand events in the physical world; as 'naive psychologists' who have theories to predict and understand the behaviour and experience of others; as 'naive sociologists' who have theories to predict and interpret social forces and so on. It is easy to see how this kind of approach attracted those psychologists who wanted to adopt the cognitive approach.

Heider distinguished between two main kinds of attribution for an event: personal attribution (where a particular individual is seen as responsible, or to blame) and impersonal attribution (where nobody is blamed or held responsible). Impersonal attributions may be made towards naturally occurring events (for example being struck by a branch falling from a tree), but could also arise from unintended actions (somebody accidentally knocking the branch off the tree). Personal attributions, however, always carry the implication of intended action (that is, somebody deliberately throwing the branch at you).

Drawing on Gestalt psychology (see Chapter 2) Heider used a great deal of visual analogy, using metaphors from its theories of visual perception. He wrote, for example, that when Joan tries to understand why Mary did something, she tries to separate the 'figure' (Mary) from the 'ground' of the social situation in which Mary acted. Heider suggested that people have a tendency to misperceive actions, because they confuse figure and ground. They conceive the figure (that is the person acting) as dominating the conceptual ground (the social situation) in parallel fashion to the way figure can dominate ground in a Gestalt analysis of visual perception. Thus people tend to be more willing than is justified to assume that actions are the *deliberate* intentions of the people involved, and less willing to attribute causes to what is going on in the social situation.

Attribution theory within social cognition

This propensity to blame the individual formed the major plank upon which attribution theory was built. Later workers expanded upon it, and drew up a number of more detailed and complex formulations about the kinds of information people use to make inferences, and the ways in which they are calculated against one another.

Correspondence inference

The first moves were made by Jones and Davis (1965), who proposed the notion of **correspondent inference**. Basically, this concerns the degree to which the actor – the person whose behaviour is being judged – is seen as behaving according to a stable and enduring disposition. Examples are: anger expressed by a person who is usually grumpy and bad-tempered, and laughter from a person who has a well-developed sense of humour. People make correspondent inferences in these circumstances (that is inferences which correspond to the assumed disposition), attributing the cause of the action – the anger or the laughter – to the person, rather than the situation.

Jones and Davis (1965) theorized about the sorts of knowledge required for making correspondent inferences, and suggested that one element was to do with **role expectations**. Jones and Davis argued that when people act in-role, according to preconceived notions of what their role should be (for example that nuns are devout, Australians brash, and professors scholarly) their behaviour will be seen as role-driven, and thus less likely to be a product of personal qualities. When people act in ways that are counter to their assumed roles (for example when a nun is brash, an Australian scholarly, or a professor devout) their behaviour is much more likely to be accredited to something peculiar to them as individuals.

A number of experiments were carried out to test this hypothesis. A good example is one conducted by Jones *et al.* (1961). When people in this study were asked to explain why job applicants in tape-recorded interviews pointedly acted counter to the job-description characteristics provided, they said it was to do with their personal characteristics. But they explained job applicants whose interviews conformed to the desired qualities as acting according to the demands of the interview situation.

Note that, unlike Heider's formulations, the concept of correspondent inference makes no claims about intentionality. All that is at issue here is whether attribution is about cause located in the *person* (intended or not) or in the *situation*. A good example is where people explain why somebody has a heart attack. If the person is seen as 'an ideal candidate' (they are overweight and take little exercise) then it is the overweight and laziness that will be seen to be the cause of the heart attack. But when a person who is a paragon of virtue health-wise is struck down, then the explanation given is that the individual must have had some specific susceptibility or have suffered some unexpected unique risk.

Kelley's 'naive statistician' model

Harold (not George) Kelley (1967) devised an even more complex and sophisticated series of parameters to the attribution process. He suggested that people base an attribution about a particular action upon estimates of three main kinds of information:

- *distinctiveness*: the extent to which the person in question normally behaves in this kind of way
- *consistency*: the extent to which the person in question has, in the past, behaved like this before in similar situations
- *consensuality*: the extent to which other people normally behave like that.

Figure 5.5
Why did Marcia eat a lentilburger for lunch?
Source: Stainton Rogers 1991: 48

DISTINCTIVENESS INFORMATION

Marcia is a vegetarian

CONSISTENCY INFORMATION

Marcia often has a lentilburger for her lunch

GREENFEAST

CONSENSUALITY INFORMATION

Most people don't eat lentilburgers

Ugh!!

MENU

All things considered, the reason Marcia ate the lentilburger is something to do with Marcia

Kelley theorized that people, when they make judgements about responsibility, act like 'naive statisticians'. Kelley saw attributional judgement as a process of weighing the different sources of evidence available in relation to each other, and carrying out a technique rather like statistical analysis of variance. The different estimates of variability in the situation are computed together, and the attribution is then calculated. When asked, for example, why Marcia ate a lentilburger for lunch, the calculation might go a bit like the situation shown in Figure 5.5 (see the previous page).

Attribution errors

The other set of well-known formulations were about the mistakes people make in their attributions; the ways in which 'naive statisticians' (that is ordinary people) are not as clever as psychologists. Nisbett and Ross (1980) describe three kinds of errors:

- **fundamental attribution error**: this is an enlargement of Heider's notion that people tend to overemphasize the personal, and underemphasize the situational causes of actions
- **actor–observer error**: this is when people (either as individuals, or as groups) assume their own behaviour to be more likely to be situationally determined, and the behaviour of others more likely to be a product of personal intentions
- **false consensus effect**: this is where people tend to assume that others are more likely to behave like them than they actually do.

Basically, this set of principles construes people as imperfect logicians, unable to overcome their own prejudices when making judgements.

More recent attribution theorists (for example Hewstone 1983) have suggested that in order to understand why this should be, we need to consider the functions – both social and psychological – of attributions. Hewstone claimed that there are three:

- the need to assume *control* over the physical and social world by being able to explain and predict what will happen. This is particularly salient with regard to misfortune, where blaming it on a person's own actions offers the hope that *you* can avoid similar misfortune by not acting so stupidly. If you see yourself as to blame for a misfortune that has happened to you, then you can mend your ways. If you blame somebody else, then you can convince yourself that *you* would never do anything so stupid.
- to promote *self-esteem*, by seeing yourself as competent, taking credit for your successes, and dismissing your failures as caused externally;

- as a means of *self-presentation* in which the act of attribution is one of portraying yourself (to yourself, and to others) in a good light.

Attribution theory

- Contemporary attribution theory is based on the work of Heider, who first proposed a distinction between personal and impersonal (situational) attribution.
- Jones and Davis (1965) proposed that attribution is determined by correspondent inference – the inferences that people make as to whether people are behaving in relation to their social role or their personal disposition.
- Kelley (1967) offered a 'naive statistician' model, where people compute distinctiveness, consistency and consensuality to work out how to attribute cause.
- Nisbett and Ross (1980) described three main kinds of attribution errors – predispositions to
  - generally site cause in the person rather than the situation
  - but site cause in the situation rather than their own behaviour
  - believe others behave more like them than they actually do.

PROCESSING-DEPTH MODELS OF SOCIAL COGNITION

In Europe, at least, social cognition is undergoing a distinct shift. A new over-arching theory is being developed that proposes that most forms of social cognition can operate in one of two distinctly and qualitatively different levels of processing:

- automatically and largely mindlessly, where cognition is heuristic – it works from 'rules of thumb' based, for example, on well-established stereotypes, schemata and scripts
- consciously, actively and purposively, where cognition is used in a thoughtful, strategic manner.

This has led to the development of a number of **processing-depth models** of social cognition. A good example is the one developed by Gilbert and his colleagues (Gilbert *et al.* 1988), based on reaction-time experiments on attribution. Subjects are presented with a stimulus on a computer screen and asked to attribute its cause – for example, whether or not a person is responsible for a particular outcome. The speed at which the subjects respond

Figure 5.6
Gilbert *et al.*'s (1988) three-stage model of attribution

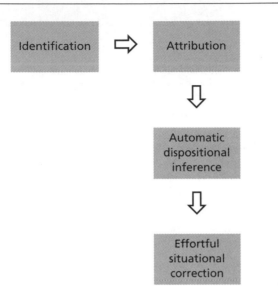

is seen as a measure of the 'depth' of processing needed to make the judgement. Using this technique, Smith and Miller (1983) found that decisions based on categorization of gender (that is based on stereotypes) were fastest, and decisions based on attributing a situational cause (that is requiring much more thought) were slowest. Gilbert *et al.* (1988) used these kinds of results as the basis of a three-stage model of attribution. This is shown in Figure 5.6.

In this model identification is a necessary first processing step. A person has to identify what is happening and who is involved before they can begin to decide who or what is responsible. This is done automatically, through reference to categorical knowledge. Then, the model proposes, there are two sequential stages of attribution. The first attributional stage is **dispositional inference**. This is also a relatively automatic and mindless process. It requires little cognitive effort (see, for example, Uleman *et al.* 1996). The second attributional stage is making a **situational correction**. Making this kind of attribution is held to require much more cognitive effort – it needs more thinking to make a decision.

Gilbert *et al.* (1988) tested their model using a divided-attention technique. Subjects watched a video of a woman anxiously having a conversation with

Table 5.1
Results obtained by Gilbert *et al.* (1988)

Distraction	Subjects just watched the video		Subjects were distracted by an attention demanding task	
Priming	Primed to see the woman as anxious	Primed to see the situation as anxiety provoking	Primed to see the woman as anxious	Primed to see the situation as anxiety provoking
Attribution	Attributed anxiety to the woman	Attributed anxiety to the situation	Attributed anxiety to the woman	Attributed anxiety to the woman

another person. Half were allowed to concentrate just on watching the video. The other half had to simultaneously carry out a distracting, attention-demanding task – they had to silently mutter lists of words to themselves while they were watching. These groups were subdivided, so that half of each sub-group were primed to view the woman's anxiety as arising from the topic she was discussing (situational attribution). The other half were primed to view her anxiety as arising from her anxious personality (dispositional inference). The results obtained are shown in Table 5.1 and show that, indeed, when distracted, subjects tend to fall back on stereotypical attribution.

Drivers for change

Three main considerations have combined to give rise to these processing depth models of social cognition: a turn to language; a recognition that people generally go about their lives in a pretty mindless way; and a turn to researching social cognition in more realistic settings.

A turn to language

In Europe, at least, while most social psychologists retain a commitment to experimental method, there are a growing number who have taken on the message that a consideration of the semantic qualities of language needs to be drawn into theorizing and built into research.

Since the 1980s a group of mainly European experimental social psychologists have begun to argue for a 'turn to language' in attribution theory. They say that classical attribution theory takes insufficient account of the extent to which attribution is articulated through language. Semin and Fiedler (1988), for instance, propose that attribution research must take account of the categories that are built into the linguistic system and, particularly, the semantic qualities of the verbs people use to describe and explain their own actions and those of others. These studies stress the complexity and subtlety of language, and how particular words convey strong implications about the causal explanation of events. Others (such as Hilton 1990) emphasize the pragmatic and strategic qualities of speech, and he argues for a 'conversational approach' to attribution that has clear links to discursive psychology.

Most processing is mindless

They also criticize classical attribution theory for the way it portrays people as living in an experiential world constantly beset by ambiguity and confusion about what is going on, desperate to know the causes of each event and constantly needing to calculate alternatives and come up with answers. Semin and Manstead (1983) argued that this is nonsense. Most of the time, they say, people go through life experiencing it as a reasonably smoothly flowing series of events, that only need to be explained or justified when something unexpected comes along. To even ask the question 'Why did she do that?' changes things dramatically, since it implies that the action *needs* to be explained (that is, it was an unwarranted action, or one that broke the rules). Consequently, simply asking people to explain an action comes across as accusatory, and so invites particular kinds of response: justifications, denials of blame, excuses. If what you want to do is to study these kinds of explanation, fine. Asking the 'why' question would be legitimate. But, Semin and Manstead (1983) argue, what cannot be done is to assume that the answers given in this situation necessarily or even probably reflect the usual way in which people understand the reasons for things, when not called upon to explicitly *explain* them.

Langer (1978) had already raised similar concerns, suggesting that when people are involved in social situations in real life, they do not usually understand it through thoughtful attributional analyses of what is going on between people. Mostly they operate pretty 'mindlessly', often by following a script.

More realistic settings

Langer and her colleagues did a number of studies to demonstrate this, including a number of clever field experiments observing how secretaries dealt with memos sent to them and how they responded to requests to 'jump the queue' to use the photocopier (Langer *et al.* 1978). These were designed to examine social cognition in situations that are much more true to real life.

This is becoming a marked trend in attributional research. Fincham and Hewstone (2001), for example, review a range of studies in which people are asked to make attributional judgements in more realistic settings, such as when people are facing problems in their close relationships (see, for example, Fincham and Bradbury 1988). These yield much more sophisticated models of attribution, that take account of the state of the relationship itself (satisfactory or unsatisfactory), the attribution pattern (relationship-enhancing or distress-maintaining), and the behaviour in question of the partner (positive or negative).

These models encompass, in particular, people's *motivation* to engage in in-depth cognition when making their attributions. Motivation is seen as a question of whether or not the attribution *matters*. When relationships are going well, for instance, the things your partner does are often not treated very seriously. Even when they do something irritating, this is passed off as relatively unimportant – as unintentional and therefore not blameworthy. But when the relationship is going badly, both positive and negative acts tend to be viewed negatively. When a partner in this situation does something good, then this is not seen as deliberate and receives no credit or praise. When they do a bad thing, this *is* seen as deliberate, as selfish and therefore as blameworthy.

This shift to more complex models that take account of meanings and salience moves closer to the kinds of model of, say, discursive psychology, that views cognition as *motivated*. The methodological approach used in discursive psychology is very different (as you saw in Chapter 4). The underlying theory base is also much more concerned with intersubjectivity. But even so, there is an agreement building up that modelling how people understand the world needs to take account of the subtlety and sophistication of human thinking that is intimately connected with language use.

Processing depth models of social cognition

Some (mainly European) experimental social psychologists have begun to develop more sophisticated models of social cognition. These

- Take much more account of the way language mediates social cognition
- View it as operating through two *kinds* of processing: superficial and automatic, or in-depth and heuristic

→

- Recognize that social cognition is much more sophisticated and complex in real life situations
- View social cognition as motivated, and hence affected by what matters and is significant.

PERSONAL CONSTRUCT THEORY

An approach that is markedly different from attribution theory, even framed as a discursive practice, is offered by George Kelly's **personal construct theory**. It is not located in the experimental social psychology frame, since its research strategy makes no claim to be experimental. However, it is very much individuo-focused, in that it is primarily a theory about how individuals build up and use 'personal constructs' to make sense of and operate within the social world. Its proponents see it as a global theory of human emotion and action as well as thinking.

Its assumptions about the way personal constructs provide the basis of understanding are not so much parts of the theory, as its basis. In other words, Personal Construct theory takes as its fundamental postulate that 'making sense of the world' is *the* basis of what it means to be a person, and underpins all of what constitutes human behaviour and experience. The basic idea (postulate) behind the theory it is simple enough: that people interpret the world by way of a series of 'personal constructs'. Kelly's (1966) own account and Bannister and Fransella's (1986) review offer more detailed descriptions, if you want to know more than the summary I provide here.

Personal Construct theory portrays people as 'naive scientists' who approach life by constructing a set of working hypotheses about what is going on and what is likely to happen, in order to plan how to proceed. These are continually tested against what actually happens and are then modified and refined. Operating in this manner allows people to live their lives in a functional, self-aware and self-controlling manner. They are thus able to tackle the complex demands of living in society, making decisions, planning action and understanding their own actions and emotions and the actions and emotions of others.

In emphasizing the person-as-scientist, Kelly was careful to say that this is just one aspect of many forms of 'constructive alternativism' that occur within an individual's understanding of the social world. His followers (see, for example, Swift *et al.* 1983) have argued that Kelly's notion of 'scientist' has often been misinterpreted as an entirely rationalizing, unemotional image. Kelly, they argue, chose the term for its liberating properties – its ability to overcome the dehumanizing 'person-as-passive-organism' image of prior forms of theorization such as behaviourism and information processing models.

In Personal Construct theory the uniqueness of each new event is made understandable by comparing it with the appropriate construct(s). Kelly and his followers have drawn up a list of descriptions as to what these are like, and how they operate, which they term **corollaries**:

- the *commonality corollary* states that people can and do experience the world in similar ways, to the extent that their construct systems are similar
- the *sociality corollary* states that people have access to each other's construct systems, which enables them to 'inhabit each other's worlds' even where they are very different.
- the *fragmentation corollary* states that there are sometimes constructs that contradict one another.

These different aspects of personal constructs are held to be crucial to allow people to operate effectively within a social world. An individual's competence as a social being depends upon how predictive their constructs are, and how appropriately they are applied. Thus while personal constructs have a lot in common with schemata, the theorization transcends some of the limitations of schema theory. It portrays people as more sophisticated, as sometimes confused and indecisive, as sharing common understandings, and as able to empathize with and understand each other.

However, the theory is ultimately limited in three main ways. First, it is primarily a *personal* construct theory. Although its commonality corollary states that people can and do experience the world in similar ways, personal construct theory emphasizes the 'personal'. In stressing the uniqueness of each individual construct system, it actually has very little to say about the ways people may construct and negotiate meanings *collectively*, or how *shared* understandings operate within the medium of culture (as, say, semiotic theory does). Personal construct theory does not deal in any depth, for example, with social processes, such as the influence of social control and the construction of knowledge by powerful groups, which is then foisted upon the less powerful. Basically, it is an *individualizing* discourse, which reifies the individual 'subject' (Henriques *et al.* 1984). If you recall from Chapter 1, psychological social psychology is inherently individuo-focused, and personal construct theory is an illustration of this.

Second, although Kelly himself argued that theories (including his own) should be treated as aids-to-understanding rather than as dogmatic assertions that they are (or ever can be) descriptions-of-what-really-is, his focus on construct bipolarity is highly specific and open to question. There are arguments for suggesting people's understanding of concepts cannot be understood just in terms of bipolar opposites. For instance, while 'good' makes sense as a concept because it is in opposition to 'bad', it also gains meaning in relation to concepts like 'fresh', 'virtuous' and 'valuable'. Terms like 'bad' and 'wicked' are even more slippery, as they can be applied in some contexts very positively – think of the term 'naughty but nice' to describe cream cakes! The constraints imposed by bipolarity are a serious problem for any theory that seeks to represent the full complexity and sophistication of human thinking.

Third, the assertion that people can only determine the accuracy of their constructs by acting upon them and thus testing them out can lead to some highly nonsensical implications. Wiggins *et al.* (1971) provide a telling illustration of the limitations of personal construct theory by considering what it says would happen when a parent sees that their child is crying. They start by supposing that, based solely on their own experience, the parent's constructs might be that either the child is in pain or it wants sweets. Personal construct theory claims that what the parent would do in this situation would be to test out one of these constructs. They might, say, give the child sweets to see if that shuts them up, and then the child might become violently sick. Once the parent has tested that construct and found it wanting, they may indeed decide to modify their construct. But the child would still be sick. This is obviously not what parents do.

Parents do not just draw upon their *own* personal constructs (derived from past experiences) in such situations. They work out what to do from a whole host of other sources of knowledge about how to treat children who are sick – such as knowledge got from books and getting advice from family, friends or health professionals. All manner of other ideas will influence their actions, including ones about risk-taking (encapsulated, for example, in aphorisms like 'better safe than sorry'). Most crucially, people do not simply choose between alternative constructs within their own cognitive system. Anybody who has ever cared for a sick child knows the enormous amount of effort you have to put into working out the possible reasons for a child crying may be, and then deciding what to do about it. Dealing with a crying child is much more than an analytic search within *individual* thought. It is an active, insightful, search after meaning which may well draw upon advice from others as well as one's own store of common-sense knowledge gained through a lifetime of exposure to everything from soap operas to helpful leaflets provided by hospitals.

Personal construct theory

Personal construct theory was devised by George Kelly.

- It portrays people as 'naive scientists' who approach life by constructing a set of working hypotheses in order to decide what to do.

- The uniqueness of each new event is made understandable by personal constructs that are derived from their own personal experience. It recognizes that people will share many constructs since they have been socialized in similar ways, and that people have access to (and can take account of) each other's constructs.
- Critics of personal construct theory point out that there are many other ways in which people learn about and make sense of the world, and do not rely just on their own experience.

FURTHER READING

Experimental social psychology

Fiedler, K. and Bless, H. (2001) Social cognition, in M. Hewstone and W. Stroeber (eds) *Introduction to Social Psychology*, 3rd edn. Oxford: Blackwell.

Fincham, F. and Hewstone, M. (2001) Attribution theory and research: from basic to applied, in M. Hewstone and W. Stroebe (eds) *Introduction to Social Psychology*, 3rd edn. Oxford: Blackwell.

These two chapters from Hewstone and Stroebe's textbook are by far the most comprehensive, balanced and sophisticated accounts of theory and research in relation to social cognition and attribution theory respectively.

Personal construct theory

Bannister, D. and Fransella, F. (1986) *Inquiring Man: The Psychology of Personal Constructs*. London: Croom Helm.

This is the standard text if you want to begin to get to grips with personal construct theory.

QUESTIONS

1 Explain what is meant by 'encoding' in social cognition, and give examples about the different forms it can take.
2 In terms of the way people deal with information overload, are they 'cognitive misers' or 'motivated tacticians'?
3 What kinds of errors do people make in social cognition and what causes them? Illustrate your answer with reference to both selective attention and attribution.

4 In the 1980s a shift was made away from traditional attribution theory to more sophisticated processing-depth models. Describe the theorizing behind this shift, and key studies that demonstrate how this new conception of attribution is different.

5 Outline the main elements of personal construct theory, and the reasons why it has been criticized.

Chapter 6

Values and attitudes

Chapter contents

A route map of the chapter

In this chapter I shall (somewhat) seek to bring values back into the frame, and this will be the first thing we will explore, looking in the first section at Rokeach's work, and then in the second at recent studies of values conducted within cross-cultural psychology.

In the remainder of the chapter the focus will be on attitudes, beginning with a section giving a general introduction to the field of attitudes, and then a section reviewing of work on attitude change.

Values

↓

Cross-cultural studies of values

↓

Attitudes

↓

Attitude change

Learning objectives

When you have completed your study of this chapter, you should be able to:

1 Define what is meant by 'values' in social psychology and describe their functions.
2 Summarize Rokeach's theory of values and the research he conducted into their links to political attitudes.
3 List the main findings of three cross-cultural studies of values, and outline their implications for social psychology.
4 Define 'attitudes', describe how they are formed and list their main psychological functions.
5 Outline the main conditions necessary for attitudes to predict behaviour.
6 Describe the theory of reasoned action and the theory of planned behaviour, listing the other elements in these models seen to be involved in influencing behaviour.
7 Describe the theory of cognitive dissonance, and list the conditions necessary for it to occur.
8 Describe two different ways in which persuasion can occur, and two processing-level models of persuasion.

INTRODUCTION

While the study of attitudes has been a key area of research and theory in experimental social psychology since Allport began working on them in the 1930s, it is generally acknowledged that attitudes have their foundation in values. Values are 'the consistent, personal assumptions we make which underpin our attitudes' (Hayes 1993: 93). Yet the study of values is, by comparison, almost absent in this field. Except for the work done by Rokeach and his colleagues in the 1970s (Rokeach *et al.* 1971; Rokeach and Cochrane 1972), the study of values has mainly been diverted off into applied fields such as political and cross-cultural psychology and market research.

VALUES

The best known and most extensive work on attitudes was done by Milton Rokeach (1973). Rokeach studied for his doctorate at Berkeley, California, and was a member of the group there studying the authoritarian personality (see Chapter 8). This was clearly influential on his choice of values as his main area of study. His doctorate was on rigidity in thinking and its links to prejudice, and his work on values was an attempt to pursue this broad agenda, but in ways that were more comprehensive than a specific focus on deviant and dysfunctional thinking.

Rokeach's theory and study of values

Rokeach formally defined a **value** as 'an enduring belief that a specific mode of conduct or end-state of existence is personally or socially preferable to [its] . . . opposite or converse mode'. He defined a **value system** as an 'enduring organization of beliefs concerning preferable modes of conduct or end-states of existence along a continuum of relative importance' (Rokeach 1976: 345). However, he pointed out that 'enduring' has to be seen as relative: '[i]f values were completely stable, individual and social change would be impossible. If values were completely unstable, continuity of human personality and society would be impossible' (Rokeach 1976: 345). In so doing, Rokeach is making it clear that values are not simply the possessions of individuals, but also operate at a much broader social and cultural level.

> Values are the cognitive representation not only of individual needs but also of societal and institutional demands. They are the joint results of sociological as well as psychological forces acting upon the individual – sociological because society and its institutions socialize the individual for the common good to internalize shared conceptions

of the desirable; psychological because individual motivations require cognitive expression, justification and, indeed, exhortation in socially desirable terms.

(Rokeach 1976: 257)

Rokeach drew some parallels between values and attitudes. For instance, he argued that values, like attitudes, have cognitive, emotional and behavioural components. However, he saw them as very different, distinguishing between attitudes and values in a number of ways; these are shown in Table 6.1.

Table 6.1
Rokeach's differentiation between attitudes and values

Attitudes	Values
A person has thousands of attitudes	A person has only a few dozen values at most
Attitudes are the organization of several beliefs around a specific object	Each value consists of a single, specific belief
Attitudes are composed of many different kinds of beliefs	Values are prescriptive or proscriptive beliefs – they implicate action
Attitudes are ephemeral – they change and differ according to context and circumstance	Values have 'a transcendental quality' – they operate consistently across objects and across situations
Attitudes can be changed relatively easily, and often quickly – sometimes in a few seconds or minutes	Values seldom undergo change, and when they do, the change takes much longer – weeks or months.
Attitudes are specific	Values are broad in their scope – they are general standards against which attitudes are judged
Attitudes are superficial	Values are foundational and perform a central organizing role in cognition
Attitudes are reflexive and responsive – they tend to react *to* situations	Values are dynamic, playing a central role in motivation and hence in directing behaviour
Attitudes only serve tangential functions in relation to identity and esteem	Values serve central and highly influential functions in relation to identity and esteem

Source: Based on Rokeach 1976

Functions of values

Rokeach listed a number of different ways in which values guide our thinking and conduct. I have modified his list somewhat, relating it directly to issues of concern to contemporary social psychology, and expanding it to include collectively held as well as individually held values.

Whether as individuals or collectively, values provide:

- a basis for *social judgement* – about our own or our group's behaviour and that of others/other groups, and for apportioning praise and blame
- a means to generate, maintain and defend our individual or group *esteem*, in part by enabling us to justify our beliefs and actions, even if they are deviant or unpopular; and in part by stirring us into action to pursue our goals
- guides to our or our group's *opinions* – the positions we should take on moral and social issues
- guides to the *attitudes* we should adopt, and how to reconcile conflicting attitudes and opinions within ourselves or among the group
- principles of *behaviour* – how to act, and how to present ourselves/our group to others
- a source of *motivation* – guiding us to act in ways that are instrumental in achieving our goals
- guides to *affiliation* – about who does and who does not share our/our group's beliefs, and with which political or religious ideology we should align
- guides to *social influence* – telling us what beliefs, attitudes, values and behaviours of others are worth challenging, protesting or seeking to change.

Classification of values

Rokeach defined two main kinds of values: instrumental (concerning modes of conduct) and terminal (concerning end-states). He then subdivided these into two kinds of instrumental values (moral and competence values) and two kinds of terminal values (personal and social). His classification is shown in Figure 6.1.

Rokeach assumed that the two kinds of values 'represent two separate yet functionally interconnected systems, wherein all the values concerning modes of behaviour are instrumental to the attainment of all of the values concerning end states' (Rokeach 1968: 351). However, it would be wrong, he argued, to see them as simple in their influence on behaviour. He recognized that particular values will conflict in different ways. For instance a person may have to choose between behaving morally or lovingly, between pursuing a logical or

Figure 6.1
Rokeach's classification of values

Instrumental values concern modes of conduct	Moral values	Values that, if transgressed, lead to feelings of guilt or wrongdoing, such as 'honesty' or 'love'
	Competence values	Values that relate to competence, such as 'intelligence', 'logical' or 'imaginative'
Terminal values concern end-states – goals or aspirations	Personal end-states	Values relating to one's own goals, such as 'salvation' or 'peace of mind'
	Social end-states	Values relating to the goals of your community, country, or even humankind in general, such as 'brotherhood' or 'world peace'

an imaginative solution to a problem, between acting politely or offering intellectual criticism. He noted that different people and different societies have different priorities in their values – for instance, some people and groups prioritize personal end-states (for example seeking salvation in a religious sense) whereas others may prioritize social end-states (for example seeking 'world peace').

Rokeach suggested that the main way in which competing values are reconciled is through individual values being organized into value systems – 'a learned, organization of principles and rules to help one choose between alternatives, resolve conflicts and make decisions' (Rokeach 1976: 352).

Rokeach's research into values and political positioning

In order to explore systematically how and why people's values differ, Rokeach and his colleagues devised a list of 18 terminal and 18 instrumental values. These are shown in Table 6.2.

Rokeach himself conducted numerous of studies into the ways in which people's values vary according to their personality, beliefs and attitudes (Rokeach 1973). In order to do this the values in Table 6.2 were each typed onto moveable labels. People were asked to work on each list separately, and to 'arrange them in order of importance to YOU, as guiding principles of YOUR life' (Rokeach 1973: 27). They were instructed to start from the value most important to them and gradually construct a rank ordered list by transferring the labels onto a grid. The labels could be moved, and subjects were told to work slowly and carefully, and move labels where necessary.

Table 6.2
Rokeach's list of values

Terminal values	Instrumental values
A comfortable life (a prosperous life)	Ambitious (hard-working, aspiring)
An exciting life (a stimulating, active life)	Broadmindedness (open-minded)
A sense of accomplishment (lasting contribution)	Capable (competent, effective)
A world at peace (free of war and conflict)	Cheerful (lighthearted, joyful)
A world of beauty (beauty of nature and the arts)	Clean (neat, tidy)
Equality (brotherhood, equal opportunity for all)	Courageous (standing up for your beliefs)
Family security (taking care of loved ones)	Forgiving (willing to pardon others)
Freedom (independence, free choice)	Helpful (working for the welfare of others)
Happiness (contentedness)	Honest (sincere, truthful)
Inner harmony (freedom from inner conflict)	Imaginative (daring, creative)
Mature love (sexual and spiritual intimacy)	Independent (self-reliant, self-sufficient)
National security (protection from attack)	Intellectual (intelligent, reflective)
Pleasure (an enjoyable, leisurely life)	Logical (consistent, rational)
Salvation (saved, eternal life)	Loving (affectionate, tender)
Self-respect (self-esteem)	Obedient (dutiful, respectful)
Social recognition (respect, admiration)	Polite (courteous, well-mannered)
True friendship (close companionship)	Responsible (dependable, reliable)
Wisdom (a mature understanding of life)	Self-controlled (restrained, self-disciplined)

Rokeach and associates carried out a large number of studies looking at, for example, how values relate to people's politics. They found few differences in terms of affiliation to political parties. But in studies that looked directly at political attitudes there were highly significant and consistent differences between what was called in the USA at that time 'conservatives' and 'liberals'. It is necessary to recognize that when this research was done, the USA was experiencing considerable political turmoil. First, the issue of race was highly volatile, and there was an active civil rights movement fighting for the emancipation of what were then called 'Blacks' and would now be called

Table 6.3
Ranking of 'equality' according to whether people express liberal or conservative attitudes

Liberal attitudes	Average rank given to equality	Conservative attitudes	Average rank given to equality
Reacted with anger to the assassination of Martin Luther King	5	Felt he brought the assassination on himself	13
Antiracist	4	Racist	14
Pro social support for the poor	5	Think poverty is the fault of the poor	13
Strongly in support of student protest	4	Strongly against student protest	12
Think the USA should withdraw from the Vietnam war	5	Think the USA should escalate the war in Vietnam	12
Think the church should get involved in social and political issues	4	Think the church should stay out of social and political issues	12

African Americans. Second, there was a great deal of civil protest against the involvement of the USA in the war in Vietnam.

The value that acted as the strongest marker between conservative and liberal standpoints was 'equality'. In a series of studies, questionnaires were used to identify attitudes to (among other things) the assassination of Martin Luther King, race, the poor, student protest, US involvement in the Vietnam war and whether the church should get involved in social and political issues. The differences in the rating of 'equality' between these two positions is highly consistent, as summarized in Table 6.3. You should note that I prepared this in a highly selective manner, drawing these data from a vast catalogue accumulated by Rokeach and his associates, in which there were very many more complex trends observed.

Similar patterns were found for behaviour – such as taking part in civil rights demonstrations. Rokeach himself rejected the liberal/conservative dichotomy, arguing that it is not useful for a number of reasons. Instead he spent much of the book developing a two-value model of ideology, that located political opinions along two dimensions – high/low equality and high/low freedom.

While Rokeach was working in the USA, his values were at the same time extensively used by Feather in Australia to study links between values and attitudes, personality and behaviour (see, for example, Feather 1971). Subsequently Feather went on to contribute to the development of expectancy-value models (Feather 1982). Feather has sustained this research ever since, continuing to study how values relate to attitudes, attributions and personality, and also influence behaviour. He has recently shown, for example, that assessing values can predict people's attitudes to 'a just world' (Feather 1991).

Rokeach's study of values

- The main theorist of values was Rokeach, who, together with various colleagues, conducted a large number of studies to explore systematic differences between different groups, and relationships between values and political viewpoints. For example liberals tended to place a higher value on 'equality' than conservatives.
- Rokeach defined two main kinds of values – instrumental and terminal.
- Rokeach saw values as having a wide range of functions, including informing social judgement, guiding opinions and attitudes, and acting as the basis for affiliation.

CROSS-CULTURAL STUDIES OF VALUES

Rokeach carried out some cross-cultural work of his own between the USA and Canada, and brought together studies conducted by Feather (1970) in Australia and Rim (1970) in Israel. He saw the results as promising, since they indicated some systematic differences. However, he recognized that 'a systematic cross-cultural approach is still some years away' (Rokeach 1973: 89). In this section we review the key studies in that development.

Hofstede's studies

In an intriguing study based on a survey conducted by a multinational company, Hofstede (1980) used its data to explore cultural differences in value-systems. In the survey, staff from the 40 countries in which this company had offices were asked to complete a questionnaire. This was administered in 1967 and then again in 1973, and asked employees a wide range of questions – about disagreements with bosses, how long they planned to work for the company, how much they valued high earnings compared to recognition, and so on. Hofstede took average scores on each item for each of the countries and used a variety of statistical techniques to look for systematic patterns. He identified four main dimensions on which they varied:

- *Power distance*, relating to the amount of respect and deference expected between staff in superior positions and their subordinates.
- *Uncertainty avoidance*, relating to the degree to which staff sought to plan their future and how much they valued stability.
- *Individualism/collectivism*, relating to whether a person's identity is defined by personal choices and achievements, or by the aspirations and success of the group to which the person belongs.
- *Masculinity/femininity*, relating to whether a person places more value on achievement or interpersonal harmony.

Hofstede (1983) subsequently enlarged the sample to cover a total of 50 countries plus three regions (East and West Africa and the Arab region) in order to try to get as comprehensive a picture as possible. The coverage was good, but it did exclude most of Africa and the communist countries such as the then Soviet Union and its satellites (such as Hungary and Poland), China and Cuba. In his analysis of data from these 53 countries/regions he identified two main cultural clusters:

- a cluster where, on average, the values expressed were high on individualism and low on power distance. In other words, the value-system was one in which people have *an individualistic focus together with low levels of deference to superiors*. The countries where these values predominated were from western Europe, North America, Australia and New Zealand. Of the 53 measures, the top five countries ranked on individualism were the USA, Australia, Great Britain, Canada and the Netherlands. The lowest five on power distance were Australia, Israel, Denmark, New Zealand and Ireland.
- a cluster where, on average, the values expressed were low on individualism and high on power distance. In other words, the value-system was one in which people have *a collective focus together with high levels of deference to superiors*. The countries where these values predominated were from Latin America and Asia. The lowest ranking countries on individualism were Guatemala, Ecuador, Panama, Venezuela and Colombia. The highest on power distance were Malaysia, Panama, Guatemala, the Philippines and Venezuela.

It is important to stress that these are *averages*, and so the data do not indicate that all Australians, for example, are brash individualists who are

These two perspectives – an individual and a relational self – are examined in more detail in Chapter 8.

irreverent in their dealings with their bosses, or that all Guatemalans are obsequious to their bosses and care more about others than themselves. Rather, the data give us some insight into the value-systems that are dominant in two different sorts of culture. Hofstede's work is useful to the extent that it provides empirical support to a broad divide between two opposed world-views – one in which there is an individualistic concept of the self, and the other in which the concept of the self is relational.

Hofstede's data were somewhat limited – not really surprising, given that he piggybacked his research onto a survey conducted for another purpose. First, all of the people who took part in the survey were employed by a company that is known to have a specific set of cultural values of its own. Second, they were drawn only from the company's 'white-collar workers' in their Marketing and Services departments. So they were hardly a representative sample of the general populations of the countries in question. What is striking is that he found such marked cultural differences, even despite these limitations.

The Chinese Culture Connection's study

A second study was conducted by an international group calling themselves the Chinese Culture Connection (1987). In order to counter the ethnocentric bias of most survey instruments designed to elicit values, the group began by asking Chinese people to list values that were fundamentally important to them. These responses were then used to construct a value scale that was administered to university students and teachers in 23 different national cultures. They then applied the same statistical techniques to the data obtained as those used by Hofstede. They also came up with four main dimensions. When a subset of the data was compared to Hofstede's, they found that three had fairly close equivalence to his dimensions, but one was new.

- *Integration*, which takes a relational view of the self and is broadly equivalent to Hofstede's individualism/collectivism. This seems to be the most culturally universal value dimension.
- *Human-heartedness*, which shares some of the elements of Hofstede's femininity (stressing values of kindness, compassion and emotional nurturance, for example) as opposed to masculinity (stressing values of conscientiousness, perseverance and thrift in order to achieve goals).
- *Moral discipline*, relating to respect for superiors and the value of diligence and hard work. This had a fair degree of equivalence to Hofstede's high power distance and uncertainty avoidance.
- *Confucian work dynamism* that values interpersonal harmony and cooperation among groups who work together and views time as elastic and expendable rather than needing to be 'saved'.

The last of these – the Confucian work dynamism dimension – did not show any correlations with Hostede's data at all. The Chinese Culture Connection claimed that it arises from the Chinese roots of its value configuration. The countries rated as strongest on this dimension were Taiwan, Hong Kong, Japan, South Korea, and Singapore.

Hofstede looked at relationships between his data and a measure of wealth (gross national product – GNP) and found that the countries high on individualism and low on power distance tended to be the richest. The Chinese Culture Connection did the same, but they found that Confucian work dynamism was most strongly positively correlated with GNP. Comparing these findings gives evidence, at a cultural level, that values influence behaviour. The rapid economic growth of countries like Japan, Taiwan, Hong Kong and Singapore has been attributed to the Confucian work ethic (Segall *et al.* 1990).

Schwartz's studies

For some time now Salom Schwartz has been working together with social psychologists in 25 countries to examine values across cultures. These studies are particularly interesting because they have included several (such as Slovakia and Poland) that have, during this time, been experiencing major social changes in the post-communist era (for example Schwartz *et al.* 2000). The group used the findings of earlier studies (including those of Hofstede and the Chinese Culture Connection) to identify 56 values operating across both Eastern and Western cultures (Schwartz 1994). They constructed a questionnaire asking respondents to rate them in terms of how much each one was 'a guiding principle in my life'. The data were analysed in a way that shows how the different items relate to each other. Separate analyses were done for each of the 60 samples included in the survey (in most countries data were collected from two groups – students and teachers). This analysis provides a refinement of the earlier analyses, as shown in Figure 6.2.

As you can see, Schwartz's analysis locates wisdom is a universal value at the core of human values. Surrounding it there is the established divide between individualism and collectivism on each side. However, these data suggest a distinction between intellectual and affective (that is emotional) individualism, and a third value-dimension, 'mastery'. These together are contrasted with collectivism, with segments relating to harmony on one side and hierarchy on the other.

If we now look at where these values are most highly endorsed, some interesting patterns emerge. Table 6.4 sets out the countries that scored highest on the broad value domains.

These patterns suggest, for example, that whereas the USA is usually regarded as the most highly individualistic country in terms of its values, this

Figure 6.2
Configuration of values obtained in Schwartz's country-level analysis
Source: Smith and Harris Bond 1993: 51

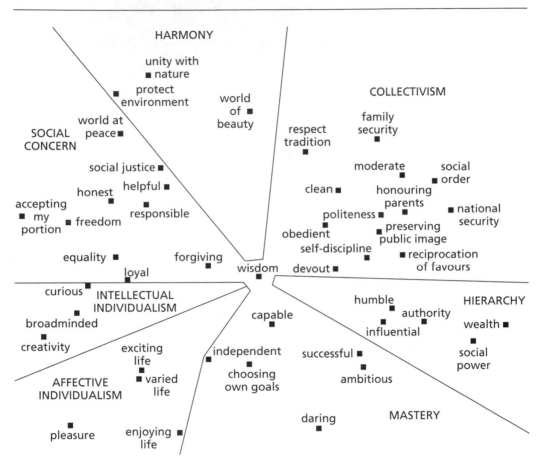

is to do with a particular aspect of individualism – mastery. In the USA the dominant value-system is one that stresses independence, self-directedness, daring, capability, ambition and success. At the same time the dominant cultural values in the USA are, in Hofstede's terms, relatively hierarchical in terms of power relations. By contrast these data identify a 'British' variant of individualism that places most value on excitement, hedonism and diversity, and a more 'European' intellectual individualism, in which the most important values are curiosity, creativity and broadmindedness.

Table 6.4
Samples scoring highest on each of Schwartz's value domains

Value	Highest scoring samples
Collectivism	Estonians and Malays, teachers from Taiwan, Turkey and Poland
Harmony	Teachers from Italy and Finland
Social concern	Teachers from Germany and Spain
Intellectual individualism	Students from the Netherlands and Italy
Affective individualism	Students from England, New Zealand and Australia
Mastery	Students from the USA, teachers from China
Hierarchy	Teachers and students from China and Zimbabwe, students from USA

Collectivism, according to this analysis, is also a complex and multifaceted value system that goes a lot further than prioritizing relatedness. It includes traditional values, such as respecting tradition and honouring parents, cleanliness, politeness, self-discipline and religious devotion. And it shows concern for social order and national security.

Again, caution needs to be applied. Remember these data were collected from students and teachers, and it is questionable how far these groups are representative of the populations as a whole in the countries surveyed. Also the data tell us about dominant value-systems, not about individuals. However, I hope you will agree they are fascinating and, crucially for the purpose of this book, tell us something worth knowing about the particularity of the dominant culture in universities in the USA.

Schwartz and his colleagues' data show very vividly just how culturally particular and specific this image is in the context of a diversity of value-systems across the world. Smith and Harris Bond (1993) argue that this is the reason why many studies conducted in the USA fail to be replicated elsewhere, even in other 'individualistic' cultures. For instance, social psychology's old chestnut – social inhibition/facilitation – appears to work very differently in different cultures. So too does social conformity (as we shall see in Chapter 9). The point they make is that what US social psychologists (who are the vast majority of experimental social psychologists) assume to be universal laws of human behaviour are, in practice, the manifestation of local norms and conventions based upon a local value-system and a local conception of the individual self.

Cross-cultural studies of values

- Studies of values by Hofstede identified two main value clusters:
  - an individualistic focus together with low levels of deference to superiors
  - a collectivist focus, with high levels of deference to superiors
- The Chinese Culture Connection identified four main dimensions on which values vary from one culture to another: in terms of integration (individualistic or collective), human-heartedness (rational or emotional), moral discipline (hedonistic or diligent) and Confucian work dynamism (time- and task-pressured or transcendental).
- Schwartz and his colleagues have produced detailed 'value maps' showing, for example, that while people in Europe and the USA both have an individualistic focus to their values, these are of different kinds.
- The results of these studies show that the Western image of the person – as an autonomous individual – is by no means universal. Social psychology needs to take this into account in its theorizing and research.

ATTITUDES

The study of attitudes has been a preoccupation of social psychology from its beginnings. Attitude is a key concept in experimental social psychology because attitudes are seen to operate at all levels of social influence:

- at an individual level, attitudes influence people's perception, thinking and behaviour
- at an interpersonal level, attitudes are a key element in how people get to know each other, and how to respond to each other; attitude change is a means by which people persuade others to act differently
- at the intergroup level, group members' attitudes towards their **ingroup** and **outgroups** are at the core of cooperation and conflict between groups.

What are attitudes?

Gordon Allport defined an attitude in Behaviourist terms as 'a mental and neural state of readiness, organized through experience, exerting a distinctive or dynamic influence upon the individual's response to all objects and situations with which it is related' (Allport 1935: 810). A more recent formulation is that an attitude is 'a psychological tendency that is expressed by evaluating a particular entity with some degree of favour or disfavour' (Eagly and Chaiken 1998: 269).

Most agree that the key elements are an **attitude object** and an evaluation towards it – attitudes are *about* something. Some kinds of attitudes are the subject of specific study by social psychologists and given particular labels. The study of negative attitudes to certain social groups is called the study of prejudice. Attitudes towards oneself are usually studied in terms of self-evaluation, and often specifically as the study of self-esteem. As you have seen already, the study of attitudes towards abstract concepts is generally called the study of values.

Generally attitudes are seen as having three main components:

- *Cognitive* components, made up of a person's understandings of and beliefs about the attitude object
- *Emotional* components, made up of a person's feelings towards and emotional reactions to the attitude object
- *Behavioural* components, made up of the person's past behaviour towards and their behavioural intentions to the attitudinal object.

A factor-analytic study by Breckler (1984), looking at students' attitudes towards snakes, showed that taking account of all three of these components was better at predicting overall attitudes than any single factor alone.

Attitude formation

It is almost too much of a truism to suggest that people form their attitudes by gaining information. It gets a lot less clichéd once we begin to consider where the information comes from.

Sources of information

Some information may be instinctive – such as feeling disgust about the smell and taste of putrefaction, which clearly has an evolutionary advantage. Evolutionary psychologists claim that people have inherent tendencies towards certain attitudes (Tesser 1993). One example is the claim that men are instinctively geared to find women with waists about one-third narrower than their hips the most attractive (Singh 1993).

The emotional elements of attitudes are most obviously informed by direct experience – events where an attitude object is accompanied by a strong emotional response. One of my friends feels revolted by coffee, which he traces back to once drinking it with sour milk that made him violently sick. Since then he even avoids being in a room where coffee is being prepared or people are drinking it. Emotional information can predominate over cognitive information. Breckler and Wiggins (1989), for example, found that if people experience strongly negative emotional reactions to seeing blood they are much less likely to donate blood, even when they know it to be a good thing to do.

Cognitive elements of attitudes are also influenced by direct experience. However, they are mainly the product of external sources of information – conversations with others, what people read in books and newspapers, see on television and so on (Fishbein and Ajzen 1975). External information often dominates over experiential information, especially that derived from hearsay (Millar and Millar 1996).

Behavioural elements arise from information about one's past behaviour. Fazio and Zanna (1981), for instance, showed that when people have regularly donated to a charity over a number of years, their approval of that charity is greater than if they have only recently donated. As we shall see, behavioural intention is also an important source of information.

Evaluating different sources of information

In many if not most cases, attitudes will be based on multiple sources of information (Breckler and Wiggins 1989). The question then arises – how is the information brought together? Theorization and research in this field has proposed two main strategies. The first is by a kind of **cognitive algebra**, where all the relevant information is weighed according to its salience and value and then a calculation is made to end up with an overall evaluation of the attitude object. Fishbein (1967), for example, proposed a precise mathematical formula. The alternative is a more **gestalt appraisal** where the 'whole' is more than just 'the sum of the parts'. Here information sources are interpreted via each other to gain a coherent, overall impression (Hamilton and Zanna 1974). For example, knowing that someone is a great artist, their outrageous rudeness might be interpreted as an aspect of 'artistic temperament' and hence regarded as insignificant compared with their flamboyant character and genius.

Resolving ambiguity and inconsistency

These strategies would both work where attitudes towards a particular object are generally consistent. But often they are not – people can have ambivalent attitudes that evaluate an object both positively and negatively. This is well encapsulated in a slogan used for selling cream cakes: 'naughty but nice'. People often have ambivalent attitudes to their indulgences – food, alcohol, being lazy, and so on. They have cognitive information about the hazards they pose, but also emotional information about how pleasurable they are.

Experimental social psychology regards the need for consistency as a powerful force on cognition and has suggested three main psychological processes that enable people to resolve inconsistency in the information they have about a particular object.

- *Social judgements* can be made to prioritize particular information sources. For example, people tend to place greater reliance on information coming from more familiar (Zajonc 1968b), more attractive (Insko 1981) or more credible (Hovland and Weiss 1951) sources.
- *Priming* can increase the impact of subsequent information. Information tends to be interpreted in the context of prior information and affected by, for example, a mind-set induced by a particular activity. For example, Tourangeau and Rasinski (1988) primed subjects in their study by asking them a series of pointed and biased questions before assessing their political attitudes. The attitudes expressed reflected the priming bias.
- *Increased depth of processing* can raise the salience of information. Depth of processing affects the extent to which information is attended to and understood. Information that is consciously and actively processed tends to have more effect than information processed automatically, and hence to influence its impact upon attitudinal evaluation (Hovland *et al.* 1953). For instance, people attend most to that information which is most personally relevant to them.

These processes have received most attention in studies of attitude change, and we will look at them in more detail later in the chapter.

The functions of attitudes

There has been considerable experimental social psychological research and theorization into the functions that attitudes serve (see, for example, Smith *et al.* 1956; Shavitt 1989). Drawing on a range of theoretical frameworks, four main kinds of function have been established:

Object appraisal function

Attitudes are seen to have an object-appraisal function (sometimes called a knowledge function) that simplifies information processing and orientates attention to particular aspects of the attitude object. For example, if you find even the idea of eating raw fish (attitude object) disgusting (evaluation), you know you hate not only sushi but also Mexican ceviche and Swedish gravlax, as raw fish is a common ingredient in all of them. Drawing on information processing theory, Smith *et al.* (1956) saw attitudes as bringing together the different elements into connected whole, making it easier to rapidly categorize – and hence be able to respond to appropriately – people, things, ideas, and events. More recent theorizing based within the social cognition framework (see, for example, Judd and Kulik 1980) suggests that attitudes function as schemas (see Chapter 5).

Instrumental function

Attitudes are held to have an instrumental function (sometimes called a utilitarian function), that helps to steer behaviour in functional ways. Based originally on the principles of social learning theory, this views attitudes as allowing people to pursue rewarding outcomes and avoid unpleasant ones. If, for example, someone knows they hate going shopping then this encourages them to act in ways to avoid shopping trips.

Social identity function

Since attitudes allow us to express values (Katz 1960), expressing attitudes enables a person to identify with and be identified by others sharing similar values. Social identity theory (see Chapters 8 and 9) stresses the role of identification with an ingroup in promoting a positive identity.

Self-esteem maintenance function

People can adopt particular attitudes as a means to distance themselves from those who threaten their self-image and to align themselves with those who enhance it. Drawing on the psychodynamic theory, Katz (1960) saw this as an **ego-defence** mechanism. From social identity theory Cialdini *et al.* (1976) claimed that identification with a prestigious ingroup allows people to 'bask in reflected glory'. Hence they theorized that positive attitudes to ingroups enable people to bolster their self-esteem and negative attitudes to outgroups allow them to distance themselves from groups who threaten their self-esteem.

Variations in the salience of functions

Shavitt (1989) recognized that attitudes will generally serve a number of functions simultaneously. Other work suggests that the salience of these functions differ between people. Snyder and DeBono (1987), for example, have gained support for their proposal that people differ in their degree of **self-monitoring**. Those who strongly monitor their behaviour to tailor it to different situations and circumstances tend to use attitudes for social identity purposes. By contrast those who engage in less self-monitoring, whose behaviour mainly reflects their own moods and disposition, tend to use their attitudes for value-expression.

Cultural differences

Evidence for cultural differences in attitudes is provided by a study comparing commercial advertisements used in the USA and in Korea (Han and Shavitt 1993). Advertising slogans in the USA stressed individualism – 'The art of being unique', 'You, only better', 'A leader among leaders'. The slogans used in Korean advertisements stressed harmonious relatedness – 'We have a way of bringing people together', 'Sharing is beautiful', 'We devote ourselves to our contractors'. Han and Shavitt showed that US and Korean subjects did indeed respond differently to the two kinds of slogan. US subjects preferred the ones that stressed individual values and the Korean subjects preferred those that centred on harmonious relationships. These differences have also been found in a study of political advertisements (Tak *et al.* 1997).

Results like these pose a challenge to experimental social psychology's theorization about the functions of attitudes, in that it tends to overemphasize the importance of functions serving self-esteem, and underemphasize those serving group-esteem. I would therefore argue that it is more useful to define attitudes as having the following four functions:

- an **organizational function**, where, by categorizing objects in the social world along evaluative dimensions, attitudes act as guides to help people – as individuals and collectively – attend to these objects, understand them and feel about them
- an **instrumental function**, where attitudes direct people to act within the social world in ways that enable them to pursue their goals, both individual and collective
- an **expressive function**, where attitudes allow individuals and collectives to communicate their beliefs, opinions and values, and, thereby, to identify with those individuals and groups who share them
- an **esteem function**, that enables individuals and collectives to achieve and maintain status, respect and honour.

Attitudes and behaviour

In the 1930s a sociologist, Richard LaPiere, took a Chinese couple on a three-month trip across the USA. They stopped at a total of 251 places like hotels, auto camps and restaurants on the trip, and only once did the staff refuse to serve them, even though people in the USA were generally hostile toward the Chinese people at the time. 'It appeared that a genial smile was the most effective password to acceptance. My Chinese friends were skilful smilers,' commented LaPiere, 'which may account in part for the fact that we received but one rebuff in our experiences' (LaPiere 1934: 232). Yet when he later wrote to all the establishments and asked if they would be willing to 'accept members of the Chinese race as guests', of the half who replied, only one said yes, all the rest (92 per cent) said they would not.

LaPiere's study is often held up to show that attitudes do not predict behaviour, though this is hardly fair. Given that the people answering the letters were not those who actually served the Chinese couple, it was hardly a study of any individual's attitudes. It remains, however, that initial experimental attempts to link attitudes with behaviour were not very successful. Reviewing what was, bluntly, a pretty awful catalogue of failure, Wicker (1969) was highly pessimistic about the possibility of ever demonstrating a simple and reliable connection between the attitudes that people express and what they actually do. In another review 20 years later McGuire called this the continuing 'scandal of social psychology' (McGuire 1986: 91).

Others (see, for example, Zanna and Fazio 1982) have been much more optimistic, arguing that in order for attitudes to predict behaviour, more thorough and subtle research design is necessary. Five main principles have been established:

1 The behaviour must be at the same level of specificity as the attitude.
2 The attitude must be held with sufficient strength to influence the behaviour.
3 The behaviour tested must be salient to the attitude at the time of testing.
4 There must be sufficient opportunities for people to act in response to the attitude.
5 Social desirability effects need to be excluded.

Attitudinal specificity

Many of the unsuccessful studies had tried to predict specific behaviour from very general attitudinal concepts. Fishbein and Ajzen (1975) have proposed a principle of correspondence – that attitudes and behaviour should be measured at the same level of specificity. When there is a high level of specificity in the behaviour observed, prediction is much better. Weigel *et al.* (1976) for instance assessed people's attitudes to general ideas (such as attitudes to 'protecting the environment') and to more specific ones (such as support for the Sierra Club, a specific organization working to protect the environment). They then gave subjects the opportunity to do volunteer work for the Sierra Club. Subjects' attitudes to protecting the environment in general were not predictive of volunteering, but support for the Sierra Club was.

Attitudinal strength

In most situations a person's behaviour will be influenced by a number of different attitudes, motives and concerns. For instance, Insko and Schopler (1967) demonstrated that although an individual may express strongly positive attitudes to the American Civil Rights movement, they may well not give money to support it because of a stronger concern to spend money on the needs of their family. Approval of the movement was insufficiently important to persuade someone to donate to it.

The relative strength of an attitude depends on a wide variety of factors (discussed in more detail in the section on attitude change). These include its power to invoke strong emotions, the extent to which the individual holding it is directly involved, and the conviction with which it is held (depending, for instance, on the source of information from which it is derived).

Attitudinal salience

Shavitt and Fazio (1991) gained evidence for the importance of salience using a priming technique. They examined students' attitudes to two drinks – 7-Up and Perrier. They hypothesized that 7-Up would be more appealing in terms of its taste, but Perrier more attractive in terms of its 'cool' image. They thus began the experiment by asking the students to rate food items on a 20-point scale, either on their 'taste' or their 'image'. They then assessed the students' attitudes towards the two drinks and their intention to buy them. Intention to buy proved a more effective measure. As predicted, students primed to focus on image evinced a significantly stronger intention to buy Perrier than 7-Up, whereas students primed to focus on taste stated a greater intention to buy 7-Up.

Behavioural opportunities

Second, many of the unsuccessful studies observed only a single behavioural expression of the attitude assessed. Given that there are many things that may influence behaviour in a particular circumstance, it is difficult to sufficiently exclude these extraneous variables to obtain a clear-cut result. Increasing the number of measures taken leads to far better predictability. In another study examining attitudes to protecting the environment Weigel and Newman (1976) gave respondents 14 separate opportunities to take pro-environmental action. These included opportunities to sign a number of petitions, to recycle their rubbish over several weeks and to recruit friends to do so too. While there were only limited (though often significant) correlations between overall support for the environment and individual pro-environment actions, an aggregate of compliance with all fourteen actions yielded a strong correlation.

Excluding social desirability effects

People are often unwilling to act out their attitudes because to do so would show them in an unflattering light. As the behaviour of the hotel and restaurant owners in LaPiere's study showed, people generally do not act in a prejudiced manner when presented with specific people in specific situations, especially when to do so would transgress social rules (such as those of courtesy). A large number of studies have demonstrated that people have a strong tendency to act in ways that make them look good, called the **social desirability effect** (Rosenburg 1969).

In order to study attitudes that may reflect badly on someone, it is necessary to use a more sophisticated approach. A good example is the study by Gaertner and McLaughlin (1983) you met in Chapter 3. They studied racist behaviour using an implicit measure (reaction times to making judgements) and inferred racist attitudes from subjects taking longer to give a positive response to a pairing of Black–smart compered with White–smart.

Expectancy value models

Bohner (2001) makes the point that the majority of studies on the links between attitudes and behaviour are based on correlations between measures. Correlation tells us that two measures are linked – but it does not tell us whether one causes the other, nor, if they do, which is the cause and which is the effect. Do attitudes make people behave in certain ways, or do their actions determine their attitudes?

To answer questions like these, experimental social psychologists decided it is necessary to develop more sophisticated explanatory theories that directly predict *how* attitudes will affect behaviour. The ones they developed located the attitude–behaviour link within more general theories of the ways people decide how to act in specific circumstances, in particular by bringing consideration of motivation into the frame.

In this field such theoretical models are generally called **expectancy-value models**. Broadly they assume that people decide between alternative courses of action through estimating the probabilities for each possible action that it will bring about benefits and/or avoid negative consequences to themselves. In other words, these models assume that people will act to optimize the consequences of their behaviour, based on their own views about what outcomes are most valuable.

The theory of reasoned action

The best known of these theoretical models has been developed by Ajzen and Fishbein (see, for example, Ajzen and Fishbein 1972; Fishbein and Ajzen 1975). In its initial formulation it was called the **theory of reasoned action**. The model differed in a number of ways from the assumption that attitudes simply trigger behaviour. First, it did not try to predict behaviour but rather the behavioural intentions that are assumed to mediate behaviour. Second, it acknowledged that attitudes are not the sole drivers determining behaviour. So the model includes a person's appraisal of what they think others will expect them to do (social norms) and their motivation to comply with these norms, and also takes account of a person's beliefs about the consequences of the behaviour and their evaluation of those consequences (values). The model is illustrated in Figure 6.3.

Figure 6.3
Schematic illustration of Ajzen and Fishbein's theory of reasoned action
Source: After Gergen and Gergen 1981

According to this model, an individual's intention to perform a given act can be worked out mathematically, by calculating the contributions to decision-making from two main sources:

- **Attitudes** towards performing the act, calculated by multiplying measures of their beliefs about outcomes and of their evaluation of the benefits of outcomes
- **Subjective norms**, calculated by measures of what they think others expect them to do (normative beliefs) multiplied by measures of their motivation to comply.

The theory of reasoned action has been shown to be much better at predicting a variety of behavioural intentions and behaviour than a simple attitude scale on its own. Examples include studies on health-related behaviours (as illustrated above) and consumer choices. A meta-analytic review of the theory's success conducted by Sheppard *et al.* (1988) looked at 87 studies and reported significant levels of prediction for both behavioural intentions and behaviour. More recent reviews (for example Sutton 1998) have also demonstrated the theory's predictive ability.

The theory of planned behaviour

The theory of planned behaviour was developed in order to fine-tune predictability. Ajzen (1991) extended the scope of the model to include an additional element – perceived behavioural control. This was done to recognize that in some situations people have only a limited ability to control what they are able to do.

Ajzen tested this new model in a study examining US business students' behavioural intentions towards and actual achievement of gaining an A grade in an examination (Ajzen and Madden 1986). They hypothesized that estimates of behavioural control – whether or not they thought they could get an A – would improve predictability, and it did, both in terms of behavioural intention and behaviour. Further they hypothesized that early in the semester the students would not be able to predict their level of behavioural control as well as they could closer to the exam. This too was confirmed in both cases. However, estimates of behavioural control are found to be less salient in situations where it is much easier to achieve the behaviour in question, such as attending a meeting (Kelly and Breinlinger 1995).

Attitudes

Attitudes
- Are evaluations of attitude objects and operate at personal, interpersonal and intergroup levels
- Have cognitive, emotional and behavioural components
- Are measured using attitude scales; the best known is a Lickert scale
- Can be seen to have four main functions: organizational (categorizing knowledge), instrumental (guiding behaviour and cognition), expressive (for communication), and esteem (both personal and collective).

Attitudes and behaviour
- Attempts to predict behaviour from general attitudes were not successful
- Predictability can be improved by excluding social undesirability effects, and/or increasing specificity or strength of the attitude, salience of the behaviour, or behavioural opportunities
- Predictability can be further improved by combining assessment of attitudes with assessment of other variables such as social norms and values.

ATTITUDE CHANGE

If attitudes are a preoccupation in social psychology, attitude change is not far short of an obsession. This arises in large part from its humaneering mission (Chapter 1) to 'make the world a better place', but also because it is a field in which social psychology's expertise can be applied to practical issues and concerns (such as advertising and political campaigning).

Cognitive consistency

Cognitive consistency is regarded as one of the main reasons why people change their attitudes. Cognitive consistency theory is based on the assumption that people will tend to organize their attitudes in ways that maintain consistency and, where inconsistencies arise, act to restore equilibrium – for example, between the attitudes they hold towards issues and their attitudes to people.

Balance theory

Heider (1946) proposed an early version of this that he called **balance theory**. In it he proposed that people seek balance in their attitudes. For example, if a man wanted to take his girlfriend – of whom he is very fond – on a trip to New York, but knew she hated the place, there would be an imbalance between his affection for her and his desire to go to New York. So, to regain balance, he could adjust his attitude to New York ('Actually, I never liked the place that much'). Or he could modify his feelings about his girlfriend ('She's getting to be a bit of a killjoy'). Or he could try to persuade her what a great place New York was really ('It has great museums – you love museums'). Any one would bring things back into balance again.

Various studies (for example Jordan 1953; Zajonc 1968a) have showed that people find balanced attitudinal situations more comfortable than unbalanced ones. Zajonc and Burnstein (1965) have also showed that people find balanced situations easier to process and remember. Balance theory has been used to explain why people tend to like others better if they share similar attitudes (see, for example, Newcomb 1961).

Cognitive consistency theory

People sometimes behave in ways that contradict their attitudes. During the Korean war, for instance, US soldiers were interned in Chinese prisoner-of-war camps. At the start of their captivity they were strongly opposed to communism. During their time there, these soldiers were exposed to considerable pressure to reconsider their attitudes. On their return home, many of them said that, while it might not work in the USA, communism 'is a good thing for Asia' (Segal 1954).

Cognitive dissonance theory was devised to account for attitude change in such situations. Its originator, Leon Festinger (1957), argued that when people realize that they have acted in ways that conflict with their attitudes they experience anxiety and tension. They need to deal with this, but they cannot go back and undo what they did. So they change the only thing they can change – their attitudes.

Festinger and Carlsmith (1959) tested this by conducting an experiment where subjects were first asked to do an incredibly boring and repetitive series of tasks. Once they had finished, the experimenter asked some of them to take the place of an assistant who had failed to turn up, who was supposed to motivate subjects in the next experimental condition. Their task was to convince the next subject that the tasks they were about to do would be interesting. There were three conditions: some subjects were not asked to lie at all, some subjects were paid $1 to lie, and some were paid $10 to lie. The subjects then all rated the experiment according to how much they enjoyed doing it. Those who did not lie and those paid $10 to lie reported enjoying the experiment, on average, at about the same level (that is not much!). Those, however, who lied and were only paid $1 rated the experiment as significantly more enjoyable.

Payment is not the only way to manipulate dissonance. Studies of **group initiation** have also shown cognitive dissonance effects. Aronson and Mills (1959), for instance, found that those women who experienced a **severe initiation** on joining a group discussion rated a taped discussion as significantly more interesting than either those who underwent no initiation or the mild initiation (who did not differ significantly from each other).

Since Festinger first proposed the theory, there has been extensive research into the process of cognitive dissonance. This has led to considerable clarification of the elements involved. The inconsistent act must

- *Matter*: While some recent research suggests that inconsistency is enough in itself (for example, Johnson *et al.* 1995; Harmon-Jones *et al.* 1996), a much larger number show that the inconsistency needs to have negative consequences (for example Scher and Cooper 1989). In particular, actions that damage self-esteem or self-worth have been found to have most impact on attitudes (for example Steele 1988). We may surmise that in relational-self cultures, undermining of group worth or violation of group honour would have the strongest effects.
- *Be volitional*: When coerced or merely lavishly rewarded for acting inconsistently, there is no dissonance because the person can explain away their behaviour. Festinger and Carlsmith's (1959) study is a good example here.
- *Make the person anxious*: Croyle and Cooper (1983) tested this by attaching electrodes to subjects' fingers to measure their arousal while they were writing counter-attitudinal essays. They found that indeed, only in dissonance conditions (that is where subjects believed they were freely choosing to write the essays) were levels of arousal raised.
- *Be seen as the cause of the anxiety*: This has been demonstrated in a number of studies. Pittman (1975) for example tricked subjects into believing the anxiety they felt was due to having to wear prism goggles while writing the essay. In this situation there was no attitude change.

Persuasion

Persuasion is where a deliberate attempt is made to change people's attitudes and is concerned with the cognitive processes involved in how that change is brought about. As with issues around the link between attitudes and behaviour, it is generally agreed among experimental social psychologists that persuasion works differently according to the level of processing involved in the change process (Petty and Cacioppo 1981).

Persuasion via automatic processing

While some attitudinal responses involve conscious judgements (Wilson and Hodges 1992), often attitudes are triggered unconsciously and automatically (Bargh *et al.* 1992). This kind of 'automatic' attitude change may affect other judgements without the person being aware of its influence. One interesting example is that people in the USA tend to like the letters in their own name better than other letters (Nuttin, 1985). Such attitudes are called **implicit attitudes**. As we saw in Chapter 5 in relation to attribution, **automatic processing** is where people take in information and respond to it with little conscious awareness or cognitive effort.

Early theorists drew from learning theory to suggest that attitudes can be changed through the process of conditioning, where associative links are made between two otherwise unrelated things. Music, for example, can be very good at creating a 'feel-good' association, and has been shown to favourably influence approval ratings of products (Galzio and Hendrick 1972). Even quite trivial and fleeting associations can have an effect. Copper *et al.* (1993) demonstrated this by showing subjects simulated news broadcasts reporting on political candidates, where they varied whether or not the 'reporter' smiled when mentioning each candidate. While the subjects' evaluations of the candidates tended mainly to reflect their own political allegiances, the smiles also had a small but significant positive impact. Smiles associated with the opponent candidate led subjects to give a slightly better rating to him, and a slightly worse rating to their preferred candidate.

Operant conditioning is where people change their behaviour in response to either a regime of rewards (called reinforcement) or punishments (negative reinforcement). An early example is where Hildum and Brown (1956) interviewed students about their attitudes about university policies. In one condition they rewarded subjects for agreeing with the policies during the interview. Every time the student said anything good about the policies, the interviewer made approving noises ('Yes', 'Right' or just 'Mm-hmm'). In the other condition students were rewarded whenever they criticized university policies. Students' views on university policies were then evinced and, sure enough, those who had been rewarded for criticizing the policies in the interview reported less favourable attitudes to the policies than those students who had been rewarded for agreeing with them.

Beware experimenter effects!

Effects like those shown in the last two studies bring home how easy it is for a researcher to influence what participants in a study say and do – called **experimenter effects**. Even though an experimenter may not intend to 'give the game away', they can do so in all sorts of subtle ways. Survey interviewers are trained, for example, to give only neutral rejoinders to interviewees' responses, in order not to contaminate the results.

A final example of automatic processing is **heuristic processing**, where people are induced to change their attitudes through their tendency to resort to simple 'rules of thumb' to assess the quality of information they are given. Examples include 'What looks good is good', 'If I feel good, it must be good', 'I agree with people I like', 'I trust people who are credible' and 'The majority is usually right'.

Just as with the other examples of automatic processing, a person does not need to be aware of using heuristics and is frequently not. Heuristics are most generally used when someone has little motivation or opportunity to get bogged down in careful deliberation – they follow the 'principle of least cognitive effort' (Bohner *et al.* 1995). People often assume that 'what is beautiful is good', for example (Dion *et al.* 1972). Mere physical attractiveness in a person tends to lead to approval of that person in general – they are seen as more able, more confident and more trustworthy (Eagly *et al.* 1991 provide a review of the evidence). Advertisements often use popular celebrities – who, by definition, are chosen because they are attractive to particular consumer groups – to endorse their products, working on both the 'what is beautiful is good' and the 'I agree with people I like' heuristics. Empirical evidence for the effects of these heuristics on attitudes has been provided, for instance, by Chaiken (1987).

There have also been numerous studies demonstrating the effectiveness of the 'I trust people who are credible' heuristic in changing attitudes. An early study by Hovland and Weiss (1951) varied the credibility of the person communicating a message intended to influence attitudes, and found that people tend to be more swayed by the expertise of the message-giver rather than the arguments used.

Persuasion via depth-processing

Two models have been developed here, one building on the other. The first, a communication model, had its origins in Information Theory Approaches. As this got refined, the focus moved to its cognitive elements. There was then a shift to a cognitive response model.

The communication model

The importance of in-depth processing for attitude change was first conceptualized as a matter of communication. Hovland and his colleagues (1953) identified three key aspects of communication that relate to persuasion: the *source* of the message (the communicator), the *message*, and the *audience* (see Chapter 4) and argued that factors pertaining to each have the capacity to determine whether attitudes can be changed.

- the source – the *communicator* – can vary, for example, in terms of their expertise, trustworthiness, **attractiveness** and so on, and in how they deliver the message (how articulate they are or how clearly or quickly they speak).
- the *message* can differ, for example, in terms of the strength of its arguments, the order in which they are presented, its contents and whether, for instance, it simply promotes a single viewpoint or offers a balanced appraisal.
- the *audience* can vary, for instance, in terms of people's self-esteem, their self-interest or whether they feel they are being manipulated or not.

Hovland and his colleagues identified four stages in the persuasion process:

Attention ➜ Comprehension ➜ Acceptance ➜ Retention

This research went on for more than 30 years, during which time they gradually documented how each of the three aspects affected the different processes (see Petty and Cacioppo 1981 for a review). Some of their findings have proved robust – for example, that expert communicators tend to gain message acceptance better than non-experts (Hovland and Weiss 1951) and that attractive communicators are more effective than unattractive ones (Kiesler and Kiesler 1969). But other findings have proven less so. Janis (1954) claimed to show that people with low self-esteem were easier to persuade than people with high self-esteem. However, subsequent work (Baumeister and Covington 1985) has suggested that this is not so. Their claim is that people with high self-esteem are persuaded, but they are less prepared to admit it.

What has endured is an acceptance within experimental social psychology that persuasion works in stages, where a series of steps need to follow one from the other to bring about attitude change. There are disagreements about what are the most crucial stages and how they work, but there is a fair consensus that the audience needs to pay attention to the message, understand its contents and actively consider what it signifies for them (Eagly and Chaiken 1984).

The cognitive response model

The approach that focuses on this latter stage – the active consideration of what the message signifies – shifted theorization about attitudes into the social cognition paradigm, where it has been developed as a cognitive response model of persuasion (see, for example, Greenwald 1968). Its assumptions are as follows:

- people actively relate the content of the message to their prior knowledge about the attitude object and their current attitude towards it. In so doing they make cognitive responses – new ideas or thoughts about the attitude object.
- it is these cognitive responses that mediate attitude change.
- the degree and direction of the change is determined by the overall number and direction of the cognitive responses. If, on balance, there are more that are favourable to the new argument than unfavourable, then attitude change will happen.

Processing level models of persuasion

As with attribution theory, since the 1980s most research in this field has been based on a recognition that persuasion generally involves two kinds of processing: superficial-processing and in-depth processing. In the attitude field, two alternative, processing level models have been devised: an elaboration likelihood model and a heuristic–semantic model.

The elaboration likelihood model

This model proposes that persuasion works via two routes: a *central route* that involves active, purposive, in-depth processing, and a *peripheral route* that operates via mindless processing such as conditioning or the use of heuristics. The two are seen as antagonistic to each other (Petty and Cacioppo 1986). According to this model, generally the peripheral route wins out, since people mostly go about their lives more or less on 'automatic', filtering out the messages with which they are bombarded. Only in exceptional situations do they stop to really think about a message they receive – situations where they are motivated and able to pay attention to it.

Motivation and opportunity thus create the conditions that encourage people to elaborate. However, when they do, the impact on their attitudes is stronger and more durable. An example is where a communicator is somebody important to you, and they express an unexpected opinion at variance to your own. The research studies conducted to develop this theory were complex and subtle, and beyond the scope of this chapter. Bohner (2001) provides a detailed review of them.

The heuristic–systematic model

This model claims that when people have to evaluate something they strive for sufficient confidence to make an informed decision:

- when they feel confident of their attitudes people are not motivated to process in-depth, and rely on heuristic processing (that is habitual 'rules of thumb') so long as they have a heuristic cue to act as a trigger.
- when they are ambivalent or uncertain, people are more likely to turn to in-depth systematic processing as long as the arguments in the message are strong and unambiguous.

In this model the threshold at which uncertainty 'kicks in' is seen to differ according to circumstances. When the judgement is important or personally very relevant, then the threshold will be low and hence **systematic processing** more likely. When buying a house or a car, for example, people usually devote considerable effort to making their choice. But when the judgement is trivial – such as choosing which flavour of ice cream to have for supper – then heuristics are more likely to carry the day. That is, unless it is somebody important coming for supper and you need to impress them! Again, the studies conducted to develop this model have been subtle and detailed, and Bohner's review is the place to go if you want to know more.

Attitude change

Cognitive consistency is where people change their attitude in line with unwarranted counter-attitudinal behaviour – for example, lie without sufficient justification.

- For it to work, the inconsistent act must matter, must be chosen, must make the person anxious, and must be explicitly associated with the anxiety.

Persuasion is where attempts are deliberately made to change behaviour through changing attitudes. Recent theorization suggests that persuasion can work in one of two ways, through:

- *Automatic attitude processes* where, for example, associations are made between the attitude object and 'feel good' music; or where heuristics (such as 'what is beautiful is good') are triggered. These are relatively easy to achieve, but tend to have a superficial effect.
- *In-depth attitude processes* where, for example, conditions are arranged so that people attend to persuasive messages. These are harder to achieve, but tend to have a stronger and more enduring effect.

Different mechanisms have been suggested to explain what it is that determines whether processing is automatic or in-depth.

FURTHER READING

Values

Rokeach, M. (1973) *The Nature of Human Values*. New York: Free Press.
> Not always easy to get hold of, this is, of course, the classic book on this subject. It is actually a pretty user-friendly read, and a fascinating glimpse, along the way, of what the world was like in the USA in the 1960s.

Smith, B. and Harris Bond, M. (1993) *Social Psychology across Cultures*. Hemel Hempstead: Harvester Wheatsheaf.
> If you want to know more about the surveys of values carried out by Hofstede, the Chinese Culture Connection and Schwartz, they are described in a lot more detail here. The book also provides an excellent review of cross-cultural psychology generally.

Schwartz, S.H. (1994) Cultural dimensions of values: towards an understanding of national differences, in U. Kim, H.C. Triandis and G. Yoon (eds) *Individualism and Collectivism: Theoretical and Methodological Issues*. Newbury Park, CA: Sage
> A fine detailed – but it is fascinating fine detail – analysis of the research programme he has led exploring values cross-culturally.

Attitudes

Hogg, M.A. and Vaughan, G.M. (1998) *Social Psychology*, 2nd edn. Hemel Hempstead: Prentice Hall.

> This textbook, in my view, provides the most accessible, balanced and comprehensive account of attitudes (and even a brief coverage of values). Chapter 4 has an extensive overview of attitudes and their measurement, and Chapter 5 gives a detailed account of research on attitude change.

Bohner, G. (2001) Attitudes, in M. Hewstone and W. Stroebe (eds) *Introduction to Social Psychology*, 3rd edn. Oxford: Blackwell.

> This is a lot more mainstream, and considerably denser. You can begin to feel a bit overloaded as he ploughs relentlessly through study after study, theory after theory. But as a scholarly and comprehensive review of attitude theory and research, it is hard to beat.

QUESTIONS

1 Should social psychologists take the study of values more seriously than they currently do?
2 What can social psychology learn from cross-cultural studies of values?
3 Under what circumstances can attitudes predict behaviour?
4 What function do attitudes serve?
5 If you wanted to plan an advertising campaign for a new product, how could different-process models of attitude change help?

Chapter 7

Constructing the social world

Chapter contents

A route map of the chapter

The chapter is divided into three sections. It begins with a section on an approach to theory and research that is (usually) located more in sociological social psychology than in critical social psychology – social representations. In this first section the history and key elements of the social representations approach are described, and these are illustrated by a study carried out in the 1960s into social representations of health and illness.

The second section covers discursive theory – that is, the theoretical basis of discourse analytical research. It starts by looking at discursive practices theory, illustrating this with a conversation analysis study of refusals to unwanted sexual advances. It then looks at discursive resources theory, and this is illustrated by the narrative approach.

The final section then works through the positions taken by discursive psychology in relation to theory and research into attitudes and attribution. From this analysis, it ends by briefly exploring the way that language can be used to 'play tricks' with agency.

Social representations

⬇

Discursive theory

⬇

Discursive approaches to attitudes and attribution

Learning objectives

When you have completed your study on this and earlier chapters, you should be able to:

1 Make a clear exposition of critical social psychology's perception of what constitutes the social world, and summarize some of the ways in which the construction of social reality has been theorized.
2 Outline the key elements of social representations theory.
3 Describe the social representations of health and illness that Herzlich identified in her study.
4 Distinguish between discursive practices and discursive resources approaches to discursive theory, and outline the key features of each.
5 Describe what is entailed in conversation analysis and give an example of how it has been applied.
6 Summarize what is meant by narrative psychology and give an example of how it has been applied.
7 Review discursive psychology's criticisms of mainstream work on attitudes and attribution, and describe its alternative approach to these psychological constructs.
8 Define what is meant by 'agency' within critical social psychology, and explain its theoretical significance.

INTRODUCTION

Critical social psychology works from the assumption that the social world is constructed, and that the constructive systems, structures and processes that create social worlds are seen to operate

- *Intersubjectively*: that is, through people's interactions with each other and their social practices towards each other, both as individuals and as collectivities
- *Semiotically*: that is, by way of the meanings and significance they accord to social events, practices and phenomena.

This ontological position starkly contrasts with that taken by experimental social psychology, that views the social world as external to and separate from people. If you remember the analogy from Chapter 1, experimental social psychology has an image of the social world as something like an ocean, in which people are immersed. Critical social psychology views the social world as more like music-making, that only exists when and because people are making it. It sees the social world as people *experience* it and the social world as people *make* it as two facets of the same thing.

Given this radically different conception of the social world, it is hardly surprising that critical social psychology approaches the topics you have covered in the last two chapters from a completely different perspective. Its theorizing is not about 'attitudes' or 'attribution', but concerned with the ways in which social worlds are produced, what produces them, and, crucially, how they 'work' – how people operate within and through them to live their lives and achieve their goals. Equally – as you have seen already in Chapters 2 and 3 – critical social psychology uses quite different research strategies, methods and analytics to gain insight and understanding of the structures, processes and practices involved both in constructing social worlds and social realities, and in operating within them.

This chapter reviews the key elements of this research and theorization. It offers a combination of two things – commentaries on and critiques of experimental social psychology's work in these fields, and also alternative theoretical frameworks to account for how the social world is 'constructed' from within rather than 'understood' from the outside.

SOCIAL REPRESENTATIONS

The term *social representation* was adopted by Serge Moscovici in the 1960s as one which could form a bridge between the sociologist Emile Durkheim's concepts of **collective representations** and **individual representations**. Potter and Wetherell (1987) have pointed out that the theory base of this concept is difficult to describe, because Moscovici's writings are fragmented and contradictory, and his followers have interpreted them in different ways. Nevertheless the concept of social representation has had a very substantial impact upon social psychology, particularly in Europe. This has been, I believe, because of its usefulness as a concept rather than an articulated theory. It offers social psychologists a framework for sophisticated theorization about the social production and manipulation of knowledge, and how this may influence and be influenced by individual thinking. As such it provides a way to span the gap between traditional concerns with subjectivity and new ones about intersubjectivity.

Moscovici drew social psychologists' attention to the way that people make sense of the world as much within the 'unceasing babble and . . . permanent dialogue between individuals' (Moscovici 1985: 18) as within individual minds. Social representations theory is semiotic in all but name, stressing the importance of shared understandings, both as a medium for communication between people and a basis for social groups to share a social world. Moscovici has claimed that it is the sharing of common social representations among a number of people that *makes* them a cohesive social group rather than a collection of individuals. In this he was going a step beyond experimental social psychology's concepts like cohesiveness and social norms (see Chapter 9) and arguing that the boundaries between one social group and another can be identified by finding out where the influence of their different social representations begin and end.

Moscovici has speculated extensively about the ways that the knowledge and images that constitute the social representations of one group get to be taken up and incorporated into the social representations of another, and changed in the process. In particular, he has been interested in the ways that the common-sense representations of 'ordinary people' take into their discourse – and in so doing distort – expert knowledge (for example scientific knowledge). Common themes with Bartlett's ideas (see Chapter 5) can be discerned, where the adoption of knowledge from one group by another consists of processes of oversimplification, of categorization, and of rationalizing. In his own earliest work (Moscovici [1961] 1976) explored the way psychodynamic concepts (for example 'complex') were taken from the domain of professional psychiatry into the discourse of everyday life. A later example of his work (Moscovici and Hewstone 1983) was about the way ideas of brain lateralization have been taken up and popularized. As a result they have now been recast as a full-blown theory about our 'intuitive' right side and 'analytic' left.

Social representations of health and illness

An example to help you get to grips with what is involved in social representations research is a study conducted by Claudine Herzlich on people's social representations of health and illness that was published in French in the 1960s but translated into English only in the 1970s (Herzlich 1973). She has, since then, gone on exploring different aspects of people's understandings of and ideas about health, illness, recovery and dying, including a fascinating analysis of social representations of plagues at different historical periods (Herzlich and Pierret 1987).

For her original study, Herzlich carried out a large number of interviews with predominantly middle-class Parisians (and a few country dwellers) which focused on health and illness. From the lengthy conversations she had with these people, she developed sophisticated descriptions of the social representations for health and illness that she saw as in use at that time in French society. Influenced by Foucault's theories and Moscovici's work on social representations of mental illness being done concurrently (Moscovici [1961] 1976), she regarded these social representations as operating both subjectively and intersubjectively. That is, she saw them in use at both the level of individual thinking and at the level of discourses functioning at an intersubjective level, including conversations, medical consultations and treatment, in the mass media and in public education campaigns.

Herzlich concluded that different understandings and explanations for health and illness are not polar opposites to each other, but quite discrete alternative conceptions. She demonstrated that individuals have access to multiple conceptions of what illness is, means and signifies, coexisting with formulations of different concepts of health.

Social representations of health

Herzlich identified these as **health-in-a-vacuum**, **reserve of health** and **equilibrium**.

Health-in-a-vacuum

This was the term Herzlich used for the notion of health as the absence of illness, of a lack of awareness of the body, and/or simply not being bothered by it, essentially a state of 'bodily silence'.

Reserve of health

This, she suggested, represents health as an asset or investment rather than a state. It has two main aspects: physical robustness or strength, and resistance to attacks, fatigue and illness. In this social representation, health is something that you 'have' that enables you to perform your job, fulfil your social obligations, defend yourself against disease, and recover from illness.

Equilibrium

The people in the study described equilibrium as 'real health' or 'health in its highest sense'. It carried the notion of positive well-being in addition to a sense of balance and harmony. Herzlich commented that although her respondents used the term 'equilibrium' frequently in their conversations, they found it hard to pin down. Overall it seemed to carry a two-level meaning: a substratum of essential harmony and balance in bodily, psychological and spiritual life – that then provides the basis for a functional sense of self-confidence, alertness, freedom, energy, and infatiguability. Thus it had both a psychological reality concerned with self-perception and a bodily reality to do with physical capability and resilience.

Social representations of illness

Herzlich's respondents distinguished between four different classes of illness: serious illnesses which may be fatal; chronic conditions; everyday, trivial illnesses like colds and flu; and childhood ailments. They also referred frequently to intermediary states between 'real' illness and 'real' health:

> There are the little troubles, the little situations of discomfort which you have more or less all the year round, headaches, the after-effects of alcohol, digestive difficulties, fatigue.
>
> (Herzlich 1973: 54)

These intermediate states were typified by links to mood (particularly depression and inertia); to their undesirable impact on relationships with others; and their tendency to be long-lasting. However, beyond this, in contrast to the well-articulated classification of aspects of health, understandings of illness were more vague, unsystematic and varied. There were attempts to distinguish illness from other states (for example accidents and physical disability) and a variety of dimensions were introduced: (for example severity, painfulness, curability). Despite this lack of clarity, however, Herzlich did identify three 'metaphors' for illness that distinguished between different social representations: illness as destroyer, illness as liberator, and illness as occupation.

Illness as destroyer

Herzlich found this image was most salient to people who were or had been particularly active or engaged in society, and for whom any interference with their professional or family role presented a serious problem. Their focus was upon the way illness could limit their ability to carry out their duties and responsibilities, and the concomitant loss of social position and subsequent social isolation they would therefore suffer whenever they were ill. Bound together in this social representation were fundamental assumptions about having obligations to others and to their work, and the ability for dependency to make them feel 'less of a person'. When people saw illness as a 'destroyer', they stressed the positive aspects of health. They responded to illness, paradoxically, both by trying to assume control (by denying it, or by keeping going as if they were not ill) and by feeling impotent (by 'giving up' when they could no longer function). People for whom this metaphor was the one guiding their behaviour avoided doctors at all costs, and would do almost anything rather than accept the label 'ill'.

Illness as liberator

This, in contrast, is a metaphor that stresses the capacity of illness to free the individual from their responsibilities or the pressures that life places upon them:

> When I'm very tired, I often wish I were ill . . . illness is a kind of rest, when you can be free from your everyday burdens. . . . For me, illness is breaking off from social life, from life outside and social obligations, it's being set free.
>
> (Herzlich 1973: 114)

The benefits of illness were seen as making possible the kind of intellectual activity that is usually prevented by the pressures of everyday life. The solitude of illness was seen in this context to be enjoyable. And there were privileges to be gained, including the sympathy and care of others. Herzlich argued that within this perception are provided the seeds of the 'invalid' personality. Bound up in it is a vision of 'being an invalid' allowing self-knowing; that experiencing illness can enrich your understanding of what matters in your life and force upon you a better and more valid set of values. Overall illness as 'liberation' is founded on the belief that experiencing illness is a route through which an individual can attain greater self-knowledge.

Illness as occupation

This metaphor is based on the assumption that when you are ill, you should see illness as a challenge – as something that you must fight with all the powers you have. It stresses that an enormous amount of strength and willpower are needed to focus all your energies on recovery. You must not worry about your other responsibilities, but concentrate on getting better. Within this conception Herzlich found there was a strong theme of 'mind over matter'.

Social representations and attitude theory

Although these three descriptions tend to read as though people could be classified according to holding one or other perception, Herzlich was at pains to point out that only some individuals tended to utilize a single representation consistently. Most people drew upon two or all three at different times in their interviews, offering complex understandings and explanations woven out of them all. This is an important distinction between attitude theory and social representations theory. Attitude theory assumes that people have a single attitude – that, for example, they are strongly racist, full stop. Social constructionist approaches view the situation as different from and vastly more complicated than this. From this perspective people can and do express a wide range of opinions, that can and do contradict each other. This is because they are drawing on different discourses at different points in a conversation to do different things.

Herzlich argued that this is true in relation to social representations. They can be used singly or in concert to, for example, make sense of illness and respond to it. But they also affect the way people see themselves and made sense of their own identity generally, even when they are well. They are, Herzlich concluded, particularly salient when people are in intermediate states between being ill and being well. Social representations thus act as resources that a person can use in different ways in different situations and in different bodily states.

The disjunction between the different kinds of representations of health and of illness meant that understandings of what makes a person healthy were different from explanations about why people get ill. Predominantly being and becoming healthy were seen as a matter of individual strength and resistance, of a capacity to adjust and find harmony between the self and the environment, in part a kind of 'natural heritage' of bodily strength, in part a product of self-fulfilment. Health was represented as something inside the individual. Illness, conversely, was construed as the result of assaults upon health from the outside such as pollution, the wear and tear of modern life, the pressures of confinement. It also included the effects of behaviour (for example staying up late, not eating sensibly). But these were usually seen as themselves a product of a particular 'way of life' – as dysfunctional responses to the root cause of ill health: the stress, fatigue and pressure of urban living (and less frequently, of country living):

> You could say that now, with the life we lead, certain diseases are increasing because our body no longer reacts because it no longer has enough resistance. . . . Modern life induces a kind of fatigue which makes us ill . . . everything to do with modern work and its conditions makes us more vulnerable to most diseases.
>
> (Herzlich 1973: 21)

Bibliographic analyses of social representations changing over time

Later work carried out with Janine Pierret (Herzlich and Pierret 1987) adopted an bibliographic approach which reviewed writings about health and illness, particularly about major 'scourges', plagues and other epidemics, from ancient times to the present, including diaries and letters as well as books and pamphlets. These sources of data showed that, irrespective of the time at which people were writing, they always made sense of bodily states of health and illness within much broader explanatory systems. These incorporated ideas about causation (such as climatic conditions and calamities like earthquakes). But they also addressed beliefs about relations within society to God, to moral codes and, from the time of the Industrial Revolution, to working conditions and the living conditions of the poor.

This later book provides a wealth of historical analysis, exploring changes over time in the way illness became individualized and medicalized. For example, concepts of plague tended to treat this as a collective scourge, understandable largely in moral terms or as the consequence of climatic variation or cosmic events (such as the appearance of comets). Later on, diseases such as consumption (tuberculosis) came to be regarded as experienced by and arising from within the individual, with the emergence of the notion of the 'sick person'. For example, despite being more widespread among the poor, it gained romantic connotations as an infliction that beset those of a passionate or artistic temperament.

Further on historically, Herzlich and Pierret traced the unfolding of a 'triumphant discourse' of the 'victories of medicine' (Herzlich and Pierret 1987: 46), due particularly to the introduction of vaccines and antibiotics. This image of an all-conquering medicine able to cure all ills was, they noted, still evident in the early stages of their research in the 1960s. But by the 1980s people had become more critical, concerned about illnesses like cancer that modern medicine seemed much less able to tackle. For some people at least, there was a recognition that health improvements related less to medical intervention than to improvements in living standards and natural changes in the disease organism. Coupled with this view have been growing expectations about the right to be sick and receive adequate treatment, and a growing conviction that 'modern life' is itself a major cause of sickness, both in terms of the pressures it imposes, and environmental factors such as pollution.

The accomplishments of social representations research

What Herzlich and her colleagues have done, therefore, has been to combine two quite different approaches to research. They have taken the data obtained in interviews and interpreted them via a social representations analysis; and they have taken historical texts and used these as data sources to trace the way that social representations change over time. As such their work is semiotic and intersubjective in its theory base. They looked both for continuity and for change; at both the historical roots of contemporary images and ideas, and at the way events have moulded and reformed them.

> Everywhere and in all periods, it is the individual who is sick, but he [*sic*] is sick in the eyes of his society, in relation to it, and in keeping with the modalities fixed by it. The language of the sick thus takes shape within the language expressing the relations between the individual and society. [Personal experiences sickness are thus] . . . woven into the collective patterns of thought that form the social reality of illness and the sick.
>
> (Herzlich and Pierret 1987: xi)

Social representations

Social representations theory was devised by Moscovici. It moves beyond not only 'attitudes' but also 'attributions', seeing them as interconnected and interwoven into broader social representations. Its main assumptions are:

- In any social group, there will be a number of shared social representations in operation. Indeed, sharing common social representations is what *makes* a social group a social group.
- The social representations available to a person enables them to make sense of their experiences and their life-world, and they use them to choose different courses of action in different situations. But, crucially, a person's social representations are not seen as locked in their individual mind. Rather they are culturally available and mediated resources, arising, for example, from the messages of the mass media, and in their interactions with experts (such as teachers or doctors).

Herzlich's study of social representations of health and illness identified three main representations of health operating in French society in the 1960s: health-in-a-vacuum, reserve of health and equilibrium. It also identified three for illness: illness as destroyer, as liberator and as occupation.

Herzlich and Pierret later examined the historical shifts and changes in social representations of illness, from the time of the plague to present day concerns about stress and cancer.

DISCURSIVE THEORY

You were introduced to discourse analysis in Chapter 3, as the main – certainly the most common – social constructionist approach to research. What holds discourse analysis together is not so much a method (there are different ways of applying it) but an analytic – a means of interpreting what is 'going on' when people communicate with each other. If you recall, there I distinguished between two main approaches:

- *Discursive practices* discourse analysis, which focuses on what people are doing and seeking to achieve when they communicate with each other
- *Discursive resources* discourse analysis, which focuses on the ways discourses operate within culture – their *textuality* and *tectonics*.

This section examines the key theoretical elements and principles upon which each of these analytical approaches are based.

Discursive practices theory

As described in Chapter 4, language is the most complex and sophisticated – and hence the most powerful – sign system, a system of signification. Social constructionism directs attention to the way that language, in particular, is used strategically to achieve particular goals. Given that they regard language as a sign system, critical social psychologists focus on speech – and the comprehension of speech – as behaviour. Research in this field studies speech behaviour in social interactions and generally uses some form of discourse analysis (as you met in Chapter 3).

   This kind of research is, by its nature, detailed and fine-grained, since it gets deeply 'into' the way language is used. It is therefore much more difficult to summarize than experimental social psychological studies. So I am going to concentrate mainly on just one illustration – a conversation analytic study. But before that I shall briefly look at discourse analysis as a semiotic approach to speech as a social practice.

Speech as a social practice

The theorization here was primarily developed by Potter and Wetherell (1987). It is mainly concerned with process rather than structure. Their interest is focused on what people *do* with discourse and what they are trying to achieve with different discursive strategies. They are much less interested in theorizing about the discourses themselves. The cornerstone of their argument has been that when people talk to each other, they use language purposefully. What they say always has a function, although this is not always explicit or obvious. The function will often have more to do with what individuals want to achieve than with what they are overtly expressing.

So, for example, when one of my guests at a dinner party said 'There are no buses round here at this time of night', I'm sure she wasn't lamenting the lack of transport provision around my home. It was obvious to me that, given the number of cocktails we had consumed, she was telling me she intended to stay the night! In discourse analysis, working out the function of talk is always a matter of interpreting it in its context, since the meaning and significance of such a statement depends on its social setting, the immediate motivations and goals of the speaker, and so on.

Potter and Wetherell (1987) challenge the assumption that people use language simply to communicate messages. People use language, they contend, in subtle, strategic ways that shift and change as the talk proceeds. They say inconsistent things and contradict themselves, and these, Potter and Wetherell argue, are often the most interesting thing going on. They describe people in their use of language as 'competent negotiators of reality' and suggest that social psychologists should stop trying to determine the universal laws of language use and instead explore the complex and sophisticated ways in which language is used to negotiate reality.

What, then, Potter and Wetherell's (1987) theory proposes is that people's language use and speech behaviour will vary according to what they are seeking to achieve at the time. In the act of expression they will construct a particular version of reality that makes sense and is functional at that moment. Thus as expressed understandings shift, moment by moment, so too will experienced reality. The understandings themselves are drawn from a repertoire of texts available via the person's broader culture or their closer social group. They are *linguistic repertoires* – used as commodities in social transactions, where people engage in complex processes of negotiation with each other over meanings and purposes. Potter and Wetherell's discourse analytic theory portrays individuals in dynamic tension between constructing reality and having it constructed for them.

In Chapter 3 you looked at an example of Potter and Wetherell's discourse analysis. The example I use here is of a different version, conversation analysis.

Conversation analysis

Conversation analysis (Psathas 1995; Sacks 1995; Hutchby and Wooffitt 1998) focuses on the units and forms of talk – such as conversational openings and closings, turn taking and repairs. It is the study of how people *use* talk in interaction, usually by scrutinizing naturally occurring talk. Examples include studies of the interactions between doctors and their patients (West 1984), and in judicial settings (Atkinson and Drew 1979). Conversation analysis is concerned with the 'natural organization' of talk (Psathas 1995) that arises from people tailoring their talk to the other person's. It looks at different kinds of conversational exchange – questions and answers, greetings, compliments and so on – and how these may be responsive to different settings and used for different purposes.

Just 'say no'

A study by Kitzinger and Frith (1999) shows the kind of thing this approach is seeking to do. In their study they examined what is going on when women seek to refuse unwanted sexual advances. To make sense of their data you will need to get to know some of the conventions used in conversation analysis for annotating text. These notations allow paralinguistic information to be included in the analysis.

Conversation analysis: transcription notations

[	overlapping speech
:	sound is drawn out (the more :::, the longer the drawing out)
text	emphasis
(.)	pause of less than 0.2 seconds
(0.2)	pause measured in seconds
.hhh	in-breath (the more hhh, the longer the in-breath)
hhh	out-breath (the more hhh, the longer the out-breath)
=	no pause
,	slight rising intonation

First Kitzinger and Frith (1999) made the point that refusing is harder *in general* than agreeing, starting off with examples of how an agreement tends to work:

Example 1
A: Why don't you come up and see me some[time
B: [I would like to.
                                          (Atkinson and Drew 1979: 58)

Example 2
A: We:ll, will you help me [ou:t
B: [I certainly wi:ll.
                                          (Davidson 1984: 116)

The overlapping speech, they point out, is typical of the immediate and direct way that people tend to talk when they are agreeing to a request (Heritage 1984: 266–7). Next Kitzinger and Frith (1999) contrast this with an example of an ordinary refusal:

Example 3

Mark: We were wondering if you wanted to come over Saturday, f'r dinner

(0.4 sec pause)

Jane: Well (.) . hh it's be great but we promised Carol already.

(Potter and Wetherell 1987: 86)

Far from being immediate and direct, this refusal is slow to be given and hedged around. There is a 0.4 second gap before Jane starts speaking, and another pause – indicated by (.) – after she uses 'Well' as a hedge. A **hedge** (sometimes called a preface) is a word or utterance like 'uh' at the start of speech, used to 'hedge around' difficulties to come. Then Jane uses a **palliative** – here an appreciation – to specifically ameliorate the potential rudeness of rejecting the invitation. Palliatives are conversational strategies used to temper the impact of what is being said. Appreciations are often used in rejections – 'That's awfully sweet of you, but', 'What a fantastic idea, but', and so on. Finally, Jane provides an **account** – here a justification for refusing. Accounts present culturally sanctioned reasons for acting (or not acting) in particular ways. In refusals, accounts convey the rationale that the person cannot (as opposed to will not or does not want to) agree to the request. Their purpose is to avoid the implication that the request is unreasonable or unattractive, and so avoid negative consequences for the relationship between the speakers.

Having used the fine-grained qualities of conversation analysis to make the point that refusals are generally problematic – and hence usually presented in ambiguous and hedged ways – Kitzinger and Frith (1999) turn their attention to the way people generally react to such refusals.

Example 4

A: hhhhh Uh will you call 'im tuhnight for me, =

B: =eYea:h

(.)

A: Plea::se,

(Davidson 1984: 113)

In this example it is clear that the person asking the favour has recognized they are not getting the kind of definite, swift agreement that means that *B* has unequivocally agreed to make the 'phone call. So *A* responds by making a more powerful plea – *Plea::se*. Kitzinger and Frith provide a number of similar examples to show that people generally have no problem in recognizing refusals, even when they are tacit and vague and sometimes include hedged or even apparent agreement. They take action accordingly, for instance, by (as above) asking again more persuasively, seeking to reassure, or to counter the excuse being used.

Kitzinger and Frith (1999) then come to the main point of their article, which is to counter the explanations usually given for miscommunication in the context of sexual advances made by men towards women. It is generally attributed to women who 'lacked effective refusal skills' (Cairns 1993: 205), in a context in which 'often men interpret timidity as permission' (cited in Turner and Rubinson 1993: 605).

These attributions, Kitzinger and Frith argue, locate the problem in *women's* communication competence rather than in that of men. Using their fine-grained analysis of refusals in ordinary settings, Kitzinger and Frith dispute this explanation, and maintain that the problem should be located in *men's* behaviour.

> Our analysis in this article supports the belief that the root of the problem is not that men do not understand sexual refusals, but they do not like them.
>
> (Kitzinger and Frith 1999: 310)

Kitzinger and Frith marshal a diversity of further evidence to support their case. One is the observation that when, in a university in Canada, posters were put up on the campus saying 'No means No', some men responded with posters of their own. The captions demonstrate incredible levels of hostility: 'No means kick her in the teeth', 'No means on your knees bitch', 'No means tie her up', 'No means more beer', and 'No means she's a dyke' (Mahood and Littlewood 1997).

Kitzinger and Frith's (1999) article demonstrates how conversation analysis can be used by social psychologists to examine how meaning is often interpreted not from the semantic qualities of language but the subtle para-linguistic ways in which it is deployed. The article also shows how, within a social constructionist paradigm, a number of different sources of data can be used together to address the way language is used strategically – for example, to warrant certain kinds of behaviour.

Discursive resources

Discursive resources theory (as described in Chapter 3) takes a much more broad-brush perspective on language. Here the approach is a bit like an ecologist who goes into a particular habitat and seeks to identify and describe the different species of animals and plants living there, and, crucially, investigates how these species co-exist together and their effects upon each other. Elsewhere (Stainton Rogers 1991) I have adopted the term *sympatricity* from Press (1980) to describe this situation – one where different discourses are in play, which compete against each other for dominance. Press (1980) uses the term to portray the way that different medical systems – biomedicine, 'alternative' or complementary medicine, Chinese Traditional Medicine, and so on – coexist together but also compete for dominance. In the West biomedicine tends to be the dominant system, but, say, in China it is Chinese Traditional Medicine that tends to dominate over Western biomedicine.

In relation to discourses, in different times, different places and different settings particular discourses will dominate. Today in the Western world it tends to be Modernism's discourses that prevail – such as discourses of Science, liberal humanism and liberal individualism. It is these discourses that dominate in the epistemological ecological setting of experimental social psychology. But in the epistemological ecology of critical social psychology, it is the discourses of Postmodernism – such as social constructionism and semiotics – that have taken over the dominant position. They are the discursive resources from which critical social psychologists have built their theories and analytics. They are antagonistic to Science, to liberal humanism and to liberal individualism. They have overgrown them and taken over the space they used to occupy.

Narrative psychology

One example of the discursive resources approach is **narrative psychology**. It focuses on the way that people tend to make sense of the world through telling stories. Stories and story-telling were extensively studied by early psychologists (for example Bartlett's 1932 experimental study of remembering stories, and Wundt's (1900–20) discussion of the role of myths and legends in his *Völkerpsychologie*) as ways of gaining insight into what we would now call social cognition. However, this approach was shunned from about the 1930s, mainly because story-telling is not very amenable to experimental research.

It came back into favour with the arrival of critical social psychology. Part of the reason is that stories are powerful ways in which we make sense of the world. We do not make sense of our lives and the things that happen in it as just 'one damned thing after another' (Gergen and Gergen 1984: 174). We strive to understand them as related to each other and as having continuity – in other words, in narrative form.

> Narratives, as omnipresent natural representational forms of human
> symbolic activity, both by their internal organization and social-cultural
> determination of their spreading . . . provide an analytical frame for the
> study of mental life as well as the study of the social conditions of these
> processes.
>
> (László *et al.* 2002: 7)

Ricoeur calls this use of narrative organization **emplotment** – the bringing together a string of incidents into a plot: 'to make up a plot is already to make the intelligible spring from the accidental, the universal from the singular, the necessary or probable from the accidental' (Ricoeur 1981: 123).

Narratives serve a **presencing function** (Heidegger 1971). That is, in Postmodern theory, a narrative is seen as a special kind of discursive practice through which past or future events (imaginary or real) are 'presenced' – put into words in order to do something – recount, entertain, inform, influence, or suchlike. Moreover, these narratives powerfully inform the ways in which we live our lives. They tell us how to 'fall in love', how to do jealousy, how to go on holiday, and so on.

Crucially, these stories in which we live are not figments of our individual imagination. They are profoundly semiotic and profoundly cultural – narrated through novels, plays and operas, both soap and serious. There is some commonality to cognitive psychology's term scripts here (Chapter 5). However, narrative psychology does not regard them as mere representations or encodings, but as powerful ways in which we *make* sense of our lives, its events, and of the world around us. They are not mere repertoires to follow, like a script. This is because they contain moral and prescriptive elements, and, crucially, implications about fact and fiction.

A good example is Jovchelovitch's (2002) study of narratives about the impeachment in 1993 of Fernando Collor de Mello, who in 1989 had been the first democratically elected president of Brazil in more than 30 years. Six months after the impeachment she interviewed 11 members of parliament. All but one of them reported their views of the impeachment by telling it as a story. By a detailed examination of these narratives she was able to build up a 'map' of the conceptual framework through which the event was understood. It included aspects of political life – as self-sacrificing or corrupt; of the politicians' views about the voting population – as ignorant and credulous, 'expecting miracles'; of their values and ethics in relation to a new era of democracy. She comments on the complexity and the contradictory nature of these narratives, and how the narrative form of organization collapses time in order to impose a meaningful structure. From this analysis she is able to offer insight into the way in which the narratives they construct profoundly affect the ways in which people make sense of the world – and, crucially, act within it.

Discursive approaches

Social constructionist social psychologists study speech behaviour using ethnographic methods, generally some form of discourse analysis. By conducting detailed and fine-grained scrutiny of the way language is deployed, they seek to gain insight into the strategies and motives involved.

Conversation analysis shows how the paralinguistic features of language can be used to signal meaning, and hence as cues to the strategies being adopted in speech.

Narrative analysis examines the ways in which people make sense of the world through organizing discrete events into a story, and how this affects their understanding of those events.

DISCURSIVE APPROACHES TO ATTITUDES AND ATTRIBUTION

Discursive psychologists have been critical of the work conducted by experimental social psychologists into attribution and attitudes. This final section briefly summarizes these objections, looking first at work on attitudes and then work on attribution.

Jonathan Potter and Margaret Wetherell gave their 1987 book the subtitle 'Beyond attitudes and behaviour'. In it they made the case for a turn to discourse analysis by arguing that this is a much better way of gaining insight and understanding into what experimental social psychologists conceive of 'attitudes' than experiments on attitude prediction and attitude change.

Potter (1996) makes four main criticisms of attitude research and theorization:

- atomism
- individualism
- variability with context
- ignoring the question of what attitudes are *for*.

Atomism

Potter argues that 'attitudes are often assumed to be scattered around in people's heads, rather like currants in a fruitcake' (Potter 1996: 135). Critical psychologists then ask the question – why? Their answer is that this is pragmatic rather than theoretical. The requirements of experimental method mean it is a lot easier to study processes and phenomena in fragmented, atomistic ways. But that does not mean that attitudes actually 'work' in isolation, merely that the experimental work on attitudes treated them as discrete. As you saw in Chapter 6, it soon became apparent that this did not work, and expectancy value models needed to be developed which brought in other elements (such as values, social norms and expectations). But even this kind of theorizing does not go far enough. The models are simply ones of richer fruitcakes, containing cherries and nuts as well as currants. Attitudes, social norms, values, and expectancies are still seen as isolated from each other. Discursive psychology views them as not just interconnected. They relate to each other in meaningful and systematic ways, and cannot be treated as discrete psychological entities that merely operate together according to an algebraic equation.

Narrative psychology provides one approach that theorizes how these different elements might be connected. Story-telling is a powerful means to integrate social norms, values, ideas about what can or should happen, how one thing connects with another in *meaningful* ways.

Individualism

Potter (1996) challenges the individualism of attitude research and theory. By assuming that attitudes are, at base, held in individual minds and merely 'influenced' by factors such as social norms and expectations, he points out that attitude researchers have studied them almost exclusively at an individual level.

Semiotic theory offers one theoretical framework to account for the ways in which individual subjectivity and collective intersubjectivity operate dialectically, in constant interplay with each other again. Social representations theory provides another, social constructionism another. What holds together the theories of critical social psychology is their aim to provide an understanding of this interplay.

Variability with context

Potter's strongest criticism, however, is that attitude research and theory cannot deal with variability. To see what he is getting at, let us look once more at the extract from Potter and Wetherell's (1987) discourse analytic study of racism that you met in Chapter 3.

> **Extract 2**
> What I would li . . . rather see is that, sure, bring them into New Zealand, right, try and train them in a skill, and encourage them to go back again.

> **Extract 3**
> I think that if we encouraged more Polynesians and Maoris to be skilled people they would want to stay here, they're not, um, as, uh, nomadic as New Zealanders are [*interviewer laughs*] so I think that would be better.

The two extracts are taken from subsequent pages of a person's interview transcript. Potter and Wetherell (1987) comment that examples like this display not so much 'variability' but stark contradiction. They then go on to argue:

> The variability in people's discourse cannot be explained merely as a product of a more *complex*, multi-faceted attitudinal structure which a more complex scale can assess, because the views expressed vary so radically from occasion to occasion. It is impossible to argue that the claim Polynesian immigration is desirable and the claim that it is undesirable are merely facets of one complex attitude. The notion of enduring attitudes, even multidimensional ones, simply cannot deal with this.
>
> (Potter and Wetherell 1987: 53)

Ignoring the question of what attitudes are for

Potter (1996) argues that there is one final 'blind spot' in traditional attitude work – which is what people use their attitudinal evaluations *for*. As you saw in Chapter 6, early theorizing proposed a whole range of different functions of attitudes. They were seen as organizational (enabling the categorization of knowledge), as instrumental (guiding behaviour and cognition and helping people to pursue their goals) as expressive (for communicating with oneself and others) and useful for esteem purposes, both personal and collective.

Yet attitude researchers today, he says, have come to virtually ignore them. Potter argues that they appear to have become completely preoccupied with just two things – working out how and when attitudes can be predictive, and working out how attitudes can be changed. They seem to have almost entirely lost sight of questions about what people *do* when they express attitudes – and what they want to achieve.

The discursive practices approach reconnects with this question. It is not at all interested in whether attitudes predict behaviour. Its concern is with, for example, the way that expressing an attitude can enable someone to justify a particular behaviour, course of action or policy. Kitzinger and Frith's (1999) conversation analysis study was crucially concerned with the ways in which certain behaviours can be warranted by a particular discursive strategy. In their analysis, when a man refuses to acknowledge a hedged refusal to his sexual advances *as* a refusal, he is doing so for a purpose – to justify pursuing his advances.

Discursive approaches to attribution

Critical social psychologists have serious problems with attribution theory for two main reasons:

- it is articulated around a distinction between attributing cause to the person or to the social situation
- it seriously underestimates the extent to which attributions are located within and articulated through the use of discursive practices and resources.

Challenging the person/situation distinction

Critical social psychologists argue that studies of social cognition 'treat linguistic materials (text, sentences and so on) as representations of the world and/or mind – of what happened, or of what somebody thinks happened – rather than as situated actions' (Edwards and Potter 1992: 77). Discursive psychology stresses that language is not simply a semantic representational system, it is a *semiotic* one – it is used to signify. And its semiotic qualities link any instance of talk into a whole network of cultural significations.

Go back and look at Chapter 5, where we were considering Marcia's lentilburger lunch (Figure 5.5). Answering the question 'Why did Marcia eat a lentilburger for lunch?' is not a matter of selecting just one of two, mutually exclusive alternatives – *either* it is to do with the kind of person Marcia is, *or* it is to do with the situation she is in. Ask a real person in a real situation that kind of question and their answer will be informed by a complex and rich set of ideas. In early twenty-first-century modern societies, one likely theme will be vegetarianism. This includes ethical concerns about the immorality of killing animals for food, both from an animal rights perspective and from ideas about the waste of resources of using animal protein as a food source. It is also likely to encompasses ideas about 'healthy eating' and the pressures (particularly on young women) to strive for a slim body and thus eat low-calorie meals.

Very soon the question of her lunch begins to take in all manner of subtle complexions, such as the marketing of 'health foods' and the effects of mass media advertising, of health education and of youth culture. Attributions in the real world (as opposed to the laboratory) are massively more complex than either classic attribution or even multiple-process models of attribution allow. Critical theorists stress that attributions are never purely matters of individual social cognition, but always the product of complex cultural and social forces providing discursive resources within and through which attributions are made.

Consequently, the 'cause' of any behaviour or event will seldom if ever be attributed unequivocally to a single site. We could ask whether it is Marcia's vegetarianism (or whatever) that led her to eat the lentilburger, or the qualities of the burger (that is, its vegetable and not meat base)? Surely it is both. But the criticism goes further than this, for, as Rommetveit (see, for example, his 1980 article) has pointed out, when we try to make sense of any action, there are many stories we can tell, all of which may have validity. He used, as an illustration, explanations about why Mr Jones was mowing the lawn. Was it to get exercise, to avoid spending time with his wife, to beautify his garden or to annoy his neighbour? Maybe it was all of them!

Attribution is made within and through discourse

Discursive psychology stresses in particular that language is used to *do* things, not simply represent concepts, ideas and understandings. And the things people do are purposive, and the purposes are much more varied than attributional theory can accommodate.

If we turn once more to Fincham's work on relationships (as described in Chapter 5 in the section on attribution), for example, while it accommodates things like whether a relationship is going well or badly, it assumed that this has a lawfully similar meaning and significance in all couple relationships. But these are not in any sense universal, but influenced by history and culture. At different historical times and in different cultures, couple relationships are understood differently.

It is very likely, for example, that where marriage is regarded as an institution rather than a source of personal fulfilment – where men and women live more separate lives, and where the roles of wives and husbands are highly gendered and specified – there will be much less agonizing over a partner's behaviour, whatever the state of the relationship. As you will see in Chapter 8, cultures vary considerably in how they understand issues of duty and responsibility in relation to individuals as compared with social groups (such as families) and hence attributional conventions will also vary considerably across cultures (Smith and Harris Bond 1993).

Moreover (as argued in Chapter 4), today, in a virtually global sense, the mass media bombard people with messages about attribution in couple relationships – about 'men behaving badly', that 'men are from Mars and women are from Venus' and so on. Newspapers as well as women's magazines carry Agony Aunt columns that minutely dissect who is and who is not to blame when relationships go wrong. Much fiction takes misattribution as its main narrative plot-line, from *Pride and Prejudice* to *Bridget Jones' Diary*. Discursive psychology thus locates attribution *within* discourse:

> The crucial point is that event description is not distinct from, nor prior to attributional work, but rather attributional work is *accomplished* by descriptions. Discursive psychology takes as a primary focus of concern, the study of talk and texts, for the situated reality-producing work that they do.
>
> (Edwards and Potter 1992: 91, emphases in the original)

Discursive psychology redefines how attribution should be studied. If we are to understand attribution we need, according to Edwards and Potter, to see attribution as work – as something that is *done*. So we must attend much more closely to the nature and content of the conversation or other exchange in which attribution work is done, and the extent to which this work is constructive. We need to recognize that the things that people say do not reflect reality but construct particular *versions* of reality according to the purposes to which the conversation is put.

> A discursive psychology of attribution proposes an active, rhetorical process, which requires at least two participants. . . . Rather than viewing the entire process from the perspective of an inference making perceiver, who passively takes versions as given, we have to examine how versions are constructed and undermined within a discursive manipulation of fact and implication. Attribution is to be studied as a public and social process, done interactionally in talk and text, where fact and attributional inference are simultaneously and rhetorically addressed.
>
> (Edwards and Potter 1992: 94)

The power of discourse to 'make' the world

> When a cat wants to eat her kittens, she calls them mice.
>
> (Old Turkish proverb)

Kitzinger and Frith (1999) identified in their study an example of what Vickers has called the **reversal of agency**. Vickers proposes that this is 'the worst kind of context stripping . . . a grammatical, theoretical and methodological trick' (Vickers 1982: 39) that beguiles the language receiver (the reader or listener) into misattributing agency.

The conventional assumption is that it is women's lack of communication skills that is the site of the 'problem' (of, say, 'date rape'). Kitzinger and Frith, in effect, argue that this is an attribution error. But it is not one located in individual cognition. It is an attribution error woven into a particular social reality. From their explicitly Feminist standpoint this social reality is a patriarchal system in which '[m]en's self-interested capacity for "misunderstanding" will always outstrip women's earnest attempts to clarify and explain' (Kitzinger and Frith 1999: 311).

Feminist analysis of patriarchal social reality

It may seem a surprising place to go, but one of the main theories of how patriarchy constructs a particular social reality is a form of psychoanalytic theory developed by Jacques Lacan. He argued for a radical change to the way psychodynamic forces are seen to originate and operate (Lacan 1966). Rather than viewing them – as Freud had done – as biologically grounded and mediated, Lacan argued that they are grounded in and mediated by culture. He drew extensively on the work of Saussure, particularly his ideas about the symbolic nature of language (see Chapter 4).

Subsequently a semiotic version of psychoanalytic theory has been generated by Feminist theorists such as Julia Kristeva ([1974] 1984). She developed a complex theoretical framework in which social reality is seen to operate at different levels. For instance, she proposed that in the 'semiotic order' of meanings and meaning-making, social reality is consciously 'made sense of', but in the 'symbolic order' it is experienced at an unconscious level – as strong emotions and feelings that can profoundly affect behaviour.

To begin with, this new, semiotic version of psychoanalytic theory was most influential in areas like Media studies. For example Laura Mulvey suggested that 'sexual instincts and identification processes have a meaning within the symbolic order which articulates desire'. In Western culture, she suggests, the symbolic order is permeated by sexual difference, where 'women are simultaneously looked at and displayed, with their appearance being coded for strong visual and erotic impact' (Mulvey 1992: 25).

Both Kristeva and Mulvey were seeking to theorize about patriarchy, which they saw as a particularly powerful social reality in which the social world has been constructed by men and for men, to serve male interests – it is, literally, a man-made world of meanings. Mulvey, for instance, drew attention to the fact that films tend almost exclusively to be made by men and for men, and in them women are almost exclusively portrayed from a male perspective.

Playing tricks with agency

Now let us go back and see what Vickers is getting at in her claim that the patriarchal social world 'plays tricks' with agency. She illustrates her case with the following statement (cited by Daly) about *suttee* – the 'custom' or 'practice' in which widows are burnt on their husband's funeral pyres. It is taken from a textbook about Hinduism:

> At first, *suttee* was restricted to the wives of princes and warriors . . . but in the course of time the widows of weavers, masons, barbers and others of the lower caste *adopted the practice*.
>
> (Walker, cited in Daly 1978: 117, emphasis added by Daly)

Vickers responded:

> Given the fact that widows were dragged from hiding places and heavily drugged before being flung on the pyre, often by their sons, this is like

saying that although the practice of being burned in gas ovens was at first restricted to political dissidents, eventually millions of Jews *adopted* the practice.

(Vickers 1982: 39, emphasis in the original)

Vickers is proposing here that language can be – and regularly is – used to 'play tricks' with meaning. The way it is deployed primes a particular interpretation of what is going on (that is contends certain facts) and, in so doing, blames the victim rather than the perpetrator (that is promotes certain values). By calling *suttee* a 'practice' or a 'custom' that is 'adopted' by widows, responsibility for their deaths is located in the women themselves rather than in those who kill them. The sense is conveyed (by using the verb 'adopting' in the textbook sentence) that it is the widows who do the doing, rather than the sons who do the doing (Vickers uses three verbs to make her point – 'dragging', 'drugging' and 'flinging').

In many ways discursive psychology as a whole is a study of attribution, in that it seeks to explicate the purposes to which talk and text are being put in the way they are deployed. A new term has been adopted for such work – the concept of **agency**. Work like that of Vickers (1982) provides a powerful framework for exploring the ways in which language is deployed to 'play tricks' with agency.

Vickers suggests that within a patriarchal social world, language is often used to obscure, deny and to reverse agency. One of her prime targets is academic text. She argues that it is, by convention, a style that is presented as academically 'pure' – objective and impersonal – in the pursuit of dis-passionate and rational scholarly report and analysis. But often in so doing it at the very least obscures agency, and often it denies it and at worst it reverses it.

People as competent negotiators of reality

The concept of agency and the use of it as an analytic within discursive psychology shifts social psychological research and theorizing about attribution into a new paradigm that takes a more radical stance on 'ordinary thinking' than attempts to apply it to 'realistic settings' like Fincham's.

Instead of concentrating on attribution *errors* and viewing the way people make sense of the world as flawed, discursive psychology regards people as 'competent negotiators of reality' (Potter and Wetherell 1987: 45) who can and do use language purposively to do 'attributional work' (Edwards and Potter 1992: 91). Like social cognition theory, this portrays the way that people understand the social world as an active and constructive process that enables them to operate effectively within it. However, where discursive psychology differs is that it does not regard this as a bumbling and bodging strategy to cope with the limitations of human cognition. It does not portray people as 'naive scientists' or 'naive physicists' or naive anyone. Instead it regards people as anything but naive – as clever and often devious.

Putting it this way, in relation to Kitzinger and Frith's (1999) article, what do you think was going on when posters were put around a campus in response to 'No means no' posters that had been placed as part of a zero tolerance campaign? These posters, if you recall, had captions reading 'No means kick her in the teeth', 'No means on your knees bitch', 'No means tie her up', 'No means more beer' and 'No means she's a dyke' (Mahood and Littlewood 1997). Do you really think these were examples of attribution errors? That the men who made the posters were suffering from a lack of proper understanding of the situation? Or do you think the making and posting of the posters was a deliberate strategy intended to exercise power?

Discursive approaches to attitudes and attribution

Potter (1996) makes the following criticisms of attitude theory:

- They *atomize attitudes* and therefore fail to explore how they interconnect, and how they relate to other evaluations such as values
- They *treat attitudes as solely operating in individual minds*, and ignore their intersubjective qualities
- They *fail to address variability* and are unable to account for it
- They are preoccupied with studying attitude change and attitude-behaviour links and *ignore* important questions about *the functions that attitudes serve*.

Criticisms of attribution theory
- Critical social psychologists suggest that attribution should be regarded as an integral part of discursive practice
- They argue that attribution is a semiotic process, mediated by culture and used in all discourse to locate agency in ways that promote the power and interest of particular groups
- Instead of seeing people as making attribution errors, they suggest that people should be seen as 'competent negotiators of reality', who use attribution strategically.

FURTHER READING

Social representations

Farr, R.M. and Moscovici, S. (eds) (1981) *Social Representations*. Cambridge: Cambridge University Press.
> This is the key text for gaining a thorough understanding of social representations theory, coming, as they say, from the horse's mouth.

Flick, U. (ed.) (1998) *The Psychology of the Social*. Cambridge: Cambridge University Press.
> A collection of chapters, covering developments in both social representations theory and social representations research. It contains a chapter by Moscovici summarizing his current views.

Herzlich, C. (1973) *Health and Illness*. London: Academic Press.
> This is a fascinating and thoroughly readable book. It is also an important one historically, being the first social psychological text on health and illness to adopt a critical perspective and highly influential in the development of critical health psychology.

Critical social psychology

Antaki, C. (1981) *The Psychology of Ordinary Explanations of Social Behaviour*. London: Academic Press.
> This was a ground-breaking book in its time, and still a good read. It critically addresses both attribution (Chapter 3) and personal construct (Chapter 9) theories. This may be a bit advanced for your purposes just now, but it is a 'have to read' if you decide to pursue critical work in relation to the topics of this chapter.

Edwards, D. and Potter, J. (1992) *Discursive Psychology*. London: Sage.
> Chapters 5 and 6 in this book provide a clear (if, at times, dense) account of attribution as addressed by discursive psychology.

Potter, J. and Wetherell, M. (1987). *Discourse and Social Psychology: Beyond Attitudes and Behaviour*. London: Sage.
> This is the 'have to read' book in this field, if you have not looked at it already.

Potter, J. (1996) Attitudes, social representations and discursive psychology, in M. Wetherell (ed.) *Identities, Groups and Social Issues*. London: Sage.
> This offers a concise and elegant critique of attitude research and theory. I would recommend this chapter as a good starting point.

Conversational analysis

Hutchby, I. and Wooffitt, R. (1998) *Conversation Analysis: Principles, Practice and Applications*. Cambridge: Polity.

>Probably the best 'how to do it' introduction to conversation analysis.

QUESTIONS

1 Outline the key features of social representations theory. Illustrate your answer with examples about social representations of health and illness.
2 'Our world is a storied world which we construct and within which we live' (Murray 1997). Do you agree?
3 What arc the main ways in which experimental and critical social psychology differ in their approach to attribution?
4 How is social reality constructed? Provide an overview of the different theories that critical social psychologists use to answer this question.
5 Explain why the concept of 'agency' is important in critical psychology. Illustrate your answer by reference to Kitzinger and Frith's (1999) study of women's refusals of sexual advances from men.

Chapter 8

Selves and identities

Chapter contents

A route map of the chapter

This is a topic where early work has become highly influential on recent theorization, so the chapter starts by reviewing the ideas developed about the self by William James, George Herbert Mead and Irving Goffman. The next section briefly takes up an issue raised in Chapter 6, where value systems were seen to vary across cultures. A key element is that there are different concepts of the self – one which thinks mainly in terms of an individual self, and another that views the self as much more relational.

There then follow three sections which each take a very different stance on the self. We begin by looking at the biologically determined self – the self that arises from our genetic heritage, moulded by evolution. Next we look at the socially determined self, based on some traditional social psychological theories about the ways that the self as moulded by social processes like learning. Then we explore, from a critical perspective, the self as intersubjective. This section begins by explaining what is meant by an 'intersubjective self'. It ends by illustrating the approach with a brief summary of the work by Michel Foucault on what he has termed 'technologies of the self'.

Historical origins of psychology's concept of 'self'

↓

An individual or a relational self?

↓

The biologically determined self

↓

The socially determined self

↓

The intersubjective self

Learning objectives

When you have completed your study on this chapter, you should be able to:

1 Outline the contributions made to our understanding of the self by James, Mead and Goffman.
2 Explain the difference between an 'individual' and a 'relational' concept of the self, and describe how these are prioritized in different ways in different cultures.
3 Summarize what is meant by a biologically determined self, and give an illustration of this viewpoint.
4 Through examples, outline social psychological theories about the ways in which the self is determined by social forces and influences.
5 Explain what is meant by an 'intersubjective self', and outline the key elements in this theorization.
6 Summarize what is meant by 'presencing practice', 'technologies of the self' and 'subject positioning', and explain their functions in the construction of the intersubjective self.
7 List the four strategies that Foucault identifies as regulating sexuality, and describe how they 'work'.

INTRODUCTION

Each of us experiences ourselves as being a 'self'. We are aware of being someone with a past, a present and a future, all of which affect who we are. We are also aware of the distinctive facets of our character that seem to have been constant since childhood, and make us the individual and unique person that we are. But as a 'self' we are not only aware of inhabiting a distinctive personal world, but also distinct social and cultural worlds. We are who we are because of our relationships to others – because we are a mother or a son, a husband or a friend, a student or a teacher. We are also who we are through belonging to different communities and our membership of other groups that reflect, construct and sustain our identity – as, for example, a social worker, a Muslim, a political dissident, a football fan, a biker, a vegetarian, or whatever.

Try it yourself

Before starting the chapter in any detail, stop for a few minutes and do the following task. Write down 20 statements to answer the question 'Who am I?' It is important that you do write at least 20 answers. When answering this question in each case, do it as if you are giving the answer to *yourself*, not another person. The order does not matter. Don't try to be systematic or logical, or think about importance. Just write down the first 20 answers that come into your head. Keep this list – it's important. We'll come back to it later.

HISTORICAL ORIGINS OF PSYCHOLOGY'S CONCEPT OF 'SELF'

More, perhaps, than with any other subject in social psychology, ideas about the self – what it means to be a person, what a person should be, what makes us who and what we are – have a long and varied history. These questions have been incorporated into all religions, traditional belief systems and folklore, as well as in the various philosophies of the world. Here we concentrate on a relatively recent history, the origins of how social psychology from its beginnings in the late nineteenth century began to conceptualize the self.

William James' theories of 'I' and 'Me'

You met William James' work in Chapter 1. Now we are going to look in greater detail at his theorization about the self. James distinguished between two aspects of the self: the 'me' which he saw as 'the self as known', and the 'I' which is, he said was 'the self as knower'. He then went on to look at different aspects of each one.

The Me – the self-as-known

James divided up the self-as-known into three main elements: the material, social and spiritual.

The *material Me*: In this James included not just the body, but also clothes, home, wealth, possessions, and works (such as his writings).

The *social Me*: James saw this as about the recognition one gets from others. People, James argued, are by nature social and gregarious and it would be impossible to have a meaningful sense of one's self without the respect and concern of others.

> No more fiendish punishment could be devised . . . than one should be turned loose in society and remain absolutely unnoticed by others. If no one turned around when we entered, answered when we spoke, or minded what we did, but if every person we met 'cut us dead' and acted as if we were nonexisting things, a kind of rage and impotent despair would ere long well up in us, from which the cruelest bodily tortures would be a relief.
>
> (James 1907: 179)

James recognized that there are multiple social selves, whereby people show different sides of themselves to different people – different selves that they show to their parents, their teachers, their friends, their customers, to those who work for them. He suggested that a man's fame or honour were crucial parts of his social self, and important influences on his behaviour. Whereas others, for example, may flee from a city infected with cholera, a priest or doctor would consider this incompatible with his honour and stay.

The *spiritual Me*: James defined this as the 'entire collection of my states of consciousness, my psychic faculties and dispositions taken concretely', and saw it as '[t]he very core and nucleus of ourself, as we know it, the very sanctuary of our life, the sense of activity which certain inner states possess' (James 1907: 181). In other words, while James recognized what we would now regard as 'the spiritual' (in terms of, say, religious faith) he was in many ways referring here to what we would now call our experiential self.

From these three aspects of the self-as-known, James said, follow a range of psychological elements such as self-appreciation, self-interest and the pursuit of self-betterment and self-respect.

The I – the self-as-knower

James notes that this is a more difficult concept: '[I]t is that which at any given moment *is* conscious, whereas the Me is only one of the things which it is conscious *of*' (James 1907: 195, emphases in the original). The difficulty is in defining what 'it' is – the soul, the transcendent ego, the spirit?

James saw a person's conscious awareness in terms of a 'stream of consciousness', in which thoughts, emotions, states, feelings, images, and ideas continually coexist together immanently – outside of our awareness and at the 'back of our minds' in a state that James called transitivity. The transitivity of consciousness, James claimed, provides the basis for an enduring, ongoing, unitary self – a self that stays the same. But at any moment some part or parts of it become substantive. We experience and act out our 'I', our self-as-knower, substantive moment by substantive moment.

> It is this trick, which the nascent thought has of immediately taking up the expiring thought and 'adopting' it, which leads to most of the remoter constituents of the self. . . . The identity which we recognize as we survey the long progression can only be the identity of a slow shifting in which there is always some common ingredient retained. . . . Thus the identity found by the *I* in its *Me* is only a loosely constructed thing: an identity 'on the whole'.
>
> (James 1907: 205, emphases in the original)

Implications for social psychology

Experimental social psychology studies James' concept of 'Me' – the self-as-known – since it is what *can* be known about the self from the kinds of self-reports that can be used as dependent variables. However, it makes no attempt to study James' concept of 'I' – the self-as-knower, since this aspect is not amenable to experimental method. It is this aspect of the self that is the focus of study for experiential psychology (see, for example, Stevens 1996). It is also the main focus for many critical social psychologists, including social constructionists and those working with a social representations approach.

Mead's theory of a social self

George Herbert Mead was a philosopher, like James (in that he worked as a professor of philosophy), but can also be considered an influential sociological social psychologist. An American, he did postgraduate training in Germany in 1889–91. His doctoral thesis (though he never finished it) was on the relationship between vision and touch, supervised by the Gestalt psychologist Wilhelm Dilthey. He gave a lecture series on social psychology at the

University of Chicago from 1900 to 1931. However, these lectures were mostly attended by sociology students, not psychologists, and Mead's influence was greatest on the development of sociology. Mead is often regarded as the originator of **symbolic interactionism**, but this is not so. The term was invented by Herbert Blumer, who took over Mead's lecture series after Mead died in 1931 (Farr 1996). Joas argues that Mead's theorization was based not on symbolic interactionism, but on the concept of 'symbolically mediated inter-action' (Joas 1985: 228). Largely ignored by psychologists until relatively recently, Mead's work is receiving renewed attention with the emergence of critical social psychology, mainly because it is semiotic in its approach (see Chapter 4).

Farr notes that it is difficult to pin down Mead's theoretical work, since he did not write it up in any systematic way and lectured without notes. The books published in his name (for example Mead 1934a, 1934b) were not written by him, but prepared from drafts he worked on but did not complete, notes taken by his students and from transcripts prepared by a stenographer they smuggled into Mead's 1927 lecture course!

Mead spent a lifetime trying to resolve the tension between the individual mind and society. Influenced both by Darwinism and by the *Völkerpsychologie* he learned in Germany and reviewed when he returned to the USA, he tried to work out how the 'self' can be understood in relation to three main determinants – human evolution, each individual's own development, and social forces and processes. He saw language as central to the way these three contributed to the construction of the 'self', and symbolically mediated inter-action as the means by which it operates. Mead's theorization about language differed fundamentally from that of behaviourists. Behaviourists like Watson (who was Mead's student) believed that language is produced by the minds of individuals. Mead believed that each individual's mind is the product of language. Like Vygotsky (Chapter 4) Mead saw language as the basic medium through which thought operates, and, given the inherently social character of language, he emphasized the importance of intersubjectivity.

Thus the 'self', according to Mead, is intersubjective, constituted through social interaction in which people have to assume the role of the other in order to gain an understanding of themselves. Thus, Mead argued, human consciousness is an awareness of self in relation to others, and therefore human consciousness is a fundamentally *social* consciousness. Like language, Mead saw this *social* self as producing – not produced by – human conscious-ness. Mead's theorization described a **reflexive self** – a self that is able to observe, plan and respond to one's own behaviour. This image is nicely conceptualized on Cooley's (1902) term 'the looking-glass self'.

Mead took James' conceptions of a separated but coexisting 'I' and 'Me' and recast them as two facets of the self that are in constant *dialectical* relation to each other (that is, in dialogue with each other). The 'I', Mead claimed, is the part of the self that responds directly and impulsively to the outside world. The 'Me' is the socialized self, the self-reflective, conventional aspect of the self that incorporates society's values, norms, ideals, and expectations. The 'Me' is the self that has internalized the standpoints and group standards embedded in a person's culture.

Implications for social psychology

As I have mentioned, Mead's professional life was conducted outside of psychology, largely dismissed by the Behaviourists who took over psychology in the USA. They saw him as engrossed in metaphysics that had nothing to offer to a 'science of mental life'. Alongside Peirce, since the early 1980s his work has been reappraised by social psychologists taking a dialectical view of human being (Marková 1987) and a semiotic approach to language (including, most notably, discursive psychologists like Potter and Wetherell 1987). More generally Mead's work has informed social constructionism, and we shall come back to it when we examine the socially constructed self at the end of the chapter.

Goffman's dramaturgical model

Irving Goffman took up Mead's ideas about social interaction and stressed that everyday life takes place in an essentially interactional world. He portrayed this world as akin to a theatre in which people are actors in the 'drama of life'. Goffman (1959) constructed a dramaturgical theory of the self in which the self arises out of acting a particular kind of role – not so much a hero or heroine, but the kind of character who is morally and socially competent and insightful.

A key concept in this theory is that of **face** – 'the positive social value a person effectively claims for himself by the line others assume he has taken during a particular contact' (Goffman 1967: 5). Goffman claimed that in social interaction, people have a mutual commitment to keep each other 'in face' by what he called **face work** (Goffman 1955). These are ritualized strategies, such as face-saving devices that serve a 'repair function' whenever the smooth flow of interaction is under threat. This kind of device enables someone who commits a social gaffe to deal with the potential embarrassment it poses, and thus to maintain the impression of being an authentically competent person.

> Each person takes on the responsibility of standing guard over the flow of expressive events. . . . He must ensure that a particular *expressive order*

is maintained – an order which regulates the flow of events, large or small, so that anything that appears to be expressed by them will be consistent with his face.

(Goffman 1967: 9)

Maintaining 'face', Goffman claimed, is not the so much goal of interaction as the very basis for it to happen and the means by which it does happen. During social interaction, according to Goffman, people act out 'lines' (as do actors in a drama) that are provided through their knowledge of social norms and rules. Goffman (alongside other ethnomethodological sociologists such as Garfinkel 1967) stressed the role of this 'interactional self' in maintaining the small-scale social order of everyday life. We shall take up these ideas again when we come to look at social interaction in more depth in Chapter 9.

Implications for social psychology

Goffman's image of the 'self' has been particularly influential on social psychologists who have adopted an ethnomethodological approach, such as Rom Harré (1977). Critical social psychologist have something of a problem with Goffman's preoccupation with interaction in rather formal settings that tend to rely on 'scripts', and hence his work fails to capture the whole range of situations in which people interact. However, his ideas have been generally influential, mainly because of its stress on the purposive nature of self-presentation.

Historical origins of the self in psychology

- James distinguished between the 'Me' – the self-as-known, made up of material, social and spiritual elements; and the 'I' – the self-as-knower, produced in the 'flow of consciousness'.
- Mead saw the 'I' and the 'Me' as in a dialectical relationship with each other, and saw the self as reflexive – able to observe, plan and respond to its own thoughts and behaviour.
- Goffman proposed a dramaturgical model of the self, in which interaction consists of 'face work' as people strive to maintain their own 'face' and protect that of others.

AN INDIVIDUAL OR A RELATIONAL SELF?

Clearly lots of different things add up and interact together to make us who we are. There are many different ways of carving these up, but for present purposes I suggest we start by thinking of three different aspects of 'self', somewhat loosely based on James' three aspects of 'Me':

- a **personal self** – the self that is self-aware of being 'Me' and conscious of one's own thoughts and feelings (as well as, possibly, aware of having some unconscious ones). This is a person's enduring self that has developed from childhood into adulthood but is still the same 'Me'. It is an individual self, with its own personality, own unique set of values, attitudes and beliefs and so on.
- a **social self** – or, perhaps, a collection of social selves that are different in different social situations. These are the selves that are defined by the social context – who a person is in private and in public, in formal situations and informal ones, and so on. This includes the self as defined by your occupation (such as being a student or doing a particular job).
- a **relational self** – the self that come from a person's interconnected relationships with others – family, friends, community, the country where they were born, and so on. This is the self defined in terms of the expectations a person has of others and they have of them, the self that exists within an interconnected network of duties, obligations and responsibilities.

Try it for yourself again

Now go back and look at the list of 20 statements about yourself that you did at the beginning of the chapter. Underneath your list, write down the three categories just mentioned: personal self, social self, relational self.

Then do your best to work out in which category each one of your statements falls, and put a tick against that category. If some statements do not fit neatly into any of them, do not worry. Count them as falling into two categories if need be, or just leave them out if they really do not fit anywhere. Now look at which category gets the most ticks. The aim is to see whether you see yourself most in terms of your personal self, your social self or your related self. Just make a note of it now, we shall come back to it later.

Cultural differences in our understanding of self

The Twenty Statements test (as this task is called) was used by Cousins (1989) to examine how concepts of the self may vary between cultures. He tested

Table 8.1

Responses to the Twenty Statements task given by US and Japanese
students

	Average % of 'personal self' answers	Average % of 'social self' answers	Average % of 'relational self' answers
US students	58	9	9
Japanese students	19	9	27

Source: After Cousins 1989

university students in Japan and the USA, and coded their responses into
several categories, three of which were broadly similar to the ones you have
just used. Cousins found a substantial difference between the responses to
the test in the two countries. Table 8.1 sets out the differences, recast in the
terminology I have used.

Cousins' results provide evidence that US students tend to have a more
individualistic sense of self, whereas Japanese students have a more relational
one. Mansur Lalljee (2000) argues that this reflects a systematic difference in
the concept of the self in different societies and cultures.

> In the West, the person is thought of as an autonomous unit, consisting
> of a set of core attributes, that are carried with the person through time
> and context . . . In Japan, India and most parts of the world other than
> 'the West', people are seen in terms of their roles and relationships, in
> terms of their activities and interests, because of the interconnected
> networks in those societies. For people living in such societies, the self
> integrally includes social relationships and social context.
>
> (Lalljee 2000: 133)

Lalljee backs up this assertion with evidence from an ingenious field study by
Semin and Rubini (1990). It was carried out in Italy, and compared the forms
of insults used in the north and the south of the country. The basis of the study
was that Northern Italy has a more individualistic culture than Southern Italy.
They predicted that insults would tend to be more personal in the north –
calling people stupid, fat, or comparing them with animals like pigs. In the
south, they argued, insults would be more likely to be about relationships
– your mother is a *****! (you know the kind of thing) and cursing family
members. The results were not entirely clear-cut, but some support for the
hypothesis was obtained.

Try it for yourself one more time

Now go back and look at what balance you found in your response to the Twenty Statements Test. Did you have more 'personal self' or 'relational self' items in your list? How far do you think your answers reflect the customs and values of your family and the community to which you feel you most belong?

Relational selves

In Chapter 6 you saw that cross-cultural examination of values provides strong evidence for there being different kinds of selves in different cultures. Wetherell and Maybin (2000) provide a different kind of evidence for culturally diverse selves. It comes from an anthropological study carried out by Kondo (1990), an ethnically Japanese woman born and raised in the USA when she was studying, working and living in Japan. For example, here is what Kondo wrote about a conversation with her landlady, following a phone call from a man she had been consulting for making contacts for her research. In it he created a situation where she felt obliged to take on a task – teaching English to a student of his – she knew would be very time-consuming and intrusive.

> I was in a foul mood the entire evening. I complained bitterly to my landlady, who sympathetically agreed the *sensei* should have been more mindful of the fact that I was so pressed, but she confirmed that I had no choice but to comply. She explained that the *sensei* had been happy to give of his time to help me, and by the same token he considered it natural to make requests of others, who should be equally giving of themselves, their 'inner' feelings notwithstanding. '*Nihonjin wa ne*' she mused, '*jibun o taisetu ni shinai no, ne.*' (The Japanese don't treat themselves as important do they? That is, they spend time doing things for the sake of maintaining good relationships, regardless of their 'inner' feelings.) I gazed at her in amazement, for her statement struck me with incredible force. Not only did it perfectly capture my own feelings of being bound by social obligation, living my life for others, it also indicated to me a profoundly different way of thinking about relationships between selves and the social world. Persons seemed to be constituted in and through social relations and obligations to others. Selves and societies did not seem to be separate entities: rather the boundaries were blurred.
>
> (Kondo 1990, as cited in Wetherell and Maybin 2000: 272)

Individual selves

The image of the individual, personal self is an incredibly powerful one in the twenty-first-century modern world. Lisa Blackman and Valerie Walkerdine describe it as one that was promoted by Thatcherism and is now 'celebrated in Blair's Britain' where we are 'all invited to be entrepreneurs of our own selves and possible achievements' (Blackman and Walkerdine 2001: 4–5). You do not need to look very far to see evidence of this.

> Stroll past the popular psychology shelves in any bookstore, and you will be encouraged to *Celebrate Your Self*, *Be Your Best*, *Know Yourself* and *Develop Your Potential*. You will be offered advice on *Making Peace With Yourself*, *Taking Control* and *How to Raise Your Self-Esteem*. And you will find that you should be *Honouring the Self*, *Asserting Yourself*, *Healing Yourself* and even *Talking to Yourself*.
>
> (Smith and Mackie 2000: 103)

This is even more so in the USA (where Smith and Mackie's book was published). But a quick glance at almost any Western woman's magazine tells much the same story in which the self is a valuable but flawed commodity and hence a do-it-yourself project in need of constant gutting out of the bits that are no longer functional, and then of updating and improvement. Put in more academic terms:

> This 'autonomous self' has the positive attributes of independence, autonomy, responsibility, self-control and forwards thinking. It is self-reliant and able to account for the choices it makes in relation to its own biography of needs, motivations, aspirations, and a desire for personal fulfilment and development. It is a self that is capable of understanding, judging and amending its own psychology.
>
> (Blackman and Walkerdine 2001: 4)

The powerful message being conveyed here is of a self that is self-made, a self that is pliable, with the potential to be anything its owner wants it to be if they are prepared to exert enough effort and control.

But – and it is a big but – there is, lurking behind and alongside this image, the contrary one: a self that is anything but self-made, but, rather, is the product of other forces outside of its own control. A great deal of human science theorization is about what these forces are and how they work. Evolutionary psychology, for example, considers human biology – in the form of our 'selfish genes' – to be the major determinant of who and what a person is and how they behave.

Sociology (especially in its subdiscipline Media Studies) takes the opposite line. Its theories argue that the idea of an 'autonomous self' is an illusion created and promoted by and through powerful social institutions such as the law, the state and the mass media as a means to exert control. You met this argument in Chapter 4, where, for example, you saw that Smythe (1994) claimed that a major goal of the mass media is to create audiences that are motivated by possessive individualism so they will desire (and hence buy) the products of capitalism.

Social psychology's view of the self

In Chapter 1 the roots of individualism were traced to Modernism. Others would argue that individualism goes further back than this, and has its roots in Judaeo-Christianity (see, for example, Dumont 1985; Rorty 1987). However, it is Modernism that is crucial here, since it is this worldview that is being globalized through the mass media (movies and television in particular) and mass communication (such as through the Internet). These are having a far-reaching impact upon cultures across the world.

As also argued in Chapter 1, social psychology itself is very much a product of Modernism. It also contributes to sustaining and promoting the Modernist worldview. One of the ways in which it has done (and continues to do) this is through the individualistic version of the self that it portrays in its textbooks. Lalljee (2000), an experimental social psychologist, is highly unusual in his inclusion of an analysis of cultural diversity in his exposition of the self. Most social psychology textbooks take the Modernist, individualized self as 'the norm' and treat any other version as exotic and other. The same goes for the vast majority of the studies they cite. Bear this in mind throughout this chapter as you read about their conclusions.

Personal, social and relational selves

We can think in terms of three different aspects of the self – a personal self, social selves and relational selves.

Cultures differ in terms of which is most salient – a relational self or an individual self.

- A *relational self* views identity as inexorably integrated with others, in terms of mutual duties and obligations, deference and authority.
- An *individual self* views people as autonomous, self-contained and self reliant, with their own concerns, motives, aspirations and desires.

THE BIOLOGICALLY DETERMINED SELF

By a biologically determined self I am concentrating on the idea that what makes us what we are is 'human nature' – our innate qualities that, in scientific terms, are encoded genetically. It is the character and personality with which we are seen to be born. In this section I illustrate theorizing about this natural self with Eysenck's theory of personality.

Eysenck's biological theory of personality

In the simplest version of his model, Eysenck claimed that people have physiological differences that are 'wired in' to their genetic make-up. These, he said, affect both their need for stimulation and in their emotional stability or instability (Eysenck 1967). These differences, Eysenck argued, result in personality differences along two dimensions: introversion–extraversion and emotionality–stability (see Table 8.2).

Eysenck's explanation for these personality differences was that **extroverts** are physiologically 'dampened'. They are much less sensitive to external stimulation than introverts, whereas **introverts** are highly sensitive to external stimulation. 'The extrovert consequently requires greater external stimulation in order to arrive at an optimal level of arousal . . . while the introvert requires less external stimulation' (Eysenck 1967: 17). One result of this, according to Eysenck, is that introverts are more susceptible to conditioning and may also be more sensitive to punishment. So, for example, introverts are more likely to be law-abiding and to follow conventional rules of behaviour; extroverts are more likely to take risks and seek excitement.

Eysenck claimed that the emotionality–stability dimension relates to a person's physiological responses to emotional stimuli, and the efficiency of their physiology in maintaining equilibrium. Individuals high in emotionality, he suggested, are more likely to show 'emotional lability and overreactivity' and will tend to be 'emotionally overresponsive and to have difficulties returning to a normal state after emotional experiences' (Eysenck and Eysenck

Table 8.2

	Extroverts tend to be	Introverts tend to be
If they are stable	Sociable, outgoing, gregarious, talkative, responsive, easy going, lively and carefree	Careful, thoughtful, peaceful, self-controlled, reliable, even-tempered and calm
If they are emotional	Touchy, restless, aggressive, excitable, changeable and impulsive	Moody, anxious, rigid, reserved and unsociable

1985: 6). Individuals high in stability, by contrast, he said, have well-tuned emotional responsiveness. They react to emotional stimuli in a measured way and their bio-feedback mechanisms return them rapidly to a stable state.

The biologically determined self

The natural self sees people as products of 'human nature', born with innate qualities, encoded genetically, that determine their basic character and personality.

Eysenck's theory of personality argues that people have innate tendencies to be either extrovert or introvert, stable or neurotic, based on the specific 'tuning' of their nervous system.

THE SOCIALLY DETERMINED SELF

Experimental social psychology is replete with research and theorization about the way that selves are determined by social influences. The vast bulk of work in this field is based on the concept of the individualistic self, and since it has been researched in the USA, gives a highly culture-specific impression that the individual self is 'the norm', when it is, in fact, just one version. Therefore I have restricted my treatment of it. Suggestions are provided at the end of the chapter if you want to know more.

Adorno's theory of socially acquired personality: authoritarianism

Adorno and his colleagues (1950) undertook one of the earliest studies of personality, shortly after the end of the Second World War, with the specific purpose of seeking to understand the anti-Semitism that had been such a central part of Nazisim. Their explicit objective was to discover what it is that leads some people to become prejudiced, in order to be able to ensure that the horrors of the Nazi regime would not be repeated.

Adorno and his colleagues found that people expressing **authoritarian personality** traits (racist attitudes, antagonism to homosexuals, very rigid ideas about what men and women should be like) tended to have had very harsh, traditional upbringings. Their parents adopted rigidly traditional gender roles. They imposed strict and inflexible rules of conduct, and applied harsh punishments for rule-breaking.

Adorno and his colleagues developed their ideas from psychodynamic theories about the impact of child-rearing practices and events in childhood upon adult personality. They concluded that authoritarianism was the product of repressed aggression. Children brought up in this manner, they argued, will experience feelings of hostility towards their parents because of their harsh treatment. But, because of their parents' repressive control, when they were children they were unable to express this anger. As a consequence, Adorno and his colleagues argued that the anger became displaced onto less 'dangerous' (from a psychodynamic point of view) targets, such as members of other races or homosexuals.

Social learning theory's account of the self

As in other fields, early work on social influences on the self was located within social learning theory. One of the best known is Daryl Bem's (1972) **self-perception theory** in which he suggested that we know who we are by observing our own behaviour.

> Individuals come to 'know' their own attitudes, emotions and other internal states partially by inferring them from observations of their own overt behaviour and/or the circumstances in which this occurs.
>
> (Bem 1972: 5)

For example, a person who attends church regularly will conclude they are religious; someone who enjoys social events and is always the 'life and soul of the party' will see themself as an extrovert (Salancik and Conway 1975; Rhodewalt and Augustsdottir 1986).

Learned helplessness

Social learning theory assumed that people learn to tackle their lives according to the rewards and punishment they have received, particularly in childhood. One well-known example is the theory of **learned helplessness** (Seligman 1975 is the standard text) devised from observations of rats in the laboratory. The rats were exposed at first to a regime where they were repeatedly punished without being able to do anything to prevent it. When, later, the regime was altered (so that they could now avoid the punishment) instead of changing their behaviour, the rats remained passive. They seemed to have lost the capacity to do anything to save themselves. They had 'learned to be helpless'.

Analogies were drawn by Seligman and his followers, to suggest that people may react to parallel situations in similar ways. People who grew up in environments where, whatever they did, they were treated badly, become, according to this theory 'eternal victims'. Either they become completely passive, seeing themselves as totally incapable to gaining life's rewards. Or they blame themselves whenever harmed by misfortune, beset by feelings of recrimination and guilt. This theory of learned helplessness has been used, for example, to seek to explain symptoms of depressive illness (for example Seligman *et al.* 1979).

Locus of control

Another, similar example is Rotter's **locus of control** construct (see Rotter 1966). According to this formulation, the way adults explain the things that happen to them is a product of their learning experiences as children. Those with early experiences of good behaviour being consistently rewarded, and bad behaviour being consistently punished, come to see themselves as 'in control'. Their successes are construed as just rewards for hard work and diligence; failure is that what they must expect if they are lazy, or do not try hard enough. Thus they learn to site control within themselves, and within their own actions. These people are termed 'internals'. In contrast, those who have had inconsistent experiences as children – who were rewarded and punished indiscriminately, irrespective of their behaviour, come, as adults, to see the things that happen to them as the consequence of chance. Their own behaviour is, from this standpoint, irrelevant – success is a matter of 'good luck', failure a matter of 'bad luck'. They site control in the vicissitudes of the outside world, and are labelled 'externals'.

Social identity theory

Couched within the social cognition paradigm, social identity theory is mostly concerned with how people relate to and relate within social groups. Therefore this theory will be considered mainly in Chapter 9.

Social identity theory focuses on people's social selves – the selves that arise from affiliation to or membership of social groups (such as religious or occupational groups) and/or social categories (such as gender or nationality). While Mead's early work included theorization about this (Mead 1934b), its 'founding father' is generally held to be Henri Tajfel (see Tajfel 1978; Tajfel and Turner 1986). Tajfel, another of social psychology's émigrés (this time from occupied France and German prison camps to England) had plenty of experience of prejudice and intergroup conflict. Tajfel set up a research group at Bristol University to develop theory and conduct research into social identity and its role in conflicts between groups, working, in particular with John Turner.

Social identity theory proposes that people's individual psychological processes (including, crucially, their identities) are transformed in group settings. People come to identify themselves with particular social groups and, thereby, to define themselves as having the characteristics of that social group. This identification is clearest in relation to large-scale, socially recognizable groups – such as being Jewish or Maori or disabled.

The construction of a social self

Turner (1982) argued that when people identify with their group, they undergo depersonalization – they abandon some of their uniqueness and engage in a process of **self-stereotyping**. Turner suggested that in order to strengthen their identification people are motivated to take on and define themselves in terms of stereotypical characteristics of the group. An example would be when a young woman who has seen herself as heterosexual adopts a new style of clothes and demeanour when she identifies herself as lesbian. Another would be a young woman who was brought up as non-religious adopts the veil and the devout demeanour when she identifies herself as Muslim. In both cases the young women cease to see how to dress and how to behave as matters of personal choice, but rather by reference to the group with which they identify.

However, Turner (1991) makes clear that such self-stereotyping can be very fluid, and shift according to the reference group. For example, yet another woman may identify herself as belonging to a reference group of 'professional women' at work, yet as a 'babe' when she goes out socializing on a 'girlie night out', and adjust her dress and demeanour accordingly. In each case she is conforming to a stereotype, but the stereotypes are different. In other words, it is important to recognize that social identity can be activated in different ways – ranging from a consistent and enduring identity to a range of dynamic and situation-specific identities.

Selves as moulded by social influences and processes

Experimental social psychology views the self as moulded by social processes (such as socialization and identification with particular social groups) and by social influences (such as the kind of upbringing a person is given).

- Adorno's theory of the *authoritarian personality* is an example of how such processes and influences are seen to work. It combines elements of psychodynamic and social learning theory. People are seen to develop an authoritarian personality through a highly rigid and traditional upbringing.

→

- *Social learning theory* claims that people acquire their personal capabilities and failings through the child-rearing regimes to which they are exposed.
- The theory of *learned helplessness* proposes that children exposed to chaotic forms of child rearing, where they are rewarded and punished indiscriminately, become, as adults, eternal victims – lacking the capacity to help themselves.
- A similar theory of *locus of control* suggests that chaotic child-rearing regimes produce adults who locate control of their lives in the external world – chance, luck and fate. By contrast, child-rearing regimes where good behaviour is rewarded and bad behaviour punished produce adults who locate control over their lives in their own actions, and are more likely to be self-motivated and self-disciplined.
- *Social identity theory* proposes that people gain their sense of identity through their affiliation with social groups. When their ingroup does well, they can bask in its reflected glory. When it does badly, this can undermine them.
- When people identify with an ingroup, their individual self gives way to a social self, and usually involves a degree of *self-stereotyping*.

THE INTERSUBJECTIVE SELF

The section is divided into two parts. The first takes you through the various elements that make up the intersubjective self, drawing mainly (but not exclusively) on a book published in the 1980s called *Changing the Subject*. Then it briefly introduces you to the theorizing of Michel Foucault, whose *History of Sexuality*, also first published in English in the 1980s, has had a dramatic impact not just upon critical social psychology, but Postmodern theory as generally applied in the human (and even in the natural) sciences. Here we look just at those aspects of his work that relate to identity, mainly identity in relation to sexuality.

Changing the subject

In 1984 a book was published that argued for a radical overhaul of psychology's view of the self – *Changing the Subject*. Its explicit agenda was, literally, to *change* our conception of both 'the subject' *of* psychology and 'the subject' *in* psychology – 'to demonstrate that the individual is not a fixed or given entity, but rather a particular product of historically specific practices of social regulation (Henriques *et al.* 1984: 12). It was written in reaction to what its authors saw as the ethnocentrism and prejudice built into experimental social psychological theories of the self. It argued that the self is not a subjective, personal, self-contained, individual entity, but a reflexive, connected, situated-in-the-world, intentional, and constantly presenced intersubjective self.

The intersubjective self

All that is a bit of a mouthful! Bear with me, and we will take each of these different elements of the intersubjective self in turn and gradually build up a picture of what is meant by an intersubjective self.

The reflexivity of the self

First, intersubjectivity takes a particular stance on the role our own subjectivity plays in the way we constitute our selves. If you recall, Mead's image of the person was as a reflexive self, stressing people's ability to observe, plan and respond to their own behaviour – to know themselves and to be self-directed. Mead also placed James' self-as-known and self-as-knower in a dialectical relationship with each other, in constant conversation. To be reflexive is to be aware and insightful, to be able, for example, to be ironic and make a joke against yourself. It is a portrayal of the self that is much more shrewd and intuitive, for example, than Goffman's face-painter.

The connectedness of the self

The second element of intersubjectivity is about how we construct and know who we are through our connected subjectivity with others – through our relationships and shared understandings with the people and the other things and abstract concepts (like religious faith) that give significance and meaning to our lives. These are as diverse as opera to soap opera, parents to pop idols, from the groups to which we belong as well as those from which we want to distance ourselves. Our **connected self** is constructed both *for* us (for example, through the duties and obligations others expect us to fulfil) and *by* us (through, for instance, emotional feelings towards another person or a pet, belief in God, or a sense of national pride).

   From an intersubjective perspective, connectedness is not just a quality of 'exotic others', though it undoubtedly has more salience in some value systems than others. It is central to all people, even those who live in a world that prioritizes the individual. To reiterate James, we could not be the selves we are 'If no one turned around when we entered, answered when we spoke, or minded what we did, but if every person we met "cut us dead" and acted as if we were nonexisting things' (James 1907: 179).

This element also has a lot in common with the idea of social identity, but the connected self is not just a matter of alliance to and identification with ingroups and hostility to outgroups. It is about a far denser and wider network of connections – to our 'significant others' and all those other others with whom we have specific relationships, including, for example, our ancestors and people who matter to us but have died or with whom we no longer have contact.

The being-in-the-world of the self

The third element of intersubjectivity is what the philosopher Heidegger ([1928] 1962) called our **being-in-the-world**. As you have seen already, experimental social psychology assumes there is a separation between two entities – the 'person' and the 'situation' (or context) in which that person operates. Persons are seen as individual, self-contained beings. They can be influenced by internal forces (whether instinct, values, attitudes, or social cognitions) and by external forces (the situation, social context, the group). But in this viewpoint the person is still thought of as pre-formed and fully present, and the situation is similarly seen as a kind of independent, objective 'frame' which exerts an independent causal effect on the person.

An intersubjective view of the self challenges this separation, arguing as follows:

- a person is never *not* in a situation that is *not* subject to 'social influence', and hence separating them creates an artificial partition, dividing up that which is inseparable. As long as they are conscious, a person is always in a state of being-in-the-world, or, as James might have put it, they are always immersed in a flow of consciousness about the world, a flow of consciousness on which the world (either/both immediately present or imagined) always-ever impinges.
- a situation is never simply an objectively present set of environmental conditions. It always-ever influences people's thoughts, experiences and actions through its significance to and meaningfulness for them. In simpler words, people are always-ever – but only ever – influenced by the situation through the way that they construe that situation.
- a person is never simply just 'there' as a timeless entity, but is constantly constructed, moment by moment, through the immanent possibilities presented by the situations that they are 'in', which are continually transformed and negotiated by the person.

Stainton Rogers *et al.* (1995) put it like this:

> people are inexorably part of, involved with, and inseparable from the circumstances that make up their world. To conceive of our selves (or whatever is denoted by the words 'I' and 'Me') as the 'inside' and the world as the 'outside' (a collection of stimuli) is to fail to recognize the extent to which we exist alongside-and-within the world. It is through and against our everyday involvements and engagements with the circumstances of our worlds (especially including other people) that we come to know ourselves.
>
> (Stainton Rogers *et al.* 1995: 55)

As I mentioned at the beginning of the section, experimental social psychology treats people as self-contained individuals who respond mechanistically to external and internal stimuli. Its theories of the 'self' therefore treat issues of concern, significance and involvement as things that 'get in the way' of being able to predict how people will behave. An intersubjective view of the self takes the opposite position. It says that if you want to know why a person is acting in a particular way, you cannot do so unless you also know what they are interested and involved in, what their concerns are, what the situation means to them.

> In short, to unproblematically separate personality from situation is to be already stepping blithely along an intellectual path which renounces our fundamental worldliness in favour of a radical objectification and subjection of all that is (i.e. either everything is subjective or everything is objective). What we mean by 'the world' here is not some external objectivity that we, as primarily detached subjectivities, strive to get to know. To us the world comprises the meaningful constitutive circumstances which are the source and target of our ongoing concerns and interests. The world is that which we are already involved with, and hence that which is significant for us: *our* world.
>
> (Stainton Rogers *et al.* 1995: 56, emphasis in the original)

The intentionality of the self

The fourth element of intersubjectivity is a perception of the person as purposive and strategic – as acting intentionally – an intentional self. In Chapter 1 I drew attention to James' understanding of the self that stressed his vision of people as intentional, and thus having free will.

> Of course we measure ourselves by many standards. Our strength and our intelligence, our wealth and even our good luck, are things that warm our heart and make us feel ourselves a match for life. But deeper than all such

Here I am following the convention of referring to myself (as I was part of the *et al.*) as just a disinterested other because I played only a small contribution in writing these words.

things, and able to suffice unto itself without them, is the sense of the amount of effort which we can put forth. Those are, after all, but effects, products and reflections of the outer world within. But the effort seems to belong to an altogether different realm, as if it were the substantive thing that we *are*, and those are but externals that we *carry*.

(James 1907: 458)

In this perspective the situations and circumstances and social influences, both those that directly impinge from the outside and those that are 'in our heads' and exert influence from the inside, are not what ultimately *determine* our actions. They are not causes. They do not produce a passive puppet that cannot move unless these external and internal forces pull the strings. Rather they provide a stage in which a range of possible actions can be acted out – but acted out intentionally through, for want of a better word, our *will*. Our actions are wilful, intended actions – or, at least, they *can* be, and (usually) are when it matters.

Here we can draw parallels with what is happening in theorization in experimental social psychology. As you saw in Chapters 5 and 6, their perception of attribution and attitudes is moving to a position where it is recognized that a lot of what we do in the ordinary, mundane, everyday living of our life is pretty mindless. We go along a lot of the time running on autopilot, in a largely pre-programmed manner. We are barely conscious of the things we say and do, and act them out virtually automatically. In such circumstances we are somewhat like robots – very efficient, but also servile to the vicissitudes of our programming that is encoded highly stereotypically and heuristically, and hence open to thinking and acting in mindless ways that can lead to mindless stupidity. To claim that people have the capacity to be intentional is not to claim that they always act with great deliberation and intention, or even that they do so most of the time. It is to claim that they *can be* intentional, and usually are, when it matters to them to be so. In other words, stressing intentionality directs our attention to the ways in which people are strategic in what they do – including constructing themselves.

When a woman says, for example, 'I am a lesbian' she is not somehow looking within herself and reporting what she has discovered there. She is actively and intentionally staking a claim, on the basis of what matters to her in her life and on what matters in the 'now' of the conversation she is having. The person she is speaking to might make a counter-claim, such as 'Well, you don't look like one and you don't act like one, and I think you are just playing at it because you think it's trendy. You're not a real lesbian, you're just a lipstick lesbian'. This person is staking a counter-claim, based on what matters to them in their life and on what matters in the 'now' of the conversation they are having.

Situations like this, where people contest or confirm their own or each other's definitions of their selves, are the norm when saying something about your self. There are formal ones – such as filling in a form to get a passport or apply for a job. In neither case do you merely look inside your self to tell who you are. The circumstance sets up an agenda, telling you what kind of claim you need to stake. There are intimate ones – sending your lover a text message that says 'You are my earth, moon and stars' or being told by your irate friend '*Who* do you think you are – my mother?' These circumstances also set their own agendas. They have what is sometimes rather grotesquely called **issuance** – there is an issue at stake, around which one or more stakes are claimed and often counter-claimed. To send a text to your lover saying 'You are my earth, moon and stars' is not some kind of pallid conveying of a description, it is sent for a purpose (I am sure you can think of all sorts of possible reasons, from the sweetly romantic to the cynical). Whenever a self (or an aspect of a self) is defined, it is done for a reason, to stake some kind of a claim, in order to achieve some sort of end. Even done mindlessly, the habitual nature of such a claim arises from a purpose, albeit, in this case, a purpose that, itself, has become habitual.

The self as constituted through presencing practices

Staking a claim is always provisional and contingent. An intersubjective perspective of the self denies the assumption that 'personality' or 'character is a static and consistent quality of being-a-person. It sees instead a *self as constituted through presencing practices*, a self that is always-ever in a state of being re-produced, both through the 'flow of consciousness' and through being-in-the-world. The analogy I have used is music-making, where the music exists only through being played. It helps, I hope, to understand what is being said here. This is probably the most difficult claim for most people to accept, because it is seen to imply that the self is entirely fragmentary, with nothing holding it together – a chameleon that is in a constant state of transformation.

To get a handle on it, you need to take all the other aspects of inter-subjectivity into your frame of reference. Crucially you need to transcend the person/situation division that, in a Modern worldview, at least, is so deeply sedimented it feels natural and incontrovertible. If you can accept that the self is in a constant state of being presenced – the self not as a thing but as a product of presencing practices – then you are more than half way there.

An example may help here. In Shakespeare's time homosexuality was not seen as an identity but as a practice, conceptualized as something that some people sometimes *did*, rather than something some people *are*. Taking an intersubjective stance on the self is to reconnect the person and the situation into an interconnected presencing *practice* (that is action) rather than regarding them as two separate entities in interaction. The person/situation distinction is seen, in this theoretical frame, as *reifying* the self.

Let us take our example of homosexuality, and tease apart what is signified by 'reification'. Here's a clear illustration of what I mean, drawn from an account of homosexuality written in the 1960s, when it was classified as an illness:

> The homosexual has been a stumbling block to many clinical theorists – especially in that he fails to respond to treatment – and he has been described as obstinate, uncooperative, etc. The profile places him actually as an anxiety neurotic, perhaps as a result of undischargeable ergic tensions, but also with a peculiar emphasis on extraversion and radicalism. Thus unlike the introverted neurotic he is compelled to 'act out' his difficulty, and to do so without conservative inhibitions.
>
> (Cattell 1966: 331)

Because this is written in the homophobic language of the 1960s and uses the terminology of Eysenck's extraversion/introversion theory, it is relatively easy to 'see through' what is going on – Cattell is staking a claim. It is that 'the homosexual' (that is, a particular category of person) is 'an anxiety neurotic' (that is has particular innate psychologically dysfunctional qualities) and therefore that he is 'compelled to act out' (that is, that he is unable to help himself behaving in a dysfunctional way). Put this all together and you have constructed homosexuality as a thing – a category of person with psychologically dysfunctional qualities that impel him to act in a dysfunctional way. All the presencing practices that *could* still today add up to being given this identity of homosexual-as-mentally-ill – acting in a 'camp manner', going to gay bars, marching in Gay Pride processions (I could go on, but you get the picture) – would be merely seen, through that identity, as forms of dysfunctional 'acting out' of a 'difficulty'. But for a gay man today in San Francisco or Sydney, they are something else entirely – the presence being practised is not an 'acting out of neurosis' but a celebration of a gay identity.

The point is, either way, presencing practices like these do not inevitably *make* a person into a homosexual. A gay man might celebrate his gay identity with pride, and through identifying with a gay community that both provides opportunity for and approval of these presencing practices. But that does not make his identity a 'real thing'.

Now all we need to do is close a loop. Throughout the book you have been exposed to the claim that, from a discursive psychology point of view, people construct their social realities through discursive practices – by purposively and strategically *doing* things whenever they use language. Discursive practices are one form of presencing practice. Staking a claim is a discursive practice that is also a presencing practice. Claiming an identity is to reproduce it through discursive practices, within situations other presencing practices (like going to gay pubs, marching in Gay Pride rallies). It is in this sense that a self is seen to be not an identity (who you are) but a practice (what you do, in relation to what your deeds mean).

Technologies of the self

Social constructionist theorizing, however, does not view identities as something that people can freely choose or construct at will. Much of it is devoted to examining the structures and forces that limit and control people's freedom to be anything they want to be. Vance (1992) makes this clear in relation to sexual identity. Social constructionism, she says, does not suggest that 'individual sexual identity is easily changeable, much like a new outfit plucked from the closet at whim; that individuals have conscious control over sexual identity; that large-scale cultural formations regarding sexuality are easily changed' or that 'individuals have an open-ended ability to construct themselves, or to reconstruct themselves' (Vance 1992: 133).

Much of Postmodern theorizing about the self has been directed, in particular, to sexual identity. I would surmise (as have others) that this is because the theorists who have been most active in this field have had a personal stake, Michel Foucault being the most notable example. Foucault was gay in a very in-your-face kind of way, during a pre-AIDS historical period when gay men were actively challenging the kind of homosexual-as-sick construction that Cattell was promoting and reclaiming their identity as one to be revelled in and taken pride in. Equally, if less visibly, some of the most active Feminist theorists in this field are self-identified separatist lesbians – that is, they claim their lesbian identities through their Feminist commitment to challenge patriarchy by not 'sleeping with the enemy'. A good example of theorization about identity from a separatist lesbian position is Kitzinger's (1987) *The Social Construction of Lesbianism*. Here, however, I concentrate on Foucault.

Regulating the self

One of Foucault's most influential concepts is the **technology of the self** – his claim that we produce our selves through treating them, almost, as technological projects, entities that must be constructed and that need to be constantly tinkered with to maintain them. However, this he saw as not a self-indulgent kind of identity-DIY, where the person concerned can simply express their own creativity and originality. Crucially for Foucault, the technological work involved is both governed by society's institutions (like in the UK you have to get planning permission to build a house) and some aspects are required by them (building regulations require you to construct it according to specific standards).

This is one half of the story – the technology of the self as directly and explicitly governed by institutional forces. The self we can build in this way is stringently constrained by the overt exercise of power. Laws against homosexuality are a good example here, and until homosexuality was decriminalized these alone exerted immense control over a person's freedom to construct themselves as a homosexual – they had to act in subversive ways to do so. But by 'institutional power' Foucault did not only mean the formal institutions like the law (that prohibited homosexual activity), education (that taught it was wrong) and medicine (that assumed that it needed to be treated and assumed the right to do so). He also included less formal elements, like pressures exerted by public opinion that stigmatized homosexuality and treated homosexuals as outcasts.

The other half of the story is self-regulation. To convey this idea Foucault adopted the metaphor of the Panopticon. This is a design for a prison developed by Jeremy Bentham, in which there is a central guard room surrounded by a number of cells in a circle around it. Each cell has a window, allowing the guard to maintain constant surveillance over the prisoners in all of the cells. This rendered the prisoners constantly under surveillance. While the guards could each look in only one direction at a time, the prisoners knew that they could be observed at any time. So if the prisoners acted in a way that the guard could punish, they did so in the knowledge that, at any time, they could be spotted. The effect is that prisoners become self-regulating. Constantly vigilant over their own behaviour, constantly aware that at any moment they could get caught out, the prisoners acted as though the guards were looking at them all the time, even though a lot of the time they were not.

Foucault claims that this self-regulation is the main way in which control is exercised. People come to act as if they are under constant scrutiny, even though most of the time they are not. In other words, institutions only need to directly and overtly exercise their governmental power occasionally and superficially. The mere fact that they have the power and can exercize it is enough to control what people do. Thus the selves that are produced through technologies of the self are highly governed and regulated. Foucault developed an extended (but incomplete – he died of HIV-induced infection before he could finish it) project of analysis and largely archival research of technologies of the self in relation to sexuality in a three-part work *History of Sexuality*.

Strategies to regulate sexuality

Foucault ([1976] 1980) began his *History of Sexuality* by observing that it is commonly assumed within Western culture that there has been a sequence of transformations of sexuality. According to this story, in the seventeenth century sexuality was relatively openly and freely acted out and discussed. By the nineteenth century sexuality had become repressed – regulated, censored and hidden away. In current times it is supposed that we have sexual liberation – a reaction against the old hypocrisy and prudery and an opening up of sexuality. Foucault argues that while there is some truth in this perception, it is only one of the stories that can be told. A counter-argument is that far from being repressed, sexuality became, over time, increasingly to *matter* – to be a site of power, a means of regulation and a source of knowledge. The task he set himself was therefore to 'define the regimes of power-knowledge-pleasure that sustain the discourse on human sexuality' (Foucault [1976] 1980: 11). He proposed that four main strategies have been used to regulate sexuality:

1 The socialization of procreative behaviour.
2 The hystericization of women's bodies.
3 The pedagogization of children's sexuality.
4 The psychiatrization of perverse desire.

The socialization of procreative behaviour

This strategy involves restricting legitimate sexuality within long-term relationships between heterosexual couples, and making these couples responsible for procreative sex and the rearing of the children that ensue from it. In this way legitimate sexuality gets doubly 'contained'. First, it gets neatly cordoned off within the confines of the normative family. And then, within the family, it gets hidden away behind the parental bedroom door. This strategy warrants what Foucault calls the 'alliance of the family' – the creation of a powerful interpersonal alliance between family members, who are seen (and see themselves) as entitled to privacy and immunity from external intervention. This acts as a normatizing force, which privatizes fertility control and child-rearing.

The hystericization of women's bodies

In this strategy women's sexuality is constituted as central to their identity – they 'are' their biology, and sexuality is at the core of their biology. In this context 'sexuality' is not just about 'having sex' but incorporates experiences like menstruation, pregnancy, childbirth, and menopause. What Foucault is implying here is that women get to be treated as 'walking wombs' (note that *hyster* is the Greek word for womb). This 'hystericization' then warrants the regulation of women, making them the legitimate objects of medical and psychological scrutiny and intervention and hence control.

The pedagogization of children's sexuality

According to Foucault this strategy works in two ways. First, it makes any sexual contact between an adult and a child into a 'monstrous crime' – one in which only a monster would engage. The second element is to regulate children's sexuality itself. These two strategies can be viewed as responses to the potential of childhood sexuality to act as a site of resistance to adult power. Foucault writes of the 'precious and perilous, dangerous and endangered potential' (1980: 104) of childhood sexuality which, being both 'natural' and, at the same time, 'contrary to nature', 'poses physical and moral, individual and collective dangers'. Consequently, he argues: the 'sex of children has become, since the eighteenth century, an important area of contention around which innumerable institutional devices and discursive strategies have been deployed' (Foucault 1980: 30). Foucault asserted that we can see this manifested, for instance, in the architecture of schools, designed to expose children to constant and vigilant surveillance. More generally, the strategy places all those in authority over children in a state of perpetual alert and exhorts them to control the sexuality of the children in their care.

The psychiatrization of perverse desire

This strategy works by pathologizing – turning into an illness – all deviations from 'normal sexuality'. Foucault was particularly concerned about male homosexuality and his terminology here highlights the particular warrant this provided for psychiatry to intervene and control homosexuality, by using a range of corrective technologies including different kinds of medical treatment: drugs to reduce libido, aversion therapy and psychoanalysis.

How the strategies work

Foucault's four strategies add up to a powerful regulatory framework, in which people's sexual identities are pretty well laid out for them. Each one provides for a particular category of person, almost an identity straitjacket into which they have to somehow squeeze their selves and make them fit the accepted model. Heterosexual adults are required to 'fit in' by adopting identities along a pre-set sequence – single (but looking for someone), dating, engaged, all leading up to married. Once married they are expected to be sexually faithful. Women's identities are further constrained in ways that require them to fulfil their biological destiny – motherhood. Children are expected to have identities where sexuality is excluded, and adults are expected to protect their innocence. Homosexuals' identity is the most restricted as all – it is cast as invalid, and anyone adopting it is 'fair game' for psychiatric control and treatment.

A useful term here is **subject positioning**. At this broad level of analysis, regulatory strategies position subjects in particular ways. For instance, a child is, through the regulatory strategy of pedagogization, positioned as asexual. But the term is used at other levels too. For example, a discourse in which adult–child sex is viewed as sexual abuse positions those who have experienced sexual abuse in their childhood as victims. As victims they are harmed, and since they are harmed, they are in need of therapy. However, there is another discourse that has been generated primarily out of the actions of self-help groups. This focuses more on the moral and criminal wrongs done to children by adults who engage them in sexuality. These offer an alternative position – survivor. Worrell (2000) has conducted a study working with a Survivors' Self-help Group, which looks in detail at the discursive 'work' involved in abandoning the subject position of 'victim' and taking on the new – and more powerful – subject position of 'survivor'.

This brings us to our last key idea in this section – that of **resistance**. Foucault stressed over and over again in his writings that the exercise of power is never simple, nor is it usually unidirectional in its impact. While society's institutions may be very powerful indeed, people can and do resist. Resistance can also be exercised in a variety of ways. One is the example above – where individuals collectively act together to encourage each other to reposition themselves. Survivors' Self-help Groups are set up to specifically challenge the power of the 'helping professions' to position them as inevitably 'damaged goods' (however well-meaning the intentions) and to therefore justify intervening in their lives and requiring them to undergo therapy.

But the list above of the traditional subject positions in relation to sexual identity is (somewhat) outdated, 20 years since Foucault assembled it. While the subject position of 'childhood innocence and vulnerability' has been, if anything, reinforced and has strengthened its grip since then, the rest are being increasingly broached, in some societies at least, through various forms of resistance. A good example is the Feminist movement, set up explicitly to resist the patriarchal powers that positioned women as 'walking wombs'.

The intersubjective self

The intersubjective self is reflexive, connected, situated-in-the-world, intentional and the product of presencing practices.

- Its **reflexivity** means that it is insightful, shrewd and intuitive, self-aware and self-monitoring.

→

- Its *connectedness* is about the way it shares subjectivity with others, through, for example, a shared system of signification.
- It is always ever in a state of *being-in-the-world*, where there is no separation between the person and the situation.
- Its *intentionality* stresses the purposive and strategic ways in which the self is presenced according to what is at stake in any situation, and the stake the person wants to claim.
- Crucially, the self is viewed as produced and perceived through *presencing practices*.

Technology of the self is a term originated by Foucault to describe the ways in which people's identities are moulded both by the overt regulatory power of society's institutions, and their self-regulation arising from surveillance. Identities, in this view, are produced by strategies of power. In relation to sexuality these are:

- The socialization of procreative behaviour
- The hystericization of women's bodies
- The pedagogization of children's sexuality
- The psychiatrization of perverse desire.

Each works through *subject positioning* – through the network of these powers creating conditions in which people adopt particular identities. They can accept the subject position provided for them by regulatory power, or they can adopt a strategy of *resistance* in order to take up another subject position to defy authority.

FURTHER READING

Relational selves

Kondo, D. (1990) *Crafting Selves: Power, Gender and Discourses of Identity in a Japanese Workplace*. Chicago: University of Chicago Press. An extended extract from this work is included in Wetherell, M. and Maybin, J. (2000) The distributed self: a social constructionist perspective, in R. Stevens (ed.) *Understanding the Self*. London: Sage.

> Kondo's account of her changing identity during the period of her anthropological studies in Japan provides a compelling illustration of the way in which selfhood is produced and maintained through culture. The extract from Wetherell and Maybin is possibly easier to get hold of, and is a fascinating and insight-provoking read, whatever your own cultural background.

Experimental social psychology

Brown, R.J. (2000a) Social identity theory: past achievements, current problems and future challenges, *European Journal of Social Psychology*, 30: 745–8.

> This article provides a comprehensive overview from a 'straight' experimental social psychology perspective.

Smith, E.R. and Mackie, D.M. (2000) *Social Psychology*. Philadelphia, PA: Taylor and Francis.

> Chapter 4 on the self is not so much further as alternative reading. It is very much the US style approach to this topic, which I have largely excluded because of its almost exclusive and uncritical focus on studies conducted in the USA. However, if this is what you want or need, this chapter is clear, comprehensive and particularly useful if you want to use it in applied settings. It has, for example, extensive coverage of self-esteem, and of coping strategies to defend against stress. Chapter 4 in this book offers a reasonably detailed and comprehensive coverage of social identity, but its main strength is, again, in its links to applied settings.

Critical social psychology

Blackman, L. and Walkerdine, V. (2001) *Mass Hysteria: Critical Psychology and Media Studies*. Basingstoke: Palgrave.

> This book provides a much deeper and broader analysis of intersubjective identity that I have been able to here. Chapter 10 – 'Post-identities: sexuality and the colonial subject' – is particularly useful. There is a great deal to get your head round in this book, but it is a sustained project of linking critical (social) psychology and Media studies and, as such, set to become an influential text. You might like to begin with Chapter 10 on Princess Diana and practices of subjectification (another way of putting subject positioning), which is a gripping read.

Foucault, M. ([1976] 1980) *The History of Sexuality*, Vol. 1. Harmondsworth: Penguin.

> If you want to begin to get to grips with Foucault, this is the book to start you off. His writing is often dense and hard going, but it is worth the effort.

QUESTIONS

1 What can the early work of James, Mead and Goffman offer to our understanding of the self today?

2 To what extent does a person's sense of who they are depend upon the culture in which they were brought up? What problems does this pose for social psychology?

3 Compare and contrast Adorno's theory of authoritarian personality and Eysenck's personality theory. Which one, in your view, provides a more convincing account of the 'self'?

4 What contribution has social learning theory made to our understanding of the self?

5 What is meant by the term 'intersubjective self'? Does it imply that people can simply choose who they want to be?

6 What contribution has Foucault made to our understanding of the self?

Chapter 9

Groups

Chapter contents

A route map of the chapter

The chapter starts by asking 'What is a group?' It examines three different kinds of groups, and gives an example of research on each kind to help you get to grips with the differences between them.

It next looks at social influence in groups, including the pressures on people in a group to conform to group pressures or rebel against it, and then the phenomenon of group polarization. The final section examines conflict between groups, and how it may be resolved.

What is a group?

⬇

Social influence in groups

⬇

Group polarization

⬇

Intergroup conflict

Learning objectives

When you have completed your study on this chapter, you should be able to:

1 Define the differences between incidental, membership and identity-reference groups, illustrating each with an example of the level and kind of group commitment involved.

2 Define 'conformity' in relation to group influence, and describe the main processes involved in this phenomenon and the influences upon it.

3 Define 'majority influence' and 'minority influence' in this context, and outline the theories and models that have been devised to explain when and how they each work.

4 Define 'group polarization' and 'Groupthink'. For each explain why they are thought to happen and the theories to explain why they occur.

5 Outline the main reasons for intergroup conflict, and the steps that can be taken to reduce it.

INTRODUCTION

This chapter is about the ways in which individuals' thoughts, feelings and actions are influenced by being part of a group, and how individuals can also affect groups. In fact social psychology takes a very broad sweep when it comes to groups – from collections of, say, four or five people brought together to do an experiment, to viewing, say, 'Chinese' as a group to which people belong, have allegiance to and from which they derive their social identity. It has studied groups ranging from boys at summer camp to nurses in hospitals, from young joy-riders to high-level executives.

WHAT IS A GROUP?

Hogg and Vaughan (1998) wryly comment that there are almost as many definitions of a 'group' as there are social psychologists! The trouble is, the term is used very differently in different contexts. For simplicity (drawing on Kelley, 1952) in this chapter I distinguish between three main meanings:

- **Incidental groups** are simply where some people are brought together for a relatively short period of time (a matter of hours at most) with minimal involvement in and commitment to each other. Examples are the kinds of 'small groups' set up to do an exercise in a training session or a workshop at a conference.
- **Membership groups** are those defined by being a member. Members may join and leave the group, but membership typically lasts some time (weeks, months or years) and members have a commitment to the group's common goals and values. Examples include work-based groups (such as a group of hospital doctors working together as a 'firm'), clubs, associations and committees.
- **Identity-reference groups** are where belonging to the group involves identification with the group, and where affiliation acts as a **reference frame** for a person to know 'who' they are – their social identity. Generally this is a long-term situation (often for many years or even permanently) and those who belong to the group will share common experiences, values and norms. Examples include ethnic identity groups (for example being pakeha or Chinese), religious communities (for example being a Muslim or a Catholic), political affiliations (for example being a socialist or a communist), nationalities and communities (for example being a Slovak or an Amish), and subcultures (for example being a Goth or a skinhead).

These three different kinds of groups vary, very broadly, in terms of their durability and the commitment of their membership, as shown in Figure 9.1.

Figure 9.1

Groups vary in their degree of commitment and conhesiveness

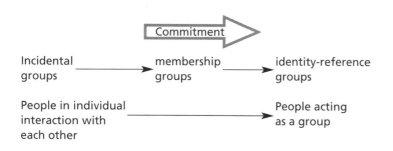

You have guessed it – it is nowhere near as simple as this. For example, membership groups are often identity-reference groups too. The distinction between being a member of a political party or pressure group and this being a person's identity-reference group is seldom clear-cut. Equally, social psychologists have studied identity-reference aspects of incidental groups. However, I think you will find the categorization helpful in that social psychologists have studied these groups in broadly different ways and, to some degree, the social psychological processes that are seen to go on within them are different.

I am going to use this section to give you a flavour of the differences between these three kinds of groups by illustrating each one with a key area of research into group processes.

Incidental groups

In social psychology the most common form of incidental group is a group convened for the purposes of an experiment! What distinguishes such groups is their low level of involvement or commitment, and generally this means that there is little, if any, group behaviour going on. A group like this is in many ways more of a collection of individuals interacting together.

The minimal group paradigm

It reality, it appears that commitment is seldom completely absent. Studies in what is called the **minimal group paradigm** have shown that almost any element of common fate is sufficient to persuade people to begin to see themselves as part of a group – by, for example, favouring members of 'their' group over members of another group. Rabbie and Horowitz (1969) demonstrated this by allocating children to groups of four by giving them badges (green or blue). In the control condition the two groups just sat together on different sides of a screen dividing greens from blues. In the experimental condition one group was given a radio and the other was not. Subsequently in both conditions the screen was removed and the children in turn read out statements about themselves, after which all the other children in both groups rated them on a number of evaluative scales. Children in the control condition showed no significant differences in their evaluations. But children in the experimental condition consistently evaluated children from their own group more favourably. However, a later study (Tajfel *et al.* 1971) showed that mere categorization as a member of a group can be enough to engender commitment, and this finding has proved extremely robust in more than 20 replications. However, it gets a lot more complicated, if, for example, group members allocate unpleasant things rather than rewards. There is considerable controversy about whether experimental effects arise from commitment to the group or some other reason. Brown (2001) provides a clear account of this dispute.

Membership groups

In real life, membership groups entail a fair degree of engagement with (and hence commitment to) the group. But experimentally created groups can be induced to behave more like membership groups, for example, when subjects are required to interact with each other and carry out a task together, as shown in Figure 9.2.

An example of experimentally observable effects of group membership are studies of social influence that either demonstrate social idling (usually called social loafing) or social energizing. These are, in other words, studies of social inhibition and facilitation applied to settings where subjects work together on a common task.

Social loafing

Most early studies in this situation found that overall task performance went down when people work together. The total output for the group was less than the sum of individual outputs that people achieve when working alone. Some of this decrement has been attributed to coordination loss – due, for example, to when people jostle or distract each other.

But over and above this a substantial number of studies have found decrements due to **social loafing** – the tendency for individuals to expend less effort on a task when they do it with others (or think they are doing so). Latané *et al.* (1979), for example, found that when people are asked to shout together as loud as they could, the amount of noise each person makes is reduced by 29 per cent in two-person groups, 49 per cent in four-person groups and 60 per cent in six-person groups. This effect has been found in almost 80 studies that have been published (see Williams *et al.* 1993 for a review). These include laboratory and field studies, with physical, cognitive, perceptual and evaluative tasks. However, the effect is most marked when the task is pretty trivial and meaningless. Where the task is important and meaningful, and/or the group members have a personal stake in the outcome, there is much less drop-off in performance.

Social energizing

It is now becoming recognized that social loafing is a consequence of working in groups with low commitment to each other and where they are required to do trivial and meaningless tasks. In other situations working as a member of a

Figure 9.2
When individuals perform tasks together as a group they become more like a membership group

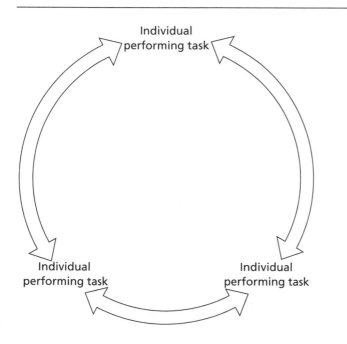

group can energize people into action rather than persuade them to loaf or to idle. We can call this opposite effect **social energizing**, where people work harder as a member of a group than alone. This is what happens when the task is important or interesting or fun (Zaccaro 1984). It also tends to occur when group members think they are competing against another group, and/or where there is strong commitment to achieving a common goal (Guzzo and Dickenson 1996).

It is worth noting that the vast majority of studies that found a social loafing effect were carried out in individualistic cultures. Smith and Harris Bond (1993) suggest that people from collectivist cultures are more likely to perform best when working together, especially when they think performance will be judged on the *group's* achievements. Here culturally normative collective values may encourage even members of incidental groups to act as if they belong to an identity-referent or membership group, at least where the task they have to do together is meaningful and important.

In collectivist cultures social energizing is thus more likely, and Smith and Harris Bond (1993) cite a number of cross-cultural studies as evidence for this. For instance, Earley (1989) compared managers in the USA and China working on an 'in basket' simulation task in which they had to deal with a rapid succession of tasks (such as rating job application forms, prioritizing interviews, and so on). Managers were told either that they were working alone and set individual targets, or that they were working as a group with group targets. US managers completed more tasks in the 'working alone' condition; Chinese managers completed more in the 'working together' condition. Similar energizing effects have been demonstrated with Taiwanese children (Gabrenya *et al.* 1985) and Japanese subjects (Matsui *et al.* 1987).

Idling or energizing?

What these differences tell us is that social loafing is not a universal quality of task performance in a group, but, again, something of an artefact of experimentally creating incidental groups. Where people are required to do pretty trivial and meaningless tasks then they are more likely to idle when working in a group than alone. This is particularly so when performing in a group where there is little or no involvement in or commitment to the group, nor any cultural norms to encourage group effort. Without any real stake in the outcome and where any individual's poor performance is less likely to be noticed, people tend to idle. By contrast, with groups that have (culturally) – or are motivated to develop (experimentally) – some degree of cohesiveness and common commitment (that is, they are or become, in effect, a membership group) and where the task is intrinsically interesting or worthwhile, then working together *as* a group is likely to be energizing.

Identity-reference groups

Identity-reference groups are where people's commitment to the group is so strong that affiliation to it is part of their identity: 'People take on the group characteristics and make these their own, at any rate for the time being, to a greater or lesser extent' (Turner 1991: 35).

A classic experimental study of an identity-reference group is a series of field experiments carried out at summer camps (often called the **Summer Camp experiments**) by Sherif and his colleagues (Sherif *et al.* 1961; Sherif 1966; Sherif and Sherif 1969). There were three of these carried out in 1949, 1953 and 1954, with slight variations in conditions and measures, but all conformed to the same general plan. Here I describe just one.

Sherif's Summer Camp experiments

The experiment was conducted with white, middle-class 11- and 12-year-old boys who did not know each other. The boys attended a summer camp – in the USA this is a common practice, providing opportunities for an activity holiday in the countryside for children (and a break for their parents!). However, unbeknown to the boys, the camp was staffed by researchers who observed the boys' behaviour in a situation deliberately structured to examine group behaviour. Sherif himself, for example, was the camp caretaker and handyman as well as leader of the experimental project team. The experiment consisted of four phases: spontaneous friendship formation, group formation, intergroup competition, and intergroup cooperation.

Spontaneous friendship formation

On arrival at the camp the boys all spent a short time together. They were free to mix with each other as they liked, and to freely choose partners for games and activities and as room-mates.

Ingroup formation

After a few days the boys were then divided into two groups. They were lodged in cabins some distance from each other and the groups were kept entirely separate. The researchers engaged the boys in activities to develop cohesiveness in the groups, getting them involved in cooperative projects like setting up a camp and cleaning a beach. Rapidly both groups became established. Leaders emerged and names were agreed for the groups – 'Bulldogs' and 'Red Devils' in this case. Soon in each group there were 'in jokes', secret codes, rules about behaviour, and sanctions agreed and imposed for those who got 'out of line'. Sound friendships were formed, and strong bonds of mutual liking and cooperation developed between group members.

Intergroup competition

Then the researchers brought the two groups together in deliberately competitive situations. A tournament was organized in which the groups competed against each other in a number of different activities for points that were manipulated so the groups were constantly neck and neck. Initial norms of good sportsmanship soon broke down and rapidly the groups became almost fanatical about winning out against each other. As the tension grew they became more and more hostile towards each other. They began to call each other derogatory names, pick fights and raid each other's camps. 'Bulldogs' put down 'Red Devils' at every opportunity and vice versa. At the same time ingroup cohesion and loyalty became stronger.

Intergroup cooperation

It would be impossible to conduct a study like the Summer Camp experiments today, given the ethical issues it raised. Even at the time, in the first study the researchers were shocked by what happened. They tried a number of strategies to tackle the incredible antagonism that had built up. They got the boys to attend religious services that preached love and cooperation, introduced a third group as a 'common enemy' and engaged the boys in joint ventures that were pleasurable, such as setting off fireworks together. None of these worked – the boys simply turned each event into a new opportunity to attack each other. In the end the researchers found one that did – creating superordinate goals that could be achieved only through cooperation between the groups. First, the researchers arranged for the water supply line to break down, in a situation where both groups had to work together to fix it. The boys did cooperate – but as soon as the water supply was returned, they went back on the warpath. However, after a series of several such cooperative ventures, the antipathy between the two groups was eventually reduced enough for most of them to choose to go home on the same bus. In subsequent studies the researchers systematically introduced an intergroup cooperation phase to reduce the hostility created.

Lessons learned

Sherif and Sherif (1969) themselves acknowledged that the Summer Camp experiments were only partially true to life, in that real conflicts between groups are much more complex, containing elements of historical feuds, power and dominance differentials, and structural, material and political inequalities. However, this research is seen as important, since it demonstrated very clearly that antagonistic and hostile behaviour can be generated by group situations. Crucially, these studies have been seen to demonstrate that human aggression is seldom simply a matter of *individual* pathology or dysfunction. It can be – and usually is – affected by the social influence of group processes.

Incidental, membership and identity-reference groups

- *Incidental groups* are characterized by people having little or no involvement in or commitment to the group, individualistic cultural norms and no real stake in what happens. Generally in such situations the impact of the group on individual behaviour is negative – social loafing – or minimal.
- *Membership groups* are where there is only moderate involvement and commitment but individuals see themselves as having some stake in the group's fortunes. The impact of the group is generally positive – encouraging group members to work harder *for* the group, and to treat other members of the group more favourably than outsiders.
- *Identity-reference groups* provide members with a locus for identification. Individuals shift from a personal to a social identity. It becomes their ingroup. In such ingroups involvement and commitment are high. Members have a strong investment in the ingroup's fortunes. Its successes and failures become *their* successes and failures. Group membership encourages cooperation within the ingroup and conflict with outgroups.

SOCIAL INFLUENCE IN GROUPS

We now move on to explore some of the group processes that experimental social psychologists have studied. We start with research into social influence, beginning with its ability to induce conformity.

Conformity

Conformity is one of the most extensively studied forms of social influence since Allport (1924) observed that groups tend to give more conservative judgements than individuals. Sherif (1936) explained this as the effect of group norms – where people tend to refer to each other and find a 'middle ground' on which to base a decision. He carried out a series of studies using the **autokinetic effect**. This is where a small bright light is shone in otherwise complete darkness, and it appears to move even though it is stationary. With no reference point to locate it, people's eye movements give the impression that it is moving. When people are asked how far it is moving, they find it very difficult to tell. When observing the effect in groups of three or four, taking it in turns to call out their estimate, Sherif observed that individuals' estimates tended to converge to the group mean after a few trials.

Norms

Norms are defined as the shared standards of conduct expected of group members. They can either be explicit (for example norms of confidentiality in juries) or implicit – the kinds of everyday, taken-for-granted conventions that oil the machinery of social interaction. Transgressing social norms can be very disruptive. In a classic study Garfinkel (1967) got students to behave at home with their families as if they were lodgers. For a period of 15 minutes they were very polite, spoke formally and then only when spoken to. Their families were puzzled and got quite angry, accusing them of being selfish, nasty and rude.

The concept of norms was used by Festinger to develop **social comparison theory** (Festinger 1954). Based on Social Learning theory, it sees norms as operating through people's propensity to want social approval and dislike social censure. For the individual, norms provide a reference frame for social comparison, and hence for guiding behaviour.

Different reference groups have different norms. Which one is followed will depend on which one is relevant to the person at the time. For instance, Tom lives in a student house, his reference group is 'students' and its norm is that only total nerds stay in on a Friday night. Tom will find it hard to resist the group pressure to go out, even if he has an urgent essay to finish. By contrast Dan lives at home with his family whose group norm is that studying is more important than going out. Dan will find it difficult to resist his family's pressure to stay home and study.

Asch's studies of conformity

In Asch's (1951) first classic experiment on conformity, male students were told they were taking part in a study of visual discrimination. They were shown a line, and three other lines to compare it with (see Figure 9.3), and then asked to say which of the comparison lines matched it.

This experiment was run with groups of seven or eight; each student had to call out their judgement in a predetermined order. In fact, all but one of the

Figure 9.3
Sample lines as used in Asch's conformity experiment

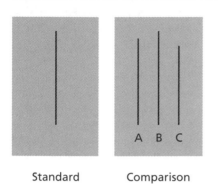

Standard   Comparison

students were stooges who called out the same wrong judgement. Only one was a real subject, who had to answer second to last. Performance was compared between this experimental condition and a control condition in which subjects made their judgements alone. In the control condition the error rate was about 1 per cent. But in the experimental condition Asch found an error rate of about 33 per cent (that is, where the subjects' responses conformed to the group's erroneous response).

There were wide individual differences. About 25 per cent of the subjects in the experiment steadfastly continued to give their own independent judgement, despite the repeated pressure of six or seven other people all giving the same (wrong) response. About 5 per cent, on the other hand, conformed to the (wrong) group response every single time. The remaining 70 per cent of subjects conformed some or most of the time. When Asch asked subjects who had conformed to report on their feelings after the experiment, they said they felt very uncomfortable. The majority said they knew they were seeing things differently from the other members of the group but felt increasingly uncertain about their own judgement. Others said they were certain they were right but went along with the group so as not to stand out. These conforming subjects said they felt self-conscious, anxious and even lonely, and feared disapproval. Even some of the independent subjects said they were emotionally affected, but felt it more important to 'stick to their guns' and do as they had been instructed (that is, give accurate estimates).

Asch (1956) went on to look at these fears of social disapproval directly by doing further experiments that changed the conditions so that 16 real subjects took part in the study with just one error-giving stooge. Now the stooge was in a minority, the subjects saw the his behaviour as ludicrous, and soon started to laugh at and ridicule him. Even the experimenter found it impossible not to burst out laughing! So it seemed to Asch that social disapproval was a major factor in the conformity. He tested this by another experiment like the first with just one subject and a majority of stooges giving wrong answers. But in this case he allowed the subject to give his responses privately, and, sure enough, the error rate dropped to 12.5 per cent.

A large number of replications of Asch's original experiment have been carried out in order to tease out the causes of conformity, each varying different aspects of the experimental conditions, and these have shown that there are a large number of influences in play. Deutsch and Gerrard (1955), for instance, in a sophisticated study varying uncertainty and group pressure, found that group pressure had the most impact. But even in their condition where the subject could directly compare the lines (low uncertainty) and had no direct contact with the group, merely observing their responses, an average of 23 per cent of responses conformed with the group's wrong answers. Other studies have varied things like the number of stooges, the confidence with which people spoke, the kind of judgement made and the extent to which the group response was unanimous. All of these affected the result, but showed evidence of some degree of conformity all the same. The most important factor, however, seems to be the isolation of being the only person in the group giving a dissenting response. Where the subject has a supporter, the tendency to conform to the group is virtually extinguished.

Who conforms?

The wide variation in conformity led to many studies investigating the personal qualities of those who conform. These found that conformers tend to have low self-esteem and a high need for social approval; to be not very bright people who are anxious and insecure and have feelings of inferiority (see, for example, Crutchfield 1955; Stang 1972). However, other studies have shown that such people may conform only in some situations, suggesting that situation is more important than 'character' (see, for example, Vaughan 1964; McGuire 1968). Just to give one illustration, a number of studies suggest that women tend to be somewhat more conforming than men (see Eagly and Wood 1991 for a meta-analytic study). However, Sistrunk and McDavid (1971) have shown that this may well be due to differential levels of uncertainty. They got women and men to make judgements that varied in terms of gender-linked knowledge (for example about mechanical tools or types of needlework), and found that women conformed less than men when making judgements about needlework, whereas men conformed less than women when making judgements about mechanical tools.

Cultural values

However, the cultural values of the people taking part in the experiment has proved to be another important variable. There have been at least 24 published replications carried out in 13 countries outside the USA and these show considerable variation in rates of conformity and independence (Smith and Harris Bond 1993). The lowest rate of conformity (14 per cent) was found with Belgian students (Doms 1983) and the highest (58 per cent) with Indian teachers in Fiji (Chandra 1973). Conformity is usually high where cultural values stress deference to authority and, more broadly, cultures where collectivist values dominate tend to be more conforming than individualist cultures (see Chapters 6 and 8).

Berry (1967) found intriguing evidence for this in a study comparing the Temne people of Sierra Leone with Inuit in Canada. Using a variant of Asch's experiment, Berry showed that the Temne were much more conforming. The Temne people make their livelihood from the collective production of a single crop. This involves close cooperation and coordination between them, and so, as one of the subjects in this study said, 'when Temne people choose a thing, we must all agree with the decision' (as reported in Berry 1967: 417). Canadian Inuit, by contrast, gain their livelihood by hunting and gathering on a much more individual basis, and so, Berry argued, group consensus is less salient and valued in their culture.

Smith and Harris Bond (1993) argue that what matters, however, are not so much cultural values as those held by a particular *group*. They illustrate this by a study that found high levels of independence with a Japanese sample – where the usual values are highly deferential to authority and collectivist (Frager 1970). This result, they suggest, may have arisen because there was, at the time, a high level of student unrest and rebellion at the university where the study was conducted. The students, they argued, responded by reference to group rather than cultural values.

Minority influence

As noted already, it is very much easier to resist conforming if you are not the only 'odd one out'. Two people can resist much better together than either one could alone. But can you go further – can you persuade the others to move to your position? Your own experience is likely to tell you that you can – sometimes, at least. And, indeed, a number of studies based on Asch's experimental paradigm have found evidence for **minority influence**, where a small minority is able to sway the judgements of the majority (see Wood *et al.* 1994 for a review).

One of the first of such demonstrations was carried out by Moscovici *et al.* (1969). In it they had students participate in a study of, ostensibly, colour

Table 9.1

Majority error rates in relation to minority influence

	Conditions – the responses made by two stooges		
	Control – no stooges	Inconsistent – stooges called 'green' only sometimes	Consistent – stooges consistently called 'green'
Error rate	0.25	1.25	8.42

Source: Moscovici *et al.* 1969

perception. The students began by taking a colour blindness test. Then those who passed were put into groups of six and shown 36 slides, all clearly blue, varying only in intensity. The task was to call out in turn the colour shown on the slide. Two of the six were stooges. In one condition (consistent) these stooges always called out that the slide was green. In a second condition (inconsistent) they called out 'green' for 24 slides and 'blue' for 12 of them. There was also a control condition in which all the subjects were 'real'; there were no dissenting stooges. The results obtained are shown in Table 9.1.

These results showed that some members of the majority in a group can be persuaded round to the judgements made by a small minority, so long as their judgements are consistent. Further studies followed, again varying the conditions, that allowed the specific elements of minority influence to be pinned down. Consistency is identified as a necessary condition, but also it matters how people interpret the behaviour of the minority group.

Models of social influence in groups

There has been a great deal of debate about the psychological processes that are involved in how social influence affects the judgements that people make in group settings. Generally there is agreement that social influence operating through two main processes: information influence and normative influence (Kelley, 1952; Deutsch and Gerrard, 1955).

- **Information influence** is where people use the group as an information source. This influence arises from people's desire to feel confident about the judgements that they make. In group settings they use the judgements of others in the group as a source of reliable information.

- **Normative influence** is where people follow group norms. This influence arises from people's desire for approval and acceptance, and their anxiety and discomfort about the possibility of being ostracized or ridiculed, or simply being seen as impolite.

However, there is strong disagreement about whether these processes are the same or different for majority and minority influence.

Same process models

In same process models, social influence (sometimes called social impact) is seen as working in the same way, irrespective of whether it is a majority influencing a minority, or a minority influencing the majority. One version (see, for example, Latané and Wolf 1981) proposes that social influence works according to a kind of cognitive algebra (rather like such models applied to reasoned action, as described in Chapter 6) where different elements contribute to an overall effect. In this model the difference between minority and majority influence is seen as nothing more than a shift in balance. For example, minority effects will not be found when the minority is heavily outnumbered, because the majority's greater numbers will strengthen the impact of normative influence. But minority influence may arise when the disparity between the majority and minority is relatively small (as was the case in the 4:2 balance in the Moscovici *et al.* 1969 study) as this will attenuate the majority's normative influence.

In another version of the single process model, information and normative influences are seen as contributing differentially in different situations. Turner and his colleagues, for example, have suggested a model that they (somewhat confusingly) call a **dual process dependency model** (Turner *et al.* 1987). This model proposes that in situations where people are confident about their own judgement and expertise, they will not be much affected by any informational influence from a minority. Equally, when people perceive the majority in the group in which they are participating as powerful – whether instrumentally (able to give rewards and punishments) or through sheer numbers, then normative influence will predominate. These are seen as operating in an additive manner. Both will generally act as levers for **majority influence** because the balance of influence is usually heavily weighted to the majority.

Strong informational influence + Strong majority normative → Majority
from the majority when their   influence from the power   influence
confidence is high   of the majority

In minority influence situations the balance gets shifted. This happens when the majority lack confidence in their own judgement, and so conflicting information from the minority can have a relatively greater impact; and when the majority is less powerful and so its normative influence is reduced.

Greater informational influence + Attenuated normative ———→ Minority
influence from minority   influence because   influence
when confidence is low   majority is not so powerful

Different process models

In different process models, majority and minority influence are seen to operate through distinctly *different* processes. These have mainly been framed within two different approaches: Moscovici's innovation model, based on his concept of social representations (see Chapter 9) and Turner's referent information influence model, based on his concept of social categorization.

Moscovici's innovation model

As you saw in Chapter 7, Moscovici developed the concept of *social representations* to explain how the new ideas of original thinkers come to influence the images, thinking, vocabulary, and beliefs of ordinary people. Social representations, in this analysis, are shared understandings and belief-structures through which people make sense of the social world. As part of this project, Moscovici ([1961] 1976) developed a specific interest in how novel ideas are transmitted and hence in the ways in which a minority can influence a majority. He saw this as a discrete process of innovation. Not surprisingly, then, Moscovici (see Moscovici and Personnaz 1980; Moscovici 1985) has contested the view that majority and minority influence operate via the same process, and proposed instead a general theory of social influence in which three processes can potentially play a part:

- **Conformity**: where the views of the majority induce the minority to comply
- **Normalization**: where a mutual compromise is reached leading to convergence
- **Innovation**: where a minority persuades the majority to adopt their viewpoint.

Moscovici's model is an early version of what, in the context of attitude change, would now be called the depth-processing model (see Chapters 5 and 6) that focuses on the impact of depth of processing. Indeed, in the mid-1990s De Vries *et al.* (1996) made a specific connection between Moscovici's theorization and this model of persuasion (see Chapter 6). If you recall, the model assumes that in much of our everyday life we do not process incoming information very deeply, but depend on heuristics to respond in a rather mindless, automatic way.

Majority influence, Moscovici claimed, works like this most of the time. It operates through the processes of conformity and normalization. Both of them are passive processes undertaken without much thought. Moscovici said they are when a person pays little attention to the perception or issue itself and instead 'concentrates all his attention on what others say, so as to fit in with their opinions and judgements' (Moscovici and Personnaz 1980: 214). By contrast minority influence, he claimed, works through a different process that he called innovation, where a minority directly challenges preconceived ideas. This sets up a conflict between people's rather mindless, taken-for-granted assumptions and a sustained, principled and coherent alternative viewpoint. This forces people to abandon heuristics (like 'the majority is generally right'), attend to the issue or perception in question, and direct processing effort to it.

Whether minority influence works or not, Moscovici claimed, depends crucially upon the **behavioural style** adopted by the minority. It has to be strong enough to get the attention of those in the majority and persuasive enough to make them think. The most effective element, he argued, is *consistency*, where the members of the minority group strongly and consistently give the same message. This disrupts the majority norm and raises doubts about it, drawing attention to a sustained, clear and coherent alternative viewpoint.

Moscovici drew on experimental evidence (for example Mugny 1982) to define further elements by which the effectiveness of consistency can be further increased. He suggested this can happen by *investment* (where the minority is seen to have made serious personal or material sacrifices to their cause) and *autonomy* (where it is seen to be acting out of principle rather than self-serving motives). At the same time he proposed that effectiveness can be undermined both by *rigidity* (where the minority are seen as too dogmatic) or *over-flexibility* (where it is seen as too willing to compromise). There is a fine line to tread, Moscovici argued, between being seen as obstinate and unyielding, and being seen as over-accommodating. If they want to change hearts and minds a minority must stick firmly to their principles but adopt an open-minded and reasonable negotiating style (Moscovici and Mugny 1983). Moscovici's model can be expressed thus:

Majority influence
Informational influence + Normative influence ⟶ Heuristic ⟶ Majority
based on taken-for-   based on *general norms*   processing   influence
granted knowledge

Minority influence

Informational influence + (Normative influence → In-depth ⟶ Minority
based on coherent,   overridden)   processing   influence
consistent minority
responses or arguments

In usual situations, majority influence will predominate, since both the information and normative influences will be the fall-back standards governing the judgements made by most members of the group. But where the minority is vocal, coherent and convincing in giving its response or making its argument, the other participants in the group will be pressed to actively process the information it supplies, overriding normative influence and potentially leading them to change their minds. Innovation, in this context, is where a sustained attempt is made to exert information influence. Real-life examples are pressure groups (such as Amnesty International and Greenpeace) that set out to sway public opinion.

Nemeth (1986) has taken this theorization further. She proposed that the effect of having a minority who express different views is it that it gets people to shift from position-relevant processing to issue-relevant information processing. In so doing, the frame of reference is, she suggested, widened up, getting people to examine a variety of alternatives. She demonstrated this effect in a study in which groups of six carried out a rather difficult discrimination task together (Nemeth and Wachtler 1983). There were two conditions: a majority influence condition (where four members of the group were stooges and called out predetermined responses) and a minority influence condition (where only two members of the group were stooges). The effect of the minority influence was that subjects were induced to consider a wider range of possible answers and came up with more correct solutions.

Turner's referent information influence model

Turner and his colleagues have proposed an alternative model. It also argues for a third form of social influence – **referent information influence** (Turner 1991). In Turner's formulation, however, this is based on social identity theory. Referent information influence is seen to operate through people's self-categorization (see Chapter 7). When they identify themselves as belonging to a particular group they then use that group's norms as standards for their own decision making. Referent information influence comes into play, then, in identity referent groups, either those set up experimentally (as in the Summer Camp experiments) or those occurring 'naturally'.

For instance, take the resistance to group pressure shown by the Japanese students in the study by Frager (1970). This can be explained by assuming that the students categorized themselves as belonging to an ingroup of 'rebellious students' in a context where student protest against authority was ongoing at the university at that time. This could have made them more likely to sustain independent (or perhaps better thought of as 'rebellious') judgements than if they had seen themselves as belonging to their more broadly culturally defined social group of 'students of low status who must defer to authority'. In Japanese culture there is a norm where the person who speaks first is viewed as having authority and therefore should be deferred to. A referent normative model suggests that in situations like this referent group (rebellious students) norm takes over from cultural group (deferential students) norm.

Conformity, in this theoretical context, is a feature of groups where there are no reference group norms in play, only the general norms of the broad culture in which the study is set. Where (as in Japan) these tend to be collectivist – stressing deference, interpersonal harmony and consensus – then, all other things being equal, people will tend to conform. Or, to put it in a less pejorative way, they tend to place their trust in cultural norms (Brown 2001). But if other norms come into play because group members have allegiance to a particular referent group (rebellious students), then they are more likely to act in ways that reflect the referent group norms – in this case, rebelliously.

Social influence processes

Conformity

- In all of the studies of conformity some people could be induced to conform to a group judgement some of the time.
- Conformity is mainly a product of being 'the odd one out'. Conditions that make this worse (for example where there are more people in the majority) lead to greater levels of conformity and conditions that alleviate it (for example having a supporter) reduce conformity.
- However, while they are billed as 'studies of conformity', in all of them there are some people who do *not* conform at least some of the time, despite social pressure to do so, and in most studies these people are in a majority.
- The processes at work that do persuade people to conform are anything but simple. They depend upon context and, in particular, on the value, salience and meaning of conformity and independence to the people concerned.

→

Minority influence

- Majorities induce minorities to conform through information and/or normative influences, both of which tend to operate at an automatic level of processing.
- However, minorities can induce majorities to shift their judgement by providing consistent alternative sets of responses or counter-arguments that require active processing.

GROUP POLARIZATION

From the previous analysis of conformity, you might expect that when groups make a decision together they are likely to come up with a compromise – a decision that reflects the average of individuals' independent views. Interestingly, this is not generally the case. Rather, the group decision tends to be more extreme – this is called **group polarization**.

The original study that identified this phenomenon was carried out for a Masters thesis (Stoner 1961). In it people were presented with a personal dilemma facing a (fictional) person and asked to advise them how to deal with it. They could make one of two recommendations to the person faced with the dilemma. One recommendation was a more appealing course of action, but risky. The other was much less appealing but carried a lot less risk. Stoner got participants in his study to first choose privately which recommendation they would make. Then they joined in a group discussion and told that the group must reach a unanimous decision about which recommendation they would offer. To Stoner's surprise, the group discussions tended to offer the risky course of action more often than individuals did privately. He called this phenomenon the **risky shift**.

The result also surprised other social psychologists – it went against their assumption that groups would be more conservative in their decisions than individuals. There followed a flurry of experiments investigating the risky shift, which showed that this was not universal. The studies found that in some situations groups do make conservative decisions, but, interestingly, when they do so these also tend to be more extreme. Group decisions are more conservative than the private decisions made by the individuals in the group. The phenomenon was thus renamed group polarization.

Group polarization (Isenberg 1986; Wetherell 1987) is defined as the tendency of group decisions to be more extreme than the mean of the individual decisions made by the members of the group. An example might be a discussion about genetically modified (GM) foods, where the group's decision is that all research and production of GM foods should be banned by law, when only two members of the group privately took this position before the discussion, and some were actually quite in favour in investing in research into GM foods. Van Avermaet defines it more precisely as where there is 'an enhancement of initially dominant position through group discussion' (Van Avermaet 2001: 427). The phenomenon has been observed in many different situations: in mock juries, negotiations, group counselling, and management teams as well as in experimental settings (see Lamm and Myers 1978 for a review).

Three main theories have been offered to explain the group polarization effect: social comparison, persuasive arguments and self-categorization theories.

Social comparison theory

Based on Festinger's original *social comparison theory* (Festinger 1954) this focuses on people's propensity to want social approval and dislike social censure. It is also sometimes called **cultural values theory** (Sanders and Baron 1977), recognizing that groups and cultures vary in the actions and behaviours that they endorse.

According to this explanation, talk in the group rapidly shows which views are valued and which ones are rebuffed by the majority. Desire for social approval will then motivate group members to shift the views they express in the direction of the socially sanctioned viewpoint, and this will soon appear to be *the group's* viewpoint. Indeed, group members may want to be seen as 'better' than the others and will therefore tend to express even more zealous views than the norm. Support is given for this by a finding that people tend to admire views that are more extreme than their own (Jellison and Davis 1973). This process can become a positive feedback loop, with speakers successively seeking to outdo each other in their endorsement for the initial group viewpoint, leading to greater and greater polarization. In this theory it is the position taken rather than the arguments expressed that brings about polarization. Polarization is seen as a process of successive 'upping the stakes', where group members vie with each other to express the group norm more emphatically.

Persuasive arguments theory

Persuasive arguments theory (also called informational influence theory) highlights the capacity for novel arguments to change people's opinions (Burnstein and Vinokur 1977). This theory assumes that at the beginning of the discussion, a range of individual viewpoints will be expressed. As this happens, people will hear new arguments that lend support to their own viewpoint and these will be perceived as further evidence to endorse it (Gigone and Hastie 1993). This will encourage them to take an even stronger position, leading, overall, to a polarization. In this theory it is the argument presented rather than the position taken that brings about polarization. Polarization is seen to be a process of mutual persuasion, where the group acts as a resource for marshalling a convincing justification for a specific decision or viewpoint.

Self-categorization theory

There is empirical evidence to support both social comparison and persuasive argument as processes involved in group polarization (see Van Avermaet 2001 for a review). However, neither can fully explain why the effect is sensitive to social context (Wetherell 1987). To address this aspect, there has recently been a turn to **social categorization theory**.

If you recall, self-categorization theory was developed by Turner and his colleagues (Turner *et al.* 1987; Turner 1991). It highlights people's tendency to identify with the group – to see it as an ingroup – and then to endorse the norms that *distinguish* their ingroup from other outgroups. In such a situation the group's norm is not defined as an average position according to what it has in common with the ingroup's beliefs and values but, crucially, how it *differs from those of outgroups*. The pressure on group members, in this theory, is not for social approval in and of itself (as social comparison theory would claim). Rather group members are motivated to demonstrate allegiance to the ingroup by distancing themselves from the views of outgroups. Social categorization theory proposes that in the course of the discussion, group members will gradually refine the group's decision or viewpoint by contrasting it with the position they assume is held by one or more outgroups.

In this theory it is the *contrast* with the assumed outgroup's position that brings about polarization. Polarization is seen to be a process of mutual self-categorization as ingroup members, where identifying with the group involves endorsing a position that marks the ingroup off as distinctive from the outgroup(s). Support for this analysis has been provided by Hogg *et al.* (1990), who carried out a study in which the reference outgroup was varied and this affected the direction of polarization. When confronted with a riskier outgroup, the group's decision became more cautious; when confronted with a more cautious outgroup, the group decision became more risky.

Implications of group polarization

Given that group decision-making is so much a part of modern life, the potential for groups to arrive at polarized decisions has serious implications. Juries, for instance, are assumed to be a means to gain considered and rational and, above all, just judgments about a defendant's guilt or innocence. Moreover, their judgments have serious consequences for the accused – in some parts of the world, literally life or death.

However, in reviewing polarization research, Brown (2001) argues that we need to be cautious about reading too much into experimental demonstrations of polarization:

> I think polarization can often be observed in social groups when a 'discussion runs away with itself'. However, formal decision-making groups do not usually exhibit such tendencies. There are several reasons for this: committees have a chairperson who directs the meeting, influences the discussion, sticks to the agenda, and so on. Also, group members may well be aware of each member's idiosyncrasies ('he always exaggerates' or 'she always brings this issue up') . . . More important in stifling any tendency towards polarization is another factor: if you are a member of, say, a management group who discuss an issue, you will be aware that you and your colleagues will have to implement the decisions taken and you are unlikely to go to unmanageable extremes.
>
> (Brown 2001: 39–40)

Groupthink

Janis (1982, for example) has documented a number of cases where high-profile groups have made military and political decisions that even the members of those groups, in hindsight, agreed were appallingly stupid and dangerous. Two often-cited examples are the Bay of Pigs invasion of Cuba in 1961 (where all the invaders were killed or captured) and the decision to launch the space shuttle *Challenger* (which exploded, killing all on board) in 1986. Janis has coined the term **groupthink** for the extreme polarization that led to these decisions.

Groupthink is what happens when a small, highly cohesive group of like-minded people becomes so obsessed with reaching consensus and so blinkered by it when they reach it, that they lose touch with reality and make a catastrophic decision. Janis argues that there are number of preconditions required for it to happen. The group has to be excessively cohesive and ideologically 'of one mind'. The decision making must be under stressful conditions and insulated from outside sources of influence and information. And the group leader must be powerful and partial.

Janis' formulations were based on a mixture of archival and interview methods, and provide compelling accounts of groupthink in action. Attempts to demonstrate it in laboratory conditions have largely been ineffective, and this may well be a phenomenon that it is simply not possible to study in the laboratory.

Group polarization

When groups make a joint decision following a discussion, there is a tendency for their joint decision to be polarized – to be more extreme than the average individual judgements of participants. There are three theories used to explain this phenomenon:

- *Social comparison theory*, where group members are seen to vie with each other to endorse more and more extremely the normative position of group
- *Persuasive arguments theory*, where group members are influenced by the additional arguments of others, further endorsing their own position
- *Self-categorization theory*, where group members are motivated to demonstrate their allegiance to the group by presenting arguments that distance the decision from that made by an outgroup.

In real-life situations polarization is moderated by longer-term influences, and the knowledge that group members have to implement the decision.

- *Groupthink* can happen, however, when a group is isolated from the outside, excessively cohesive and ideologically 'of one mind', the decision is made under stressful conditions and the group leader is powerful and partial. This can lead to the group losing touch with reality and making a catastrophic decision

INTERGROUP CONFLICT

When we deal with each other individually, we can be civilized . . . but when we deal with each other in groups, we are like savage tribes in the Middle Ages.

(Berri 1989)

This is a quotation from Nabith Berri, who was, at the time, a leader of one of the factions fighting in the Lebanon. In this section we shall explore what social psychology can tell us about whether he is right – are groups where people have invested their identity inevitably doomed to be in conflict with each other? You have already had a brief introduction to research into intergroup conflict at the beginning of the chapter when you examined Serif's Summer Camp experiments. Here we briefly explore this further, looking in particular at theorization about conflict between groups arising from social identity theory.

Competition and conflict

In the Summer Camp experiments Sherif and his colleagues demonstrated that conflict tends to arise when groups are placed in highly polarized competitive situations.

Boys will be boys?

It looks as though these findings are surprisingly robust, even across cultures. Yet a similar study conducted by Tyerman and Spencer (1983) in the UK, carried out in a Boy Scout camp did not produce intergroup conflict. However, the situation was very different. The Boy Scouts is a long-standing membership organization for adolescent boys. It is run on quasi-military lines in which local groups are called 'patrols' and usually meet every week to engage in activities together, with one or more adult leaders. They usually go away to camp each year, where a number of patrols are brought together but live in separate tents. They engage in many activities in patrols, but also regularly take part in competitions together. Tyerman and Spencer (1983) argued that the lack of hostility was because behaviour in the camp was regulated by strong and long-established social norms, which continued to operate during the camp period.

However, Diab (1970) ran a camp similar to Sherif's in the Lebanon and the antagonism generated in the competitive phase was so extreme it proved impossible to continue the camp into the superordinate goals phase. The boys taking part were ten Christian and eight Muslim 11-year-olds, and Diab and his colleagues found that while initial friendship patterns did tend to follow religious lines, there was a fair degree of cross-over. The boys were allocated randomly to groups and, like the 'Bulldogs' and 'Red Devils', they too soon chose names for themselves – 'The Friends' and 'Red Genie'. However, the group cultures were very different from each other, as these names suggest. 'The Friends' soon became highly cooperative and affable towards each other and set about 'having fun'. 'Red Genie', by contrast, just as rapidly became aggressive and mean, stealing from each other and 'The Friends'. In the competitive situation, 'Red Genie' 'played dirty' and competed with hostility, and were mostly ahead until, in the final stage, 'The Friends' passed them and won the tournament. 'Red Genie' became so aggressive at this point – stealing knives, threatening others with them and attempting to leave the camp by force – that the experiment was terminated.

Smith and Harris Bond (1993) argue that we should not read too much into what was a single study with a small group. They draw a general conclusion that intergroup conflict tends to arise where groups are thrown together in isolated settings for short periods, in situations where social norms mitigating against conflict are largely absent.

Before we end this section, it is worth making a significant point – have you noticed that all the studies mentioned so far were conducted with boys? It is interesting to speculate why girls' groups were not studied, or even mixed gender groups. In part this reflects psychology's sexism (an issue taken up in Chapter 10) in that a large proportion of psychological studies have been restricted to studying male behaviour. But it is worth asking the question – would girls have behaved in the same way? Some feminists would argue that conflict of this kind is an overwhelmingly male propensity – whether experimentally induced or in real life. This opens up a whole can of worms that social psychologists seem to have erred away from addressing – which, when you think about it, is surprising, given its implications. Maybe this is a case when, genuinely, 'more research is needed'.

Social identity theory and intergroup conflict

As you have seen, social identity theory claims that ingroups tend to favour ingroup members and discriminate against members of outgroups. This idea has been developed to try to explain intergroup conflict.

The explanation starts from the assumption that once group members identify with the ingroup, they gain a social identity in which esteem is gained through affiliation with it. They are therefore motivated to view the ingroup as having high status in relation to outgroups. One way of doing this is to accentuate intergroup differences – to distance the group from outgroups – and then to denigrate the outgroup.

Most theorization has gone on with regard to ingroup of low status. Hogg and Vaughan (1998) suggest that what happens hinges first of all on whether an individual believes it is possible for them to make a shift from a low-status to a higher-status group. If so, they are not motivated to invest in their low-status ingroup, but rather to concentrate their efforts on social mobility. Where, however, they feel they have no chance of 'jumping ship', the only way to gain a positive social identity is to invest in their current low-status ingroup. In situations of social stability the ways in which they can do this are:

- find alternative ways of demonstrating ingroup competence – even if they are transgressive ones such as joy riding
- seek to change the value accorded to the ingroup
- identify other groups that are of even lower status than themselves and act to distance themselves from them.

Demonstrating ingroup value

Emler and his colleagues (Emler and Hopkins 1990; Emler and Reicher 1995) have looked for evidence of outgroup discrimination by low-status groups by studying youths engaged in petty crime. They concluded that one motivation for criminality is that it enables youths to impress their ingroup peers – other under-achievers at school. By identifying with others in the same position, showing off to them by criminal activity, and denigrating the 'swots' who do well at school, they can find in their ingroup membership an alternative source of a positive identity. Other examples suggested by Brown (2001) are 'punks' and 'crusties'. Groups like these refuse to engage in the 'rat race', and rather establish their own value by setting different standards as to what should be valued, among the ingroup at least.

Improving social respect for the ingroup

An example given here by Hogg and Vaughan (1998) is the promotion of the slogan 'Black is beautiful'. Brown (2001) points to the demands for social change by feminists.

Denigrating groups even lower in the pecking order

Interestingly, somewhat counter-intuitively, it seems that high-status ingroups tend to show greater ingroup favouritism than low-status ingroups (for example Crocker and Luhtanen 1990). However, there is some evidence of this with low-status groups. Vanneman and Pettigrew (1972), for example, found that among 'poor white trash' in the USA, racist attitudes and support for right-wing politicians tended to be strongest among those who felt the greatest social deprivation.

The effects of conflict

Intergroup conflict has been extensively studied in laboratory settings as well as the kinds of field experiments we have looked at so far. These studies have shown that when acting in groups, people tend to be more competitive (Insko *et al.* 1990) and more aggressive (Insko and Schopler 1998) than when they do the same task on their own. The stronger the identification with the group, the more these effects spiral upwards (Rehm *et al.* 1987), especially so where there is competition for scarce material resources (Taylor and Moriarty 1987). Groups also fight over social resources such as respect and esteem (Tajfel and Turner 1979).

Deutsch (1973) has outlined three characteristic consequences of intergroup conflict:

- *Communication between the groups becomes unreliable and impoverished.* Either available communication channels are not used or are used in ways that deliberately mislead the other. In consequence, neither group trusts the information they get from the other group.
- *Norms of trust and fair play break down.* The groups become highly sensitive to any differences between them and treat any similarities as if they do not exist. Differential perceptions build up, each group viewing its own behaviour as benevolent and fair but the behaviour of the other group as malicious, hostile and unfair. This leads to suspicion of the other group's motives, a breakdown of trust and fair play, and hence a refusal to address any attempt by the other group to defuse the situation.
- *Conflict becomes a matter of principle.* The groups each become convinced that the only resolution to the conflict is for them to impose a solution on the other group, by force if necessary. Each side therefore seeks to increase its own power while undermining the power and legitimacy of the other group. In the process the dispute gets escalated, shifting from a clash over a few specific issues to all-out conflict over moral principles and superiority.

These were all demonstrated in a study by Blake and Mouton (1984), in which corporate executives took part in what they thought was a 'training programme'. They were assigned complex problem-solving tasks and told that as part of the training programme their performance would be evaluated by experts. They were not, however, explicitly told they would be in competition. Team spirit was rapidly established and group members were soon to be found huddled together at breaks and mealtimes planning strategy. While there was not the level of acted-out antagonism found between the boys in the summer camps, intergroup antagonism between these professional men also soared as time went on. At the end of the programme, representatives from all the groups were brought together to evaluate each other's performance. Almost always these meetings ended in impasse, the representatives unwilling to concede that other groups' solutions were as good as their own. When facilitators intervened to impose a judgement, the losing team angrily accused them of being biased and incompetent. Tempers sometimes got so high the experiment had to be abandoned.

Looking at the minimal group experiments described at the beginning of the chapter, it appears that ingroup membership tends to lead to the downgrading of outgroups, disliking them and discrimination against them.

Conflict resolution

A study by Worchel (1979) has shown that while working for superordinate goals can reduce intergroup conflict, this works only if the project is successful. If it fails antagonism can be multiplied rather than reduced. Other factors that social psychological research has established for conflict reduction include the following:

- *Changing perceptions*, through education or by the use of media. A good example was the 1966 television docu-drama, *Cathy Come Home*, which changed attitudes in the UK towards homeless people.
- *Redrawing the category boundaries*. This can be achieved, for example, by creating conditions where the groups come to perceive themselves as belonging to a common group together. Alternatively arrange for social categories (such as gender) to cut across the group boundaries.
- *Increasing contact between the groups*, for example by providing community projects and events that bring warring groups together on neutral ground. Contact needs to be sustained, involving, and officially supported and works best when groups are of roughly equal status.

Intergroup conflict

Social identity theory claims that conflict between groups arises from situations where group members are motivated to emphasize intergroup differences, to distance their ingroup from the outgroup, and then to denigrate the outgroup. This tends to happen most with high-status groups.

Members of **low-status groups** will usually, if they believe they can 'jump ship' to a higher status group, invest in making this shift rather than in the ingroup. If they cannot, they can adopt one of three strategies:

- Find ways (often transgressive) of demonstrating ingroup competence
- Find ways to increase perceptions of ingroup value
- Find groups even lower in the 'pecking order' to disparage.

The *effects of conflict* are that communication and norms of trust and fair play break down, and conflict becomes a matter of principle.

Intergroup conflict can be reduced by:

- Engagement in successfully pursuing superordinate goals
- Changing 'hearts and minds' through education and propaganda

- Crossing or changing category boundaries
- Increasing contact between the groups. Contact needs to be sustained, involving, and officially supported and works best when groups are of roughly equal status.

FURTHER READING

Experimental social psychology

Brown, R.J. (2000b) *Group Processes: Dynamics Within and Between Groups*, 2nd edn. Oxford: Blackwell.

> A thoroughly scholarly book that offers a comprehensive and up-to-date review of research and theory in this field.

Hewstone, M. and Stroebe, W. (eds) (2001) *Introduction to Social Psychology*, 3rd edn. Oxford: Blackwell.

> Given that groups are important in European social psychology, it is not surprising that there are three chapters in this book on groups. Together they provide a thorough and meticulous coverage of the field. Chapter 13 by Van Avermaet is on social influence in small groups. Chapter 14 by Wilke and Wit is on group performance. Chapter 15 by Brown is on intergroup relations.

Hogg, M.A. and Vaughan, G.M. (1998) *Social Psychology*, 2nd edn. Hemel Hempstead: Prentice Hall.

> There are two chapters on groups, Chapter 7 on basic group processes, and Chapter 8 on leadership and group decision-making. This is much less dense than Brown's chapter, and easier reading.

QUESTIONS

1 'To be a group, there needs to be more than just a collection of individuals.' Illustrate your answer with examples of research in connection with different kinds of groups.
2 'Many hands make light work.' Is this true? Illustrate your answer with empirical evidence to support the argument you make.
3 To what extent do cultural norms influence what goes on in groups?
4 What are the explanations given for minority group influence?
5 What is groupthink, and how can it be avoided?
6 Why do groups get into conflict with each other, and how can this conflict be resolved?

Chapter 10

Where next for social psychology?

Chapter contents

A route map of the chapter

This is quite a daunting agenda, and I cannot do much here other than make a couple of suggestions about how we might begin.

In the first section I consider an issue that has bubbled throughout this book – the ethnocentrism of a social psychology that does most of its research in highly specific cultural contexts, and what we should do about that. In this section I explore two forms of psychology's racism. First there is the out-and-out obvious kind that I think we can all agree is a nasty blot on psychology's history. Then I look at an institutional form of racism that, I believe, still permeates the discipline. I conclude this section by offering some suggestions about how we can do something about this.

In the second section I explore how critical and experimental social psychologists can learn something from each other, and might even find ways of working together in the research they do. To do this I take up Shank's (1998) suggestion of juxtaposing apparently incomparable things (see Chapter 4). In this case, I juxtapose examples of experimental and critical research, and show they actually have more in common than you might think. In each case there is no summary box distilling the section, but instead practical suggestions about what social psychologists might do next.

> **Tackling social psychology's ethnocentrism**
>
> ↓
>
> **Working together**

Learning objectives

When you have completed your study on this chapter, you should be able to:

1 Review social psychology's racist history and describe some of the influences on its (virtual) eradication.
2 Define what is meant by 'institutional racism' and suggest ways in which it can be tackled by social psychology.
3 Suggest some ways in which social psychological research could be improved.
4 Juxtapose experimental and critical research studies, and use this device to gain greater insight into the similarities and differences between the two approaches.
5 Indicate how critical and experimental social psychologists might be able to work together to promote a more effective, useful and theoretically informed approach to our subject.

INTRODUCTION

In this chapter I look at where I think social psychology is going and give my suggestions about where I think it *ought* to be going. As someone who 'jumped ship' some time ago from cognitive psychology to critical social psychology, you might expect me to use the chapter to make a sustained case that what social psychologists should be doing is abandon all that experimental stuff, give up on their love affair with Science and get themselves properly trained as discourse analysts. But that is not what I am going to do, for two rather contrary reasons.

First, while I think that kind of argument might impress some of my friends, it would be pretty pointless. I doubt that a single experimentalist would take any notice. Second, I am not convinced it would be the right course to take. As I said at the beginning of the book, I genuinely believe that both approaches have something to offer our understanding of the social aspects of what people feel, think and do. So instead, what I am going to do is make some suggestions about the lessons that Goliath can learn from David, and even some that David could learn from Goliath.

No, I am not going all 'fluffy bunny' on you (do read the introduction to Chapter 1 if none of this is making any sense right now). I am saying that I think social psychology needs to take a good, hard look at what it is doing. It needs to make some real changes. I do not believe that the differences between experimental and social psychology can be resolved by integration. But I do believe that their protagonists should stop behaving like a couple of self-satisfied ingroups calling each other names, and begin to get into more serious and fruitful debates about their subject. In other words, I think we should try some of the recommendations for resolving intergroup conflict set out in Chapter 9:

- Both camps should engage in cooperatively pursuing a superordinate goal – reassessing social psychology's project and finding better ways to take it forward. There are, I believe, some real problems to be tackled and it might just be that we can make a better job of it by working together on it.
- Those of us in the minority, low-status ingroup (critical social psychology) should actively strive to change the perceptions of the high-status ingroup (experimental social psychology). We should pursue this through education and, well, if not propaganda, at least by making a much better job of getting them to understand what it is we are doing and why. And, while we are at it, we should keep ourselves better informed about developments in the other field. One of the great things about writing this book is that it has forced me to do just that. I have learned a lot. For their part, the high-status ingroup should stop

distancing themselves from us, take us seriously and make a real effort to inform themselves sufficiently about our theories and methods to make informed decisions about their merits.

- We should work at crossing category boundaries. One way to do this might be to encourage alliances between experimental and critical social psychologists working in the same general fields, or who have some other common agenda. One area where this is already working quite well is among Feminist psychologists, whose common cause has proved sufficient to get them talking (and even, sometimes, working together) across the experimental/critical divide.

- We really do need to increase contact between the two groups. The trend is currently to go in the other direction. Increasingly, in my experience, experimental and critical psychologists publish in separate journals (the high-status ingroup doing a pretty good job at keeping their low-status outgroup out, I have to say). The books that experimental social psychologists produce almost without exception ignore the very existence of critical social psychology, and critical social psychologists produce books that start with a ritual hatchet job on the opposition, then move on swiftly to offering the better alternative. A student who wanted to know about both had no choice but to go and buy two books (until this one, of course)! We mainly go to different conferences, or, when we do get to attend the same one, we boycott the papers of our outgroups. I have even noticed that people seem to drink in the bar and dance at the disco only with their ingroup confederates! We need to think of ways in which, in a sustained and meaningful manner, we can begin to engage in serious debate, one that actually gets us beyond merely ritually attacking each other's position. And for that we need some help from social psychology's officialdom (you know who you are).

TACKLING SOCIAL PSYCHOLOGY'S ETHNOCENTRISM

Mainstream social psychology has been under sustained attack for some time now about its prejudices. These include an almost entire exclusion of women up until about the 1970s, treating them almost as though they were not really people at all and not worth carrying out experiments on (this may, on consideration, have been a benefit). If you do not believe me, go back through the book and make a note of just how many of social psychology's early studies were conducted with only boys or men as subjects.

But if you want a really bizarre example, try this one. So extreme was this tendency to exclude women from the frame that one of the most famous personality tests – the Minnesota Multiphasic Personality Inventory (MMPI) – was developed using only men's responses. This is even more weird, because it had a specific sub-scale (Mf) designed to test for 'masculinity' and 'femininity'. The two poles were not 'validated' as you would expect, by comparing men's and women's responses. Instead (wait for it – you are not going to believe this) it was done by contrasting responses from a large group of male heterosexual soldiers (to locate the 'male' end) with the responses of 13 homosexual men (to locate the 'female' end)! (See Stainton Rogers and Stainton Rogers 2001 for a more detailed discussion of the sexism involved in the development of scales of masculinity and femininity.) And, believe me, it gets a lot worse when you begin to look at the sexism behind its early theorization.

Another of its prejudices has been its dressing up of social deprivation and inequality as a mere 'variable', and its incredibly patronizing and pejorative treatment of people who do not conform to its liberal, middle-class values. Here go back and look at the theories of learned helplessness and locus of control briefly outlined in Chapter 8, and see what you make of them (see Stainton Rogers 1991 for a detailed analysis of this bigotry in relation to locus of control).

However, here I am going to focus on social psychology's racism – or ethno-centrism if you want a more comfortable word – and what I think we need to do about it. My justification for this is that I believe it is a much more intractable problem, for reasons I shall describe. That being so, I also think it *has* to be tackled. This is not just because any self-respecting group should attend to its prejudices, but rather because I think social psychology is unsustainable unless we do. Without coming over as melodramatic, I sincerely believe that the future of social psychology as a viable discipline is at stake here.

The real problem lies, I contend, not in overt racism. While there is still a way to go, except in a few pockets of resistance (some work recently published 'demonstrating' the inferiority of the Rom, for example – I will not lend it credence by citing it) social psychology's explicit and aggressive racist beginnings have largely been consigned to the history books, where one hopes it will remain. No, the problem lies in its **institutional racism**. I believe this is almost entirely unintended, but it is having a pernicious effect nonetheless.

The racist origins of social psychology

If you go back to Chapter 1 and look at McDougall's theory of social evolution, it is clear that it was profoundly racist. He regarded the behaviour of 'savages' as almost entirely determined by instinct. Only in modern, civilized societies, he concluded, is it possible for individuals to progress to a higher plane of moral conduct, since only there are the social rules sufficiently complex and flexible for individuals to acquire the capacity for self-regulation.

But it is much worse than that. For example, in the 1919 edition of his *Introduction to Social Psychology*, he introduced a new chapter on 'The sex instinct'. In it he contrasted 'civilized' treatment of the female sex with 'primitive' societies, where men regard women as nothing more than an object capable of stimulating their erogenous zones; where a woman is 'merely the chief of many "fetish objects"' (McDougall 1919: 419). The consequence, he argues, will be 'an unrestrained and excessive indulgence of the sexual appetite . . . for both sexes'. In a footnote he then goes on to say:

> It has often been maintained, and not improbably with justice, that the backward condition of so many branches of the negro race is in the main determined by the prevalence among them of this state of affairs.
>
> (McDougall 1919: 419)

Scientific racism

According to Richards (1997) McDougall took a more extreme and explicit racist and supremacist stance than most of his colleagues in England. This may have been one of the reasons why he moved to work in the USA, where **Scientific Racism** was endemic at the time. Richards defines 'Scientific Racism' as based on evolutionary theory, that took the position that humankind has a common ancestry where:

> [d]ifferent 'racial stocks' could be understood as diverging from a main stem at various times in the long distant past, with some subsequently failing to evolve as far as others. Tree diagrams of this became commonplace. The 'biologisation' of human diversity was thus consolidated; not only physical appearance but temperament and culture reflected a people's innate evolutionary status. It was easy to draw up the rankings; White Europeans at the top, Chinese, Indians and perhaps Arabs jostling for silver and bronze medal placings and at the bottom Australian aborigines, Bushmen, Hottentots and Tiera del Fuegans lapped so often it was hardly worth considering them as any longer participating in the event.
>
> (Richards 1997: 13)

Scientific Racism was the theory upon which the discipline of **Racial Psychology** was built, in an explicit quest to document the superiority of the white race. To do so psychologists engaged in some amazing theoretical contortions, in which the better performance of 'black people' on some tasks (such as reaction time) was held up as 'evidence' for their inferior level of development. This allowed them to argue:

> That the Negro is, in the truest sense, a race inferior to that of the white can be proved by many facts, and among these by the quickness of his automatic movements as compared with those of the white . . . the Negro is, in brief, more of an automaton than the white man is.
>
> (Bache 1895: 481)

The history of racism in psychology is a highly complex one with subtle twists and turns that were often nudged and sometimes required by local politics. For example, Richards (1997) suggests that one of the greatest inducements for the abandonment of overtly racist theorizing was the horrors of Nazi genocide. This shocked the academic community into retrenching from its complacent acceptance of racist assumptions about the superiority of one 'race' over another. As Richards takes great pains to point out, throughout its history, psychology (along with the other human sciences) was always divided. There were always a brave few who challenged racism, even though they were sometimes in a very small minority.

Nonetheless, an examination of some of the arguments used to support racist theorizing is illuminating. There is not room here to go into this in detail, but I cannot resist giving the following example, in part because I think it tells us something about the logic of contemporary psychological theorizing in some quarters, but mostly because it is so breathtakingly ludicrous. Richards calls it 'one of the most hilariously ridiculous pieces of Psychology ever to have appeared' (Richards 1997: 179). Produced in the 1930s in Germany during the rise of Nazism, this is Richards' abbreviated summary from *Psychological Abstracts* of a paper by Jaensch (1939), the title of which translates as 'The poultry-yard as a medium for research and clarification in problems of human race differences'.

> The superiority of Nordic races is reflected in the race differences among chickens. The Nordic chick is better-behaved and more efficient in feeding than the Mediterranean chick, and less apt to over-eat by suggestion. The poultry-yard confutes the liberal-bolshevik claim that race differences are really cultural differences because race differences in chicks cannot be accounted for by culture.
>
> (as cited in Richards 1997: 179)

I am not quite sure what makes this come across as so preposterous, since all Jaensch is doing is inferring principles of human nature from the behaviour of chickens in the poultry-yard. Is this really all that far from inferring nomothetic principles of human learning from the behaviour of rats running through mazes in the laboratory, as Behaviourism does? Or inferring nomothetic principles of, say, human gender differences from the behaviour of anything from ants to primates as does contemporary Evolutionary psychology (where a very small but nasty core of racists continue to hang out)? Maybe it is the elision of human 'races' and chicken breeds that does it, and Jaensch's patently obvious Nazi political agenda writing in Germany in 1939. But this is precisely the kind of 'knowledge' that Postmodernism claims is the wolf of politics dressed up in the sheep's clothing of Science. By juxtaposing a patently preposterous claim like this one with the claims made by Evolutionary psychology, a Postmodern analysis makes its case that Science is a story-telling practice, in which:

> [L]ife and social sciences in general . . . are story-laden; these sciences
> are composed through complex, historically specific storytelling
> practices. Facts are theory-laden; theories are value-laden; values are
> story-laden. Therefore facts are meaningful within stories.
>
> (Haraway 1984: 79)

Psychology's institutional racism

The term institutional racism is possibly one of the most misunderstood in contemporary popular discourse, in Britain at least. This arises from its usage in relation to the police, in the McPherson Report (2001) following the bungled investigation of the murder of a black young man, Stephen Lawrence, where the conclusion was reached that policing in Britain is 'institutionally racist'.

Institutional racism differs profoundly from the kind of overt racism in the examples given above. It is a much more subtle form of racism in that it is not *intended* to be prejudiced – though its impact can be nearly as damaging as out-and-out blatant racism. It is an *unconscious* racism that permeates the worldview of otherwise well-meaning and well-intentioned people, subtly distorting their thinking and hence their behaviour.

I will bite the bullet and give you an example of my own institutional racism. I have a friend whose wife is Indian and a senior academic in the field of politics. When we first met we began to ask each other questions and I asked her what her field was. She replied that at the time it was mainly concentrated on political dissent in China. My knee-jerk thought was 'What's an Indian doing studying China?' Fortunately for me I did not actually come out with this incredibly racist question, but I have to admit, to my shame, that I did think it. I immediately reminded myself that the question would not have occurred to me if, say, she had been Australian or from the USA. The heuristic stereotype that led to my racist thinking was that 'we' (that is, white people) are at liberty to study exotic others, whereas 'they' (that is, exotic others) are not.

By admitting this, the point I am trying to make is that nobody is immune to prejudice. It is built into the way we think (see Chapter 5). Everyone is the victim of their own socialization, in the sense that in providing them with heuristic, 'automatic' categories for carving up the world, it leads them into stereotypical thinking. Nobody can entirely escape from their own prejudice, though one can learn a sensitivity to it and, as I did, (sometimes) stop yourself from explicitly expressing it and (somewhat) modify your behaviour – which is what antiracist training is intended to achieve. The McPherson Report was not accusing the police in general of being overtly racist, though it did acknowledge that some police officers are. It was saying that a racist, stereotype-distorted mind-set is endemic among police officers (as it is within the white community as a whole), and this leads to racist behaviour. However unintended, institutional racism results in different treatment by the police of white and black suspected criminals, and white and black crime victims alike.

Throughout this book I have built up a case that social psychology is institutionally ethnocentric, at the least, and this verges into institutional racism. What I mean by this is that social psychology's knowledge – as expressed in its textbooks, the topics it studies and the people it uses as subjects in them – is based on two racist fallacies. The first is a kind of **head-in-the-sand fallacy**, in which social psychologists simply assume that what they discover from their biased samples mainly of students, mainly from US campuses, are data that allow them to build and refine universally nomothetic theories about social psychological processes and phenomena. These, they believe, are psychologically pure – clean and unsullied by any irritating extraneous influences from these students' socialization or enculturation. In particular, they assume that social psychology is immune to the fundamental attribution error, which leads to a prioritization of the importance of individual, a decidedly Western preoccupation.

The second is an **Us and Them fallacy** that is based on the stereotypical view that there are two kinds of people. First of all there is 'Us', a group of almost exclusively white people, for whom nomothetic laws of human behaviour and experience can be developed to explain social psychological processes and phenomena outside of culture. Then there is 'Them' – exotic and colourful others, for whom these nomothetic laws do not apply because they have 'culture', and it is this 'culture' that determines what they do and how they see the world.

The need to develop methods and theories that address culture

My first suggestion for where social psychology needs to go, therefore, is that it has either to give up on its endeavour entirely and leave the field to anthropologists. Or it has to tackle the problem if it is to survive. What it does at present is that it plays the head-in-the-sand card and ignores the influence of culture altogether. Or it plays the purist game of hiking off any treatment of culture into cross-cultural psychology. This will not do. Social psychology has to get down to devising methods and theories that acknowledge that cultural factors are inherent elements within *all* social psychological processes and phenomena. It needs to formulate research designs and approaches that regard cultural conventions not as extraneous influences to be excluded, but inevitably part of what is studied.

This was a strong reason why some people developed social constructionist methods. By the nature of an abductory approach that derives theory from data, cultural influences are not excluded, and can be addressed whenever they arise. Wetherell and Potter's (Wetherell and Potter 1992) discourse analytic research into racism is a good example, but there is plenty else. The Chinese Culture Connection group's approach is inspirational, in the way it began by sampling values from Chinese people instead of merely translating standard English-language scales (which is what much cross-cultural psychology research has done). This strategy was taken up by Schwartz and his colleagues, who sampled widely and thoroughly across cultures to arrive at the values they used in their studies.

Social representations research offers another fruitful approach. Indeed, it is specifically designed to explore the relationship between social, cultural and subcultural groups and their social representations (such as conventions for determining appropriate ways to behave in different situations). More than that, its theorization is directly relevant to issues of culture, and how knowledge is transmitted between different cultural groups (see, for example, Doise *et al.* 1999).

However, I would argue that the way forward has to be more accommodating than suggesting that social psychologists dump experiments and move over, en bloc, to adopt discursive or social representations methods. If it is to accommodate continued experimentation, then the research endeavour needs a serious overhaul.

I have a specific, pragmatic suggestion to make here. It is that we build on the real progress that has been made in Feminist psychology. Feminist psychologists have developed approaches to research that are sensitive to difference, especially differential power. They offer ways for researchers to do research that not only acknowledge the differences between the researcher and the people who take part in their studies, but also are frank about the researcher's limitations in working with issues and people they can never fully understand. Best of all, they provide practical advice about how to go about this. It is time, I contend, to draw the expertise they have gained into the mainstream, and stop seeing it as relevant only to 'women's subjects' and Feminist researchers. Here is a brief summary of the main principles they have developed, rewritten to apply directly to issues over culture and with some additions of my own. Suggestions are made in the further reading section for where to find out about Feminist research methods in more detail.

Strategies for research

- Research should be carried out into *topics that relate directly to issues raised by cultural difference*. This should be carried out within and by those who belong to social psychology's Establishment, published in its journals and not hiked off as a less valued 'specialist' activity on the fringe, or even worse, seen as only appropriate for certain groups to study. Those who have the power to decide what research gets funded and published should use this power to encourage and stimulate such research – if, for no other reason, that we are sadly lacking knowledge in this field at the moment and we need it if social psychology is to tackle its own ignorance.
- Research should be undertaken on *institutional racism*. Given this concept is so poorly understood, social psychological expertise with studying stereotyping and prejudice could make a real contribution to public understanding of the problem and its potential solutions.
- Where culture is not the focus of research, the research must nonetheless always be pursued in ways that are aware of and *sensitive to culture and context*. Researchers must stop pretending that a study carried out with only one cultural group can have any credence as a study of nomothetic laws of human behaviour. Information about the cultural setting should be provided in any report, including relevant details of the participants in the study. Information about ethnic group should not be restricted to just those studies or people who are not-white.
- Researchers must be *reflexive*, acknowledging their own engagement with and investment in the topic under study and reporting on their experiences during the research and its impact upon them. They must stop portraying themselves as dispassionate, objective scholars who have no stake in what they do.
- The way in which research is carried out must be *informed by ethics of difference*. In particular researchers must acknowledge and address the power relationship between themselves as researchers and those with whom the research is conducted,

treating them as participants in rather than subjects of the process. They must stop 'tricking' or deceiving the participants. Rather they should seek to engage them in the research process, including its planning and execution. They should negotiate with participants about what is done with the data, giving them a degree of control over what is reported and how it is interpreted. Researchers should acknowledge their limitations and actively make use of advisers drawn from the researched group, with whom they consult at all stages in the process.

- Researchers should become more open about the *multiplicity of methods* available, and should consider combining several methods in a single study. They should be willing to consider methods drawn from disciplines such as anthropology, sociology and social geography and adapt them for use in psychological research (and vice versa).

- Researchers should be *explicit about their agendas* if they plan to use their research to stimulate social change, and, where they do, use methods and approaches tactically – for their potential to make an impact.

- In recognizing difference, researchers should seek to explore and *gain insight into variability* rather than try to 'iron it out'. They therefore need to develop methods that can accommodate variability and difference.

WORKING TOGETHER

While integration is not possible, this does not mean that psychologists from the different camps cannot call a truce and seek to work together. To show how this might be pursued I am going to make use of Shank's suggestion (Chapter 7) that it can be informative to juxtapose things that do not usually go together. I would like to try this by comparing a couple of studies from the experimental paradigm with a couple from the critical approach.

Experimental and critical studies of prejudice juxtaposed

First, let's juxtapose the experiment on racial prejudice carried out by Gaertner and McLaughlin (1983) in which they used reaction times as an implicit measure of racism (see Chapter 3) with the Kitzinger and Frith (1999) conversation analysis study of women's refusals of sexual advances (see Chapter 7).

There are several similarities between them. They are both looking at processes that are automatic and not under conscious control. In the Gaertner and McLaughlin experiment this was categorization, in the Kitzinger and Frith study it was the subtle, unconscious paralinguistic features of conversations. Also both are studies of prejudice – racism in the Gaertner and McLaughlin experiment, and sexism in Kitzinger and Frith's study. In both pieces of research the researchers wanted to use unconscious, mindless behaviour to gain evidence for prejudicial thinking.

But there is, I suggest, a third, less obvious similarity. Gaertner and McLaughlin have a clearly and explicitly articulated hypothesis they want to test. Kitzinger and Frith do not say they have one – but I think they do, in all but name. The contentions that underpin how they go about selecting the data to support their case are that women do not lack refusal skills when dealing with unwanted sexual advances. Neither do men lack the skills to understand a hedged refusal. Rather 'the root of the problem is not that men do not understand sexual refusals, but they do not like them' (Kitzinger and Frith 1999: 310).

In, literally, other words, Kitzinger and Frith wanted to demonstrate that there was a *difference* in the way men react to ordinary refusals and sexual refusals. It is implied rather than said that when a man does something like ask a mate around to watch football and have a beer, the man is perfectly capable of reading a hedged refusal. He is able to know what is meant by the pauses, mutterings and the warrant encoded in a statement like 'I'd like to, mate, but, um, well, I promised Jason's lot I'd go round to theirs'. So a similar refusal by a woman is not something he is incapable of decoding. It is something he wants to resist. Hence, the study is an 'experiment' to the extent that it had a prediction that Kitzinger and Frith provide evidence to support. Finally, both studies' hypotheses were falsifiable. Data could be produced in either case to disprove the conclusions they reach.

There are certainly differences between the two approaches. The data providing support for their 'hypothesis' in each case was gained very differently. For a start, Kitzinger and Frith did not get their data experimentally. In fact they did not do any empirical work at all, but mine other people's data instead. However, I would argue that there is a crucial difference: it is that Gaertner and McLaughlin's study demonstrates prejudice, but it goes no further. It cannot tell us anything much other than the people concerned could be shown to have thinking that is influenced by racial prejudice – important information to have, certainly, but it takes us little further. Kitzinger and Frith's study is a demonstration, too, in a way. It tells us something we would not know without their painstaking analysis.

But the study itself also implies and the article makes explicit that certain kinds of action can be taken to tackle the prejudice. They specifically argue, for example, that campaigns to teach women to 'just say no' are not the solution to the problem. I am skating on thinner ice here, I realize, because in many reports of experimental studies the authors make specific links to practical issues and recommendations about how to address them. However, I would suggest that critical research is more explicitly intended and directed towards 'making the world a better place'. First, as I noted in Chapter 2, this is because many critical psychologists have an overt world-changing mission. Second, and more speculatively, I think it is because critical theory, in its focus on intersubjectivity, is inherently more connected to the 'real world'.

Experimental and critical studies of group behaviour

Here I am going to juxtapose Stenner's (1993) study of jealousy with Blake and Mouton's (1984) field experiment, in which corporate executives took part in what they thought was a 'training programme' but actually were observed to gain insight into intergroup conflict.

At first you may find it hard to see any similarities, until I remind you that Stenner got some of his data by bringing groups of people together to write jealousy scenarios. He used the scenarios (alongside other data) to gain access to alternative accounts of jealousy. I told you about two of them, if you remember: 'jealousy as natural', and 'jealousy as psychological immaturity'. So, first similarity: both used incidental groups. Second, and more importantly, both made use of the extensive social knowledge (including knowledge of social norms) of these people as essential elements to make the study 'work'. In Stenner's case he wanted to gain access to their stock of social knowledge as his data. For Blake and Mouton it was equally important, but a means to an end – their executives' expectations about and knowledge of competition meant that even though they were not told to compete, they did. Both also made use of the group process. This time it was Blake and Mouton who wanted it as the basis of their data. For Stenner it was a means to an end – he used the group's willingness to cooperate as the means by which they produced the scenario.

An interesting similarity here, by the way, is that neither study used a control group. Blake and Mouton's study was less of an experiment than a demonstration. So, too, was Stenner's, in a way. His overall project was taxonomic – gaining coherent accounts of the different discourses on jealousy that people can use as discursive resources. So, no hypothesis-testing in either of them.

Differences? The most striking one is that Blake and Mouton's demonstration is self-contained, whereas Stenner was doing something typical of critical research – bringing together a variety of methods that included Q methodology and reading historical texts to gradually build up a taxonomy of jealousy discourses.

Lessons and suggestions

My purpose in adopting juxtaposition here is to provide a basis for some suggestions about how social psychologists from the two camps might begin to break down the barriers and antagonism between them. Here they are:

Strategies for methodological reconciliation

The distinctiveness between experimental and critical social psychological research is nowhere near as great as it is often made out to be. There is real potential, I believe, for synergy. Theoretically I think the 'two tribes' cannot and will never agree. They are incommensurate theoretical paradigms based on radically different ontologies and epistemologies. They cannot be integrated. But there is scope for cooperation at the level of doing research.

- How about Kitzinger and Firth getting together with some people who have the equipment to do reaction time experiments? (Perhaps they have already done this and if so, pardon my ignorance.) How about experimentalists getting together with some discourse analysts to take the study of intergroup conflict further? Maybe some of them have – if so, again, my apologies for my ignorance. But if not, experimentalists working in this field could, I believe, gain enormously from getting some meaty discourse-analytic data to add to those they already have.
- [a] Finally, how about a strategy of having journal special issues or conferences or something like that, where the connecting theme is not the approach to social psychology but the issue? Often critical and experimental social psychologists study the same issue, but pass each other like ships in the night. A conference on a common theme might be an excellent superordinate task to begin the reconciliation.

FURTHER READING

Racism in psychology

Richards, G. (1997) 'Race', Racism and Psychology: Towards a Reflexive History. London: Routledge.
> This does what it says on the tin! It is a very detailed and painstaking, scholarly account of 'race' and racism in psychology,

which also strives to be even-handed. It is not a one-sided diatribe, but a real attempt to understand these issues and to make suggestions about how to tackle them.

Feminist research methods

Reinharz, S. (1992) *Feminism Research Methods in Social Research*. Oxford: Oxford University Press.

This is, in my view, the most useful and coherent account of Feminist research methods, and my inspiration for the suggestions I made at the end of the first section.

QUESTIONS

1 What is meant by 'institutional racism', and how is it manifested in contemporary social psychology?
2 What can social psychology learn from Feminist research methods?
3 Choose an example of an experimental social psychological study and juxtapose it with any example of a critical social experiment. Choose different ones from those juxtaposed in this chapter. Describe each one briefly, and then juxtapose them. Describe their similarities and their differences, and say what these can contribute to our understanding of the relative merits and applicability of the two paradigms.
4 'Experimental and critical social psychology are two argumentative ingroups devoting most of their time to emphasizing the differences between them.' Discuss this assertion, and suggest strategies that could be adopted to reduce the conflict.

Glossary

Abduction is a 'logic of research' in which hypotheses are generated through identifying and seeking to explain anomalies or data that do not fit the current theory.

Account as used as a technical term in conversational analysis, is a culturally sanctioned justification or explanation or behaving in a certain way.

Actor–observer error: in attribution theory, this is when people assume their own behaviour to be more likely to be situationally determined, and the behaviour of others more likely to be a product of personal intentions.

Affiliation is used in social psychology in social identity theory to refer to identification with an ingroup.

Agency is the location of the cause of an effect.

Analytics are strategies and procedures to interpret data – to analyse them.

Associative networks is a term used in social cognition to describe the way connections between categories are organized semantically.

Attitude is any feeling towards or opinion about something or someone that is evaluative.

Attitude object is anything a person can express an attitude towards.

Attractiveness is a term used in group theory that is not do with physical attractiveness, but is about group members developing bonds of liking for and affiliation with other group members.

Audience is a term used in studies of social influence to describe the people observing the behaviour under study.

Authoritarian personality is one in which the person adopts highly rigid views, which are usually strongly prejudiced.

Autokinetic effect is where a small bright light is shone in otherwise complete darkness, and it appears to move even though it is stationary.

Automatic processing (sometimes called mindlessness) is where people take in information and respond to it with little conscious awareness or cognitive effort.

Balance theory claims that people seek balance in their attitudes, so that they are consistent.

Behavioural style is a term used in Moscovici's theory of minority group influence, and describes whether, for example, the minority are consistent or not.

Behaviourism assumes that *all* behaviours are learned though experience.

Being-in-the-world is a term adopted by Heidegger (1928/1962) to describe the way that people are always ever engaged with and in the world. It makes explicit the claim that there can never be a separation between people and situations, that one cannot be present without the other.

Big Q is qualitative research conducted within a social constructionist approach, where the aim is to gain insight and understanding rather than test a hypothesis. There is no attempt to pre-code categories of response.

Body language is a form of non-verbal communication, in which ideas and messages are signified by stance, gestures and so on.

Bottom-up processing is processing driven by stimulus input.

Categorization is where similar things are classified together and treated as an entity.

Cocktail party phenomenon is where you can, for example, spot your own name in a conversation, even though you are not attending to it. It shows that extraneous noise is being processed, if only superficially.

Cognitive algebra is where all the relevant information is weighed according to its salience and value and then a calculation is made to end up with an overall evaluation (for example, of the attitude object).

Cognitive consistency is where people adjust their attitudes in ways that maintain consistency.

Cognitive miser describes a person processing information in ways that restrict the expenditure of cognitive resources.

Cognitive psychology grew out of disillusionment with information processing models of human thinking. It stresses the active, meaning-making and meaning-interpretation qualities of human communication, thinking, memory and so on.

Cognitive strategies are those where people direct the way they process information, in order to serve a particular function or optimize their performance.

Collective representations are those that are shared *between* people. It is a term adopted by Durkheim for representations shared among people, as opposed to those unique to individuals.

Conditions is a term that, when used in relation to experiment, has to do with the settings in which variables are being manipulated. In the simple case of an experiment to find out if something (X) affects behaviour, there are two conditions: an experimental condition (where X is applied) and a control condition (where it is not).

Conformity where the views of the majority induce the minority to comply.

Confounding variables are ones that the experimenter does not intend or want to vary but may affect the results of an experiment.

Confucian work dynamism is a term used by the Chinese Culture Connection to describe set of values that stress interpersonal harmony and cooperation among groups who work together and views time as elastic and expendable rather than needing to be 'saved'.

Connected self is a version of the self where it is seen in terms of relationships with others (for example, kinship ties and responsibilities).

Construct is the term used to describe the abstract, theoretical concepts being studied.

Conversation analysis is a form of discourse analysis that focuses on the units and forms of talk – such as conversational openings and closings, turn taking and repairs.

Corollary is a term used in personal construct theory to describe its basic assumptions and principles.

Correspondent inference is from attribution theory and concerns the degree to which the person whose behaviour is being judged is seen as behaving according to a stable and enduring disposition.

Critical social psychology is the term I have adopted in this book to describe a collection of approaches that contest experimental social psychology. These include social constructionist, postmodernist, discursive, and narrative approaches to social psychology. Its main elements are a rejection of Scientific method as the means to gain knowledge, a claim that social psychology is always an ideological endeavour, and a view of the social world that contends it is constructed through people's meaning-making not something 'out there' waiting to be discovered.

Crowd psychology is an early branch of psychology developed in France and Italy in the late nineteenth century. It was based on the notion that 'crowds' and 'mobs' appear to act as though they have a single mind – called the 'group mind'. Acting in this way, it was thought, reduces people to the 'lowest common denominator', almost as if, as a mob, they become like a primitive animal.

Cultural values theory recognizes that groups and cultures vary in their values, especially the actions and behaviours that they endorse.

Demand characteristics are cues in the experimental setting that may lead to bias.

Dependent variable is the variable in an experiment that is used to observe the effect of the independent variable.

Descriptive interviewing is an approach that aims to give participants in a study the opportunity to speak for themselves without interpretation.

Descriptive research uses an inductive approach, and is intended to provide the basis for an accurate description of the phenomenon in question.

Dialectical is where things are in a reciprocal relationship to or interaction with each other.

Disclaiming is a term used in discourse analysis, referring to discursive strategies to deny something (for example, that you are racist).

Discourse analysis is a generic term applied to a range of semiotic methods for scrutinizing text – which can be talk, writing or even visual images – to gain insight into its meanings and what it is being used to signify.

Discursive practices discourse analysis tends to be very specific in its application. It focuses on what a particular text element – such as a short extract of talk – is being used to achieve. More broadly this approach examines the ways in which discourse is used strategically – to do things like persuade, impress or undermine another person.

Discursive psychology is a generic term applied to approaches that assume that social reality is constructed by subjective and intersubjective 'effort after meaning', where discourse is seen as the main means by which people construct, communicate and interpret meaning.

Discursive resources discourse analysis takes a 'broad-brush' approach, looking at discourse in an almost ecological way. It is less concerned with what a particular person says at a specific time and more concerned with the ways different discourses interact with each other, mutate over time, gain dominance in certain settings and cultural locations. For example, this approach traces the ways in which new discourses (such as feminism) have posed a challenge to the dominant discourse of patriarchy.

Dispositional inference is a stage in attribution, where a judgement is made based on a stereotype (for example, 'women are emotional').

Double-blind experiment is where both subject and experimenter do not know the experimental hypothesis or the condition under test.

Dual process dependency model explains social influence in groups as operating in terms of a person's confidence in their own judgement. When they are confident, they act according to it – but when they lack confidence, they follow group norms.

Ego-defence is from psychodynamic theory, and is a strategy to protect the ego from being undermined or harmed.

Emblem is a gesture that stands in for speech, such as a soldier's salute or a police officer's upheld hand signalling 'stop'.

Emotional labour is the hard work involved in presenting a cheery face for hours on end, however obnoxiously the customers are behaving.

Empiricism is the basis of scientific epistemology, where objective data are the sole means to gain valid knowledge.

Emplotment is where a string of incidents are woven together to form a narrative, so that they become a meaningful story.

Epistemology is a theory of knowledge.

Equilibrium is a term used by Herzlich (1973) to describe a social representation of health where it is seen as a state of positive well-being, where body and soul are in harmonious balance.

Esteem function is the way an attitude that enables individuals and collectives to achieve and maintain status, respect and honour.

Ethnolinguistic groups are groups defined by their ethnic commonality and their use of a common slang or patois.

Ethnomethodology is an approach to research that works in naturalistic settings and is informed by Critical Realist ontology and epistemology.

Evolutionary psychology is rooted in evolutionary biology and sociobiology, and claims that human behaviour is moulded by evolution and encoded in the genes.

Exemplar-based memory is where storage and processing are based on specific exemplars.

Expectancy-value models assume that people decide between alternative courses of action through estimating the probabilities for each possible action that it will bring about benefits and/or avoid negative consequences to themselves.

Experimental scenario is where an experiment is 'set' to create the experimental conditions.

Experimental subjects are the people taking part in an experiment.

Experimenter effects are where researchers act in ways that affect the outcome of the experiment, in unintended ways.

Explanation is to 'smooth over' – it is where the causes of effects are identified, and complexity is 'ironed out'.

Explication is to 'unfold' – it is where insight is the goal, not explanation.

Expressive function is where attitudes allow individuals and collectives to communicate their beliefs, opinions and values and, thereby, to identify with those individuals and groups who share them.

Externalization when used in social constructionist theory is about the way that cultures, societies and social groups of different kinds make sense of – and therefore 'make' – their social worlds, including a whole range of social institutions and constructs.

Extreme case formulation is a term used in discourse analysis, where someone is seeking to justify taking or recommending a particular action by expressing the worst case scenario.

Extroverts according to Eysenck (1978), are people who are physiologically 'dampened' and hence seek arousing stimulation. They are risk-takers, for example, and enjoy extreme sports.

Face is a term used by Goffman to describe the positive social value a person effectively claims for themselves by the line others assume they have taken during an interaction.

Face work goes on in social interaction, where people have a mutual commitment to keep each other 'in face'.

False consensus effect is where people tend to assume that others are more likely to behave like them than they actually do.

Falsification is seeking to disprove a rule or a theory's predictions.

Field experiments are experiments carried out in naturalistic settings rather than the laboratory.

Field theory is a term used in Gestalt theory, where behaviour is seen to be influenced by the 'psychological field' or 'social climate' in the same way that the perceptual field influences what a person sees.

Focus groups are where a group is brought together in order to explore attitudes and opinions; they are often used in market research.

Foucauldian discourse analysis is another term for discursive resources discourse analysis, where the analysis is at the level of discourses operating intersubjectively.

Fundamental attribution error is where people tend to overemphasize the personal causes, and underemphasize the situational causes of actions.

Gaydar is a kind of cultural radar that allows gay people to recognize whether another person is gay or straight.

Gaze has (at least) two meanings. In non-verbal communication it has to do with the way people look at each other. In Postmodern theory, it is about the semiotic 'lens' through which people view the world – such as a 'male gaze' or a 'Feminist gaze'.

Gestalt appraisal is based on the whole of something not just its constituent parts.

Gestalt psychology is an approach that views context for the way that people perceive objects – including social objects; the 'figure' is viewed in relation to the 'ground'.

Grounded theory is not only a general term to refer to research where theories are developed from interpretation and analysis of the data (rather than the other way around) but also a specific research method (described in detail in Chapter 3).

Group dynamics is a field of study developed by Lewin in the 1940s. It concerns the ways in which individuals act differently when they are part of a group, compared with when they are acting alone. For example, working on a task together as a group can either have the effect of making individuals work harder (social energizing) or less hard (social loafing), according to circumstances.

Group initiation is where in order to join a group the person is expected to participate in an activity or ritual – such as swearing an oath.

Group norms are the norms endorsed by the group – as opposed, say, to cultural norms.

Group polarization is where a group decision is more extreme than the average when group members make the decision individually.

Groupthink is what happens when a small, highly cohesive group of like-minded people becomes so obsessed with reaching consensus and so blinkered by it when they reach it, that they lose touch with reality and make a catastrophic decision.

Head-in-the-sand fallacy is where social psychologists assume that what they discover from studying samples of US students are universally nomothetic theories about social psychological processes and phenomena.

Health-in-a-vacuum is a social representation of health where it is seen as an absence of illness.

Hedge (sometimes called a preface) is a word or utterance like 'uh' at the start of speech, used to 'hedge around' difficulties to come.

Heuristic processing is where information is processed using 'rules of thumb' (such as the majority are usually right).

Human science disciplines are those that study some aspect of people, such as anthropology and economics.

Human-heartedness is a value dimension varying from values of kindness, compassion and emotional nurturance to values of conscientiousness, perseverance and thrift.

Hypothetico-deductive method are methods of research based on making deductions from the testing of hypotheses.

Hypothetico-deductivism is the process of making deductions from the testing of hypotheses.

Identity-reference groups are where belonging to the group involves identification with the group, and where affiliation acts as a reference frame for a person to know 'who' they are – their social identity.

Idiographic means specific to particular instances, as opposed to generally lawful.

Illustrator is a posture or gesture that accompanies speech, generally reinforcing its message, such as using your hand to point directions.

Implicit attitudes are attitudes based on stereotypical thinking, that *can* affect other judgements without the person being aware of their influence.

Implicit measures are measures in an experiment that infer a person's thinking (including their unconscious thinking) rather than test it directly by self-report.

Impression formation is how people form their first impressions of others.

Impression management is a conscious or unconscious attempt to control the impression you make on others in social interactions.

Incidental groups are where two or more people are merely together for a relatively short period of time and have minimal involvement in and commitment to each other.

Independent variable this is the variable in an experiment that is varied by the experimenter.

Individual representations are those that are unique to the person.

Individuo-centred approach focuses on the ways in which social grouping, social institutions and social forces are determined by the behaviour of individuals and the processes going on within individual minds.

Information influence is where people use the group as an information source.

Ingroup is the group to which a person belongs.

Initiation: see **group initiation**.

Innovation is a term from Moscovici's theory of minority influence, where a minority persuades the majority to adopt their viewpoint.

Institutional racism differs profoundly from overt racism; it is a much more subtle form of racism in that is not *intended* to be prejudiced – though its impact can be as damaging as out-and-out blatant racism.

Instrumental function is where attitudes direct people to act within the social world in ways that enable them to pursue their goals, both individual and collective.

Integration is the term used by the Chinese Cultural Collective to describe whether the self is seen in individualistic or relational terms.

Internalization when used in social constructionist theory is where the objectified social world becomes known and understood by individuals through processes of socialization and enculturation.

Interpersonal distance is the distance at which two people interact; intimates get up close, friends less so, and strangers prefer to keep their distance.

Intersubjective is subjectivity (experiencing, thinking, perception) that is based upon common impressions, symbols, ideas and understandings shared between people rather than being the products of individual minds.

Introspectionism is the exploration of thought processes by, literally, individuals internally reflecting on their own experiences of remembering, perceiving and so on.

Introverts, according to Eysenck (1978) are people who are physiologically sensitized and so avoid arousing stimulation. They are risk-avoiding, for example, and prefer a quiet and predictable life.

Issuance is the property of something to 'be an issue' – that is, to be something about which people are concerned and/or have contested views.

Laboratory experiments are conducted in controlled settings. In social psychology this is often just an ordinary room.

Langue is that aspect of language that is its abstract system of syntax and semantics, and that is virtual and outside of time.

Leakage is where non-verbal cues that indicate a person is being dishonest.

Learned helplessness is a term adopted by Seligman (1975) to describe people whose childhood experiences taught them that they have no control over their destiny. So, he argued, in adulthood they are incapable of helping themselves – they are passive and incapable.

Liberal humanism is an ideology that gives priority to the well-being and well-functioning of a 'good society', in which individuals have a duty to contribute to the good of society through collective effort.

Liberal individualism is an ideology that gives priority to a person's individual autonomy and freedom. In it institutions like the Church or the state are seen to have little or no right to intervene in how an individual chooses to live their life.

Lickert scale is a scale consisting of a set of statements, and boxes (or whatever) that people mark to indicate, say, their agreement with the statement – for example ranging from 'strongly agree' to 'strongly disagree'.

Linguistic repertoires is a term used by Potter and Wetherell (1987) to describe the discursive resources people draw upon to achieve particular ends.

Little q is qualitative research conducted within an experimental approach where categories of response are pre-coded, and hence measures are obtained.

Locus of control is about whether a person sites control in themselves or in chance, luck or fate, seen to be a product of their learning experiences as children.

Low-status groups are social groups consisting of marginalized or socially excluded people (for example, 'the underclass') or those regarded by an in-group as inferior (for example, 'gypsies').

Major histocompatibility complex (MHC) is genetic material that contains information that allows for the recognition of genetic similarity and is the basis of the immune response.

Majority influence – informational influence based on taken-for-granted knowledge.

Market research is where research is carried out in order to inform commercial decisions – for instance, to find a new brand name for a product or discover what kinds of people are most likely to be interested in a new service.

Mass media are forms of collective communication such as television and newspapers.

Matched-guise technique is where a series of tape-recorded speech extracts are recorded, all spoken by the same highly skilled actor but each one in a different accent or dialect. Subjects in the study give their impression of the speaker by responding to different evaluative dimensions.

Membership groups are groups that people join and can leave; in such groups people see themselves as having a stake in the group's fortunes and are can be strongly committed and involved.

Micropolitics of power is a term devised by Foucault to describe the complex webs of power and resistance that operate in people's relations with one another, whether as individuals or as groups.

Mindlessness (sometimes called automatic processing) is where people take in information and respond to it with little conscious awareness or cognitive effort.

Minimal group paradigm is where social effects are studied in incidental groups. Almost any element of common fate seems to be sufficient to persuade people to favour members of 'their' group over members of another group.

Minority influence is where a small minority is able to sway the judgements of the majority.

Mnemonic strategies are ways of memorizing information by making it meaningful.

Modernism is the name given to a set of ethical beliefs and values, practices and endeavours, that were developed in Europe and the USA during the historical period of the Enlightenment in the eighteenth century.

Moral discipline is a set of values relating to respect for superiors and the value of diligence and hard work.

Morphemes are the units of speech composed of phonemes, and are usually words.

Motivated tactician is a term used to describe cognition where different processing strategies are used tactically, to optimize the chances of achieving goals.

Narrative psychology explores the ways in which people make sense of the social world and their lives within it through constructing knowledge into a story.

Natural sciences are those that study the natural (as opposed to the human) and include physics, chemistry and biology.

Negative bias is where, once a negative impression is formed about someone, it tends to persist and lead to negative evaluation.

Nomothetic means lawful, that is relating to people systematically acting in similar ways.

Normalization is a term from Moscovici's theory of minority influence, where the minority and majority members of a group agree on a compromise judgement.

Normative influence is where people in a group follow group norms.

Norms are defined in experimental social psychology as the shared standards of conduct expected of group members.

Null hypothesis is devised in an experiment as that which falsifies the experimental hypothesis.

Objectification is one of the 'moments' in the social construction of reality, whereby ideas, concepts and so on are taken to be 'real things'.

Observational measures are those taken from direct observation of the behaviour of subjects that is relevant to the research question.

Ontology is the branch of philosophy concerned with what things 'are' – their 'being-in-the-world'. A good example is the different ontological positions taken by experimental and critical social psychology over the nature of the social world. Experimental social psychology sees it as something separate from people – an external medium within which individual people operate. Critical social psychology sees the social world as a product of human thought and action.

Operalization describes the way a construct is 'made operational' (that is, useable) in the form of variables that can be measured in a particular study.

Operant conditioning is a process whereby people change their behaviour in response to either a regime of rewards (called reinforcement) or punishments (negative reinforcement).

Opinion polls are studies of public attitudes, as used, for example, by political parties to find out about voting intentions in the period before elections.

Organizational function is where, by categorizing objects in the social world along evaluative dimensions, attitudes act as guides to help people – as individuals and collectively – attend to these objects, understand them and feel about them.

Outgroup is any group other than a person's in-group, but usually refers to the comparison group(s) in a study of social identity.

Palliative is a term used in discourse analysis; it is where someone seeks to ameliorate potential rudeness of, say, rejecting the invitation.

Paradigm shift is where one paradigm is overthrown and replaced by another, in which radically different questions are asked and methods used, and theorization is based on different assumptions.

Paralanguage is the non-linguistic elements of speech, things like ums and ahs, grunts and sighs, speed, tone and pitch of voice, and so on.

Parole is that aspect of language that operates in a speech community, such as English or French.

Patois is a developed and inclusive way of talking that has not only a particular accent, but also its own grammar and terminology, such as Rastafarian.

Personal construct theory is primarily a theory about how individuals build up and use 'personal constructs' to make sense of and operate within the social world.

Personal self is the self that is self-aware of being 'you' and conscious of your own thoughts and feelings.

Persuasion is where a deliberate attempt is made to change people's attitudes and is concerned with the cognitive processes involved in how that change is brought about.

Persuasive arguments theory proposes that group polarization works through people taking notice of additional arguments that support their own opinion, this making it stronger.

Phenomenological causality is a term adopted by Heider to describe the ways in which people attribute the causes of events and things that happen to them, including locating agency in people and in nature.

Phenomenological methods are those where people seek to report their subjective experiences.

Pheromones are chemicals exuded (for example by sweat glands) that communicate through the sense of smell.

Phonemes are the basic, meaningless sounds in spoken language, like the 'th' at the beginning of 'think, or the 'oo' at the end of 'kangaroo'.

Positivism is the epistemological position that there can be a straightforward one-to-one relationship between things and events in the outside world and people's knowledge of them.

Postmodernism is a reaction and challenge to Modernism. It disputes Modernism's claim that there is a singular objective knowledge that can be gained through scientific inquiry. Rather, Postmodernism regards all knowledge as socially constructed. It contends that there are many knowledges, each one arising from different standpoints (that is, that knowledge is always *positioned* by the person or group promoting it). Postmodernism is fundamentally concerned with the relationship between knowledge and power – what actions, for example, a particular knowledge allows and what it prevents.

Power distance is a value dimension relating to the amount of respect and deference expected between superiors and their subordinates, and the formality of social interactions.

Preface: see **hedge**.

Presencing function is where some action (such as constructing a story) is carried out in order to make something 'real' – to bring it to our attention as a 'real thing'.

Presencing practices are where some kind of social reality is made and/or made real. For example, a Gay Pride procession presences a particular form of homosexuality – one that is celebratory (as opposed, say, to one which presences homosexuality as an illness).

Primacy effect is where the first information in a list has a greater effect than information later in that list.

Priming is where prior information or other manipulation of experimental conditions affects subsequent behaviour.

Processing depth models of social cognition view it as operating in one of two distinctly and qualitatively different levels of processing. Information processing about something that is mundane and unimportant tends to be 'mindless' and automatic. But information processing that matters or is out of the ordinary tends to be carried out in-depth and with careful consideration.

Prototypes are abstract representations of idealized categories, rather like mental blueprints.

Proxemics is the study of the distance that people adopt when communicating with each other.

Psycholinguistics views language as the main medium for thought, and examines the ways in language affects thinking.

Psychological social psychology studies how social events and phenomena influence the ways in which individual people feel, think and act. It is concerned with the psychological processes (such as social perception and cognition) that go on within individual minds.

Qualitative research is where behaviour is observed rather than measured. Little q qualitative research is where it is used experimentally, and is coded according to predetermined categories. Big Q qualitative research makes no attempt to measure or pre-categorize what is being observed.

Quasi-experiment is another name for field experiment, where researchers capitalize upon situations where relevant factors are being varied naturally.

Racial psychology was the study of psychological differences between different races in an explicit quest to document the superiority of the white race.

Received pronunciation is that pronunciation of a language assumed to be the standard, and is often accorded a higher status than, for example, a regional accent.

Recency effect is where items at the end of a list are remembered or have more effect that items in the middle.

Reference frame is a set of norms that a person uses as a reference point to judge their own.

Referent information influence is seen to operate through people's self-categorization. When they identify themselves as belonging to a particular group they then use that group's norms as standards for their own decision making.

Reflexive self is the part of a self that is able to observe, plan and respond to one's own behaviour.

Reflexivity is being self-aware, and able to, for example, judge one's own behaviour or thinking and gain insight.

Reification is where an abstract idea or a number of coexisting ideas or events get conceptually turned into a 'thing'. An example is pre-menstrual tension.

Relational self is the self that comes from interconnected relationships with others, such as family or community.

Representativeness is about making sure that the people taking part in the study are representative of the people the researcher wants to find out.

Reserve of health is a social representation of health based on the idea that health is a resource or an investment.

Resistance is a term adopted by Foucault to describe the strategies that people use to resist power being exercised over them.

Respondents is the name given to the people taking part in a survey.

Retroduction is a logic of inquiry that seeks to identify systematic regularities in social action and social phenomena, in order to speculate about the structures and mechanisms underlying them.

Reversal of agency is a term devised by Vickers to describe the misattribution of agency, where, for example, a 'victim' is blamed for the harm done to them and the perpetrator absolved of responsibility for the harm they did.

Risky shift is where, in group discussions, the group adopts a more risky decision than the individuals did privately.

Role expectations are those that require people to act in accordance to preconceived notions relating to their role.

Scary bridge study was a field experiment where subjects' arousal was varied naturally – they were interviewed either on an ordinary bridge or a very scary one.

Schema is a cognitive structure that represents knowledge about a concept, including its attributes and the relations among these attributes.

Science: using a capital letter indicates that this is a science that uses a hypothetico-deductive approach to gaining knowledge.

Scientific racism is a theory that assumes that humankind has a common ancestry, but some races are more advanced than others.

Script is a well-rehearsed and well-remembered repertoire for action, sometimes viewed as a schema about an event.

Selection task problem was devised by Wason to examine people's tendencies to make induction errors when problem solving.

Selective attention is where someone has to divide their attention between two or more tasks, and prioritizes one of them.

Self-categorization theory is where a person identifies with a social group, and hence categorizes themself as a member of that group.

Self-esteem refers to the attitudes that people hold towards themselves.

Self-monitoring is about the way people monitor their behaviour to tailor it to different situations and circumstances.

Self-perception theory argues that people know who they are by observing their own behaviour.

Self-presentation is about how you portray yourself (to yourself, and to others) in a good light.

Self-report measures are where subjects respond directly to questions – for example, by completing a questionnaire.

Self-stereotyping is where a person identifies with a social group, and categorizes themself as a member of that group, and adopts the stereotypical behaviour and persona expected of members of that group.

Semantic describes those aspects of language to do with the meanings of words, sentences and utterances.

Semiotics is the study of signs and symbols and how they convey significance and meaning.

Severe initiation is an initiation into a group that involves pain, discomfort and/or embarrassment. It can be a powerful means to establish loyalty to the group.

Sign systems are systems of signifiers and signifieds, whereby messages about meaning are communicated.

Significant difference is a technical term in statistics. A difference is significant if it is sufficiently large that, statistically, it is very unlikely to be a matter of coincidence or chance.

Signification is the process of using signs to communicate significance and meaning.

Signified is that aspect of something (such as an article of clothing) that refers to what it is intended to mean.

Signifier refers to the physical characteristics of the sign.

Signifying act is when a person expresses a sign or symbol by the articulation of a message. This can be in language, but also by an act (such as marching in a Gay Pride rally).

Situated identity is where a person's identity is determined and defined by the situation.

Situational correction is a stage in attribution where a person corrects their stereotyped view of a disposition, and take into account the influence of the situation or context.

Social attraction in group theory is where inter-individual liking is based upon group norms.

Social categorization theory highlights people's tendency to identify with the group – to see it an ingroup – and then to endorse the norms that distinguish their ingroup from other outgroups.

Social cognition comprises the processes involved in perceiving, understanding and responding to the social world. As a concept it is based on the general principles of cognitive psychology.

Social cohesion model defines a number of stages by which people move from acting independently to acting as a group.

Social comparison theory argues that people want social approval and dislike social censure, and so comply to group norms.

Social constructionism is the term generally used for approaches to social psychology that are informed by Postmodernism. Its main emphasis is upon the way that reality is constructed through social processes – another way of putting this is intersubjectively.

Social desirability effect is where people act in ways that make them look good.

Social desirability is the tendency for people to want to think well of themselves and want others to see them in a good light, and may affect the way they behave. This can cause problems in experiments.

Social energizing is where people work harder as a member of a group than alone.

Social facilitation is where the effect of doing a task in front of others tends to improve performance.

Social identity is the identity a person gains as a member of an in-group; it is a sort of socio-cultural 'glue' which plays a significant role in sustaining social and cultural groups.

Social influence is about the ways that other people and social processes between people can affect a person's behaviour.

Social interaction is where people are acting in relation to each other.

Social learning theory assumes that people's behaviour is the product of learning – for example, it is determined by the rewards and punishments they receive in their childhood.

Social loafing is where individuals expend less effort on a task when they do it with others (or think they are doing so).

Social perception is concerned with the ways in which people make sense of the social world of other people (in their actions both as individuals and groups).

Social representations is a concept developed by Moscovici to refer to the shared understandings and belief-structures, through which people make sense of the social world. According to Moscovici's theory of social representations theory, a social group is a group with common, shared, social representations.

Social self is the self that arises and is acted out in a social situation.

Sociobiology is a theory that human behaviour is moulded by evolution; people behave in ways that maximize their reproductive potential.

Socio-centred approach is one that focuses on the ways in which the behaviour and experiences of individual people are determined by their membership of social groups and social institutions and by social forces.

Sociolinguistics is the study of language in experimental social psychology; it focuses on how language is used in social situations.

Sociological social psychology studies how people act together and interact to produce social phenomena (such as crowd behaviour). It is concerned with how social processes (such as group cohesion and social identity) arise from social forces (such as the influence of group norms).

Sociology of science is the sociological study of how science works in practice – by, for example, observing scientists working in a laboratory.

Speech is the term in English used to mean *parole*: that which is particular to the use of language in a specific situation.

Speech style is the manner in which people speak in different contexts (for example talking to children or adults).

Stereotyping is where something is categorized according to an overgeneralized and often negative category, as in sexist stereotyping.

Stooge is a member of the experimental team, briefed to act as if they are a subject in an experiment in ways that establish one of the experimental conditions. For example, in studies of compliance, stooges give wrong answers.

Stream of consciousness: in a person's stream of consciousness, James proposed, all manner of thoughts, emotions, states, feelings, images and ideas continually coexist at some level.

Structuralism is the global, all-encompassing study of the architecture of meaning – of what meanings can be constructed, by whom and how and why and from what.

Subject positioning is where a person is positioned through strategies of regulation. An example is a person who was abused in childhood, who may be positioned as a 'victim' by the actions and expectations of people like counsellors or psychiatrists.

Subjective norms are composed of other people's expectations and a person's own motivations to comply with them.

Substantivity is when a transitive state becomes actual – for example, when we notice, we realize, we recognize, we become aware of *something*.

Summer Camp experiments were Sherif's classic experimental studies of group cooperation and conflicts carried out with boys attending US summer camps.

Survey research is where data are gathered by asking people to fill in questionnaires, or they are interviewed – face to face, by telephone or by email.

Symbol is a sign where its meaning is based upon a shared ideology or institution. Examples include flags and religious symbols like the cross in Christianity.

Symbolic interactionism is a sociological theory, focusing on the ways in which people interact with each other through expressing and sharing meaning.

Syntactic rules are the linguistic rules that determine how words are fitted together.

Systematic processing is processing that involves conscious and systematic thought, as opposed to automatic processing; it is demanding but much more strategic and insightful.

Talk is a term used by discourse analysts to refer to any sort of speech, usually naturally occurring, such as in meetings or counselling sessions.

Team-building exercises are designed to build the 'team spirit' and solidarity that leads to effective teamwork. They usually engage people in cooperative tasks, sometimes in extreme conditions (such as white water rafting).

Technology of the self is a term adopted by Foucault to convey the ways in which a 'self' is constructed through regulatory control – for example, through strategies for controlling and regulating sexuality (see Chapter 8).

Tectonics is a term adopted by Curt to refer to those aspects of discourse that relate to how it is produced, maintained and promoted, and how discourses vie against and impinge upon one another.

Text when used as a technical term is any human product or action that signifies something. Although it is usually language, it can be, for instance, a painting or a building.

Textuality is a term adopted by Curt to refer to those aspects of discourse that have to do with its semiotic qualities, and hence its potential to wield power.

Theory of reasoned action is where people's behaviour is seen to be a product of their attitudes plus other elements including subjective norms and values.

Thingification is another (uglier but easier to understand) term for reification, the process whereby ideas get turned into things.

Top-down processing is where information stored in memory (such as schema) is used to enable higher order, more complex thinking processes.

Transitivity is where thoughts are immanent rather than substantive – outside of our awareness and at the 'back of our minds'.

Us and Them fallacy is the stereotypical view that studying white people can tell you about social psychological processes and phenomena, whereas the study of black people is the domain of cross-cultural psychology.

Utilitarianism is an ideology developed by Jeremy Bentham (1748–1832), in which it is held that the most ethical way to behave is in a manner that brings the greatest good for the greatest number of people.

Values are stable and enduring convictions – often moral principles – that people hold about what matters to them and/or what they believe to be good or bad, worthwhile or worthless.

Value system is where values are organized together.

Variable is where a construct is defined in a way that can be measured.

Verification involves seeking to verify that a rule or a theory's predictions are supported.

Visual dominance behaviour is where a person expresses or seeks to impose dominance by the use of eye gaze (such as 'staring someone out').

Völkerpsychologie is an early branch of psychology developed in Germany in the late nineteenth century. Difficult to translate exactly, it is the psychological study of the way the 'folk' or ordinary people in a particular society tend to share a similar worldview – they have similar opinions and beliefs.

Western is a term which, when capitalized, does not describe the geographical western area of the world. Rather it refers to the industrialized, rich areas of the world that include Australia and New Zealand. However, it does not just denote relative wealth and the accessibility of advanced technology – this is also true of the richer countries on the Pacific rim. Crucially 'Western' refers to places where the dominant culture is one that has emerged from Western (as opposed to Eastern) religious beliefs and a more general worldview of individualism.

References

Abelson, R.P. (1981) The psychological status of the script concept, *American Psychologist*, 36: 715–29.

Abrams, D. and Hogg, M. (1988) Comments on the motivational status of self-esteem in social identity and in-group discrimination, *European Journal of Social Psychology*, 18: 317–34.

Adorno, T.W., Frenkel-Brunswick, E., Levinson, D.J. and Sandford, R.N. (1950) *The Authoritarian Personality*. New York: Harper.

Aiello, J.R. and Jones, S.E. (1971) Field study of the proxemic behaviour of young children in three subcultural groups, *Journal of Personality and Social Psychology*, 19: 351–6.

Ajzen, I. (1991) The theory of planned behaviour, *Organizational Behaviour and Human Decision Processes*, 50: 199–211.

Ajzen, I. and Fishbein, M. (1972) Attitudes and normative beliefs as factors influencing behavioural intentions, *Journal of Personality and Social Psychology*, 21(1): 1–9.

Ajzen, I. and Madden, T.J. (1986) Prediction of goal-directed behavior: attitudes, intentions and perceived behavioral control, *Journal of Experimental Social Psychology*, 22: 453–74

Alexander, R.D. (1974) The evolution of social behaviour, *Annual Review of Ecology and Systematics*, 5: 325–83.

Allport, F.H. (1920) The influence of the group upon association and thought, *Journal of Experimental Psychology*, III: 159–82.

Allport, F.H. (1924) *Social Psychology*. Boston: Houghton Mifflin.

Allport, G.W. (1935) Attitudes, in G. Murchison (ed.) *Handbook of Social Psychology*. Worchester, MA: Clark University Press.

Allport, G.W. (1954) *The Nature of Prejudice*. Reading, MA: Addison-Wesley.

Allport, G.W. (1968) The historical background of modern social psychology, in G. Lindzey and E. Aronson (eds) *The Handbook of Social Psychology*, Vol. 1, 2nd edn. Reading, MA: Addison-Wesley.

Allport, G.W. and Vernon, P.E. (1931) *A Study of Values*. Boston: Houghton Mifflin.

Allport, G.W., Vernon, P.E. and Lindzey, G. (1960) *A Study of Values*. Boston: Houghton Mifflin.

Antaki, C. (1981) *The Psychology of Ordinary Explanations of Social Behaviour*. London: Academic Press.

Antaki, C. (1988) *Analysing Everyday Explanations: A Casebook of Methods*. London: Sage.

Archer, J. (2000) Evolutionary social psychology, in M. Hewstone and
W. Stroebe (eds) *Introduction to Social Psychology*, 3rd edn. Oxford:
Blackwell.

Argyle, M. (1988) *Bodily Communication*. London: Methuen.

Argyle, M. and Henderson, M. (1985) *The Anatomy of Relationships*.
Harmondsworth: Penguin.

Argyle, M. and Ingham, R. (1972) Gaze, mutual gaze and proximity,
Semiotica, 6: 32–49.

Armistead, N. (1974) *Reconstructing Social Psychology*. Harmondsworth:
Penguin.

Aronson, E. (1999) *The Social Animal*, 8th edn. New York: Worth/Freeman.

Aronson, E. and Mills, J. (1959) The effects of severity of initiation on liking
for a group, *Journal of Abnormal and Social Psychology*, 59: 177–81.

Asch, S.E. (1946) Forming impressions of personality, *Journal of Abnormal
and Social Psychology*, 41: 258–90.

Asch, S.E. (1951) Effects of group pressure on the modification and
distortion of judgements, in H. Guetzkow (ed.) *Groups, Leadership and Men*.
Pittsburgh, PA: Carnegie Press.

Asch, S.E. (1952) *Social Psychology*. Englewood Cliffs, NJ: Prentice Hall.

Asch, S.E. (1956) Studies of independence and conformity: a minority of one
against a unanimous majority, *Psychological Monographs*: *General and Applied*,
70, 170 (whole no. 416).

Atkinson, J.M. and Drew, P. (eds) (1979) *Order in Court: The Organization of
Verbal Interaction in Judicial Settings*. London: Social Sciences Research
Council.

Bache, G.M. (1895) Reaction time with reference to race, *Psychological Review*,
2: 475–86.

Bales, R.F. and Slater, P.E. (1955) Role differentiation in small decision-
making groups, in T. Parson and R.F. Bales (eds) *Family, Socialization and
Interaction Process*. Glencoe, IL: Free Press.

Banner, L.W. (1983) *American Beauty*. Chicago: University of Chicago
Press.

Bannister, D. and Fransella, F. (1986) *Inquiring Man: The Psychology of Personal
Constructs*. London: Croom Helm.

Bargh, J.A. (1997) The automaticity of everyday life, in R.S. Wyler and
T.K. Krull (eds) *Advances in Social Cognition*. Mahwah, NJ: Erlbaum.

Bargh, J.A., Chaiken, S., Govender, R. and Pratto, F. (1992) The generality of
the automatic attitude activation effect, *Journal of Personality and Social
Psychology*, 62: 893–912.

Barsalou, L.W. (1985) Ideals, central tendency and frequency of instantiation
as determinants of graded structure in categories. *Journal of Experimental
Psychology: Learning Memory and Cognition*, 11: 629–54.

Barthes, R. ([1957] 1967) *Elements of Semiology*. New York: Hill and Wang (originally published in French).

Barthes, R. (1985) *The Grain of the Voice: Interviews, 1962–1980*, trans. L. Coverdale. New York: Hill and Wang.

Bartlett, F.C. (1932a) *Psychology and Primitive Culture*. Cambridge: Cambridge University Press.

Bartlett, F.C. (1932b) *Remembering*. Cambridge: Cambridge University Press.

Batson, C.D., Duncan, B.D., Ackerman, P., Buckley, T. and Birch, K. (1981) Is empathic emotion a source of altruistic motivation?, *Journal of Personality and Social Psychology*, 40: 290–302.

Baudrillard, J. (1988) *America*. London: Virago.

Baumeister, R.F. and Covington, M.V. (1985) Self-esteem, persuasion and retrospective distortion of initial attitudes, *Electronic Social Psychology*, 1(1): 1–22.

Bem, D. (1972) Self-perception theory, in L. Berkowitz (ed.) *Advances in Experimental Social Psychology*, Vol. 6. New York: Academic Press.

Benson, P.L., Karabenick, S.A. and Lerner, R.M. (1976) Pretty please: the effects of physical attractiveness, race and sex on receiving help, *Journal of Experimental Social Psychology*, 12: 409–15.

Bentler, P.M. and Speckart, G. (1979) Models of attitude–behaviour relations, *Psychological Review*, 86: 452–64.

Berger, C.R. and Calabrese, R.J. (1975) Some explorations in initial interaction and beyond: toward a developmental theory of interpersonal communication, *Human Communication Research*, 1: 99–112.

Berger, P.L. and Luckmann, T. (1967) *The Social Construction of Reality*. Harmondsworth: Penguin.

Berri, N. (1989) as quoted in editorial, *Indianapolis Star*, 12 September.

Berry, J.W. (1967) Independence and conformity in subsistence level societies, *Journal of Personality and Social Psychology*, 7: 415–18.

Bhaskar, R. (1979) *The Possibility of Naturalism: A Philosophical Critique of the Contemporary Human Sciences*. Brighton: Harvester.

Billig, M. (1982) *Ideology and Social Psychology: Extremism, Moderation and Contradiction*. Oxford: Blackwell.

Billig, M. (1987) *Arguing and Thinking: A Rhetorical Approach to Social Psychology*. Cambridge: Cambridge University Press.

Billig, M. (1997) Rhetorical and discursive analysis: how families talk about the Royal Family, in N. Hayes (ed.) *Doing Qualitative Analysis in Psychology*. Hove: Psychology Press.

Blackman, L. (2001) *Hearing Voices: Embodiment and Experience*. London: Free Association Books.

Blackman, L. and Walkerdine, V. (2001) *Mass Hysteria: Critical Psychology and Media Studies*. Basingstoke: Palgrave.

Blaikie, N. (2000) *Designing Social Research: The Logic of Anticipation*. Cambridge: Polity.

Blake, R.R. and Mouton, J.S. (1984) *Solving Costly Organisational Conflicts*. San Francisco, CA: Jossey Bass.

Bohner, G. (2001) Attitudes, in M. Hewstone and W. Stroebe (eds) *Introduction to Social Psychology*, 3rd edn. Oxford: Blackwell.

Bohner, G., Maskowitz, G. and Chaiken, S. (1995) The interplay of heuristic and semantic processing of social information, *European Review of Social Psychology*, 6: 33–68.

Bowlby, J. (1969) *Attachment and Loss, Vol. 1: Attachment*. London: Hogarth Press.

Bowlby, J. (1980) *Attachment and Loss, Vol. 3: Loss*. London: Hogarth Press.

Breckler, S.J. (1984) Empirical validation of affect, behaviour and cognition as distinct components of attitude, *Journal of Personality and Social Psychology*, 47: 1191–205.

Breckler, S.J. and Wiggins, E.C. (1989) Affect versus evaluation in the structure of attitudes, *Journal of Experimental Social Psychology*, 25: 253–71.

Brehm, S.S. (1992) *Intimate Relationships*, 2nd edn. New York: McGraw-Hill.

Brickman, P. (1980) A social psychology of human concerns, in R. Gilmour and S. Duck (eds) *The Development of Social Psychology*. London: Academic Press.

Broadbent, D. (1958) *Perception and Communication*. New York: Pergamon.

Broverman, I.K., Vogal, S.R., Broverman, D.M., Clarkson, F.E. and Rosenkranz, P.S. (1972) Sex-role stereotypes: a current appraisal, *Journal of Social Issues*, 28(2): 59–78.

Brown, P. and Fraser, C. (1979) Speech as a marker of situation, in K.R. Scherer and H. Giles (eds) *Social Markers in Speech*. Cambridge: Cambridge University Press.

Brown, R.J. (1978) Divided we fall: an analysis of relations between sections of a factory work-force, in H. Tajfel (ed.) *Differentiation between Social Groups: Studies in the Social Psychology of Intergroup Relations*. London: Academic Press.

Brown, R.J. (2000a) Social identity theory: past achievements, current problems and future challenges, *European Journal of Social Psychology*, 30: 745–78.

Brown, R. J. (2000b) *Group Processes: Dynamics Within and Between Groups*, 2nd edn. Oxford: Blackwell.

Brown, R.J. (2001) Intergroup relations, in M. Hewstone and W. Stroebe (eds) *Introduction to Social Psychology*, 3rd cdn. Oxford: Blackwell.

Brown, S.R. (1980) *Political Subjectivity: Applications of Q Methodology in Political Science*. New Haven: Yale University Press.

Bruner, J. (1957) On perceptual readiness, *Psychological Review*, 64: 123–52.

Burgoon, J.K., Buller, D.B. and Woodall, W.G. (1989) *Nonverbal Communication: The Unspoken Dialogue*. New York: Harper and Row.

Burman, E. (1994) *Deconstructing Development Psychology*. London: Routledge.

Burman, E. (1998) Deconstructing feminist psychology, in E. Burman (ed.) *Deconstructing Feminist Psychology*. London: Sage.

Burman, E. and Parker, I. (1993) *Discourse Analytic Research: Repertoires and Readings of Texts in Action*. London: Routledge.

Burnstein, E. and Vinokur, A. (1977) Persuasive argumentation and social comparison as determinants of attitude polarization, *Journal of Experimental Social Psychology*, 13: 315–32.

Burr, V. (1995) *An Introduction to Social Constructionism*. London: Routledge.

Buss, A.R. (1979) *A Dialectical Psychology*. New York: Irvington.

Buss, D.M. (1989) Sex differences in human mate preferences: evolutionary hypotheses tested in 37 cultures, *Behavioral and Brain Sciences*, 12: 1–49.

Buss, D.M. (1990) Evolutionary social psychology: prospects and pitfalls, *Motivation and Emotion* 14: 265–86.

Buss, D.M. (1994) *The Evolution of Desire: Strategies in Human Mating*. New York: Basic Books.

Cairns, K. (1993) Sexual entitlement and sexual accommodation: male and female responses to sexual coercion, *Canadian Journal of Human Sexuality*, 2: 203–14.

Cartwright, D. (1979) Contemporary social psychology in historical perspective, *Social Psychology Quarterly*, 42: 82–93.

Cattell, R.B. (1966) *The Scientific Analysis of Personality*. Chicago: Aldine.

Chaiken, S. (1987) The heuristic model of persuasion, in M.P. Zanna, J.M. Olson and C.P. Herman (eds) *Social Influence: The Ontario Symposium*, Vol. 5. Hillsdale, NJ: Erlbaum.

Chalmers, A.F. (1999) *What is this Thing Called Science?*, 3rd edn. Buckingham: Open University Press.

Chandra, S. (1973) The effects of group pressure in perception: a cross-cultural conformity study, *International Journal of Psychology*, 8: 37–9.

Chinese Culture Connection (1987) Chinese values and the search for culture-free dimensions of culture, *Journal of Cross-Cultural Psychology*, 18: 143–64.

Chomsky, N. (1957) *Syntactic Structures*. The Hague: Mouton.

Cialdini, R.B., Borden, R.J., Thorne, A., Walker, M.R., Freeman, S. and Sloan, L.R. (1976) Basking in reflected glory: three (football) field studies, *Journal of Personality and Social Psychology*, 34: 366–75.

Clark, R.D. and Hatfield, E. (1989) Gender, differences in receptivity to sexual offers, *Journal of Psychology and Human Sexuality*, 2: 39–55.

Clifford, M.M. (1975) Physical attractiveness and academic performance, *Child Study Journal*, 5: 201–9.

Coch, L. and French, J.R.P. (1948) Overcoming resistance to change, *Human Relations*, 1: 512–32.

Cooley, C.H. ([1902] 1922) *Human Nature and the Social Order*, rev. edn. New York: Scribner's Press.

Copper, C., Mullen, B., Adrales, K., Asuncion, A., Gibbons, P., Goethals, G.R., Riordan, V., Schroeder, D., Sibicky, M., Trice, D., Worth, L. and Lippsitt, N. (1993) Bias in the media: the subtle effects of the newscaster's smile, in G. Comstock and F. Fischoff (eds) *Media Behaviour*. Newbury Park, CA: Sage.

Cosmides, L. (1989) The logic of social exchange: has natural selection shaped how humans reason? Studies with the Wason selection task, *Cognition*, 31: 187–276.

Cousins, S.D. (1989) Culture and self-perception in Japan and the United States, *Journal of Personality and Social Psychology*, 56: 124–31.

Cozby, P.C. (1973) Self-disclosure: A literature review. *Psychological Bulletin*, 79: 73–91.

Cranston, M. (1953) *Freedom: A New Analysis*. London: Longman.

Crocker, J. and Luhtanen, R. (1990) Collective self esteem and in-group bias, *Journal of Personality and Social Psychology*, 58: 60–7.

Croyle, R. and Cooper, J. (1983) Dissonance arousal: physiological evidence, *Journal of Personality and Social Psychology*, 45: 782–91.

Crusco, A.H. and Wetzel, C.G. (1984) The Midas touch: the effects of interpersonal touch on restaurant tipping, *Personality and Social Psychology Bulletin*, 10: 512–17.

Crutchfield, R.A. (1955) Conformity and character, *American Psychologist*, 10: 191–8.

Cunningham, M.R. (1986) Measuring the physical in physical attractiveness: quasi-experiments on the sociobiology of female facial beauty, *Journal of Personality and Social Psychology*, 13: 35–67.

Curt, B. (1994) *Textuality and Tectonics: Troubling Social and Psychological Science*. Buckingham: Open University Press.

Daly, M. (1978) *Gyn/Ecology: The Metaethics of Radical Feminism*. London: The Women's Press.

Davidson, J. (1984) Subsequent versions of invitations, offers, requests and proposals dealing with potential or actual rejection, in J.M. Atkinson and J. Heritage (eds) *Structures of Social Action: Studies in Conversational Analysis*. Cambridge: Cambridge University Press.

Davidson, L.R. and Duberman, L. (1982) Friendship: Communication and interaction patterns in same-sex dyads, *Sex Roles*, 8: 809–22.

Davis, J.H. (1973) Group decision and social interaction: a study of social decision schemes, *Psychological Review*, 80: 97–125.

Dawkins, R. (1976) *The Selfish Gene*. Oxford: Oxford University Press.

Deutsch, M. (1973) *The Resolution of Conflict*. New Haven, CT: Yale University Press.

Deaux, K. and Wrightsman, L.S. (1988) *Social Psychology*, 2nd edn. Belmont, CA: Brooks/Cole.

Deutsch, M. and Gerrard, H.B. (1955) A study of normative and informational social influences upon individual judgement, *Journal of Abnormal and Social Psychology*, 51: 629–36.

De Vries, N.K., De Dreu, C.K.W., Gordijn, E. and Schuurman, M. (1996) Majority and minority influence: a dual role interpretation, in W. Stroebe and M. Hewstone (eds) *European Review of Social Psychology*, Vol. 7. Chichester: Wiley.

Diab, L.N. (1970) A study of intragroup and intergroup relations among experimentally produced small groups, *Genetic Psychology Monographs*, 82: 49–82.

Dion, K.K. and Bersheid, E. (1974) Physical attractiveness and peer perception among children, *Sociometry*, 37: 1–12.

Dion, K.K., Bersheid, E. and Walster, E. (1972) What is beautiful is good, *Journal of Personality and Social Psychology*, 24: 285–90.

Doise, W., Spini, D. and Clémence, A. (1999) Human rights studied as social representations in a cross-cultural context, *European Journal of Social Psychology*, 29(1): 1–30.

Doms, M. (1983) The minority influence effect: an alternative approach, in W. Doise and S. Moscovici (eds) *Current Issues in European Social Psychology*, Vol. 1. Cambridge: Cambridge University Press.

Douglas, M. (1966) *Purity and Danger*. London: Routledge and Kegan Paul.

Downs, A.C. and Lyons, P.M. (1991) Natural observations of the links between attractiveness and initial legal judgements, *Personality and Social Psychology Bulletin*, 17: 541–7.

Drew, P. (1995) Conversational analysis, in J.A. Smith, R. Harré and L. Van Langenhove (eds) *Rethinking Methods in Psychology*. London: Sage.

Duck, S. (1988) *Relating to Others*. Milton Keynes: Open University Press.

Dumont, L. (1985) A modified view of our origins: the Christian beginnings of modern individualism, in M. Carrithers, S. Collins and S. Lukes (eds) *The Category of the Person: Anthropology, Philosophy, History*. Cambridge: Cambridge University Press.

Dunant, S. (ed.) (1994) *The War of the Words: the Political Correctness Debate*. London: Virago.

Dutton, D.G. and Aron, A.P. (1974) Some evidence for heightened sexual attraction under conditions of high anxiety, *Journal of Personality and Social Psychology*, 30: 510–17.

Eagly, A.H. and Chaiken, S. (1984) Cognitive theories of persuasion, in L. Berkovitz (ed.) *Advances in Experimental Social Psychology*, Vol. 17. New York: Academic Press.

Eagly A.H. and Chaiken, S. (1993) *The Psychology of Attitudes*. Fort Worth, TX: Harcourt Brace Jovanovich.

Eagly, A.H. and Chaiken, S. (1998) Attitude structure and function, in D.T. Gilbert, S.T. Fiske and G. Lindzey (eds) *The Handbook of Social Psychology*. New York: McGraw-Hill.

Eagly, A.H. and Wood, W. (1991) Explaining sex differences in social behaviour: a meta-analytic perspective, *Personality and Social Psychology Bulletin*, 17: 306–15.

Eagly, A.H., Ashmore, R.D., Makhijani, M.G. and Longo, L.C. (1991) What is beautiful is good, but . . . : a meta-analytic review of research on the physical attractiveness stereotype, *Psychological Bulletin*, 110: 109–28.

Earley, P.C. (1989) Social loafing and collectivism: a comparison of the United States and the People's Republic of China, *Administrative Science Quarterly*, 34: 563–81.

Edwards, D. and Potter, J. (1992) *Discursive Psychology*. London: Sage.

Edwards, D., Ashmore, M. and Potter, J. (1993) Death and furniture: the rhetoric, theology and politics and theory of bottom line arguments against relativism. Mimeograph, Discourse and Rhetoric Group, Loughborough University.

Edwards, J. and Chisholm, J. (1987) Language, multiculturalism and identity: a Canadian study, *Journal of Multilingual and Multicultural Development*, 8: 391–407.

Ekman, F. (1973) Cross-cultural studies of facial expression, in P. Ekman (ed.) *Darwin and Facial Expression*. New York: Academic Press.

Ekman, P. and Friesen, W.V. (1974) Detecting deception from the body or the face, *Journal of Personality and Social Psychology*, 29: 188–98.

Ekman, F., Friesen, W.V., O'Sullivan, M., Chan, A., Diacoyanni-Tarlatzis, J., Heider, K., Krause, R., Lacompte, W.A., Pitcairn, P.E., Riccibitti, P.E., Scherer, K., Tomita, M. and Tzavaras, A. (1987) Universals and cultural differences in the judgement of facial expressions of emotion, *Journal of Personality and Social Psychology*, 53: 712–17.

Ellis, W.D. (1938) *A Source Book of Gestalt Psychology*. New York: Harcourt Brace.

Emler, N. and Hopkins, N. (1990) Reputation, social identity and the self, in D. Abrams and M. Hogg (eds) *Social Identity Theory: Constructive and Critical Advances*. London: Harvester Wheatsheaf.

Emler, N. and Reicher, S. (1995) *Adolescence and Delinquency: The Collective Management of Reputation*. Oxford: Blackwell.

Erikson, E. (1963) *Childhood and Society*. New York: Norton.

Exline, R.V., Ellyson, S.L. and Long, B. (1975) Visual behaviour as an aspect of power role relationships, in P. Pliner, L. Krames and T. Alloway (eds) *Nonverbal Communication of Aggression*, Vol. 2. New York: Plenum.

Eysenck, H. (1967) *The Biological Basis of Personality*. Springfield, IL: C.C. Thomas.

Eysenck, H.J. and Eysenck, M.W. (1985) *Personality and Individual Differences*. New York: Plenum.

Fann, K.S. (1970) *Peirce's Theory of Abduction*. The Hague: Martinus Nijhoff.

Farr, R.M. (1996) *The Roots of Modern Social Psychology*. Oxford: Blackwell.

Farr, R.M. and Moscovici, S. (eds) (1981) *Social Representations*. Cambridge: Cambridge University Press.

Fazio, R.H. (1990) Multiple processes by which attitudes guide behaviour: The MODE model as an integrative framework, in M.P. Zanna (ed.) *Advances in Experimental Social Psychology*, Vol. 23. New York: Academic Press.

Fazio, R.H. and Zanna, M.P. (1981) Direct experience and attitude-behaviour consistency, in L. Berkowitz (ed.) *Advances in Experimental Social Psychology*, Vol. 14. San Diego, CA: Academic Press.

Feather, N.T. (1970) Educational choice and student attitudes in relation to terminal and instrumental values, *Australian Journal of Psychology*, 22: 127–44.

Feather, N.T. (1971) Value differences in relation to ethnocentrism, intolerance of ambiguity and dogmatism, *Personality*, 2: 349–66.

Feather, N.T. (1982) *Expectations and Actions: Expectancy–Value Models in Psychology*. Hillsdale, NJ: Erlbaum.

Feather, N.T. (1991) Human values, global self-esteem and belief in a just world. *Journal of Personality*, 59: 83–106.

Feather, N.T. (1995) Values, valences and choice: the influence of values on the perceived attractiveness and choice of alternatives, *Journal of Personality and Social Psychology*, 68: 1135–51.

Feingold, A. (1992) Good looking people are not what we think, *Psychological Bulletin*, 111: 304–41.

Fenton-O'Creevy, M. (2001) Leadership in the New Organisation, Block 2.

Festinger, L. (1954) A theory of social comparison processes, *Human Relations*, 7: 117–40.

Festinger, L. (1957) *A Theory of Cognitive Dissonance*. Stanford, CA: Stanford University Press.

Festinger, L. and Carlsmith, J.M. (1959) Cognitive consequences of forced compliance, *Journal of Abnormal and Social Psychology*, 58: 203–10.

Festinger, L., Schachter, S. and Back, K. (1950) *Social Pressures in Informal Groups: A Study of Human Factors in Housing*. New York: Harper and Row.

Fiedler, K. and Bless, H. (2001) Social cognition, in M. Hewstone and W. Stroeber (eds) *Introduction to Social Psychology*, 3rd edn. Oxford: Blackwell.

Fincham, F.D. and Bradbury, T.N. (1988) The impact of attributions in marriage: an experimental analysis, *Journal of Social and Clinical Psychology*, 9: 31–42.

Fincham, F.D. and Bradbury, T.N. (1991) Cognition in marriage: a program of research on attributions, in W.H. Jones and D. Perlman (eds) *Advances in Personal Relationships*, Vol. 2. London: Jessica Kingsley.

Fincham, F. and Hewstone, M. (2001) Attribution theory and research: from basic to applied, in M. Hewstone and W. Stroebe (eds) *Introduction to Social Psychology*, 3rd edn. Oxford: Blackwell.

Fishbein, M. (1967) A consideration of beliefs and their role in attitude measurement, in M. Fishbein (ed.) *Readings in Attitude Theory and Measurement*. New York: Wiley.

Fishbein, M. and Ajzen, I. (1975) *Belief, Attitude, Intention and Behaviour: An Introduction to Theory and Research*. Reading, MA: Addison-Wesley.

Fiske, S.T. (1980) Attention and weight in person perception: the impact of negative and extreme behaviour. (See Fiske and Taylor, 1991.)

Fiske, S.T. and Taylor, S.E. (1991) *Social Cognition*, 2nd edn. New York: McGraw-Hill.

Flick, U. (ed.) (1998) *The Psychology of the Social*. Cambridge: Cambridge University Press.

Flick, U. (2002) *Introduction to Qualitative Research*, 2nd edn. London: Sage.

Ford, C.S. and Beach, F.A. (1951) *Patterns of Sexual Behaviour*. New York: Harper and Row.

Fornäs, J. (1995) *Cultural Theory and Late Modernity*. London: Sage.

Foucault, M. ([1976] 1980) *The History of Sexuality*, Vol. 1. Harmondsworth: Penguin.

Fox, D. and Prilleltensky, I. (1997) *Critical Psychology*. London: Sage.

Frager, R. (1970) Conformity and anti-conformity in Japan, *Journal of Personality and Social Psychology*, 15: 203–10.

Freud, S. (1905) *Three Contributions to the Theory of Sex*. New York: Dutton.

Frick, R. W. (1985) Communicating emotions: the role of prosodic features, *Psychological Bulletin*, 97: 412–29.

Gabrenya, W.K., Wang, Y.E. and Latané, B. (1985) Social loafing on an optimising task: cross-cultural differences among Chinese and Americans, *Journal of Cross-Cultural Psychology*, 16: 223–42.

Gaertner, S.L. and McLaughlin, J.P. (1983) Racial stereotypes: associations and ascriptions of positive and negative characteristics, *Social Psychology Quarterly*, 46: 23–30.

Galzio, M. and Hendrick, C. (1972) Effect of music accompaniment on attitudes, *Journal of Applied Social Psychology*, 2: 350–9.

Garfinkel, H. (1967) *Studies in Ethnomethodology*. Englewood Cliffs, NJ: Prentice Hall.

Gates, M.F. and Allee, W.C. (1933) Conditioned behaviour of isolated and grouped cockroaches on a simple maze, *Journal of Comparative Psychology*, 15: 331–58.

Gerard, H.B. and Mathewson, G.C. (1966) The effects of severity of initiation on liking for a group: a replication, *Journal of Experimental Social Psychology*, 2: 278–87.

Gergen, K. (1973) Social psychology as history, *Journal of Personality and Social Psychology*, 26: 309–20.

Gergen, K.J. and Gergen, M.M. (1981) *Social Psychology*. New York: Harcourt Brace Jovanovich.

Gergen, K.J. and Gergen, M.M. (eds) (1984) *Historical Social Pyschology*. Hillsdale, NJ: Erlbaum.

Gigone, D. and Hastie, R. (1993) The common knowledge effect: information sharing and group judgement, *Journal of Personality and Social Psychology*, 65: 959–74.

Gilbert, D.T., Pelham, B.W. and Krull, D.S. (1988) On cognitive busyness: when person perceivers meet persons perceived, *Journal of Personality and Social Psychology*, 54: 733–40.

Giles, H. and Coupland, N. (1991) *Language: Contexts and Consequences*. Buckingham: Open University Press.

Glaser, B.G. and Strauss, A.L. (1967) *The Discovery of Grounded Theory: Strategies for Qualitative Research*. Chicago: Aldine.

Goblot, E. (1901) *Le Vocabulaire Philosophique*. Paris: Armand Colin.

Goffman, E. (1955) On face-work: an analysis of ritual elements in social interaction, *Psychiatry*, 18: 213–31.

Goffman, E. (1959) *The Presentation of Self in Everyday Life*. New York: Doubleday.

Goffman, E. (1963) *Behaviour in Public Places*. New York: Free Press.

Goffman, E. (1967) *Interaction Ritual: Essays on Face-to-face Behaviour*. Garden City, NY: Anchor.

Gonzalez-Crussi, M. (1988) *On the Nature of Things Erotic*. London: Picador.

Gough, B. and McFadden, M. (2001) *Critical Social Psychology: An Introduction*. Basingstoke: Palgrave.

Graumann, C.F. (1988) Introduction to a history of social psychology, in R. Gilmour and S. Duck (eds) *The Development of Social Psychology*. London: Academic Press.

Graumann, C.F. (2001) Introducing social psychology historically, in M. Hewstone, and W. Stroebe (eds) *Introduction to Social Psychology*, 3rd edn. Oxford: Blackwell.

Greenwald, A.G. (1968) Cognitive learning, cognitive response to persuasion, and attitude change, in A. Greenwald, T. Brock and T. Ostrom (eds) *Psychological Foundations of Attitudes*. New York: Academic Press.

Gribbin, M. and Gribbin, J. (1998) *Being Human: Putting People in an Evolutionary Perspective*, 2nd impression. London: Phoenix.

Grimshaw, A.D. (1981) Talk and social control, in M. Rosenburg and R.H. Turner (eds) *Social Psychology: Sociological Perspectives*. New York: Basic Books.

Grujic, L. and Libby, W.L. Jnr (1978) Nonverbal aspects of verbal behaviour in French Canadian French–English bilinguals. Paper presented at the meeting of the American Psychological Association, Toronto, September.

Guzzo, R.A. and Dickenson, M.W. (1996) Teams in organizations: recent research on performance and effectiveness, *Annual Review of Psychology*, 47: 307–38.

Haire, M. and Grune, W.E. (1950) Perceptual defenses: Processes protecting an organised perception of another personality, *Human Relations*, 3: 403–12.

Hall, E.T. (1966) *The Silent Language*. New York: Doubleday.

Hamilton, D.L. and Zanna, M.P. (1972) Differential weighting of favourable and unfavourable attributes in impressions of personality, *Journal of Experimental Research into Personality*, 6: 204–12.

Hamilton, D.L. and Zanna, M.P. (1974) Context effects in impression formation: Changes in connative meaning, *Journal of Personality and Social Psychology*, 29: 649–54.

Han, S. and Shavitt, S. (1993) Persuasion and culture: advertising appeals in individualistic and collectivistic societies, unpublished manuscript, Champagne, IL: University of Illinois at Urbana.

Haney, C., Banks, W.C. and Zimbardo, P.G. (1973) Interpersonal dynamics in a simulated prison, *International Journal of Criminology and Penology*, 1: 69–97.

Haraway, D.J. (1984) Primatology is politics by other means, in R. Bleier (ed.) *Feminist Approaches to Science*. London: Pergamon.

Harding, S. (ed.) (1987) *Feminism and Methodology*. Milton Keynes: Open University Press.

Harmon-Jones, E., Brehm, J.W., Greenberg, J., Simon, L. and Nelson, D.E. (1996) Evidence that the production of aversive consequences is not necessary to create cognitive dissonance, *Journal of Personality and Social Psychology*, 70: 5–16.

Harré, R. (1977) The ethogenic approach: theory and practice, in L. Berkowitz (ed.) *Advances in Experimental Social Psychology*, Vol. 10. New York: Academic Press.

Harré, R. (1979) *Social Being: A Theory for Social Psychology*. Oxford: Blackwell.

Harré, R. and Secord, P.F. (1972) *The Explanation of Social Behaviour*. Oxford: Blackwell.

Hastie, R., Penrod, S.D. and Pennington, N. (1983) *Inside the Jury.* Cambridge, MA: Harvard University Press.

Hauck, P. (1981) *Jealousy: Why it Happens and How to Overcome It.* Philadelphia: Westminster.

Hayes, N. (1993) *Principles of Social Psychology.* Hove: Psychology Press.

Heidegger, M. ([1928] 1962) *Being and Time.* Oxford: Blackwell.

Heidegger, M. (1971) *Poetry, Language, Thought.* New York: Harper and Row.

Heider, F. (1946) Attitudes and cognitive organisation, *Journal of Psychology,* 21: 107–12.

Heider, F. (1953) *The Psychology of Interpersonal Relations.* New York: Wiley.

Heider, K. (1976) A conversation with Fritz Heider, in J.H. Harvey, W.I. Ikes and R.F. Kidd (eds) *New Directions in Attribution Research I.* Hillsdale, NJ: Earlbaum.

Hempel, C. (1968) *Philosophy of Natural Science.* Englewood Cliffs, NJ: Prentice Hall.

Henley, N.M. (1977) *Body Politics: Power, Sex and Nonverbal Communication.* Englewood Cliffs, NJ: Prentice Hall.

Henriques, J., Hollway, W., Urwin, C., Venn, C. and Walkerdine, V. (1984) *Changing the Subject: Psychology, Social Regulation and Subjectivity.* London: Methuen.

Heritage, J. (1984) *Garfinkel and Ethnomethodology.* Cambridge: Polity.

Herzlich, C. (1973) *Health and Illness.* London: Academic Press.

Herzlich, C. and Pierret, J. (1987) *Illness and Self in Society.* Baltimore: Johns Hopkins University Press.

Hewstone, M. (1983) Attribution theory and common-sense explanations: an introductory overview, in M. Hewstone (ed.) *Attribution Theory: Social and Functional Extensions.* Oxford: Blackwell.

Hewstone, M. and Stroebe, W. (eds) (2001) *Introduction to Social Psychology,* 3rd edn. Oxford: Blackwell.

Hilgard, E.R. (1953) *Introduction to Psychology.* London: Methuen.

Hilton, D.J. (1990) Conversational processes and causal attribution, *Psychological Bulletin,* 107: 65–81.

Hodge, R. and Kress, G. (1988) *Social Semiotics.* Cambridge: Polity.

Hofstede, G. (1980) *Culture's Consequences: International Differences In Work-related Values.* Beverly Hills, CA: Sage.

Hofstede, G. (1983) Dimensions of national cultures in fifty countries and three regions, in J. Deregowski, S. Dzuirawiec and R. Annis (eds) *Explications in Cross-Cultural Psychology.* Lisse: Swets and Zeitlinger.

Hogg, M.A. (1992) *The Social Psychology of Group Cohesiveness: From Attraction to Social Identity.* London: Harvester Wheatsheaf.

Hogg, M.A. (1993) Group cohesiveness: a critical review and some new directions, *European Review of Social Psychology,* 4: 85–111.

Hogg, M.A. and Turner, J.C. (1987) Social identity and conformity: a theory of referent informational inference, in W. Doise and S. Moscovici (eds) *Current Issues in European Social Psychology*, Vol. 2. Cambridge: Cambridge University Press.

Hogg, M.A., Turner, J.C. and Davidson, B. (1990) Polarised norms and social frames of reference: a test of the self-categorisation theory of group polarisation, *Basic and Applied Social Psychology*, 11: 77–100.

Hogg, M.A. and Vaughan, G.M. (1998) *Social Psychology*, 2nd edn. Hemel Hempstead: Prentice Hall.

Hollander, E.P. (1971) *Principles and Methods of Social Psychology*, 2nd edn. Oxford: Oxford University Press.

Hollway, W. (1989) *Subjectivity and Method in Psychology: Gender, Meaning and Science*. London: Sage.

Hovland, C.I. and Weiss, W. (1951) The influence of source credibility on communication effectiveness, *Public Opinion Quarterly*, 15: 635–50.

Hovland, C.I., Janis, I.L. and Kelley, H.H. (1953) *Communication and Persuasion*. New Haven, CT: Yale University Press.

Hutchby, I. and Wooffitt, R. (1998) *Conversation Analysis: Principles, Practice and Applications*. Cambridge: Polity.

Ibáñez, T. and Iñiguez, L. (1997) *Critical Social Psychology*. London: Sage.

Ikes, W. (1981) Sex-role influences in dyadic interaction: a theoretical model, in C. Mayo and N. Henley (eds) *Gender and Non-verbal Behaviour*. New York: Springer-Verlag.

Inglehart, R. (1990) *Culture Shift in Advanced Industrial Society*. Princeton, NY: Princeton University Press.

Insko, C.A. (1981) Balance theory and phenomenology, in R. Petty, T. Ostrom and T. Brock (eds) *Cognitive Responses and Persuasion*. Hillsdale, NJ: Erlbaum.

Insko, C.A. and Schopler, J. (1967) Triadic consistency: a statement of affective-cognitive-conative consistency, *Psychological Review*, 74: 361–76.

Insko, C.A. and Schopler, J. (1998) Differential distrust of groups and individuals, in C. Sedikedes, J. Schopler and C. Insko (eds) *Intergroup Cognition and Intergroup Behaviour*. Mahwah, NJ: Erlbaum.

Isenberg, D.J. (1986) Group polarisation: a critical review, *Journal of Personality and Social Psychology*, 50: 1141–51.

Izard, C. (1971) *The Face of Emotion*. New York: Appleton-Century-Crofts.

Jaensch, E.R. (1939) Der Hünerhof als Forschungs- und Aufklärungsmittel in menschlichen Rassenfragen, *Zeitschrift für Tierpsycholgie* 2: 223–58.

James, W. (1890) *The Principles of Psychology*, Vol. 1. New York: Holt.

James, W. (1907) *Psychology*. London: Macmillan.

Janis, I.L. (1954) Personality correlates of susceptibility to persuasion, *Journal of Personality*, 22: 504–18.

Janis, I.L. (1972) *Groupthink: Psychological Studies of Policy Decisions and Fiascos*. Boston: Houghton Mifflin.

Janis, I. (1982) *Groupthink*, 2nd edn. Boston: Houghton Mifflin.

Janoff-Bulman, R. and Frieze, I.H. (1987) The role of gender in reactions to gender victimization, in R.C. Barnett, L. Beiner and G.K. Baruch (eds) *Gender and Stress*. New York: Free Press.

Jellison, J.M. and Davis, D. (1973) Relationships between perceived ability and attitude extremity, *Journal of Personality and Social Psychology*, 27: 430–6.

Jensen-Campbell, L.A., Graziano, W.G. and West, S.G. (1995) Dominance, prosocial orientation, and female preferences. Do nice guys really finish last?, *Journal of Personality and Social Psychology*, 68: 427–40.

Joas, H. (1985) *G.H. Mead: A Contemporary Re-examination of his Thought*. Cambridge: Polity.

Johnson, R.W., Kelly, R.J. and LeBlanc, B.A. (1995) Motivational basis of dissonance: aversive consequences or inconsistency, *Personality and Social Psychology Bulletin*, 21: 850–5.

Jones, E.E. and Davis, K.E. (1965) A theory of correspondent inferences: from acts to dispositions, in L. Berkovitz (ed.) *Advances in Experimental Social Psychology*, Vol. 2. New York: Academic Press.

Jones, E.E., Davis, K.E. and Gergen, K. (1961) Role playing variations and their informational value for person perception, *Journal of Abnormal and Social Psychology*, 63: 302–10.

Jones, E.E. and Goethals, G.R. (1972) Order effects in impression formation: attribution, context and the nature of the entity, in E.E. Jones, D.E. Kanouse, H.H. Kelley, R.E. Nisbett, S. Valins and B. Weiner (eds) *Attribution: Perceiving the Causes of Behaviour*. Morristown, NJ: General Learning Press.

Jones, E.E. and Sigall, H. (1971) The bogus pipeline: a new paradigm for measuring affect and attitude, *Psychological Bulletin*, 76: 349–64.

Jordan, N. (1953) Behavioural forces that are a function of attitudes and cognitive organisation, *Human Relations*, 6: 273–87.

Jourard, S.M. (1966) An exploratory study of body accessibility, *British Journal of Social and Clinical Psychology*, 5: 221–31.

Jourard, S.M. (1971) *Self-disclosure*. New York: Wiley.

Jovchelovitch, S. (2002) Social representations and narrative: stories of public life in Brazil, in László, J. and Stainton Rogers, W. (eds) *Narrative Approaches in Social Psychology*. Budapest: New Mandate.

Judd, C.M. and Kulik, J.A. (1980) Schematic effects of social attitudes on information processing and recall, *Journal of Personality and Social Psychology*, 38: 569–78.

Katz, D. (1960) The functional approach to the study of attitudes, *Public Opinion Quarterly*, 24: 163–204.

Kelley, H.H. (1950) The warm–cold variable in first impressions of persons, *Journal of Personality*, 18: 431–9.

Kelley, H.H. (1952) Two functions of reference groups, in G.E. Swanson, T.M. Newcomb and E.L. Hartley (eds) *Readings in Social Psychology*. New York: Holt, Rinehart and Winston.

Kelley, H.H. (1967) Attribution theory in social psychology, in D. Levine (ed.) *Nebraska Symposium on Motivation*, Vol. 15.

Kelly, C. and Breinlinger, S. (1995) Attitudes, intentions and behavior: a study of women's participation in collective action, *Journal of Applied Social Psychology*, 25: 1430–45.

Kelly, G.A. (1966) A brief introduction to personal construct theory, in D. Bannister (ed.) *Perspectives in Personal Construct Theory*. London: Academic Press.

Kent, G.G., Davis, J.D. and Shapiro, D.A. (1978) Resources required in the construction and reconstruction of conversation, *Journal of Personality and Social Psychology*, 36: 137–41.

Kidder, L.H. and Fine, M. (1987) Qualitative and quantitative methods: when stories converge, in M.M. Mark and L. Shotland (eds) *New Directions in Program Evaluation*. San Francisco, CA: Jossey-Bass.

Kiesler, C.A. and Kiesler, S.B. (1969) *Conformity*. Reading, MA: Addison-Wesley.

Kinder, D.B. and Sears, D.O. (1985) Public opinion and political action, in G. Lindzey and E. Aronson (eds) *Handbook of Social Psychology*, Vol. 2. New York: Random House.

Kitzinger, C. (1986) The construction of lesbian identities, unpublished doctoral dissertation, University of Reading.

Kitzinger, C. (1987) *The Social Construction of Lesbianiam*. London: Sage.

Kitzinger, C. and Frith, H. (1999) Just say no? The use of conversational analysis in developing a feminist perspective on sexual refusal, *Discourse and Society*, 10(3): 293–316.

Klein, P. (1988) *Psychology Exposed: Or the Emperor's New Clothes*. London: Routledge.

Kleinke, C.L. (1986) Gaze and eye contact: a research review. *Psychological Bulletin*, 100: 78–100.

Knapp, M.L. (1978) *Nonverbal Communication in Human Interaction*, 2nd edn. New York: Holt, Rinehart and Winston.

Knapp, M.L., Hart, R.P. and Dennis, H.S. (1974) An exploration of deception as a communication construct, *Human Communication Research*, 1: 15–29.

Kondo, D. (1990) *Crafting Selves: Power, Gender and Discourses of Identity in a Japanese Workplace*. Chicago: University of Chicago Press.

Kraut, R.E. and Poe, D. (1980) Behavioural roots of person perceptions: The deception judgements of customs officers and laymen, *Journal of Personality and Social Psychology*, 39: 748–98.

Kristeva, J. ([1974] 1984) *Revolution in Poetic Language*, trans. M. Waller. New York: Columbia University Press.

Kuhn, T.S. (1970) *The Structure of Scientific Revolutions*, Vol. 2, no. 2, 2nd edn. Chicago: University of Chicago Press.

Lacan, J. (1966) *Écrits*. Paris: Seuil.

Lacan, J. (1977) *Ecrits: A Selection*, trans. A. Sheridan. London: Tavistock.

LaFrance, M. and Mayo, C. (1976) Racial differences in gaze behaviour during conversations: two systematic observational studies, *Journal of Personality and Social Psychology*, 33: 547–52.

Lalljee, M. (2000) The interpreting self: a social constructionist perspective, in R. Stevens (ed.) *Understanding the Self*. London: Sage.

Lalljee, M. and Cook, M. (1973) Uncertainty in first encounters, *Journal of Personality and Social Psychology*, 26: 13–22.

Lambert, W.E., Hodgson, R.C., Gardner, R.C. and Fillenbaum, S. (1960) Evaluation reactions to spoken language, *Journal of Abnormal and Social Psychology*, 60: 44–51.

Lamiell, J.T. (1998). 'Nomothetic' and 'idiographic': contrasting Windelbrand's understanding with contemporary usage, *Theory and Psychology*, 8(1): 23–38.

Lamm, H. and Myers, D.G. (1978) Group induced polarization of attitudes and behaviour, in L. Berkowitz (ed.) *Advances in Experimental Social Psychology*, Vol. 11. New York: Academic Press

Langer, E.J. (1978) Rethinking the role of thought in social interaction, in J.H. Harvey, W.I. Ikes and R.F. Kidd (eds) *New Directions in Attribution Research II*. Hillsdale, NJ: Erlbaum.

Langer, E.J., Blank, A. and Chanowitz, B. (1978) The mindlessness of ostensibly thoughtful interaction: the role of 'placebic' information in interpersonal interaction, *Journal of Personality and Social Psychology*, 36: 635–42.

LaPiere, R.T. (1934) Attitudes and actions, *Social Forces*, 13: 230–7.

László, J., Ehman, B., Péley, B. and Pólya, T. (2002) Narrative psychology and narrative content analysis, in J. László and W. Stainton Rogers (eds) *Narrative Approaches in Social Psychology*. Budapest: New Mandate.

Latané, B., Williams, K.D. and Harkins, S.G. (1979) Many hands make light work: The causes and consequences of social loafing. *Journal of Personality and Social Psychology*, 37: 822–32.

Latané, B. and Wolf, S. (1981) The social impact of majorities and minorities, *Psychological Review*, 88: 438–53.

Laughlin, P.R. and Ellis, A.L. (1986) Demonstrability and social combination processes on mathematical intellectual tasks, *Journal of Experimental Social Psychology*, 22: 177–89.

Lazarus, R.S. (1991) *Emotion and Adaptation*. Oxford: Oxford University Press.

Leventhal, H. and Hirshman, R.S. (1982) Social psychology and prevention, in G.S. Sanders and J. Suls (eds) *Social Psychology of Health and Illness*. Hillsdale, NJ: Erlbaum.

Lewin, K. (1936) *Principles of Topological Psychology*. New York: McGraw-Hill.

Lewin, K. (1947a) Frontiers in group dynamics, *Human Relations*, 1: 5–42.

Lewin, K. (1947b) Group decisions and social change, in T.M. Newcomb and E.L. Hartley (eds) *Readings in Social Psychology*. New York: Henry Holt.

Lewin, K. (1951) *Field Theory in Social Science*. New York: Harper and Row.

Lewin, K., Lippitt, R. and White, R.K. (1939) Patterns of aggressive behaviour in experimentally created 'social climates', *Journal of Social Psychology*, 10: 271–99.

Linder, D.E., Cooper, J. and Jones, E.E. (1967) Decision freedom as a determinant of the role of incentive magnitude in attitude change, *Journal of Personality and Social Psychology*, 6: 245–54.

Lindesmith, A.R., Strauss, A.L. and Denzin, N.K. (1999) *Social Psychology*, 8th edn. London: Sage.

Lindner, G.A. (1871) *Ideen zur Psychologie der Gesellschaft als Grundlage der Sozialwissenschaft*. Vienna: Gerold.

Lorber, J. (1994) *Paradoxes of Gender*. New Haven, CT: Yale University Press.

McDougall, W. (1919) *An Introduction to Social Psychology*. London: Methuen.

McGarty, C. and Haslam, S.A. (eds) (1997a) *The Message of Social Psychology*. Oxford: Blackwell.

McGarty, C. and Haslam, S.A. (1997b) Introduction and a short history of social psychology, in C. McGarty and S.A. Haslam (eds) *The Message of Social Psychology*. Oxford: Blackwell.

McGuire, W.J. (1968) Personality and susceptibility to social influence, in E.F. Borgatta and W.W. Lambert (eds) *Handbook of Personality: Theory and Research*. Chicago, IL: Rand-McNally.

McGuire, W.J. (1986) The vicissitudes of attitudes and similar representational constructs in twentieth century psychology, *European Journal of Social Psychology*, 16: 89–130.

McPherson, W. (2001) *The Stephen Lawrence Inquiry*. London: HMSO.

Mahood, L. and Littlewood, B. (1997) Daughters in danger: the case of 'campus sex crimes', in A.M. Thomas and C. Kitzinger (eds) *Sexual Harassment: Contemporary Feminist Perspectives*. Buckingham: Open University Press.

Manstead, A.S.R. and Semin, G. (1980) Social facilitation effects: more enhancement of dominant responses?, *British Journal of Social and Clinical Psychology*, 19: 119–36.

Manstead, A.S.R. and Semin, G. (2001) Methods in social psychology: tools to test theories, in M. Hewstone and W. Stroebe (eds) *Introduction to Social Psychology*, 3rd edn. Oxford: Blackwell.

Marková, I. (1987) *Human Awareness*. London: Hutchinson.

Marsh, A. (1976) Who hates blacks?, *New Society*, 23 September: 649–52.

Marsh, P., Rosser, E. and Harré, R. (1974) *The Rules of Disorder*. London: Routledge and Kegan Paul.

Maslow, A.H. (1954) *Motivation and Personality*. New York: Harper and Row.

Maslow, A.H. (1964) *Religions, Values and Peak Experiences*. Columbus, OH: Ohio State University Press.

Matsui, T., Kakuyama, T. and Onglatco, M.L. (1987) Effects of goals and feedback on performance in groups, *Journal of Applied Psychology*, 72: 407–15.

Mead, G.H. ([1934a] 1977a) *Mind, Self and Society: From the Standpoint of a Social Behaviourist*, ed. C.W. Morris. Chicago: University of Chicago Press.

Mead, G.H. ([1934b] 1977b) *On Social Psychology*, ed. A. Strauss. Chicago: University of Chicago Press.

Mehrabian, A. (1972) Nonverbal communication, in J. Cole (ed.) *Nebraska Symposium on Motivation*, Vol. 19. Lincoln, NV: University of Nebraska Press.

Middlemist, R.D., Knowles, E.S. and Mutter, C.F. (1976) Personal space invasions in the lavatory: suggestive evidence for arousal, *Journal of Personality and Social Psychology*, 33: 541–6.

Milgram, S. (1963) Behavioural study of obedience, *Journal of Abnormal and Social Psychology*, 67: 371–8.

Milgram, S. (1965) Some conditions of obedience and disobedience to authority, *Human Relations*, 18: 57–76.

Milgram, S. (1974) *Obedience to Authority*. London: Tavistock.

Millar, M.G. and Millar, K.U. (1996) The effects of direct and indirect experience on affective and cognitive responses and the attitude–behaviour relation, *Journal of Experimental Social Psychology*, 32: 561–79.

Miller, G.A. (1953) What is information measurement?, *American Psychologist*, 8: 3–11.

Morawski, J.G. (1990) Towards the unimagined: feminism and epistemology in psychology, in R.T. Hare-Mustin and J. Marecek (eds) *Making a Difference: Psychology and the Construction of Gender*. New Haven, CT: Yale University Press.

Moreland, R.L. and Levine, J.M. (1982) Socialization in small groups: temporal changes in individual-group relations, in L. Berkowitz (ed.) *Advances in Experimental Social Psychology*, Vol. 15. New York: Academic Press

Moreland, R.L., Levine, J.M. and Cini, M. (1993) Group socialization: the role of commitment, in M.A. Hogg and D. Abrams (eds) *Group Motivation: Social Psychological Perspectives*. Hemel Hempstead: Harvester Wheatsheaf.

Moscovici, S. ([1961] 1976) *La Psychoanalyse: son image et son public*. Paris: Presses Universitaires de France.

Moscovici, S. (1980) Towards a theory of conversion hejaviour, in L. Berkowitz (ed.) *Advances in Experimental Social Psychology*, Vol. 13. New York: Academic Press.

Moscovici, S. (1985) Society and theory in social psychology, in J. Israel and H. Tajfel (eds) *The Context of Social Psychology: A Critical Assessment*. New York: Academic Press.

Moscovici, S. and Hewstone, M. (1983) Social representations and social explanations: from the 'naïve' to the 'amateur' scientist, in M. Hewstone (ed.) *Attribution Theory: Social and Functional Explanations*. Oxford: Blackwell.

Moscovici, S. and Mugny, G. (1983) Minority influence, in P.B. Paulus (ed.) *Basic Group Processes*. New York: Springer-Verlag.

Moscovici, S. and Personnaz, B. (1980) Studies in social influence: minority influence and conversion behaviour in a perceptual task, *Journal of Experimental Social Psychology*, 16: 270–82.

Moscovici, S., Lage, E. and Naffrechoux, M. (1969) Influence of a consistent minority on the responses of a majority in a colour perception task, *Sociometry*, 32: 365–80.

Mugny, G. (1982) *The Power of Minorities*. New York: Academic Press

Mulvey, L. (1975) Visual pleasure and narrative cinema, *Screen*, 16(3): 6–18.

Mulvey, L. (1992) Visual pleasure and narrative cinema, in *The Sexual Subject: A Screen Reader in Sexuality*. London: Routledge.

Murphy, G. (1929) *A Historical Introduction to Modern Psychology*. London: Kegan Paul, Trench, Trubner.

Murphy, G. and Murphy, L.B. (1931) *Experimental Social Psychology*. New York: Harper.

Murray, M. (1997) A narrative approach to health psychology, *Journal of Health Psychology*, 2 (1): 9–20.

Nash, J. (1985) *Social Psychology: Self and Society*. St Paul, MN: West.

Neisser, U. (1966) *Cognitive Psychology*. New York: Appleton-Century-Crofts.

Nemeth, C. (1986) Differential contributions to majority and minority influence, *Psychological Review*, 93: 1–10.

Nemeth, C. and Wachtler, J. (1983) Creative problem solving as a result of minority versus majority influence, *European Journal of Social Psychology*, 13: 45–55.

Newcomb, T.M. (1961) *The Acquaintance Process*. New York: Holt, Rinehart and Winston.

Nisbett, R.E. and Ross, L. (1980) *Human Inference: Strategies and Shortcomings of Social Judgement*. Englewood Cliffs, NJ: Prentice Hall.

Nuttin, J.M. (1985) Narcissism beyond Gestalt and awareness: the name letter effect, *European Journal of Social Psychology*, 15: 353–61.

Oppenheim, N. (1992) *Questionnaire Design, Interviewing and Attitude Measurement*. London: Pinter.

Ouellette, J.A. and Wood, W. (1998) Habit and intention in everyday life: the multiple processes by which behaviour predicts future behaviour, *Psychological Review*, 124: 54–74.

Parker, I. (1989). *The Crisis in Modern Social Psychology, and How to End It*. London: Routledge.

Parker, I. (1992) *Discourse Dynamics: Critical Analysis for Social and Individual Psychology*. London: Routledge.

Parker, I. (1997) Discursive psychology, in D. Fox and I. Prilleltensky (eds) *Critical Psychology: An Introduction*. London: Sage.

Perinbanayagam, R.S. (1985) *Signifying Acts*. New York: Aldine de Gruyter.

Peirce, C.S. (1940) Abduction and induction, in J. Buchler (ed.) *The Philosophy of Peirce: Selected Writings*. London: Routledge and Kegan Paul (republished in 1955 as *Philosophical Writings of Peirce*. New York: Dover).

Petty, R.E. and Cacioppo, J.T. (1981) *Attitudes and Persuasion: Classic and Contemporary Approaches*. Dubuque, IA: Brown.

Petty, R.E. and Cacioppo, J.T. (1986) *Communication and Persuasion: Central and Peripheral Routes to Attitude Change*. New York: Springer.

Petty, R.E., Cacioppo, J.T. and Goldman, R. (1981) Personal involvement as a determinant of argument-based persuasion, *Journal of Personality and Social Psychology*, 41: 847–55.

Pittman, T.S. (1975) Attribution of arousal as a mediator of dissonance reduction, *Journal of Experimental Social Psychology*, 11: 53–63.

Poletiek, F. (2001) *Hypothesis-testing Behaviour*. Hove: Psychology Press.

Popper, K. (1959) *The Logic of Scientific Discovery*. New York: Basic Books.

Posner, M.I. (1966) Components of skill performance, *Science*, 152: 1712–18.

Potter, J. (1996) Attitudes, social representations and discursive psychology, in M. Wetherell (ed.) *Identities, Groups and Social Issues*. London: Sage.

Potter, J. and Wetherell, M. (1987). *Discourse and Social Psychology: Beyond Attitudes and Behaviour*. London: Sage.

Potter, J. and Wetherell, M. (1995) Discourse Analysis, in J.A. Smith, R. Harré and L. Van Langenhove (eds) *Rethinking Methods in Psychology*. London: Sage.

Potter, J., Edwards, D. and Wetherell, M. (1993) A model of discourse in action, *American Behavioural Scientist*, 36(3): 383–401.

Press, I. (1980) Problems in the definition and classification of medical systems, *Social Science and Medicine*, 14b: 45–57.

Price, S. (1993) *Media Studies*. London: Pitman.

Psathas, G. (1995) *Conversational Analysis: The Study of Talk-in-action*. Thousand Oaks, CA: Sage.

Rabbie, J.M. and Horowitz, M. (1969) Arousal and ingroup–outgroup bias by a chance win or loss, *Journal of Personality and Social Psychology*, 13: 269–77.

Reason, P. and Rowan, J. (1981) *Human Inquiry: A Sourcebook for New Paradigm Research*. Wiley: Chichester.

Rehm, J., Steinleitner, J. and Lilli, W. (1987) Wearing uniforms and aggression: a field experiment, *European Journal of Social Psychology*, 17: 357–60.

Reinharz, S. (1992) *Feminism Research Methods in Social Research*. Oxford: Oxford University Press.

Rhodewalt, F. and Augustsdottir, S. (1986) Effects of self-presentation on the phenomenological self, *Journal of Personality and Social Psychology*, 50: 47–55.

Richards, G. (1997) *'Race', Racism and Psychology: Towards a Reflexive History*. London: Routledge.

Ricoeur, P. (1955) The model of the text: meaningful actions considered as texts, *Social Research*, 38, 530–47.

Ricoeur, P. (1981) *Hermeneutics and the Human Sciences*. Cambridge: Cambridge University Press.

Rim, Y. (1970) Values and Attitudes, *Personality*, 1: 243–50.

Ringleman, M. (1913) Recherches sur les moteurs animés: travail de l'homme, *Annales de l'Institute National Agronomique*, 2nd series, 12: 1–40.

Roberts, H. (ed.) (1981) *Doing Feminist Research*. London: Routledge.

Rokeach, M. (1968) *Beliefs, Attitudes and Values: A Theory of Organisation and Change*. San Francisco, CA: Jossey-Bass.

Rokeach, M. (1973) *The Nature of Human Values*. New York: Free Press.

Rokeach, M. (1976) The nature of human values and value systems, in E.P. Hollander and R.G. Hunt (eds) *Current Perspectives in Social Psychology*, 4th edn. New York: Oxford University Press.

Rokeach, M. and Cochrane, R. (1972) Self-confrontation and confrontation with another as determinants of long-term value change, *Journal of Applied Social Psychology*, 2: 283–92.

Rokeach, M., Miller, M.G. and Snyder, J.A. (1971) The value gap between police and policed, *Journal of Social Issues*, 27, 155–71.

Rommetveit, R. (1980) On 'meanings' of acts and what is meant and made known by what is said in a pluralistic world, in M. Brenner (ed.) *The Structure of Action*. New York: St Martin's Press

Rorty, A.O. (1987) Persons as rhetorical categories, *Social Research*, 54(1): 55–72.

Rorty, R. (1980) *Philosophy and the Mirror of Nature*. Oxford: Blackwell.

Rosenberg, S., Nelson, C. and Vivekanathan, P.S. (1968) A multidimensional approach to the structure of personality impressions, *Journal of Personality and Social Psychology*, 39: 283–94.

Rosenburg, M. (1969) The conditions and consequences of evaluation apprehension, in R. Rosenthal and R.L. Rosnow (eds) *Artefact in Behavioural Research*. New York: Academic Press.

Ross, E.A. (1908) *Social Psychology*. New York: Macmillan.

Rotter, J.B. (1966) Generalised expectancies for internal versus external control of reinforcement, *Psychological Monographs*, 80(1): 1–28.

Ruckmick, C.A. (1912) The history and status of psychology in the United States, *American Journal of Psychology*, 23: 517–31.

Rushton, J.P. (1989) *Altruism, Socialisation and Society*. Englewood Cliffs, NJ: Prentice Hall.

Sachdev, I. and Bourhis, R.Y. (1990) Ethnolinguistic vitality: Some motivational and cognitive considerations, in M.A. Hogg and D. Abrams (eds) *Group Motivation: Social Psychological Perspectives*. Hemel Hempstead: Harvester Wheatsheaf.

Sacks, H. (1995) *Lectures on Conversation: Volumes I and II*, ed. G. Jefferson. Oxford: Blackwell.

Salancik, G.R. and Conway, M. (1975) Attitude inference from salient and relevant cognitive content about behaviour, *Journal of Personality and Social Psychology*, 32: 829–40.

Sanders, G.S. and Baron, R.S. (1977) Is social comparison relevant for producing choice shifts?, *Journal of Experimental Social Psychology*, 13: 303–14.

Sanders, G.S., Baron, R.S. and Moore, D.L. (1978) Distraction and social comparison as mediators of social facilitation effects, *Journal of Experimental Social Psychology*, 14: 291–303.

Sanna, L.J. and Shotland, R.L. (1990) Valence of anticipated evaluation and social facilitation, *Journal of Experimental Social Psychology*, 26: 82–92.

Sarbin, T. (1986) *Narrative Psychology: The Storied Nature of Human Conduct*. New York: Praeger.

Sasfy, J. and Okun, M. (1974) Form of evaluation and audience expertness as joint determinants of audience effects, *Journal of Experimental Social Psychology*, 10: 461–7.

Saussure, F. de (1959) *A Course in General Linguistics*. New York: McGraw-Hill.

Saussure, F. de (1974) *Course in General Linguistics*, ed. J. Culler, trans. W. Baskin. London: Fontana.

Scher, S. and Cooper, J. (1989) Motivational basis of dissonance: the singular role of behavioural consequences, *Journal of Personality and Social Psychology*, 56: 899–906.

Scherer, K.R. (2001) Emotion, in M. Hewstone, and W. Stroebe (eds) *Introduction to Social Psychology*, 3rd edn. Oxford: Blackwell.

Schlenker, B.R. (1980) *Impression Management: The Self-concept, Social Identity and Interpersonal Relations*. Monterey, CA: Brooks/Cole.

Schwartz, S.H. (1992) Universals in the content and structure of values: theoretical advances and empirical tests in 20 countries, in M.P. Zanna (ed.) *Advances in Experimental Social Psychology*, Vol. 25. San Diego, CA: Academic Press.

Schwartz, S.H. (1994) Cultural dimensions of values: towards an understanding of national differences, in U. Kim, H.C. Triandis and G. Yoon (eds) *Individualism and Collectivism: Theoretical and Methodological Issues*. Newbury Park, CA: Sage.

Schwartz, S.H. and Bilsky, W. (1987) Towards a psychological structure of human values, *Journal of Personality and Social Psychology*, 53: 550–62.

Schwartz, S.H. and Bilsky, W. (1990) Towards a theory of the universal content and structure of values: extensions and cross-cultural replications, *Journal of Personality and Social Psychology*, 58: 878–91.

Schwartz, S.H., Bardi, A. and Bianchi, G. (2000) Value adaptation to the imposition and collapse of communist regimes in East-Central Europe, in S.A. Renshon and J. Duckitt (eds) *Political Psychology: Cultural and Cross-cultural Foundations*. London: Macmillan.

Schwarz, N. and Clore, G.L. (1988) How do I feel about it? Informative functions of affective states, in K. Fiedler and J. Forgas (eds) *Affect, Cognition and Social Behaviour*. Toronto: Hogrefe.

Sears, D.O. (1983) The person–positivity bias, *Journal of Personality and Social Psychology*, 44: 233–50.

Sears, D.O., Peplau, L.A. and Taylor, S.E. (1991) *Social Psychology*, 7th edn. Englewood Cliffs, NJ: Prentice Hall.

Sebok, T.A. and Umiker-Sebok, J. (1983) 'You know my method': a juxtaposition of Charles S. Peirce and Sherlock Holmes, in T.A. Sebok and U. Eco (eds) *The Sign of Three*. Bloomington: Indiana University Press.

Sedgwick, P. (1982) *Psychopolitics*. London: Pluto.

Segal, H.A. (1954) Initial psychiatric findings of recently repatriated prisoners of war, *American Journal of Psychiatry*, 61: 358–63.

Segall, M.H., Dasen, P.R., Berry, J.W. and Poortinga, Y.H. (1990) *Human Behavior in Global Perspective: An Introduction to Cross-Cultural Psychology*. New York: Pergamon.

Seligman, M.E.P. (1975) *Helplessness: On Depression, Development and Death*. San Francisco: Freeman.

Seligman, M.E.P., Abramson, L.Y., Semmel, A. and von Baeyer, C. (1979) Depressive attributional style, *Journal of Abnormal Psychology*, 88: 242–7.

Semin, G.R. (1997) The relevance of language to social psychology, in C. McGarty and S.A. Haslam (eds) *The Message of Social Psychology*. Oxford: Blackwell.

Semin, G.R. and Fiedler, K. (1988) The cognitive functions of linguistic categories in describing persons: social cognition and language, *Journal of Personality and Social Psychology*, 54: 558–68.

Semin, G.R. and Manstead, A.S.R. (1983) *The Accountability of Conduct: A Social Psychological Analysis*. London: Academic Press.

Semin, G. and Rubini, M. (1990) Unfolding the concept of person by verbal abuse, *European Journal of Social Psychology*, 20: 463–74.

Shank, G. (1994) Shaping qualitative research in educational psychology, *Contemporary Educational Psychology*, 19: 340–59.

Shank, G. (1998) The extraordinary ordinary powers of abductive reasoning, *Theory and Psychology*, 8(6): 841–60.

Shank, R.C. and Abelson, R.P. (1977) Scripts, plans and knowledge, in P.N. Johnson-Laird and P.C. Wason (eds) *Thinking: Readings in Cognitive Science*. Cambridge: Cambridge University Press.

Shannon, C.E. (1948) A mathematical theory of communication, *Bell Systems Technology Journal*, 27: 379–423, 623–56.

Shannon, C. and Weaver, W. (1949) *The Mathematical Theory of Communication*. Urbana, IL: University of Illinois Press.

Shavitt, S. (1989) Operationalizing functional theories of attitude, in A.R. Pratkanis, S.J. Breckler and A.G. Greenwald (eds) *Attitude Structure and Function*. Hillsdale, NJ: Erlbaum.

Shavitt, S. and Fazio, R.H. (1991) Effects of attribute salience on the constancy between attitudes and behaviour predictions, *Personality and Social Psychology Bulletin*, 17: 507–16.

Sheppard, R.H., Hartwick, J. and Warshaw, P.R. (1988) The theory of reasoned action: a meta-analysis of past research with recommendations for modifications and future research, *Journal of Consumer Research*, 15: 325–43.

Sherif, M. (1936) *The Psychology of Social Norms*. New York: Harper and Row.

Sherif, M. (1966) *In Common Predicament: Social Psychology of Intergroup Conflict and Cooperation*. Boston, MA: Houghton Mifflin.

Sherif, M. and Hovland, C.I. (1961) *Social Judgement*. New Haven, CT: Yale University Press.

Sherif, M. and Sherif, C. (1969) *Social Psychology*. New York: Harper and Row.

Sherif, M., Harvey, O.J., White, B.J., Hood, W. and Sherif, C. (1961) *Intergroup Conflict and Cooperation: The Robbers' Cave Experiment*. Norman, OK: University of Oklahoma Institute of Intergroup Relations.

Shiffrin, R.M. and Schneider, W. (1977) Controlled and automatic human information processing II: perceptual learning, automatic attending and general theory, *Psychological Review*, 84: 127–90.

Shotter, J. (1984) *Social Accountability and Selfhood*. Oxford: Blackwell.

Shotter, J. and Gergen, K.J. (1989). *Deconstructing Social Psychology*. London: Routledge.

Showers, C. and Cantor, N. (1985) Social cognition: a look at motivated strategies, *Annual Review of Psychology*, 36: 275–305.

Siegel, A.E. and Siegel, S. (1957) Reference groups, membership groups and attitude change, *Journal of Abnormal and Social Psychology*, 55: 360–4.

Singh, D. (1993) Adaptive significance of female physical attractiveness: role of waist-to-hip ratio, *Journal of Personality and Social Psychology*, 65: 293–307.

Sistrunk, F. and McDavid, J.W. (1971) Sex variables in conforming behaviour, *Journal of Personality and Social Psychology*, 2: 200–7.

Smith, B. and Harris Bond, M. (1993) *Social Psychology across Cultures*. Hemel Hempstead: Harvester Wheatsheaf.

Smith, E.R. and Mackie, D.M. (2000) *Social Psychology*. Philadelphia, PA: Taylor and Francis.

Smith, E.R. and Miller, F.D. (1983) Mediation among attributional inferences and comprehension processes: initial findings and a general method, *Journal of Personality and Social Psychology*, 44: 492–505.

Smith, E.R. and Zaraté, M.A. (1992) Exemplar-based model of social judgement, *Psychological Review*, 99: 3–21.

Smith, M.B. (1969) *Social Psychology and Human Values*. Chicago: Aldine.

Smith, M.B., Bruner, J. and White, R.W. (1956) *Opinions and Personality*. New York: Wiley.

Smythe, D. (1994) *Counterclockwise: Perspectives on Communication from Dallas Smythe*, ed. T. Gubacl. Boulder, CO: Westview.

Snyder, M. and DeBono, K.G. (1987) A functional approach to attitudes and persuasion, in M.P. Zanna, J.M. Olson and C.P. Herman (eds) *Social Influence: The Ontario Symposium*, Vol. 5. Hillsdale, NJ: Erlbaum.

Snyder, M. and Swann, W.B. Jnr (1978) Behavioural confirmation in social interactions: from social perception to social reality, *Journal of Experimental Social Psychology*, 14: 148–62.

Snyder, M., Tanke, E.D. and Berscheid, E. (1977) Social perception and interpersonal behaviour: on the self-fulfilling nature of social stereotypes, *Journal of Personality and Social Psychology*, 35: 656–66.

Stainton Rogers, R. (1995) Q methodology, in J.A. Smith, R. Harré and L. Van Langenhove (eds) *Rethinking Methods in Psychology*. London: Sage.

Stainton Rogers, R., Stenner, P., Gleeson, K. and Stainton Rogers, W. (1995) *Social Psychology: A Critical Agenda*. Cambridge: Polity.

Stainton Rogers, W. (1991) *Explaining Health and Illness: An Exploration of Diversity*. Hemel Hempstead: Harvester Wheatsheaf.

Stainton Rogers, W. (1995) Does critical social psychology mean the end of the world?, in T. Ibañez and L. Iniguez (eds) *Critical Social Psychology*. London: Sage.

Stainton Rogers, W. (1996) Critical approaches to health psychology, *Journal of Health Psychology*, 1(1): 556–9.

Stainton Rogers, W. (2002) Psychology as telling stories, in J. László and W. Stainton Rogers (eds) *Narrative Approaches in Social Psychology*. Budapest: New Mandate.

Stainton Rogers, W. and Stainton Rogers, R. (2001) *The Psychology of Gender and Sexuality*. Buckingham: Open University Press.

Stang, D.J. (1972) Conformity, ability and self-esteem, *Representative Research in Social Psychology*, 3: 97–103.

Steele, C.M. (1988) The psychology of self-affirmation: sustaining the integrity of the self, in L. Berkowitz (ed.) *Advances in Experimental Social Psychology*, Vol. 21. San Diego, CA: Academic Press.

Stenner, P.H.D. (1992) Feeling deconstructed? With particular reference to jealousy, unpublished doctoral dissertation, University of Reading.

Stenner, P.H.D. (1993) Discoursing jealousy, in E. Burman and I. Parker (eds) *Discourse Analytic Research: Repertoires and Readings of Texts in Action*. London: Routledge.

Stephan, C.W. and Stephan, W.G. (1990) *Two Social Psychologies*, 2nd edn. Belmont, CA: Wadsworth.

Stevens, R. (1996) The reflexive self: an experiential perspective, in R. Stevens (ed.) *Understanding the Self*. London: Sage.

Stoddart, D.M. (1990) *The Scented Ape: The Biology and Culture of Human Odour*. Cambridge: Cambridge University Press.

Stoner, J.A. (1961) A comparison of individual and group decisions involving risk, unpublished Masters thesis, Cambridge, MA: MIT.

Strodtbeck, F.L., James, R. and Hawkins, C. (1957) Social status in jury deliberations, *American Sociological Review*, 22: 713–18.

Stryker, S. and Statham, A. (1986) Symbolic interaction and role theory, in
G. Lindzey and E. Aronson (eds) *Handbook of Social Psychology*, 3rd edn,
Vol. 1. New York: Random House.

Sutton, S. (1998) Predicting and explaining intentions and behaviour: how
well are we doing?, *Journal of Applied Social Psychology*, 28: 1317–38.

Swift, D.J., Watts, D.M. and Pope, M.L. (1983) Methodological
pluralism and personal construct psychology: a case for pictorial
methods in eliciting personal constructions. Paper presented to the
Fifth International Conference on Personal Construct Psychology, Boston,
MA.

Tajfel, H. (1972) La catégorization sociale, in S. Moscovici (ed.) *Introduction à
la Psychologie Sociale*, Vol. 1.

Tajfel, H. (ed.) (1978) *Differentiation between Social Groups: Studies in the Social
Psychology of Intergroup Relations*. London: Academic Press.

Tajfel, H., Billig, M.G., Bundy, R.P. and Flament, C. (1971) Social
categorization and intergroup behaviour, *European Journal of Social
Psychology*, 1: 149–78.

Tajfel, H. and Turner, J.C. (1979) An integrative theory of intergroup
conflict, in W.G. Austin and S. Worchel (eds) *The Social Psychology of
Intergroup Relations*. Monterey, CA: Brooks/Cole.

Tajfel, H. and Turner, J. (1986) The social identity theory of intergroup
behaviour, in S. Worchel and W.G. Austin (eds) *Psychology of Intergroup
Relations*. Chicago: Nelson.

Tak, J., Kaid, L.L. and Lee, S. (1997) A cross-cultural study of political
advertising in the United States and Korea, *Communication Research*, 24:
413–30.

Tarde, G. (1903) *The Laws of Initation*, trans. from the French 2nd edn by
E.C. Parsons. New York: Holt.

Taussig, M. (1980) Reification and the consciousness of the patient, *Social
Science and Medicine*, 14b: 3–13.

Taylor, D.A. and Moriarty, B.F. (1987) In-group bias as a function of
competition and race, *Journal of Conflict Resolution*, 31: 192–9.

Tesser, A. (1993) The importance of heritability in psychological research: the
case of attitudes, *Psychological Review*, 100: 129–42.

Tiffin, J., Knight, F.B. and Josey, C.C. (1940) *The Psychology of Normal People*.
Boston: Heath.

Toffler, A. (1981) *The Third Wave*. London: Pan.

Tourangeau, R. and Rasinski, K.A. (1988) Cognitive processes underlying
context effects in attitude measurement, *Psychological Bulletin*, 103:
299–314.

Triplett, N.D. (1898) The dynamogenic factor in pacemaking and
competition, *American Journal of Psychology*, 9: 507–33.

Turner, J.C. (1982) Towards a cognitive redefinition of the social group, in H. Tajfel (ed.) *Social Identity and Intergroup Relations*. Cambridge: Cambridge University Press.

Turner, J.C. (1991) *Social Influence*. Pacific Grove, CA: Brooks/Cole.

Turner, J.C., Hogg, M.A., Oakes, P.J., Reicher, S.D. and Wetherell, M.S. (1987) *Rediscovering the Social Group: A Self-Categorization Theory*. Oxford: Blackwell.

Turner, J.S. and Rubinson, L. (1993) *Contemporary Human Sexuality*. Englewood Cliffs, NJ: Prentice Hall.

Tyerman, A. and Spencer, C. (1983) A critical test of the Sherifs' robbers' cave experiments: intergroup competition and cooperation between groups of well acquainted individuals, *Small Group Behaviour*, 14: 515–31.

Uleman, J.S., Newman, L.S. and Moskowitz, G.B. (1996) People as flexible interpreters: Evidence and issues from spontaneous trait inference, in M.P. Zanna (ed.) *Advances in Experimental Social Psychology*, Vol. 29. San Diego, CA: Academic Press.

Van Avermaet, E. (2001) Social influence in small groups, in M. Hewstone and W. Stroebe (eds) *Introduction to Social Psychology*, 3rd edn. Oxford: Blackwell.

Vance, C. (1992) Social construction theory: problems with the history of sexuality, in H. Crowley and S. Himmelweit (eds) *Knowing Women*. Cambridge: Polity.

Van Hooff, J.A. (1972) A comparative approach to the phylogeny of laughter and smiling, in R. Hinde (ed.) *Non-verbal Communication*. Cambridge: Cambridge University Press.

Vanneman, R.D. and Pettigrew, T.F. (1972) Race and relative deprivation in the urban United States, 13: 461–86.

Vaughan, G.M. (1964) The trans-situational aspect of conforming behaviour, *Journal of Personality*, 32: 335–54.

Vickers, J. and McCalla (1982) Memoirs of an ontological exile: the methodological rebellions of feminist research, in A. Miles and G. Finn (eds) *Feminism in Canada: From Pressure to Politics*. Montreal: Black Rose.

Vygotsky, L.S. (1962) *Thought and Language*, eds and trans. E. Haufmann and C. Vakar. Cambridge: MIT Press.

Walkerdine, W. (1990) *Schoolgirl Fictions*. London: Verso.

Walster, E., Aronson, V., Abrahams, D. and Rottmann, L. (1966) Importance of physical attractiveness in dating behaviour, *Journal of Personality and Social Psychology*, 4(5): 508–16.

Wason, P.C. (1966) Reasoning, in B. Foss (ed.) *New Horizons in Psychology*. Harmondsworth: Penguin.

Wason, P.C. (1968) Reasoning about a rule, *Quarterly Journal of Experimental Psychology*, 20: 273–81.

Wedekind, C., Seebeck, J., Bettens, F. and Paepke, A. (1995) MHC-dependent mate preferences in humans, *Proceedings of the Royal Society of London*, B 260: 245–9.

Weigel, R.H. and Newman, L.S. (1976) Increasing attitude–behaviour correspondence by broadening the scope of the behavioural measure, *Journal of Personality and Social Psychology*, 33: 793–802.

Weigel, R.H., Vernon, D.T.A. and Tognacci, L.N. (1976) Specificity of the attitude as a determinant of attitude-behaviour congruence, *Journal of Personality and Social Psychology*, 30: 724–8.

Wertheimer, M. (1923) Untersuchungen zur Lehre von der Gestaldt, II. *Psychol. Forsch*, 4: 301–50.

Wessely, S. (1996) Chronic fatigue syndrome: summary of a report of a Joint Commission of the Royal Colleges of Physicians, Psychiatrists and General Practitioners, *Journal of the Royal College of Physicians of London*, 30(6): 497–504.

West, C. (1984) *Routine Complications: Troubles with Talk between Doctors and Patients*. Bloomington, IN: Indiana University Press.

Wetherell, M. (1987) Social identity and group polarization, in J.C. Turner, M.A. Hogg, P.J. Oakes, S.D. Reicher and M.S. Wetherell (eds) *Rediscovering the Social Group: A Self-Categorization Theory*. Oxford: Blackwell.

Wetherell, M. (ed.) (1996) *Identities, Groups and Social Issues*. London: Sage.

Wetherell, M. (1998) Positioning and interpretative repertoires: conversational analysis and post-structuralism in dialogue, *Discourse and Society*, 9(3): 387–413.

Wetherell, M. and Maybin, J. (2000) The distributed self: a social constructionist perspective, in R. Stevens (ed.) *Understanding the Self*. London: Sage.

Wetherell, M. and Potter, J. (1992) *Mapping the Language of Racism: Discourse and the Legitimation of Exploitation*. Brighton: Harvester Wheatsheaf.

Whitcher, S.J. and Fisher, J.D. (1979) Multidimensional reaction to therapeutic touch in a hospital setting, *Journal of Personality and Social Psychology*, 37: 87–96.

Whorf, B.L. (1956) *Language, Thought and Reality*. Cambridge, MA: MIT Press.

Wicker, A.W. (1969) Attitudes versus actions: the relationship of verbal and overt behavioural responses to attitude objects, *Journal of Social Issues*, 25(4): 41–78.

Wiggins, J.S., Renner, K.E., Clore, G.L. and Rose, R.J. (1971) *The Psychology of Personality*. Reading, MA: Addison-Wesley.

Wilke, H. and Wit, A. (2001) Group performance, in M. Hewstone and W. Stroebe (eds) *Introduction to Social Psychology*, 3rd edn. Oxford: Blackwell.

Wilkinson, S. (1997) Prioritizing the political: feminist psychology, in T. Ibáñez and L. Iñiguez (eds) *Critical Social Psychology*. London: Sage.

Williams, K.D., Karau, S.J. and Bourgeois, M. (1993) Working on collective tasks: social loafing and social compensation, in M.A. Hogg and D. Abrams (eds) *Group Motivation: Social Psychological Perspectives*. London: Harvester Wheatsheaf.

Willig, C. (2001) *Introducing Qualitative Research in Psychology: Adventures in Theory and Method*. Buckingham: Open University Press.

Wilson, E.O. (1975) *Sociobiology: The New Synthesis*. Cambridge, MA: Harvard University Press.

Wilson, T.D. and Hodges, S.D. (1992) Attitudes as temporary constructions, in L.L. Martin and A. Tesser (eds) *The Construction of Social Judgements*. Hillsdale, NJ: Erlbaum.

Wood, W., Lundgren, S., Ouellette, J.A., Busceme, S. and Blackstone, K. (1994) Minority influence: a meta-analytic review of social influence processes, *Psychological Bulletin*, 115: 323–45.

Woolgar, S. (1988) *Science: The Very Idea*. Chichester: Ellis Harwood.

Worchel, S. (1979) Co-operation and the reduction of intergroup conflict: some determining factors, in W.G. Austin and S. Worchel (eds) *The Social Psychology of Intergroup Conflict*, Monterey, CA: Brooks/Cole.

Worrell, M. (2000) The discursive construction of child sexual abuse, unpublished doctoral dissertation, The Open University.

Wundt, W. (1897) *Outlines of Psychology*. New York: Stechert.

Wundt, W. (1900–20) *Völkerpsychologie: eine Untersuchung der Entwicklungsgesetze von Sprache, Mythus und Sitte* (10 volumes). Leipzig: Winter.

Young, A. (1980) The discourse on stress and the reproduction of conventional knowledge, *Social Science and Medicine*, 10: 147–56.

Zaccaro, S.J. (1984) Social loafing: the role of task attractiveness, *Personality and Social Psychology Bulletin*, 10: 99–106.

Zajonc, R.B. (1968a) Cognitive theories in social psychology, in G. Lindzey and E. Aronson (eds) *The Handbook of Social Psychology*, 2nd edn, Vol. 1. Reading, MA: Addison-Wesley.

Zajonc, R.B. (1968b) Attitudinal effects of mere exposure, *Journal of Personality and Social Psychology*, 9 (monograph supplement 2, part 2).

Zajonc, R.B. and Burnstein, E. (1965) The learning of balanced and unbalanced social structures, *Journal of Personality*, 33: 153–63.

Zanna, M.P. and Fazio, R.H. (1982) The attitude–behaviour relation: moving toward a third generation of research, in M.P. Zanna, E.T. Higgins and C.P. Herman (eds) *Consistency in Social Behaviour: The Ontario Symposium*, Vol. 2. Hillside, NJ: Erlbaum.

Zimbardo, P.G., Banks, W.C., Haney, C. and Jaffe, D. (1973) The mind is a formidable jailer: a Pirandellian prison, *The New York Times Magazine*, 8 April: 38–60.

Zuckerman, M., DePaulo, B.M. and Rosenthal, R. (1981) Verbal and non-verbal communication of deception, in L. Berkowitz (ed.) *Advances in Experimental Social Psychology*, Vol. 14. New York: Academic Press.

Index

(Note: numbers in **bold** are in the glossary)